THE AMERICAN POET

Weedpatch Gazette
For 1992

Samuel D. G. Heath, Ph. D.

iUniverse, Inc.
New York Bloomington

The American Poet
Weedpatch Gazette For 1992

iUniverse books may be ordered through booksellers or by contacting:

iUniverse
1663 Liberty Drive
Bloomington, IN 47403
www.iuniverse.com
1-800-Authors (1-800-288-4677)

ISBN: 978-1-4401-6015-8 (sc)
ISBN: 978-1-4401-6016-5 (ebook)

Printed in the United States of America

iUniverse rev. date: 07/13/2009

CONTENTS

CHAPTER ONE	1
CHAPTER TWO	18
CHAPTER THREE	39
CHAPTER FOUR	60
CHAPTER FIVE	81
CHAPTER SIX	102
CHAPTER SEVEN	123
CHAPTER EIGHT	144
CHAPTER NINE	166
CHAPTER TEN	187
CHAPTER ELEVEN	190
CHAPTER TWELVE	204
CHAPTER THIRTEEN	221
CHAPTER FOURTEEN	242
CHAPTER FIFTEEN	263
CHAPTER SIXTEEN	281
CHAPTER SEVENTEEN	302
CHAPTER EIGHTEEN	323
CHAPTER NINETEEN	344
CHAPTER TWENTY	365
CHAPTER TWENTY-ONE	384
ABOUT THE AUTHOR	405

CHAPTER ONE

JANUARY

Isaiah 45:22

"The crisis is arrived when we must assert our rights, or submit ... till custom and use shall make us ... tame and abject slaves. ..." George Washington to his friend and neighbor Bryan Fairfax, a royalist, after the "Boston Tea Party."

Sam Adams, often referred to as the Father of the American Revolution, applauded his "gang," ill disguised as Indians, on a crisp, December night in 1774, for tossing three shiploads of the King's tea overboard into Boston Harbor. On guard that night, keeping lookout was John Hancock, a compatriot of Adams'. The two were to become the Crown's "Most Wanted." Paul Revere was to save them from capture at a later time.

History records the fact that King George III was not an evil man. Far from it, he evidenced much of a character that most would find laudable. According to Churchill, he was one of the most conscientious sovereigns to ever sit the English throne.

It was not despotic "Kingliness" that led to the Revolutionary War and cranked up the presses of Paine and Jefferson. It was a host of "little" things like the sugar and stamp acts, the grinding away, by petty bureaucrats, of personal dignity and the rights to forge a man's own destiny without undue governmental intrusion. It was the actions of these little tyrants, like our own building inspectors, corrupt cops, judges, "faceless bureaucrats" that attempted, and still attempt, to make us "... tame and abject slaves." It is indeed, "Custom and use," that system of evil laws and all forms of penurious taxation that prevent any hope or vision, that rob men of their manhood, rob women of their special place of homemaker and tender nurturer of children, rob children of their right to be children, that is killing us as a nation.

From Columbus, Bradford, Eliot, Penn, Adams, the "Molly Pitcher's," and Betsy Ross's, Witherspoon, Asbury, Webster, our history has had its roots in a thousand men and women who had a profound belief in God, His Word and the destiny of this nation. It is a tragic loss to mine and the younger generation that so little is now taught or even known by those who purport

1

to teach, about the History of The United States of America. And, in all, it is a noble history of noble men and women.

I have commented on the fact that mine was the last generation of readers; this, largely because of the film and TV industries together with the change from pre war agrarian populations to post war urban. The changes over the last fifty years have been deadly to families and reading in general. Much of what is called "critical thinking skills" was lost in the process. Critical thinking requires ability and practice in the area of reading and reflection on what is read. The reading must challenge to be effective. Therefore, it has to cover a broad spectrum, not just one, specialized area. The highest thought processes, involving imagination, are enforced in such a manner.

As a "simple honorary Okie" I may lack the verve and panache of my "betters" but I know something of the effects of the literature that has impacted our course as a nation. I also know that American literature is one of the richest in the history of the world. It is a truism that "The pen is mightier than the sword." It is for that reason that, some years ago, I left off speaking engagements and took up the pen. Notwithstanding the fact that we have become a nation of non-readers, it is still my hope that my printed words will accomplish the task I have set.

My distinct advantage was being raised without TV and in settings that promoted reading. My grandparents made sure books surrounded my brother and me and the radio and literature were marvelous mediums to encourage imagination and dreams. The "How To" genre was well represented also. On the mining claim, lacking electricity or plumbing, I learned much as a child in the "How To" category. It also made reading the essential means of entertainment and the source of knowledge to satisfy curiosity.

James Fenimore Cooper is a name, like so many others, tragically lost to our young people. The writer, famed for his "Leatherstocking Tales" and the riches of imagination he provided for millions of readers is little known to, or past, my generation. Oh! But how I thrilled as a child as I would read of the great forests, of the constant battle between good and evil with good, invariably gaining the triumph, as the Deerslayer, (Natty Bumppo) also known as Hawkeye and his companion, Chingachgook, and the noble Uncas did battle in the name of honor and righteousness.

The wooded mountains and their teeming creatures would come alive in my imagination as Cooper skillfully weaved his tales of derring-do. I would stalk the trails of the wilderness with the honest, courageous and upright Hawkeye and his Indian companion as they fought evil men and explored this native and unspoiled vastness.

But Cooper was far more than a gifted "teller of tales." He was an American and his commentaries are of far more significance than the tales he wove. Cooper recognized the many evils of his day and rightly addressed them in much of his writing. For example: "What the world of America is coming to, and where the machinations of its people are to end, the Lord, He only knows.... towns and villages, farms and highways, churches and schools, in short all the inventions and deviltries of man, are spread across the region." Thus it was that Cooper foresaw the evil that government, even then, was capable of. And because he loved the wilderness, loved the country where men could be men and could work, explore, dream and hope, he warned of the evils he saw coming upon the land.

It was in the creation of Leatherstocking that Cooper evidenced hope that the wisdom of natural virtue, the desire for good that such wilderness as he describes where men could roam free of the restraints of the selfishness evidenced in the "villages" and "settlements," free from the evils of petty tyrants, bureaucrats, would prevail.

Cooper wrote: "The doctrine that any one may do what he please with his own, however, is false...Thus, he, who would bring his money to bear upon the elections of a country like this, abuses his situation, unless his efforts are confined to fair and manly discussions before the body of the people... In this country, it is the intention of the institutions, that money should neither increase nor lessen political influence...If left to itself, unsupported by factitious political aid, but sufficiently protected against the designs and rapacity of the dishonest, property is an instrument of working most of the good that society enjoys. It elevates a national character, by affording the means of cultivating knowledge and the tastes; it introduces all above barbarism into society; and it encourages and sustains laudable and useful efforts in individuals. Like every other great good, its abuses are in proportion to its benefits...A people that deems the possession of riches its highest source of distinction, admits one of the most degrading of all influences to preside over its opinions. At no time, should money be ever ranked as more than a means, and he who lives as if the acquisition of property were the sole end of his existence, betrays the dominion of the most sordid, base and groveling motive, that life offers.

"The principle of individuality, or to use a less winning term, of selfishness, lies at the root of all voluntary human exertion. We toil for food, for clothes, for houses, lands and for property, in general. This is done, because we know that the fruits of our labor will belong to ourselves, or to those who are most dear to us. It follows, that all which society enjoys beyond the mere supply of its first necessities, is dependent on their rights of property."

But, as I have pointed out, forcefully, in previous epistles, the evil system we live with today precludes a man doing with his own property as he wishes. The "State" has robbed us of the hope of building for those we love and, if exorbitant taxes are not paid, the "State" will be the beneficiary of all we have worked for, not our children and those most dear to us.

Farewell old friends, my soul brothers and heart's companions, James Fenimore Cooper and Hawkeye. Farewell to your vast, virginal mountains of forests, abundant wildlife and crystal, pure lakes, rivers and streams. Farewell your voice of warning that the loss of such that gave dignity to men would be sold to the "villages" and "settlements" where "deviltry" would prevail in seeking the "Almighty Dollar!" with all its attendant corruption, devastating taxes and devastating, mountainous system of emasculating laws and codes.

Cooper also leaves a legacy in regard to the media to which we would do well to heed: "This is a terrible picture to contemplate, for when the number (newspapers and, today, TV) of prints is remembered, and the avidity with which they are read is brought into the account, we are made to perceive that the entire nation, in a moral sense, breathes an atmosphere of falsehoods. There is little use, however, in concealing the truth; on the contrary, the dread in which publick men and writers commonly stand of the power of the press to injure them, has permitted the evil to extend so far, that it is scarcely exceeding the bounds of a just alarm, to say that the country cannot much longer exist in safety, under the malign influence that now overshadows it. Any one, who has lived long enough to note changes of the sort, must have perceived how fast men of probity and virtue are losing their influence in the country, to be superseded by those who scarcely deem an affectation of the higher qualities necessary to their success. This fearful change must, in a great measure, be ascribed to the corruption of the publick press, which as a whole, owes its existence to the schemes of interested political adventurers."

It is a tragedy for our nation that conscience has become a "vestigial organ" of politicians. I would call them all Asses but for the fact that I know of a few exceptions and, further, that would be defaming to that, comparatively, noble beast. The festering, suppurating sore that is now Washington, D.C. with its enormous crime rate, its black, woman mayor, its beehive activity of every kind of corruption imaginable, is a heritage of those that have sought their own gain at the expense of an entire nation.

I have to assume that the only reason the drug problem in our country is not solved in common sense fashion is the result of the need by that "shadow government," that system that operates behind the scenes like the C.I.A. and the "Doomsday" government which continues to use the enormous profits from an "illegal" drug business to finance itself. As with the BCCI, these shadowy, unaccountable groups have the billions of dollars with which they give no account to Congress or the people. How appropriate that the trail of slime these creatures leave invariably leads to the halls of Congress where it is effectively lost, commingled as it is with so many others like the CFR (Council on Foreign Relations) and Trilateral Commission.

I wish everyone would support the National Rifle Association in its continued battle to keep our right to bear arms intact. There are many organizations that are attempting to stem the tide of evil men who are threatening Americans and dooming any hope of a future for our children. Are you too "busy" to be involved in the battle? If so, you deserve the despotic reign of evil which so surely will come to pass if good men and women remain "too busy."

The drama of human tragedy is played out, daily, not in the courts of the wealthy and powerful, but in the lower courts of commissioners, of the traffic courts where the poor invariably find themselves. Forced to drive without insurance, forced to drive vehicles in need of repairs, the poor are bound to, eventually, find they have no chance in a system that will grind them into ever increasing poverty. It is a system that will make criminals of otherwise decent people. It will force them to drink, it will force them to give up or deny them employment unless they drive illegally.

Try to build your own home, or even make a modest improvement in your present one, no matter how humble, and face the army of codes, regulations and bureaucrats that will, with the state's blessing, sunder your family and force you, rather, onto the streets and the dole. You might, in all reason, rather a "tent in the wilderness" than a crushing load of debt that will prevent any hope for the future but the "system" says NO!

Thoreau wrote: "For eighteen hundred years, though perchance I have no right to say it, the New Testament has been written; yet where is the legislator who has wisdom and practical talent enough to avail himself of the light which it sheds on the science of legislation?" Where indeed? I see none in our Congress, our Oval Office or High Court.

When it comes to a confrontation between the Almighty Dollar and The Truth, I'm reminded of the words of Herman Melville in a letter to Hawthorne: "Dollars damn me and the malicious Devil is forever grinning in upon me, holding the door ajar. ... What I feel most moved to write, that is banned - it will not pay. Yet, altogether, write the other way I cannot. ... Try to get a living by the Truth - and go to the Soup Societies." This great writer, the author of Moby Dick, Billy Budd and so much more, living out the truth of his fateful statement, reduced to working obscurely for almost twenty years as a customs inspector, living in perpetual poverty.

Melville, like me, had a real grasp of the position The Truth holds in society. It doesn't pay since, for the many, it has no "practical" value. Hence, Pilate's question was not far off the mark. To quote Melville: "But Truth is the silliest thing under the sun. Try to get a living by the Truth - and go to the

Soup Societies. Heavens! Let any clergyman try to preach the Truth from its very stronghold, the pulpit, and they would ride him out of his church on his own pulpit banister. It can hardly be doubted that all Reformers are bottomed upon the truth, more or less; and to the world at large are not reformers almost universally laughing-stocks? Why so? Truth is ridiculous to men. Thus easily in my room here do I, conceited and garrulous, reverse the test of my Lord Shaftesbury." Melville's remarks are to be taken in the context of the position of The Truth as opposed to the "half-truths" by which men live and deceive themselves. In such a comparison, the "Noble Lies" and "Fairy Tales" that comprise the "truth" for most make The Truth fare badly, even appearing "ridiculous" and, "of no practical value!"

It was his high and, even sacrificial love of The Truth that led Melville to say: "I have come to regard this matter of Fame as the most transparent of all vanities. I read Solomon more and more, and every time see deeper and deeper meanings in him. I did not think of Fame, a year ago, as I do now. ... Lord, when shall we be done growing?"

Where the William Bradford that could say, in all sincerity and without a taint of hypocrisy: "God, it seems, would have all men to behold and observe such mercies and works of His providence as these are towards His people that they in like cases might be encouraged to depend upon God in their trials, and also to bless His name when they see His goodness towards others. Man lives not by bread only. It is not by good and dainty fare, by peace and rest and heart's ease in enjoying the contentment's and good things of this world only that preserves health and prolongs life; God in such examples would have the world see and behold that He can do it without them; and if the world will shut their eyes and take no notice thereof, yet He would have His people to see and consider it."

It has to be openly admitted that even that great patriot, Benjamin Franklin, when having had to deal with the pettiness of small-minded men came to his last years saying, of the mass of them, to Joseph Priestly in 1782: "Men I find to be a sort of being very badly constructed, as they are generally more easily provoked than reconciled, more disposed to do mischief to each other than to make reparation, more easily deceived than undeceived and having more pride and even pleasure in killing than begetting one another." As to the "begetting" Franklin adds: "A virtuous one it would be, and a vicious one the killing of them, if the species were really worth producing or preserving; but of this I begin to doubt."

And so it was that Franklin, the great patriot, tired and worn from having fought for so long on the side of liberty, gave vent to his despair of the meanness of small souls who failed to come up to the mark of the greatness of that liberty; and in words not even uttered by that great ecclesiastical contemporary who could preach so movingly on the subject of God's righteous wrath against all sin, called the "Supreme Pontiff of human damnation," Jonathan Edwards.

Yet, Franklin, in the cruelty of so-called "modern historians," called of them the "Philistine of the Republic's history," could say:

"And now I speak of thanking God, I desire with all humility to acknowledge that I owe the mentioned happiness of my past life to His kind providence, which lead me to the means I used and gave them success. My belief of this induces me to hope, though I must not presume, that the same goodness will still be exercised toward me, in continuing that happiness, or enabling me to bear a fatal reverse, which I may experience as others have done; the complexion of my future fortune being known to Him only in whose power it is to bless to us even our afflictions."

It needs be pointed out that Franklin's early dissatisfaction with organized religion in general and led to much opprobrium in this regard, reflects my own conclusion in that area; to wit: "... discourses were chiefly either polemic arguments, or explications of the peculiar doctrines of our sect, and were all to me very dry, uninteresting, and unedifying, since not a single, moral principle was inculcated or enforced, their aim seeming to be rather to make us Presbyterians than good citizens."

Reflecting my own long-held view of organized religion Franklin said:

"I never doubted, for instance, the existence of the Deity; that he made the world, and govern'd it by his Providence; that the most acceptable service of God was the doing good to man; that our souls are immortal; and that all crime will be punished, and virtue rewarded, either here or hereafter. These I esteem'd the essentials of every religion; and, being to be found in all the religions we had in our country, I respected them all, tho' with different degrees of respect, as I found them more or less mix'd with other articles, which, without any tendency to inspire, promote, or confirm morality, serv'd principally to divide us, and make us unfriendly to one another."

It did not help matters that Franklin was astute enough to make the observation that: "... a perfect character might be attended with the inconvenience of being envied and hated; and that a benevolent man should allow a few faults in himself, to keep his friends in countenance." I can say, in all good faith and truthfulness, that I have made great personal strides in fulfilling Franklin's advice on that particular score. I would add: "Perfection is not monotony."

It is my many failings and failures that so promote good will on the part of those that are "perfect" of my acquaintance, to those that look upon my fallen conditions and "sinful" practices that, as with Franklin, enable them to see themselves as: "At least I'm better than he!" And so, in that regard,

Ben and I fulfill a valuable service in making the "saints" pleased and full of their own "redeeming qualities of righteousness." I will leave it to history and God's fair judgment whether "honest pagans" like Franklin and myself are doing battle where it counts, whether ours is a "field of honor," as opposed to the "saints struggling against the powers of darkness" from the comfort and safety of their pews!

It should be mentioned that at the end of his life, Franklin's last public service was his attendance at the Constitutional Convention where this "Philistine of the Republic," not a "man of the cloth," called the members to ask God to bless and guide in their deliberations. Were it not for his wisdom and trust in God, the reputation and esteem in which he was held, we may well not have had the unanimity of purpose, divinely led, which resulted in that greatest document of history, our Constitution and, indeed, the Republic which we have inherited and, sadly, have so betrayed. And, I note, it was this same "Philistine" that was elected, in 1788, president of the first antislavery society in America, his last public act the signing of an appeal to Congress calling for the speedy abolition of slavery; but alas he failed and for the sake of profits our Founding Fathers may have planted the seed of our destruction by refusing to abolish slavery. Would that so many "good Christians" were as equally "good Philistines" as Benjamin Franklin!

It grieves me that Melville did not find the solacing friendship with Hawthorne that he so obviously sought. Both had such an understanding of the dark side of human nature, such genius for exploring, like Poe, the magnetism and glory of evil. But "Ye damn-ed whale!" was too overt for Hawthorne, who lacked the passion of Melville. And so it is that Moby Dick leads us to the storm but the Scarlet Letter and Twice-told Tales to the nuances, not that they are lacking in Melville, of evil. But, sadly, the personalities were too disparate and Hawthorne could not respond equally to Melville's fire; his "*Sturm und drang.*"

I have found it so in my own life that my "fire" may kindle the passions of my listeners for a time but unless there is an accompanying conviction resulting in a change of mind and behavior, the "seed" is "snatched away," the "Grail" becomes tawdry, even ridiculous, when I am out of sight. Few men indeed have the "fire" of conviction that results in action, particularly when, like The Truth, it has no perceptible pecuniary results. In other words, "It don't pay!" The Widow's mite has long ceased to weigh heavily on the scales of the treasury of this world system. "It don't pay!"

A friend has accused me of being a man of ponderous speech with a "thousand yard stare." Tain't so! I can "Aw shucks, Ain't" and "Shoot far" ('fire' to the non-cognizante) and "pint" my finger with the best of my Okie peers. As for a far-off look, I admit I engage in a lot of "looking" at things that seem, indeed, far off. And, I have to admit I use one of those sixteen cylinder words when occasion demands I must. But druther not. Tain't nothin t' be shamed of. I like a language that "lives."

Speaking of living, here is a headline for you:

LOCAL HIGHSCHOOL TEACHER SHOT 148 TIMES IN CASE OF MISTAKEN IDENTITY!

I was on my way to a meeting out at Edwards Air force Base. It was late afternoon and I was traveling in one of the more remote areas of the base-no traffic on the road. It was about an hour before sunset and the desert was beautiful and serene. I was driving my old Chevy pickup, coffee cup and cigarette doing their usual duty when, suddenly, a base police car came zooming up behind me, lights and siren going. Having learned, thanks to the California Highway Patrol, and why should the base police be any different, that obeying the speed laws is no guarantee of not getting a ticket, I dutifully and resignedly pulled off to the side of the road.

The minion of the law stayed in his "unit" for some time jawjacking into his mike. He finally got out and, hand on his gun, slowly came up to the rear of the driver's side of my truck. I had my window down and the officer, staying well behind the door, unusual I thought, asked for my license and registration. I had to bend backward out of the window of the truck to hand them to him. He seemed to be exceptionally cautious about advancing any further to me than absolutely necessary. As he walked away toward his car, and he walked backwards, never taking his eyes from me, a CHP unit pulled up behind his car. That officer joined the base cop. Then another base unit pulled up. There were now three units and all the cops were conversing, watching me all the while. It dawned on me that I must fit the description of some dangerous criminal.

Realizing that it might take some time for them to sort things out, I lit another cigarette and reached for my coffee cup. Empty! Oh, well, I had my thermos but it had rolled under the seat of the truck. You know, there is a something humorous even in our dark parts; hence my "Macabre Toys Incorporated" idea. Another CHP unit arrived and on its heels, another base car. I was surrounded. It occurred to me, that, in spite of my innocence, if I were to make a sudden lunge for the thermos under my seat, I might make the headlines, hence, the one I suggested at the start of this story. There were about twelve, itchy-fingered cops watching my every move. I had to chuckle at my predicament and decided, in a more lucid moment, that If I wanted my thermos I had better not make any sudden moves in its acquisition. No one, not even a bomb disposal officer, has ever moved more deliberately and cautiously in the retrieval of an object.

Did it occur to me to go without my coffee? No. Did I think it worth getting salivated, air-conditioned by .38s, .357s, 9 m.m. and double-ought buck just to have my thermos? No. Then why, for Heaven's sake? It was the "principle" of the thing. Damn it! I was innocent! And they had no right to deprive me of my coffee just because they thought I might be an escaped ax murderer or had assassinated the pope! Oh, well, I got my thermos successfully, no shots fired, but I did notice a few, anticipatory looks and knew how "game" must feel during hunting season.

The conference seemed to be coming to an end and one of the officers moseyed over and, returning my license and registration, said that I had been stopped because a stolen vehicle matching mine had been reported seen in my general area. What a let down. Couldn't it have at least been someone who had held up a gas station? Were twelve cops so bored they had to congregate to catch a simple car thief? Or, maybe, they just weren't telling me the straight scoop? In any event I went merrily and late to my meeting where I was able to regale my compeers with my close call in becoming a headline and making "Film at Eleven!"

"Someday we'll laugh about all this" may be true in many cases but it isn't likely in the face of today's happenings. The news is too grim and holds too many "doomsday" scenarios to be any contender for laugh awards.

Are we doomed to become a polyglot, mongrel nation, without a definitive heritage and culture, doomed to fall to a second-rate power among other nations because we have lost any pride or hope? If we fail to recover those things that were peculiar to "America," those things that were peculiarly, Euro-Christian, is there any hope that, looking to a "mixed multitude," a sea of black, brown and yellow faces will turn this nation around and restore its greatness? I think not. No nation in history has been able to do so. A single culture, a single race, makes a nation. America has succeeded, by the blessing of God, to do more than any nation in history in an attempt to overcome the stigma of "racism" and include so many diverse nationalities in its makeup. But, unless common values adhere, unless a common culture is preeminent, we cannot survive.

The single factor that contributed most to our success, a strong, common faith in God, in Jesus Christ and the Bible, is no longer the case. It was our religious heritage that provided the "glue" that enabled us to succeed where so many others failed. When a common morality and common values were rooted in the National Textbook, The Bible, we were able to do what no other nation in history has ever done. We were able to take in hoards of mixed peoples, albeit all of European ancestry, and build a nation. But, the overriding principles and leadership, the authority, was, as a constant, the view of men who held to Jesus Christ and The Bible.

I am presently staying with my friends in Bakersfield, my hometown. We have had some rain and the air is marvelously clear. The clouds are glorious, downy, feathery, ranging from brilliant white to various shades of gray with pastel blues breaking through. There is snow on the mountains round about. While winter has wrought its peculiar effect on the flowers and plants, there is always the promise of spring. It may be that Nature, with its promise of renewal, has lulled us into a complacency that life will get better through great, impersonal forces beyond our ken.

But it is a false hope. Action is required in the human arena. My friend's wife was telling me of some friends, missionaries from Brazil, whose children, after viewing some of our TV shows, became physically ill. I can believe it. If I think of it too much, it makes me sick. We have become jaded, inured, anesthetized, and thoroughly complacent to the mayhem, pornography, perversion, crime and violence of this "entertainment" medium. But those who have not been "inoculated, immunized," by long association, such as the young, are its victims.

My own generation is to blame for not passing on the lessons of history to our children, thinking, as we did, that the same things were being taught in the schools that we had learned. But, did we in fact really learn? I purposely included a glaring, historical error in fifty copies of last month's "epistle" as an experiment. Not one single individual contacted me concerning it! I know there are many plausible explanations for this but suppose the most horrifying reason should prevail, that the people simply did not know it was an error? Is my own generation as abysmally ignorant of our history as a nation? If so, maybe that is why we didn't see how the damage was being done when our children were not learning to read, write and cipher, when our children were obviously not conversant with the worthy literature of our past? How was it that my generation got so caught up in materialistic "values" that our children were let to "go to hell," that they were sacrificed on the "Altar" of State Education?

We "got busy" about all the wrong things. We allowed wicked men and women in the universities and government to gain power over us and our children, eroding, little by little, the liberty we so took for granted. We allowed our heroes to become objects of scorn and derision, our values to be sneered at, all in the high-sounding rhetoric of "multi-cultural equality!"

But our children and we now face corruption at all levels in all our institutions of society from the churches to the presidency. The rot is everywhere. In California, Cranston's remarks to the Senate come home in the education spectra as our State Superintendent's wife, Nancy Honig quits "milking" a cushy "perk" as the head of her "educational consulting program," QED, amid an investigation by state and federal authorities. Why should Bill and Nancy be immune from the "everybody does it" morality? Why shouldn't Honig's exalted and lucrative "business" as the State Superintendent of Schools spill a little gravy over to his wife; how far have we come from Horace Mann with his calvinistically inspired, lofty ideals and the "Old Deluder Satan" Act of 1647 in Massachusetts and its proud heritage of public education?

But, after all, the Honig's are at least "polite" about their graft unlike "Yahweh ben Yahweh" (an undoubtedly spurious nom-de-plume) who is the head of a black supremacist group dedicated to building a religious empire in the ghetto, accused of a reign of terror and dispatching "death angels" to kill defectors and those that resist a cushy real estate scheme. Thanks to the "entertainment" media, we have become so accustomed to theft, pornography, and violence that we hardly notice where "Beany and Cecil" left off and the "Playboy channel" began.

A very dear man, a Christian brother, recently took me to task, but gently so, for using some mild expletives in my writing. He made the point that I have made as well a number of times, that Clark Gabel's notorious "Damn" opened the floodgates to the common usage of all forms of profanity and vulgarisms. I cannot but agree with his chastening. On the other hand, my own justification is the necessity, as a responsible writer, to be real and to deal realistically, with all those that know me and never to hide behind some phony facade of religiosity. It need hardly be pointed out that some people's "That's nice" is equal to the most profane or vulgar expression "worldly" people are capable of. Sadly, given my own numerous failings, as with Franklin's, I fight demons of far greater dimensions than the use of an occasional, mild expletive, and I can only ask those, like this dear brother, to pray for me and follow the Lord's admonition that we are to love one another "warts and all." After all, The Lord isn't finished with me yet.

In Omaha Nebraska, two police officers are surrounded and beaten badly by eight men, the surrounding crowd of about fifty people, mostly Negro, laughing and cheering them on and cursing one person who tried to help. Thanks to the media, perhaps this is revenge for Rodney King? Is it any wonder that the "Pasadena Vikings" and other police feel they must organize in the face of such lawlessness? Did I make a mistake in turning down that offer, some years past, to head a "Posse Comitatus?"

A word to the churches: It would make a lot more sense to me if you would send your missionaries to America than Africa. Isn't it ironic that the Bible is now welcome in Russia but effectively banned in our schools? Maybe Russia will be sending missionaries to us? But, I suppose, since "religion" has become such a laughingstock in this country, it's easier for our "saints" to "hear the call" and go to Africa. Or, maybe, America has been "evangelized." I doubt this. I rather think that America, at least its professing "Christian" population, has no real stomach for the battle. Just what would our nation do, faced with a handful of Nathan's, Elijah's or John the Baptist's? Is God so pressed for a "few good men" that He must say: "I sought for a man but I found none!"?

Admittedly, the "Franklin's" make poor Elijah's; those of us, like Franklin, susceptible to the frailties of the flesh, imbibing "spirits" and engaging in coarse conversation and friends, living as though this world and our calling means honest perspiration and study, are ill-suited to the "high calling" of "prophet." But don't you sometimes wonder, as I do, if God isn't just a little tired of "business as usual" in the churches? I also have to admit that, over the years, I have become somewhat coarse in my view of what religionists seem to consider their "struggle" with the "powers of darkness." Plain manna simply doesn't cut it and Daniel's "pulse" seems to have disappeared in favor of the dainty fare of the king. Also, it would seem that, according to my lights, the churches have proven Jesus incorrect in his assessment of the situation; you really can serve two masters. God and money speak the same language after all. Just ask Oral Roberts, et al., or, for that matter, most any priest, preacher or rabbi. Of course, don't take their word for it; look closely at how they live!

It may well be that those of us who have deep convictions concerning subjects such as abortion as contraception will have to bow to Thoreau's dictum on Civil Disobedience. Perhaps, as James Dobson points out, the future will, as with Hitler's regime, declare us the "heroes" of our posterity. But none of us who are truly convinced in our souls and minds of the righteousness of a just cause will act on things in order to become heroes or to make names for ourselves. We will be the ones who, like Luther, "... *kann nicht anders*" in such cases. I do know this; no nation has, or can, survive the murder of babies by abortion as a means of contraception or homosexuality being given legislative protection.

I was able, unexpectedly, to spend this last Christmas with my daughter Karen. She is a very beautiful and extremely talented girl. She has the most beautiful singing voice I have ever heard. I hope she will be able to find success in utilizing her gifts. Her brother, Michael, is very intelligent and talented as well. We were able to visit friends living in Mi Wuk village in Sonora and the trees and mountains were beautiful. We went up to the snow and had a lovely time of it. The Stanislaus River was marvelous; many good-looking trout pools where the river curved around large boulders.

I love my children and, no matter the heartache that comes with parenting, what a cruel loss it would be if I had been one of those that subscribed to the murder of innocent, unborn babies. But this satanic evil of murdering babies as a means of contraception is one that must be confronted by the leadership.

No matter what the "polls" say, there will be a "Nuremberg" sometime in the future, and most certainly at "God's Assize," and the issues of homosexuality and abortion as contraception will be two of its most prominent features. But only those who really believe in God and have that honest fear of His righteous justice and judgment will act accordingly. So much for the many that "say, and do not!"

We read in the Psalms: "When the foundations are being destroyed, what can the righteous do? The wicked freely strut about when what is vile is honored among men." You leaders, from Mr. Bush on down, do you understand the implications of this?

It will take an enormous amount of courage on the part of those in the seats of authority to honestly address the problems we face as a nation. The polyglot multitudes will scream "Racism!" when it is pointed out that abortion and other crimes, welfare abuse, prison population, are largely "colored" affairs. It stands to reason, therefore, that issues, such as the death penalty, should impinge on a disproportionate number of colored criminals since they figure, disproportionately, in the criminal population.

Marilyn Savant, a most knowledgeable and astute lady, when asked what she considered posed the greatest threat to our nation replied: "The hyphenated American!" I repeat what I have said: "The hyphenated American is no American!" America's roots are, to repeat, Euro-Christian. All attempts to inculcate so-called "Multiculturalism" by way of legislative means will come down on the heads of those "minorities" and their leadership in dreadful acts of violence, even as we witness the same things happening in all other parts of the world. "I am proud to be a Black, Mexican, Jew, Croat, Armenian, etc.," does not play to an American culture. It plays in Africa, Mexico, Israel, Croatia and Armenia. Neither will it play in France, Ireland, China, Japan, etc. If not, why here in America? It is insane to even think such a thing as "multiculturalism" will ever be an American theme! One must, therefore, carefully consider the goals and objectives of the media and the "special privilege crowd" and its "leadership" which is trying to force it down our throats. If there is a conspiracy of evil that is threatening to destroy our nation it begins with this monstrous lie, this cruel hoax that is creating havoc and raising false hopes among minorities and engendering hatred, anger and frustration among real Americans.

"Yankee ingenuity" is a phrase well known. "Yank" is still used throughout the world in a Caucasian context. Notwithstanding the fact that there are many, good, colored Americans, once they start beating the drum of calling attention to their color, once they start crying for special attention, once they start agitating for special privilege, once they start hyphenating their ethnicity, they cease to be American. They have divorced themselves from our noble history and alienated themselves from America's Heartland.

I like Pat Buchanan. But as the "media" try to "tar" him, I have to wonder if he will stay the course. Recently, the papers picked up a quote of his from his Nixon years. Pat had said that efforts to integrate American society may result in perpetual friction and problems could arise "as the incapable are played consciously by government side by side with the capable (Boston Globe)." He was absolutely right of course.

Now, what shall we say to those black and brown minorities, those that presently have no hope or whose hopes are the cruel ones born of false shepherds like Farrakhan, Rangel and Willie Brown? What does the white power structure; the wealthy and elite have to offer? So far, nothing more than continued government pay-offs that lead ever further into national debt, utter dependence on welfare hand-outs and the concomitant resentment, anger and frustration of the, largely white, taxpayers; and this "golden goose" is about "cooked." Patronage! That is the ugly truth of it. The leadership is "paying those people" to "stay in their place!"

And speaking of "leadership," Congress got another $5,000 pay raise this month, six months after the infamous $23,000 raise they gave themselves. To quote "Moonbeam," ex-California Governor Brown: "A Christmas bonus six months after the infamous midnight pay raise is greedy and totally unearned. This action demonstrates contempt for the American people and just how out of touch these politicians are." Well-said Jerry!

There is a new CW song making a hit: "We're Working For The Japanese!" This does not bode well as a sign of Americans' frustration with the arrogant and high-handed methods of the Japanese of doing business that, effectively, cuts the throats of American businesses. But single-culture nations such as Japan easily despise "mongrel" nations like the U.S. It is a distinctive of their own cultures to conceive of us as inferior, being "mixed blood." And what does our "leadership" consider an appropriate quid pro quo? I have to suspect that Mr. Bush's present overseas jaunt is more in the seeking and "informing" of "allies" than the expressed agenda. And that, if true, I deem most ominous, particularly by a man who faces the certainty, that unless he "pulls a rabbit out of the hat," he will be a one-term president. That is a dangerous motive for someone like George Bush.

It would serve well to bear in mind, at all times, that human nature has not changed since time immemorial, that people do the same things and for the same reasons, that they always have, whether for good or evil. Further, in spite of what Marxist, Socialist, Leftist "historians" of all stripes, both here and abroad, have tried to do in defaming our Founding Fathers and the good men following, a factual account will always portray them as men and women with a profound belief in God and reliance on His blessing and help. And it was far more than mere lip service.

I can't help wishing, at times, that I possessed Joseph's "cup of divination" or some other, worthy crystal ball; a "Urim and Thummim" that would help me see the future or know the mind of God on some of these issues. We have God's Word and that should be sufficient but, yet, I can't help but wish at times that I were more in tune with His thoughts on some things. It is fortunate that we know His mind on the subject of highest importance; that we are to treat others as we wish to be treated, that, in honoring and obeying Him, we can trust all the consequences to His hands.

But, since we are made in His image, I suspect He expects us to deal with issues as the "gods" He made us; a tremendous responsibility and truly exciting possibilities. Issues such as homosexuality God leaves no doubt about. He is unmistakably clear on these things. But slavery? Our nation, good men and women on both sides, fought the bloodiest Civil War in history on this score. Good men on each side were no less fervent in their cause than those opposing them. In truth, did the great tragedy of this war solve the problems, were they resolved? Far from it! One form of slavery was overcome to make way for another, perhaps, even crueler.

Were the fields and plantations a fair trade for the crime and drug-infested ghettos and barrios? No! Then what? Is the patronage of welfare more to be desired than the kind of slavery that the war brought to an end? Or, is that the only choice? It is at present. The cruel evils of a slavery that sunders families, that robs men and women of any hope, of any dignity, that subjects human beings to dehumanizing mechanisms, has to be abhorrent to all civilized men and women. Yet, that is the system of government we all live under at present. The system is simply more overt in its reckoning with the poor and minorities. In spite of the "tokenism" extending even to our highest court, minorities can never hope to realize any real power in a nation that must exercise a dominant ethic and culture to function and survive.

What, then, is the answer to the heart's cry of black and brown people who, as human beings, want the same things the rest of us want? Will "education" prevail? Not likely. Perhaps it would have a chance if that education was of the kind that made "Americans," but the kind that enforces ethnic differences is doomed to failure. "Home of the Free and the Brave!" That only applies to Americans! "Old Glory!" For who? Especially when our flag by the "wisdom" of our Supreme Court can be burned or otherwise soiled with impunity; who, really, would wish to die for a symbol so despised? "Shoot if you must, this old gray head, but spare your country's flag she said!" And Stonewall Jackson replied: "Who touches a hair of yon gray head, Dies like a dog! March on!"

he said. So wrote John Greenleaf Whittier of Barbara Frietchie. Now thought romantic gibberish; but not to me as a child when I learned it in school.

Nor were Old Ironsides, The Preamble and so many more only so much "romantic gibberish" to me as a child. I was an American and proud of it! Pride in my country and its history was mine in childhood. At what perverse turn of society did such learning become "provincial, ignorant, anachronistic, parochial, misanthropic, misguided, prejudiced, etc.?" Just when did pride in a nation become shame; and for what reasons? When did honest, hard-working people give the reigns of power and authority to those that despise every principle of the foundations of America? When did "One Nation Under God" become a travesty?

As I drive the cities, I see more and more "street people," more and more "homeless" and I am struck by the thought that, but for the grace of God, there go I! And, few of us are that far removed from the possibility. The recent, senseless murder of a man who stopped to help someone with a sign on their car saying "Help;" won't that prevent more and more people from attempting to aid those in real distress? Of course! The murderer was an out of work electrician, according to the news report. As with Killeen Texas and so much other, senseless, killing, are we to expect more and more people to "snap" under the pressure of a system of government that continues to enslave and rob us of any dignity, of any hope of a future? Of course!

It is a certainty that we must close our borders; a nation that cannot control its borders is lost. We must regain a national identity and purpose, our integrity and pride in our history and our leadership. My "campaign" for president is serious on these things, if for no other reason than to call attention to them. We must return property rights to the people, face the issues of abortion, homosexuality, pornography, "multiculturalism" and all forms of perversion; we must deal with those issues that are destroying us as a nation, all those things that both history and common sense tell us must be done. If we fail to do so, we must anticipate those "Final Solutions" that I have written of that are born of expediency and from which all vestiges of freedom and liberty will be removed. And that will be the final betrayal of our proud past and any hope for our future.

CHAPTER TWO

THE OKIE INTELLECTUAL

II Corinthians 11:7-9

Our grandparents had taken Dee Dee and me to a Christmas program at The American Legion Hall in Bakersfield. I was about four and my brother three years old. Some lady was on stage singing when I turned to Dee Dee and said in a loud voice: "Dee Dee, I think that lady is a painted hussy!" Dee Dee replied: "I think she's a painted hussy too!" One can only imagine the embarrassment of our grandparents as everyone within hearing range burst out laughing at Dee Dee's and my somber pronouncement concerning the character of the lady in question. Now neither my brother Ronnie nor I had any idea what a painted hussy was. Having heard the phrase a number of times, perhaps we had learned to equate it with any woman who dressed in a certain way and wore makeup. But, living a generation "behind the times" with our maternal grandparents, we children were exposed to a morality that society has long since repudiated to our destruction.

It has been a tragedy to watch my own children robbed of a society of decency, hope, adventure and romance; of individual freedom and liberty. While we, the "great unwashed," have our noses rubbed in a "schlock drama of one-dimensional players" (Meg Greenfield) called the Presidential Primaries, we sense that there is nothing that these men can, or will, do to turn our nation back to God Who is our only hope. Admittedly, it is a whole lot easier (and safer) and a whole lot more fun to "play" with ideas than to act on them; to "plunder" philosophies than to live by their dictates. Our churches and political "leadership" reflect this "play-acting" admirably.

For example, Christian doctrine teaches that we are saved by the grace of God through faith in Jesus Christ, not by any works of our own. It is also sound doctrine that works of righteousness are the "fruit" of all who are truly saved from their sins. In short: "If we talk the talk, we are to walk the walk."

As an accused "heretic," I have some strange ideas about what passes for a belief in God by the "elect." I have called many things into question that have found acceptance among the "saints" through what I have named "blind orthodoxy." Those that have read my books know what I am talking about. I have just stated what I believe to be sound doctrine. Now I share one of my, at the very least, "heterodox" thoughts. The ability to love and forgive as God commands is based on our own sin and failures and looking at them honestly. Repentance is nothing more than a Holy Spirit conviction of these things which leads the honest individual to a realization that he needs God's mercy and forgiveness; that, by the Law, he stands condemned. And, Christian doctrine has it what the Law cannot do through the weakness of the flesh God has done for us through His Son and given us eternal life through our acceptance of His great Gift of love. (John 3:16). It was by such a mechanism of "introspection" that the great Apostle to the Gentiles, Paul, could, in all honesty, consider himself to be the "chief of sinners... not worthy to be called an Apostle." The "missing dimension" in the great majority of people is the refusal to accept blame for their own selfishness. They will blame others for their sinfulness, never admitting fault in themselves, never honest with themselves, never getting the "timber" out of their eye. So far, good, sound doctrine. Now for the "heterodox" thought; just how, do you suppose, did God come to understand this process of loving and forgiving; how was it that only the sacrifice of His own Son became the mechanism of our salvation?

We learn many things through marriage and parenting that can't seem to be learned in any other way. We learn to sacrifice our own desires for the benefit of others. We learn to set aside our own interests for the sake of the good of family. In brief, we learn to be unselfish and think of others before ourselves, to love "sacrificially." That is the ideal.

The grief and heartache that comes to the parent of a rebellious child is impossible to describe. It is not that the loving parent is trying to cheat the child by the parent's insistence on obedience. The parent only treated him as ordinary parents raising an ordinary boy. It is obvious that for learning to be needed, one must make a presumption of ignorance. Of what, I ask, was the Son of God ignorant that He had to learn by "the things which He suffered?" The doctrine of his incarnation was definitely essential for learning what it is to "walk in the flesh." He had to "taste" death to understand that. He had to grow through the experiences of childhood and "childishness." He had to be "tested" in every way that we are and yet be found without sin.

This is a subject which would require a book to do justice. In this limited space I offer only the thought that God, Himself, needed to "learn" to love these "men" who He had created in His own image, these men and women who would be His "adopted" children, joint heirs with Christ, that He, by offering His only begotten Son, proves He did learn and He knows the depth of the love that He commands we are to have for Him and others.

The failure of the love of God to take root in a person's life is evidenced by that person's selfishness. It is only the love of God that enables us to live for others; to put their welfare above our own, seeking their benefit before our own. It is, then, a simple matter to understand God's righteous wrath in sending the betrayers of such love, as with an adulterous marriage partner or a willful and rebellious child, to hell in judgment of their sin.

It is evident that I have engaged in "heresy" to claim that God "learns." But I take my stand on God's own Word in the matter. No honest reading of the Bible allows of any other interpretation. God is far more "human" than religionists give Him credit. It is only in this context that much of Scripture makes any sense at all. It is only in this context that "made in His image" makes any sense.

Is the whole subject of evil to be understood in any other context? I think not. I contend that it is at least possible that God Himself has "learned" by His own "mistakes" and "failures." The entire subject of Satan and evil, of the heartache and suffering of this evil world-system only makes sense in this way of understanding the nature of God. It is also the only way I can find to make sense of the huge responsibility God has placed on us, as human beings, to "be perfect just as He is perfect." Not a perfection of men's definition, but by the definition God supplies by an honest reading and understanding of His own Word together with His natural creation.

It is just such teaching that has cut me off from organized religion. My many years among the "saints" have led me to the conclusion that they are far more comfortable with their traditional "noble lies" and "fairy tales" than having to take God at His Word and think for themselves; far better to accept the "traditions of men" than confront their own ignorance let alone act on what they profess to believe. The whole thing is a sham and mocks the One they profess to love. I am trying to make them face their own self-willed, unbelieving, ignorant hypocrisy just as Jesus did those of his time! Look at the "thanks" he got!

Before you consign me to the "outer reaches," I have spent my own time in "sighs and tears" coming to such an understanding. As with Jesus Himself, I have "learned obedience" by suffering as any child must. The righteous do, indeed, enter into life through much tribulation. And, "He who would save his life in that which is to come must lose it in this one."

As a parent I have made many mistakes and suffered many failures. Unlike our Heavenly Father, I have succumbed to punishing my children in anger on occasion. Unlike Him, I haven't always sacrificed my own desires in favor of family. But the "human condition" still remains relevant to the argument as a whole. I have, in spite of many failures and mistakes, even my own sinfulness, learned to love and forgive. But only, as with the Apostle

Paul who kept the clothes of those that were stoning Stephen and who went on to persecute the churches, by looking honestly into my own vile heart and accepting my own guilt rather than trying to pass it off on to others.

After his "Damascus," the Apostle sat at the foot of Sinai pondering and agonizing until he was able to take up the work he once persecuted. And so it was that the great Apostle to the Gentiles, the great "doctrinaire" of the Church, searching his own vile heart honestly, was able to write the definitive word on the subject of love. In "walking the walk," I have learned to take responsibility for the consequences of my own actions; that God has no "magic wand" by which those consequences are "waved away." In just such a manner I continue to love my own children no matter what they do. But, as God must also, I often wish I could shield them from the consequences of their own sin and rebellion; I often grieve for what they must suffer by disobedient choices and wish fervently I had a "magic wand," that I could "kiss it and make it all better."

I wish I knew what those loved ones gone on before me know. They are the "experts" in matters I can only make educated guesses about. I wish I still had the love and companionship and counsel, the security of great-grandma, grandma, grandad, my daughter Diana, my brother Ronnie, but, they are with The Lord and I remain to "cumber" the earth and, like you, do the best I can with imperfect knowledge; doing the best I know how to help others and my country; to learn and dispel my own ignorance about so many things.

I spent years preaching my heart out to others, including my children, to no avail. I hadn't learned the hard lesson that the individual makes the choice; I cannot do it for him. Each of us must learn the things that really count in the same fashion as Jesus; by the things which we suffer. So it is that love may cover a multitude of sins but the consequences of those sins, those we must suffer even if forgiven.

It seems I am on target about Iran. The Mideast continues to be a powder keg, presently leading all contenders in a dangerous world. Israel is attacking Lebanon and following its Zionist agenda. Iran is involved in a massive rearmament rivaling Iraq prior to the Kuwait invasion. The two nations, Israel and Iran, are bound to "duke" (nuke?) it out eventually. Iran is also hiring Russian nuclear experts and buying high-tech planes, tanks and Soviet submarines. The West, completely ignorant of the religious fanaticism of Moslems and Zionists, is unable to deal with the problem intelligently.

It is now well-known that Desert Storm was utter chaos and was won largely because Iraq was so much more inept than UN forces and the sheer weight of material thrown at it. Jack Anderson accurately called the war, after the first 72 hours, a kind of "controlled chaos," and the Air Force's command center in Riyadh a "Black Hole." Communications were deplorable, the military having to resort to courier's hand delivering pictures to battlefield units. Reports of casualties and strength were hugely inaccurate.

If it were only as simple as bombing and shooting, that would be one thing. But it isn't that simple. Religious fanaticism never is. Iran does not have the weakness of a Hussein. The Iranian leadership, like the Israeli, is dedicated to a religious philosophy that transcends any single leader. It considers itself the true follower of Mohammed and "Death to the Infidel" is taught from cradle to grave just as it is with the Zionists. There is no room for any form of accommodation to Western thought in these belief systems no matter how, for political reasons, they try to present a "moderate face" to the world at large.

Poor old Mike Tyson; how could he, with a slightly above room-temperature I.Q. possibly figure out the "system?" All he had to go on was the fact that women threw themselves at him and society approves the use of women as "objects" as they sell themselves so cheaply. Now a smiling picture of Miss Washington adorns the cover of the Feb. 24 issue of People Magazine. Quote: "I didn't do it for fame. It was the right thing to do." Just another man proving my point women control and destroy immoral men through the use of their sex. And considering what our nation has become, with adultery and fornication simply quaint "anachronisms," who can blame them? The latest edition of Random House Webster's Dictionary now shows "Womyn" as an alternate spelling for those wishing to get rid of the "men." With "Thelma and Louise" and Pamela Smart running interference, the "privileged class" of Males is being made to pay the price of what it "owes" the "poor, oppressed women." Besides Tyson/Washington, just look at the "successes" of recent "victims" who have "had to come out" and "courageously" do the "right thing:" Anita Hill, Anne Mercer, and Gennifer Flowers. Unsafe sex in America can now, at last, be legitimately defined as any relationship with a woman by a man with anything worth the woman's going after.

I can well understand the frustration women face because of the historical record. God placed man over woman. He made it clear that this was judgment for Eve's sin of rebellion. Since I have made this position so clear in my books, I won't belabor it here. Suffice it to say, women face an impossible task in our society due to their own abrogation of God's clear commands. They must deal with the historical record of men as leaders, artists and poets, writers and possessed, in general, with a great deal more of the creative gifts than women. God intended a cooperative union, not a competitive one. But He also commanded the man to lead and part of His judgment was that a man was to be responsible for such leadership no matter how a woman might try to circumvent it. In the irony of God's judgment, men have had their hands full ever since trying to exercise this leadership. It hasn't helped that, in far too many instances, men still try to blame God and Eve for their own miserable failures in exercising responsible leadership.

"The plain fact is that California's Anglo and black population is growing so quickly - some 2,000 people a day - because of continued high foreign immigration, both legal and illegal, and very high birth rates among recent immigrant groups. The only way to significantly slow population growth would be to impose much tougher controls on immigration, both directly at the borders and indirectly through means such as higher penalties on employers for hiring undocumented workers, and a much broader program of state-sponsored birth control that would contradict the cultural traditions and religious teachings of many who, through immigration, are contributing to population expansion. It's pointless to engage in a debate over population control that would create friction among ethnic, economic and age groups, especially since enactment of draconian control policies is not politically feasible. What's important is to do what Wilson says he's doing: devise some strategies to manage growth until economic, environmental or other factors impose their natural limit on the state, whatever that may be." Dan Walters, syndicated columnist.

What Mr. Walters hints at is what I have so plainly stated many times; those "other factors" will, indeed, impose their "natural" limit on this state and all others as well. And, while "draconian" measures may not be "politically feasible," those "natural limits," which are draconian beyond his conception, will take a most unnatural, evil form in "Final Solutions" like those I have written and warned of for years. Even now, with Nazi Germany as the example, a new "Holocaust Memorial" is opened at the villa in Wannsee, the birthplace of the Nazi concept of the "final solution." The present "ambiguity" of Germans about this period of their past lends credence to the fears that the "beast" slumbers but is not dead. A recent poll showed 42 percent of Germans believe that the Nazi regime had "positive attributes." Curiously, the "liberal" German leadership claimed the shrine at Wannsee was to be a repudiation of those Nazi ideals. It is, instead, a shrine to them. Is it remotely possible that the leadership knew this?

"Coincidentally," Berlin is wrestling with the future of the remains of Hitler's bunker. Just three blocks away, the Brandenburg Gate and Potsdamer Platz will be rebuilt into their prewar glory. The bunker is a "natural" for a shrine for the New Reich. Reminds me of what Zionists are planning for the "New Temple." Wonder how this competition is going to work out?

The history of our nation is deeply rooted in Biblical ethics. But, as with the Civil War, those ethics can easily be distorted to accomplish the most evil desires of evil men and women. In spite of this ugly fact, it cannot be denied that our culture is Caucasian Anglo-Saxon Protestant. All attempts to accommodate the corrupt Mexican form of so-called "Christianity," Muslimism, Buddhism, Judaism, etc. are doomed and will only be further excuses for the New Reich to exercise its philosophy of racial and religious "purification."

To add to the New Reich's agenda, only about four in ten children in major cities are properly vaccinated. In some cities, the figure is only ten percent. Of course, the statistics reflect one of the more ominous impacts of minority problems and "culture." Negroes and Hispanics don't seem to know how important vaccinations are. But the result of such irresponsibility and ignorance is the specter of many diseases which were once under control, becoming epidemic once more. Consider the impact on an already, impossibly over-burdened and expensive health care system. The New Reich has no problem here. It fits the agenda perfectly. Let the "undesirables" and "incapables" kill each other off, let them putrefy and die like flies in the stench of L.A. and N.Y.

What do you suppose the "nut," Harry Bodine," accomplished by trying to shoot judge Howard Broadman because of the judge's order that a drug and child abusing, Negro, welfare "mother" have a Norplant implant? Bodine says he tried to shoot the judge because of "religious conviction" against birth control. Yet, under the circumstances, the judge acted reasonably and humanely. Birth control is essential among minorities. If a device like Norplant is not exercised, the "natural order" will prevail. The "leadership" knows full well that there is no "liberal" solution to problems such as this. One example of the helplessness of the "system" to deal with the problems in any humane way is the problem of graffiti. You say: "How's that?" I'll explain.

Graffiti clean up now costs L.A. about $16 million a year. Architects and designers like Daniel Mellinkoff and Brian Murphy, along with several others, say: "Let's make friends with this... The initial reaction is shock but people get used to it." In other words, "If you can't lick em, join em." They could be right. Just consider what Hitler's Germany got "used to!" Consider the filth and garbage we have already gotten "used to" on TV! Extrapolated to the other problems that defy legitimate and civilized solutions, let's let the "animals" deface and destroy at will until "something" breaks. Then, we can "fix" it! Though writers like Thoreau, Melville and I find ourselves "bottomed on the Truth," (it don't pay) we take the long view that there is a reward for faithfulness to that Truth and to write other, we cannot. Of course it helps immensely that Jesus tells us that that is the way the Truth will always be treated. And, if they treated him the way they did how, he says, should we expect to be treated?

But the Truth requires "preachers" who will be true themselves. Too often the Truth, face to face with evil, is so awful in all its import that the message is alloyed with "noble lies" and "fairy-tales" to make it palatable. An example is my statements of the government using "fiat" money; that we are a bankrupt nation. Now, as a statement of fact, this can easily be verified in every household in America. The historicity of this "bankruptcy" goes back to the unconstitutional founding of the "Federal Reserve System" that Jefferson warned would, indeed, be the ruin of our economy.

In the simplest language, the Federal Reserve, not our government, prints money as a private, lending institution at the government's request. This "paper" is then "loaned" to the government at interest. This interest accounts for a national debt that has pauperized the nation. The fact that the interest goes to private lenders seems to go unnoticed by the leadership which continues to "request" that more and more "paper" be printed. In short, your "Federal Reserve Notes" are virtually worthless since they have no foundation in any commodity such as gold or silver but were "borrowed into existence" and made working Americans virtually "wage-slaves" to the bankers.

Andrew Jackson and Abraham Lincoln worked to kill this power of "bankers" who, they recognized, would strangle our nation. Harking back to Jefferson's warning, it must be recognized that congress failed to take the warning seriously and, worse, became guilty of involving this nation in international finance which is disproportionately Zionist. I quote from The Patriot: "In 1913, the bankers were able to get the Federal Reserve Act through congress which puts the nation in bondage to the bankers perpetually. The opposition to the Federal Reserve Act, which became 'law' in 1913 was so great that the only way they could get it passed was by cunningly bringing it up for a vote on Christmas eve when most senators were home on leave."

The "children of Abraham" are all those that believe in God. In the words of the Apostle Paul: "A man is not a Jew if he is only one outwardly; and circumcision is circumcision of the heart, by the Spirit, not by the written code. Such a man's praise is not from men, but from God." Romans 2:28, 29. It would amaze not a few so-called "Christians" that God calls those that believe in Him "Jews," the true children of Abraham whose faith is in Him not in the Law. This is what distinguishes the use of the term "Zionist" from Jews who, like any Gentile unbeliever, takes no form of religious conviction or active participation in any direction. It is, properly, the Zionist that has his roots in "Those Jews," that put Jesus on the cross and persecuted the early disciples. The Apostle Paul was a good Zionist until his conversion.

One of the earliest leaders of the Rothschild banking family in the eighteenth century: "Let me control the wealth of any nation and I care not who makes its laws." He did not count on Hitler! While it is a truism that, in most cases, the "bottom line" is economics, we, in this nation, are having to face the cruel truth that "liberalism" and great, "social programs" can only flourish in a thriving economy. When times get so hard as they are now, ideologues come to the fore offering "solutions" that would be unthinkable in a good economy.

When things get as bad as they are now, the New Reich seizes on the opportunity to advance its agenda. While economics provides the leverage, it is an ideology that provides the motive force for action. It helps immensely for "scapegoats" to make their presence blatantly onerous, to make themselves the "righteous targets" of an outraged populace. Every "special privilege" group will fall to the ideology of "righting injustice" and "curing" the problems of our nation. The "Us versus "Them" industry is flourishing on university campuses. Donald Kao, a student activist, is busy "selling" his ideology of "White is oppressive and bad! White 'owes' us" (the "us" being any one of color). His "program" is succinct and direct. To quote Kao from U.S. News: "White people are the privileged class. If you are feeling comfortable or normal, then you are probably oppressing someone, whether that person is a woman, a gay or whatever. We probably won't rid our society of racism until everyone strives to be abnormal."

Kao bills himself as a "diversity consultant" and universities are actually paying him to set up classes that teach White is bad; White, especially White Male, a double whammy, "owes" the "oppressed." As usual, university leadership, like the vast majority of all "educational leadership," has its head where the sun never shines and actually thinks they can promote such blatantly, discriminatory racism and never suffer any consequences. Wrong!

The Japs have a new word: Kenbei. It denotes gut-level contempt for America. The word was coined by a Japanese novelist, Yasuo Tanaka. Mr.Tanaka came up with this shortly after the Gulf War which was about as popular in Japan as it was in Iraq. The "beat" goes on! The Zionists have an outstanding propaganda machine. FLAME, operating as a tax exempt "educational" organization and advertising in publications like U.S. News and World Report will, for a donation, send you information about why the Jews, not the Arabs, have the only right to the West Bank. They will tell you a great deal more than that as well. You will "discover," according to Zionists, why Israel is the only "hope" for the world and the only "legitimate" contender for world "peace" and "leadership!"

Working hard on a "partnership" for the "New World Order," theologians are coming to terms with science. With the help of the new revelations of the Dead Sea Scrolls, it is obvious to the leadership in organized religion that God must be defined in "legitimate" scientific methodology. Since the Bible, with the help of the Scrolls, has been assigned the roll of an anachronistic book of "legends," liberal theologians are free to pick and choose what constitutes "truth." Interestingly, Germany led in this "search" and the influence of those

German theologians and scientists, together with Charles Darwin, laid the foundation for the present drive to accommodate religion and science. The "Beast" is very much alive.

To quote Darwin: "I look at everything as resulting from designed laws, with the details left to the working out of what we may call chance. Not that this notion at all satisfies me. I feel most deeply that the whole subject is too profound for the human intellect." That great scientist, Stephen Hawking: "If we do discover a complete theory of everything (the "unification" theory)... we shall all, philosophers, scientists and just ordinary people, be able to take part in the discussion of why it is that we and the universe exist. If we find the answer to that, it would be the ultimate triumph of human reason...for then we would truly know the mind of God."

One cannot fault the desire to "know the mind of God." It is inherent in our very being, in every look toward a starry sky or the contentedness of a warm and fragrant summer night in the wilderness of desert or forest, in the love of men and women and the magic of a baby. But to look to "nature" alone, apart from God's Word and His determinate work is to be tragically, even satanically, flawed in coming to understanding. It is, in short, the "wisdom of this world," and, as such, woefully deficient and utterly "disinterested" in the God-given needs and faculties of His children.

But, in the need of a fallen, sinful condition, men must find a way out that will relieve them of the huge responsibility of accountability to a "personal God." That "way" will allow for some such amalgam of religion and science which will accommodate any who wish to "worship" but such worship will be of men (or "That Man") who will promise to allow them to live as they please without the restraints of conscience or sacrificial love.

One of the few good things about my being in Merced so much lately is the chance to visit my old friend, Bill Cox. Bill is addicted to horses and the outdoors. He is one of those rare individuals with a lot of common sense and I value his counsel and friendship.

We were sitting in his place at his ranch in Stevinson where he keeps his horses. We were discussing the Founding Fathers and agreed no devices of men in their wildest imaginations could have made it happen. The history speaks for itself. That such a diverse group of men could have had such vision and purpose, could have acted in such concert in the face of virtually impossible circumstances, defies any other explanation but it being miraculous when one examines the individual, single acts of providence, every act of selflessness and heroism, studies the obstacles one by one that were overcome, scrutinizes each and every item that ultimately came together to form this union of states into this great Republic, one must be found dumb in the face of it all. You are left with only one thought: "It couldn't have happened!" But it did!

Can it possibly happen again? Is it possible to gather our nation together with a righteous, singleness of such purpose once more? Because of their failure to abolish slavery I think not. I look in vain for such men as those early ones in whom the cry for liberty, freedom and justice burned so fervently as to light the fires of rebellion to the evil men and system of injustices they faced. It certainly cannot happen at the behest of the religious charlatans, those "performers" like Roberts and snake-oil salesmen like Schuller or the "flaccid leadership" of main-line churches. They constitute a joke to the whole world and a stench in the nostrils of God. There is no "Jonah," no matter how reluctant, to call, with all the power and authority of God, our own "Nineveh" to repentance in sackcloth and ashes.

To my "professing Christian friends" out there, to love someone means you live for that one. You want the closeness of companionship; you strive to please them in every way; you constantly want to be with them and speak with them, sharing the closeness of intimate contact and your innermost secret hopes, dreams and thoughts. You WORK at the relationship and there is no doubt in anyone's mind that you are sincere because of your "works." This is what makes adultery such a monstrous thing; it is the betrayal of this love commitment and trust to which you have entrusted all your own heart and soul; your very being. And for some of you to tell me you "love God" while I see the sheer hypocrisy of your claim! We must all stand before Him one day and give an account for such a claim. Real love is tested by fire. Most of you will not stand the flames due to the lack of any of the real "fire" of God in your own lives. And many of you are already in league with Satan, doing nothing for this nation which you have the temerity to call your country! "I know not what course others may choose, but as for me, give me liberty or give me death!" And thousands of other voices rose to the challenge of this young "fanatic" and took by force of arms what would not be granted in any other way.

"Taxation without representation" was a rallying cry of the Colonial Army. For over a hundred years, our nation has had to suffer from the evil men who have forced this nation into bankruptcy, forced us to beg from other nations, sold out the ideals that better men and women died for, robbed our posterity of any hope of a future. Taxation without representation; it has made us a nation of those "tame and abject slaves" the Father of our country warned about.

There is, at least, some honor to be found in the battlefield. To die in a righteous cause was no sham to those that gave us our much vaunted liberty and future ones who fought and died to keep hold of it. Now to have to face daily the dishonoring of those brave ones; to have to stand in judgment of them as do-nothings I say: "NO!" I will not!

If ever a system of evil needed to be confronted it is the one ruling our nation today. If ever a system of injustices needed redress, it is the one we presently are slaves to. If ever a system so dishonored God it is that of this nation. There is far too much to commend the epithet of Islam: "America; the Great Satan!" I am a most reluctant "revolutionist." No path has been so strewn with obstacles to Truth as the one I have, kicking all the way, been literally forced to choose. I am the most devout of cowards, the most unwilling of prophets but, yet, *"Ich kann nicht anders. Hier, Ich stande!"*

From this great Republic, founded on God's Word and honor, the Gospel went out in a way never before seen. The greatest of blessing was ours, the greatest nation in history with the greatest of natural resources, gifted with its great leaders, preachers, inventors, scientists, artists, writers and poets. The corruption of this great country is more than I can anymore endure.

I sorrow to read the history of our nation; the histories of those far-visioned men and women who paid the price for liberty, to read those immortal documents which came from the pens of the Founding Fathers, filled with such wisdom of government that they continue to stun the reader and, once read, stir to such fury that such wisdom is now so corrupted and despised. Such betrayal screams for retribution, for God's vengeance and judgment.

I am serving notice on that "Supreme Court," the host of politicians and all others that despise God, my country and its noble dead, its ideals of liberty and freedom; I am your unrelenting enemy! You who would make "one" of the polyglot, mongrel hoards that despise God, heritage, culture and ideals and those that paid the price for them; you that think that by fiat of law you will still be able to steal my children's hope of a future others died for; I will not, as long as I have breath, let you get away with it! I will fight all of you to the death! If you imprison me I will shout for liberty and justice through the bars. A man may well lose his courage. He cannot lose his heart's cry for his children. It is not a matter of courage, for in that my heart would fail, but of righteousness and the honor of God, for a future for all our children.

For those that think my statements extreme, please consider the fact that it is obvious that our "house" is on fire. Not to announce the warning in unmistakable language would be unthinkable and, at the least, a failure to do what is imminently reasonable: shout FIRE!

While Americans have recently been flooded with bad news, the case of BCCI should make my point admirably. If we keep the fact that this was a, largely Arab, undertaking, the results are disquieting beyond the face of it as horrible as that is.

BCCI operated in 69 countries, bilking a million depositors, most of whom could not afford the loss, particularly third-world nations. Notwithstanding Stephen Pizzo's book, Inside Job, which I recommended to all of you, the fact that our own Justice Department took over two years to act at all and is presently loath to pursue indictments paints an ugly picture of graft and corruption throughout the leadership of our nation. It is estimated that over one-hundred of our "politicians," called the "Black Network," were riding this gravy train through bribes.

Even "sainted" Jimmy Carter and his close friend, the "Godfather of the Democrats," Clifford, are found to be "friends" of BCCI! The loss of any vestiges of integrity in our government are sunk in this cesspool of intrigue of Drugs, Weapons, Prostitution (including eight-year-old girls), Extortion, Graft, Corruption of governments and wholesale Bribery. Because the evidence in the case is so overwhelmingly involved with so many highly placed government leaders, the Justice Department knows it may well rock our nation in such a way that they hope the "Whole thing will go quietly away" and that Abedi and Pakistan will take the "heat." Justice knows that the "establishment" has lost control in leadership and is, frankly, unable to deal with the problem. The wholesale corruption of the leadership presented an ideal opportunity for BCCI because the actual "NEED" for an organization such as this actually existed. The CIA needed it; international police have made it happen. The history speaks for itself. That such a diverse group of men could have had such vision and purpose, could have acted in such concert in the face of virtually impossible circumstances, and defies any other explanation.

If one examines the individual, single acts of providence, every act of selflessness and heroism, studies the obstacles one by one that were overcome, scrutinizes each and every item that ultimately came together to form this union of states into this great Republic, one must be found dumb in the face of it all. You are left with only one thought: "It couldn't have happened!" But it did!

Can it possibly happen again? Is it possible to gather our nation together with a righteous, singleness of such purpose once more? I look in vain for such men as those early ones in whom the cry for liberty, freedom and justice burned so fervently as to light the fires of rebellion to the evil men and system of injustices they faced. It certainly cannot happen at the behest of the religious charlatans, those "performers" like Roberts and snake-oil salesmen like Schuller or the "flaccid leadership" of main-line churches. They constitute a joke to the whole world and a stench in the nostrils of God. There is no "Jonah," no matter how reluctant, to call, with all the power and authority of God, our own "Nineveh" to repentance in sackcloth and ashes.

To my "professing Christian friends" out there, to love someone means you live for that one. You want the closeness of companionship; you strive to please them in every way; you constantly want to be with them and speak with them, sharing the closeness of intimate contact and your innermost secret hopes, dreams and thoughts. You WORK at the relationship and there is no doubt in anyone's mind that you are sincere because of your "works." This is what makes adultery such a monstrous thing; it is the betrayal of this love commitment and trust to which you have entrusted all your own heart and soul; your very being. And for some of you to tell me you "love God" while I see the sheer hypocrisy of your claim! We must all stand before Him one day and give an account for such a claim. Real love is tested by fire. Most of you will not stand the flames due to the lack of any of the real "fire" of God in your own lives. And many of you are already in league with Satan, doing nothing for this nation, blessed and built of God, which you have the temerity to call "your country!" "I know not what course others may choose, but as for me, give me liberty or give me death!" And thousands of other voices rose to the challenge of this young "fanatic" and took, by God's blessing and force of arms, what would not be granted in any other way.

"Taxation without representation" was a rallying cry of the Colonial Army. For over a hundred years, our nation has had to suffer from the evil men who have forced this nation into bankruptcy, forced us to beg from other nations, sold out the ideals that better men and women died for, robbed our posterity of any hope of a future. Taxation without representation; it has made us a nation of those "tame and abject slaves" the Father of our country warned about.

If ever a system of evil needed to be confronted it is the one ruling our nation today. If ever a system of injustices needed redress, it is the one we presently are slaves to. If ever a system so dishonored God it is that of this nation. There is far too much to commend the epithet of Islam: "America; the Great Satan!" I am a most reluctant "revolutionist." No path has been so strewn with obstacles to Truth as the one I have, kicking all the way, been literally forced to choose. I am the most devout of cowards, the most unwilling of prophets but, yet, *"Ich kann nicht anders. Hier, Ich stande!"*

The greatest of blessing was ours, the greatest nation in history with the greatest of natural resources, gifted with its great leaders, preachers, inventors, scientists, artists, writers and poets. The corruption of this great country is more than I can anymore endure. I sadden to read the history of our nation; the histories of those far-visioned men and women who paid the price for liberty, to read those immortal documents which came from the pens of our Fathers, filled with such wisdom of government that they continue to stun the reader and, once read, stir to such fury that such wisdom is now so corrupted and despised. Such betrayal screams for retribution, for God's vengeance and judgment.

I am serving notice on that "Supreme Court," the host of politicians and all others that despise God, my country and its noble dead, its ideals of liberty and freedom; I am your unrelenting enemy! You who would make "one" of the polyglot, mongrel hoards that despise God, heritage, culture and ideals and those that paid the price for them; you that think that by fiat of law you will still be able to steal my children's hope of a future others died for; I will not, as long as I have breath, let you get away with it! I will fight all of you to the death! If you imprison me I will shout for liberty and justice through the bars. A man may well lose his courage. He cannot lose his heart's cry for his children. It is not a matter of courage, for in that my heart would fail, but of righteousness and the honor of God, for a future for all our children.

For those that think my statements extreme, please consider the fact that it is obvious that our "house" is on fire. Not to announce the warning in unmistakable language would be unthinkable and, at the least, a failure to do what is imminently reasonable: shout FIRE! While Americans have recently been flooded with bad news, the case of BCCI should make my point admirably. If we keep the fact that this was a, largely Arab, undertaking, the results are disquieting beyond the face of it as horrible as that is.

BCCI operated in 69 countries, bilking a million depositors, most of whom could not afford the loss, particularly third-world nations. Notwithstanding Stephen Pizzo's book, Inside Job, which I recommended to all of you, the fact that our own Justice Department took over two years to act at all and is presently loath to pursue indictments paints an ugly picture of graft and corruption throughout the leadership of our nation. It is estimated that over one-hundred of our "politicians," called the "Black Network," were riding this gravy train through bribes.

It wasn't BCCI's owning American banks like Independence and First American that brought about its downfall. It was, primarily, two things: the greed of its leaders and Zionist pressure. The greed factor is quite understandable but what caused the Zionists to act? Simple; BCCI was Arab controlled, made large amounts of money available to Moslem terrorists and terrorist organizations and countries like Libya. The challenge to the Zionist agenda was too great to let BCCI continue.

Since the media is largely Zionist controlled, it is easy to see that it will not let Justice off the hook but will do all it can to keep the heat on it until the right "deals" are struck which will satisfy Zionist ends. I found it quite ironic that the "sting" took place in Miami with its large Jewish population. I don't believe this was mere "coincidence." Those of us who make it our business to keep in contact with a few "gray" organizations take it as a given that the majority of police forces are heavily imbued with "vigilantes," but BCCI was an opportunity for the largest vigilante force in the world, the CIA, to act on so many fronts. The "need" was there. It isn't just the leadership of our own nation that has lost control, the nations of the whole world face as bad, or worse. Now, without the help of BCCI, those that "need" the instrumentation of such an organization are forced, once more, to do business with the Zionist controlled world bankers.

I like George Will most of the time. A couple of recent "beauts" are worth passing on to you: "Life is priceless. It sounds good but is inapplicable as policy. Times have changed; for the worse, naturally." George failed to give credit to the French philosopher of "Night Flight" but his statement "... For the worse, naturally," is a somber reflection of a thinking man's attitude in these horrific days. If George thinks any "change" is going to be for the worse, it speaks volumes and only reinforces my own protracted warnings of what lies ahead for us. The fact that we nod our heads when the statement "Life is priceless" is made doesn't obviate the fact that it just isn't applicable as policy, for, as Saint-Exupery stated, "We live as though there were something of more importance, but what thing?"

I'm glad Gary hasn't cut me off his mailing list. I often find something of value in his newsletters to pass on to others. Most recently, he mentioned the story of Joseph in Egypt. He makes the point that, since God deliberately placed Joseph in this position, it was to serve His purpose. And so it did.

Gary points out a "double standard" at work in this history. I know Gary strongly disagrees with many of my own thoughts about the nature and works of God but he, probably unwittingly, gives a most telling evidence of one of my points here; that God does, indeed, condone slavery in some instances and has "experimented" with this issue.

Now Joseph, in order to save Egypt, had instituted virtual slavery of all the Egyptians in order to save the nation from the deadly famine that encompassed the world at this time. It was this famine that forced the removal of Jacob to Egypt and, eventually, the bondage of the Israelites and the demonstration of the power of God in their liberation. You would do well to study this whole concept in the Bible for yourself. Keep the distinction which God makes between indentured servitude and legal slavery in mind when you do so. It is most enlightening.

Dan Walters recently wrote of California's "rigid class structure." He mentions a Wall Street Journal article which talks about Great Britain's role in the European economy: "England's rigid class structure, its exclusive education system and its welfare state all reinforce a stagnant status quo. 'We're drifting into the backwaters of Europe,' economic historian John Saville is quoted as saying. 'If things don't change, we'll become an ill-educated outpost with nothing to sell but our heritage.' Californians should pay attention to Britain's malaise, because their state shows signs of emulating it."

But, as many economists are now pointing out, "Rhetoric won't end recession!" The fact that virtually no one believes any of the campaign "promises" of leading politicians leaves only "rhetoric" without any sign of substantive change for the better. And even though Pat Buchanan promises needed changes while the Democrats tell us "we are all part of the team (read perverts, minorities and convicted murderers included)," I doubt even he has any idea of how such changes such as the economy, Zionist influence and controlling our borders is to be accomplished. Joseph in Egypt is an apt illustration of what is presently working in our own society and, particularly, in California. We now have a rigid class structure as I have often pointed out. The gap between the "haves" and "have-nots" has become so pronounced that there is simply no denying it. The have-nots are slaves already. Our "Pharaoh" is an evil system of government that keeps them in "their place" by welfare "pay-offs." Now this could only go so far, as Joseph found out. In a short time, the people of Egypt had to turn over their lands and then their own persons to Pharaoh in order to exist.

In California we have reached the point of no return. Taxation together with high illegal alien and minority birthrates and immigration have pauperized the state. We have simply run out of options short of slavery. Now, it can be argued vis-à-vis Egypt, that slavery isn't all bad. Was Joseph immoral, as Gary points out, because he became an advocate of slavery when faced with our own impossible circumstances? Was I being immoral when I broached the same subject some time ago? No. I, like Joseph, was simply being pragmatic.

When I warned of those "Hitlerian" so-called "solutions" as being the only viable courses of action left open to us, was I advocating them? Of course not! But that broad streak of Platonic pragmatism that runs through my being leaves no room for wishful thinking in the face of indisputable fact. These things are going to happen because they are the only courses of action left. With George, I concur that "change" will be for the worse in the face of a Godless and adulterous generation. I find it of great interest that even some Negro leaders are of this same point of view! You will have a lot of trouble digesting this tidbit but I will share the thinking of one in particular; Jeffery M. Johnson. Mr. Johnson says, I would think jokingly: "One of the things that slavery guaranteed was 100 percent employment." In the context of Mr. Johnson's speech it isn't funny. He claims Black males are a "dying species." He is a nationally recognized expert on urban education and management. His contention is that the Black male is the "New Bald Eagle" and may need the same efforts by government to save from extinction. He says: "Every institution that is supposed to make a difference in his (the black male) life has failed... They have failed him in terms of not being able to keep his attendance in school. They have failed him in the sense of not being able to give him something to do productively."

I might ask Mr. Johnson how this differs from the same prospect for Caucasians? I know; it would be a difference in numbers alone. But both white and black face the same bleak prospects. However, it is a fact that Negro young men are far more likely to be killed in violent confrontations than whites. Hearken to my own "racist" statements of a "white-dominated" power structure against which minorities are bound to lose to in "class struggles." At least Mr. Johnson recognizes the facts and openly admits that the only "black hope" is for Negroes to compete legitimately for wealth and power within a Caucasian-dominated society. That is a breath of refreshingly pure wisdom from a Negro leader.

I have to wonder if slavery, as I mentioned some time ago, wasn't preferable, even kinder, to what minorities have to deal with now in the "more liberal" environment of the ghettos and barrios? I wonder what Benny Carter and Lena Horne would say if they could have given voice to their honest convictions. When I listen to the magic Big Band sound of Carter and Lena's "I Surrender Dear" there are visions of the antebellum gentility, where, unlike the North, chivalry, manners, a man's word and integrity were more than clichés and women enjoyed their rightful place and were cherished and protected for their virtuousness. It took the "rape and pillage" by the "Carpetbaggers" and "Scalawags" of the North of the South, men like John Patterson, to inculcate the violence, racial hatred and prejudice that became commonplace where it never existed before. It took the destruction of a better society where Negroes were in far better circumstances than they have today to bring the real shame to our nation we face now. For a more enlightened view of the whole matter, I refer you to "The Tragic Era" by Professor Claude Bowers. It's over 500 pages of facts that stultify the mind. The brutality of the North's treatment of the South will make you sick. You are left wondering at the shame of it all. But it serves well in getting at an understanding of what ultimately came to pass in the South and our whole nation as a consequence of the Civil War. You will also be possessed of a greater understanding of my apologetic for the Klan of that time of our history.

Had the founding fathers followed Franklin's advice to exclude slavery and Zionists by the Constitution who knows what the future might have been? But we cannot fault them for not foreseeing a time when freedom of religion would result in the chaos of every kook having a field day all in the name of God! Those great men couldn't possibly have known that their own efforts would be so distorted, as with God's own Word, as to make room for a hundred God despising religions and perverts being given government aid, even government assistance, protection, special privilege and subsidy.

Can you possibly imagine the anguish of Hamilton, Madison or Jay in view of what our Judiciary has become? "...and that an ordinary degree of prudence and integrity in the national councils will insure us solid advantages from the establishment of the proposed judiciary, without exposing us to any of the inconveniences which have been predicted from that source. Publius." How could they, with their conception of European, English, Christian foundations and culture, have possibly entertained any thought of the evils instituted by that very "limited" Judiciary so divorced from Christian ideals and far removed from any semblance of the "prudence" and "integrity" of these "Federalist" authors!

By the Lord's goodness I was able to get away to the cabin for a short time recently. A large, saucy gray squirrel and a couple of cottontails greeted me when I drove up. As I got out of the car, I could hear the quail calling. The air was crisp and fragrant with pine and the odor of new grasses and wildflowers, thanks to recent snow and rain. The sun was out in brilliance while puffs of fleecy clouds dotted the higher mountains round about. I had tried to contact a couple of my friends to join me but, sadly, they were too "busy" to bother with an old man's foolishness of simply enjoying God's renewal of strength and purpose through His great creation.

The lake has filled nicely promising good fishing. The springs, brooks and streams are running with crystal, cold water. There is still no magic like the ripple on the surface of a pond or pool from a rising trout taking a fly while I watch from a stand of pines, granite boulders and shrubs.

I managed to bring a few of my needed books back with me. They are, in my dotage, the "friends" that, like good music and art, never fail. I look forward to the time, when, by God's grace, I can remove to the cabin or a similar place and "finish my course."

Much as my legs and back now trouble me while driving any distances, I still enjoy traveling. Right now I drive the San Joaquin a lot and still marvel at the "breadbasket" of California. The state faces insurmountable problems but, I know, if our leaders had the courage to do so, there would be hope of renewal. Sadly, it would take such courage that is not "policy" or "politically sensible" to do the job that I fear it is not likely; but if more and more welfare recipients complain about not getting enough to pay their cable TV bill or braces for their kid's teeth?

James Boswell, in his dedication to Sir Joshua Reynolds states: "The world, my friend, I have found to be a great fool, as to that particular, on which it has become necessary to speak very plainly. I have, therefore, in this Work (on Samuel Johnson) been more reserved; and though I tell nothing but the truth, I have still kept in my mind that the whole truth (remember

Melville?) is not always to be exposed...though malignity may sometimes be disappointed of its gratifications."

It has fallen to my unhappy lot not to be able to avail myself of Boswell's sage advice. In spite of the fact that the Truth does not pay, I cannot but expose the lie and, to do that, it must be met with Whole Truth. And, while in my case, malignity is not disappointed of its gratification, to do other is beyond me. There is no solace in my doing the job that so many weak-hearted, cowardly and hypocritical "brethren" fail to do. I grieve for their loss and the Lord's loss, not for my trials and "wounds" by the "enemy," even the most grievous, those I suffer from my own "household" and "Joseph's brethren."

> *Her smile's a gift frae 'boon the lift,*
> *That maks us mair than princes;*
> *A sceptred hand, a king's command,*
> *Is in her darting glances;*
> *The man in arms 'gainst female charms*
> *Even he her willing slave is,*
> *He hugs his chain, and owns the reign*
> *Of conquering, lovely Davies.*
> *The Charms of Lovely Davies by Robert Burns*

Where the society gone that not only produces the "Burns'" but the appreciation of their fine and gentle sentiments; the virtues of real romance? What loss, what loss, what tragic, grievous loss!

> *Let her be as the loving hind and pleasant roe;*
> *let her breasts satisfy thee at all times and be*
> *thou ravished always with her love.* Prov. 5:19

So speaks God of the "wife of your youth," never to forsake her or her to forsake you. That is God's ideal and command. That is real romance. Now our schools pass out condoms, our young people laugh at Burns and Browning (if they ever hear of them) and live with the fear of AIDS. God will not be mocked!

My own often caustic, sometimes sardonic and, occasionally, rapier wit is well-tested in these times. I wish Sam or Will Rogers were available with their genius at pricking the balloons of pompous asses. But the world is a far more dangerous place today, fast becoming inimical to life, full ripe for the prophesied *Gotterdammerung*, let alone any promotion of gentleness and romance. Perhaps they might not fare as well as I. It isn't that Socrates, Galen, Aurelius, Locke, Berkeley or Hume are no longer relevant; they are simply, as with the God of Joseph, unknown in this Babylon; our "Egypt." It isn't that we no longer need to heed the wisdom of past generations; as Thoreau and others warned, we are "too busy" for the things that make humanity unique and valuable and, having become "too busy," we now have time only for war and Pharaohnic slavery that at least promises bread.

Philosophical, even pragmatic truth, as with the Gospel, has always been poor pay. God says: "Why do you waste your substance on that which is not bread?" So it is that even the "Bread of Life" is disdained by this generation that is "too busy," for those for whom the "cares of this world and the deceitfulness of riches" have choked The Word of Truth and a sinful world continues to choke on it.

Look for more about Japan's version of Jim Baker, Mr. Ikeda and his S.G.I. and its American "campus," SOKA. Japanese leaders are alarmed by his successes as he enlists the aid of the Japanese Mafia and his Brown Shirts and call him a combination of Baker, Hitler and Stalin. There was a simple dignity among my Okie "kin" as my brother and I were exposed to it in our early travels across this nation. The labor camps are deeply etched in my mind. John Steinbeck and Woody Guthrie did them some justice but you had to live it to learn its lessons. I will share some of these with you in the next newsletter. I yearn for "Walton's Mountain" and "Mayberry."

CHAPTER THREE

THE OKIE INTELLECTUAL

MAY, 1992A

II Timothy 3:12

I just returned to Bakersfield from a quick trip to Lancaster. I really enjoy the drive. Going out, I took 178 to Comanche and headed for highway 58. The iron birds were bobbing their heads, sucking the black nectar for industry but, intermixed, were the orchards, row crops and vineyards. We have just enjoyed some thundershowers and the air, clean and scented, was filled with white, puffy clouds; a glorious morning.

Heading East on 58, the drive over the hills through Tehachapi, the green of the mountains, trees, grass and fields spoke peace to my soul. Descending to Mojave and then on highway 14 toward Rosamond, the desert was especially beautiful and traffic was light, allowing my mind to soak in the tranquil magnificence of the wide vistas that I have always loved and never tire of. I longed, once more, for the simplicity of earlier years when I and the children or a buddy would take our Colts and Rugers and chase pesky jackrabbits in the great "Empty." I recalled flying out of Fox in the Alon or Stinson and winging all over the Mojave, the trips to Apple Valley and Palm Springs, to Kernville and other places just for the sheer joy of it.

In the reverie of a tape of forty's tunes and precious memories, the knowledge of what had just transpired in L.A. and other places seemed distant and unreal. Reality was the music and escaping to those times when life was simpler and people were kinder, when there was time to enjoy all those things that wind up in the archives of the mind.

But the "teacher and preacher" was insistently prodding for a place of dominance. So it was that I had to forcefully speak to that gentler part and take, once more, the roll of the writer, composing things in my mind that are the harder part of my humanity. "It's a dirty and thankless task but someone has to do it!" Why me, Lord? And the Lord seems to insist, "Because you know!" So, in obedience to Him and, returning to Bakersfield with my notes, I sit once more at this infernal device and put the thoughts into words that I always hope will make a difference. Here goes:

The recent riots have been a wellspring of excruciating, national soul-searching. We are seeing ourselves as people really are in all our fears, ignorance and prejudices; in short, the truly, human condition and it's an ugly thing to have to face.

U.S. News has its cover in stark colors of red, white and black declaring in large letters: RACE AND RAGE! Newsweek vies with a young, angry, gesticulating Negro against a wall of flames and in large letters: AMERICA ON TRIAL - FIRE AND FURY! Articles and letters proliferate screaming the obvious: We are a nation divided and it's getting worse, not better!

Cultural Anthropologists are drowning in a sea of information that has only one bottom line: Multiculturalism is a failed experiment. The historical imperative of human nature and nations will never allow of it. When those Negroes mobbed a car, mistaking a light-colored "one of their own" screaming: "He's white, kill him, kill him!" it speaks more to the fact of our condition in this nation and the entire world than all the glib phrases of all the sociologists and liberals combined.

The august Kerner Commission, founded to examine the causes and offer solutions which emanated from the Watts Riot 25 years ago declares, after considering the recent riots: "Our nation is moving to two societies, one black, one white - separate and unequal." But you who subscribe to my epistles heard it first from me and at no expense to the taxpayers.

I read the silliness of James Q. Wilson, writing for the Wall Street Journal, as he makes the ridiculous, tired, party-line statement: "To Prevent Riots, Reduce Black Crime!" Right on, Mr. Wilson, and, pray tell, just how do we do that? Silly me! Of course! As Mr. Wilson points out with his gift for erudition, all we have to do is soak the taxpayers more and more for more and more failed "social experiments" which will make taxpayers more and more angry and frustrated! Now why couldn't I have figured that out?

But I can't get past the niggling doubt that a few hundred more billions are going to overcome the salient fact that the Negroes that do make it to "White Standards" still think of all those they leave behind in the process as "Niggers!" I certainly faced this fact while teaching at Watts when the Negro teachers beat the kids out the door when the last class bell rang so they could leave the crime-ridden neighborhood and get to the safety of their better, and safer, class environments in Downey, Hollywood and Alhambra. As one said to me when I asked about living in the Projects: "Are you crazy? That place is for the niggers!"

We come face to face with another unassailable fact: While the looters were a mixed bag, the hatred was directed, predominantly, toward a white system and white people. Granting that the Vu decision was already burning in Negro consciousness Asian businesses were hit hard because they were seen as the "haves" and, simply, and unfortunately, just convenient.

As monstrous as it is, there we were, face to face with the Beast as we watched, repeatedly, the beating of Rodney King, as we watched the wheels of "justice" turn for Stacey C. Koon, Laurence M. Powell, Theodore J. Briseno and Timothy E. Wind, four white officers. Then we watched as the Beast took things into its own hands and the fires, killing and looting began. We watched as Negroes took their revenge against a city and Reginald Denny, a white truck driver; we watched as the "thin, glass pane" separating races shattered and watched Asian victims try to defend themselves against the hoard of vandals. We watched as L.A. Police retreated from the violence and let the Beast have its way with a city. Then we watched as the troops moved in, belatedly, to try and restore order and the arrests of over 13,000 people took place. We watched as an estimated, nearly 40,000 jobs and tax base of a city go up in $700,000,000 flames, adding greatly to the financial burden of an already bankrupt State. Insane!

An ultra-conservative backlash will find fertile soil to offer Draconian "solutions" to these problems and "killing the poor" becomes the only viable alternative to our fiscal woes. Oh, of course, no one is going to come right out and say: "Kill the poor!" But taxing them out of existence or making them slaves to the State amounts to the same thing. In brutal fact, it has always been God or Satan. When men's hearts are so steeped in darkness that night becomes their dawn, there is only one course of action left; kill or enslave the poor.

None will heed the warning that exchanging The Bible, the Old Deluder Satan Act and McGuffey for Catcher in the Rye and Evolution as fact, that Affirmative Action, legalized discrimination against Caucasians, burgeoning social welfare costs etc. have alienated an entire society and removed any true compass heading for standards of justice and morality. As I have said for years of education in particular, I say now for our whole system of government and society: "We could not have designed a system for failure any better if we had done so intentionally!"

The hard things I have been saying for so many years have been an attempt to get people to look at themselves and our nation honestly, to admit that our national course has been headed in this very direction of national suicide and destruction. Forsaking the ancient landmarks of Plymouth Colony and the founding fathers, we live with the natural result and express surprise that the lines in front of subsidized ignorance, poverty and immorality grow ever longer! But, as with my, and others, warnings concerning a failed educational system, no one of any real authority gave heed and we now live with the abysmal results.

Dear, old McGee said: "The mountain should do better than propagate the mouse population. Wind is not the child of the church of Jesus Christ or of any Christian organization that is true to the Book. The Word of God produces legitimate children of God." But the churches are too busy producing "wind and mice" in the comfort and safety of their pews, of listening with itching ears to comfortable sermons, to even notice the real warfare going on.

The insanity of refusing to accept reality shows itself in such madness as Santa Cruz banning bigotry by a wide-ranging ordinance that fuels the very fire it attempts to extinguish. Crazy! This in the face of recent events and everyone engaging in "Straight Talk on Race" and the burgeoning evidence that a conspiracy of silence has attended the actual facts concerning AIDS, that the "noble experiment" has resulted in escalating illegitimate births, disease, crime, drugs, ignorance, fear and bigotry and a failed justice, economic, government and educational system; in short, fertile soil for anarchy and a Ross Perot to "heal" the problems.

In regard to race, I quote John Kerry from his Yale speech: "We cannot equate fear of crime or concern about deteriorating schools with racism and then expect those we have called 'racists' to invest in the very neighborhoods they have fled!"

The logic of such Platonic reasoning flies in the face of the emotions of the Beast; we will have none of it! When injustice is so blatant that the only possible course of action is the unleashing of the Beast, blood is the required sacrifice and nothing else of lesser quality will sate his appetite. Love, repentance, restitution, forgiveness are the purview of God and His children; they are weak anomalies, completely incomprehensible to the Beast, to the children of the Devil.

Several people, most recently by a young friend that used to be a student of mine, have called my writings "inflammatory". But, I would ask, as would the Apostle Paul, Luther, Paine, Franklin, Melville and Thoreau, "Since when has Truth ever been anything else but?" We always stand as Pilate, torn between the Truth of Jesus or the Lie of Satan; there has never been any middle ground for decision and it is a battle to the death with no quarter asked or given. I, admittedly, have faint hope of the churches re-awakening to this inescapable fact to which they only give lip service at best. Resist unto blood? We aren't even resisting to the point of perspiration!

The "Cruel Hoax" I have written of has come to its logical conclusion. Has it really been forty years since I lived in Camelot? That long for the "Dream" to come to fruition as the Nightmare of inescapable reality? It was easy to become lulled into a sense of "All is right with the world and God is in His Heaven" during my Weedpatch, National Forrest and South Bay days.

But Birmingham lay ahead and the results of misguided legislative action at "forced equality" were seed thoughts in the liberal climate of that time. Now we live, worry, are enraged and kill as a result of the bitter fruit of what was sown.

Now Robert J. Samuelson of Newsweek has just cause to worry about a Perot candidacy. But, dear Bob, your own ethnicity aside, your "liberal" fears fall on the deaf ear of the New Reich and you will find yourself a target, as I do, of that New World Order.

I have to wonder if Mr. Wilson, as with Samuelson and Spike Lee will ever accept their own contributions to the rage and anger that has erupted? Or, will they, as Wilson writes, continue to try to make us "rednecks" the cause of all our woes? Will they continue the tired line of trying to make us feel guilty for being rightly afraid for our own Caucasian children, for being afraid of a bunch of young, angry, criminal Negroes or Mexicans, of being afraid of going into "certain neighborhoods" day or night, of crying out for justice against those that are largely responsible for the vanishing middle class? That group, largely Caucasian, that has paid the costs for all the privileges such as medical and dental even the poorest minority enjoys which, in most cases, middle class Caucasians cannot receive or afford is not supposed to be enraged itself?

Speaking of being afraid of driving or walking through neighborhoods, try comparing the "discrimination" of being stopped by a policeman because you are Negro or Mexican with the actual death and violence that actually happens for being Caucasian and in the "wrong place!" Oh yes, it does happen in certain places for minorities as well, but not at nearly the numbers as Caucasians. "Kill him, kill him, he's white!" That is what is heard out of all proportion to "Kill him because he's Negro or Mexican!" And a Caucasian America will react to just that kind of threat and be damned because of being rightly angry and afraid.

Ignorance breeds prejudice and poverty. Not a unique statement. But I carry it a step further than most people mean by it. Ignorance of The Bible and the history of our nation are breeding immorality and destruction. Can we ever recapture those values that made this the greatest nation the world has ever seen? Can leadership be found that will make the necessary sacrifices to, once more, instill hope of a future in our young people? I hope my following words together with the books I have already written will do their part in the plan to do what needs, desperately, to be done before it is too late.

EDUCATION IN AMERICA

I promised to once again address myself to the issue of education after a long silence. So, blowing the dust off my research and bringing myself current in my experience and reading, I tackle the project in the hope of making some sense of an extremely complex subject.

Without any apology, I am decidedly Christian in my approach and recommendations. For that reason, I introduce the subject with some observations that, in my thinking and experience, must be aired and considered for the reader to have a clear idea of what has happened to education in this nation and what will have to be done to turn the disaster around.

It is a fact that each generation needs its history taught and learned all over. It is also a fact that when that history is corrupted and twisted to evil ends, the results, as with Hitler's Germany, ends in death and destruction.

It took the "revisionists" to make our heroes and their goals ignoble. While it is true enough that great men and women of our past have often been romanticized and painted larger than life, the truth of Plymouth Colony, our Revolution and the men and women that gave us the greatest and freest nation the world has ever seen is in fact, larger than life.

The fact that what became "Public Education" became so because of the noble purpose of teaching morality has been lost to the past generations. The fact that reading was taught in order for people to read the Bible has been lost to us together with the fact that the Bible was our national textbook for generations. It wasn't that long ago that virtually every classroom had the Ten Commandments posted and school began with prayer and reading from the Bible. And it was not "prayer" to some unknown "deity" or some Islamic, Jewish or Hindu mishmash but prayer to the God of the Bible!

Certainly the history of education is there for anyone to read for themselves; but few do so. But very few will find, in modern histories, the full account of the prominence of God's Word in shaping what would become the greatest educational system the world had ever seen.

But to understand what happened to bring us to this sorry pass we live with today, the betrayal of those early ideals, you have to understand what has happened in the churches. For this reason, I have to provide a frame of reference that might be called the psychology of Christianity. While it will appear that I have "lost my way," I ask you that have little or no background in "Churchology" to bear with me as I provide the needed parameters for the fullest understanding of what went wrong.

I will, undoubtedly, appear narrow and "preachy" in much of what I need to write, especially in this needed, prefatory material. But, because of the subject matter, that is unavoidable. Just hold on to the thought that I am going somewhere and all this is necessary to arrive at the proper destination. Further, since education was, predominantly, the purview of the churches in the beginning, what ultimately went wrong and what is ultimately needed to fix it will lie at their doorstep.

"You can't please everybody" is an inescapable truism. I have been denounced by the religious for being too irreligious and by the secular for being too religious. To many, I am neither fish nor fowl; to some in both camps, I am a self-excommunicated heretic. In short, because of the national shame of the condition of education, I must be doing something right to have so many "experts" mad at me.

But, because the problem is, in the words of General MacArthur: "Basically theological!" I cannot but begin by laying some basic "religious" groundwork. All you "fellow heathen" out there please bear with me and, I trust, I will eventually get to the "good" part.

Division among believers is of Satan. The divisive spirit is contrary to the work of The Holy Spirit. If there is to be any work of consequence done by God's people it must be done in the spirit of love and unity. But this cannot be a cooperation bought at the cost of sound doctrine (teaching).

If we can accept as a given that the Lord's people are woefully ignorant of true, Biblical scholarship (and I do not believe this has to be proven) then we can easily accept the contention that such a lack easily leads many into grievous errors and makes them susceptible to false teachers.

It is small wonder that such people will have trouble properly instructing their own children. Yet many of these same people are teaching in schools, Sunday schools and even, to our shame and hurt, in pulpits.

I recently had a mathematics teacher ask me what an exponent was. This is like a mechanic asking what a piston is or a housekeeper what a broom is.

While such ignorance on the part of someone who should not only know better, but is well paid to know, is almost beyond credulity, it is the kind of ignorance that is rampant among believers (and our state schools).

I do not mean the kind of ignorance that cannot name the books of the Bible, cannot find certain passages or does not memorize "key" verses, does not attend church faithfully or does not seem to care for others. I mean the hurtful kind of ignorance that makes believers unfruitful, divisive, covetous, envious, joyless and, in general, of no use to God in the building of His Kingdom.

Before we can properly approach the question of Godly education we need, desperately, to clear the air concerning some specific areas of religious prejudice and ignorance, even antagonism to God's Word. We need to be aware that it exists in Christian schools also.

Having personally started three Christian schools, I have had to review a small mountain of Christian instructional material. While there are some very worthy works, the vast preponderance is either worthless or downright heretical.

As a psychologist and educator, I have discovered the same plight with most of the Christian books about parent-child relationships (I except most of Dobson's); they simply display either a woeful ignorance of what God says or choose to distort it.

Unless we apply the criteria of Deuteronomy, we have an exercise of man's autonomous reason as opposed to God's wisdom (That is, we think we know better than God). God has promised us that if we will do things His way, He will bless and keep (Proverbs 22:6 and many similar passages). We do not know better than God. To excuse ourselves from God's clear statements because of circumstances of culture, time, peer involvement, etc., is to be without excuse.

If we would be ruthlessly candid with ourselves we might admit that we think the Lord's way is too hard or that He simply does not understand our peculiar circumstances. While no believer would consciously admit to this, isn't that what is actually being said?

There is a generation already that is without natural affection, disobedient to parents and ridiculing the beliefs of their elders. This did not happen because of keeping God's Word and applying it. It happened because people thought they could interpret God's Word in a comfortable and careless fashion.

The Godly home or school is one that honors God's Word and applies it literally in the fashion God intended. But, in altogether too many cases there is only a veneer of religiosity or even hypocrisy at work.

For example: to tell a small child that God sees and hears all we say and do, better be augmented by the life of the teller. In too many cases, again, we see lip service only, rather than doers of the work.

The practical, and God's Word is imminently practical, application of God's Word in raising and educating our children deserves more attention than it has received from Bible scholars. But in point of fact, too few are truly qualified to do the work.

At appointed times the Israelites were to cleanse all leaven from their houses. I will suggest you first of all take a similar approach in both the home and the school.

The root of the problem is, as I have said, the lack of sound doctrine among believers. I point out the obvious fact that even as parents, in too many cases, have entrusted the value structuring of their children to state schools, believers, sending their children to Christian schools, have been guilty of the same thing.

God says parents bear the responsibility of such instruction, not some institution. But too many religious leaders have failed to denounce unbiblical teaching and heresy leaving parents to their own floundering devices to sort out the truth. It is very easy to point out the obvious fact of parental responsibility and ignore the tremendous responsibility church leadership shares in this.

God established the Church and its leaders, in part, as an entity that would lead the flock. Such Godly leadership is sorely lacking today. Where the trumpet gives an uncertain sound, the people are left wandering.

It is to you, my brothers and sisters that I presume to present the challenge of this message. The Remnant lives largely in your camp. You are the ones who know the Truth and are vitally concerned that your lives count for God. You are the ones that want a part in building the Kingdom, that want to honor God, that hunger and thirst after righteousness, that want to be a channel of the Holy Spirit.

But the plain fact of the matter is that you too often appear to be more concerned about getting others to subscribe to your "purity" of doctrine than showing the world you are Christians by your love (John 13:35). I believe most strongly in the absolute necessity of preaching and teaching sound doctrine, but "strong meat belongs to those who by reason of use have their senses exercised to discern both good and evil." (Hebrews 5:14). That "use" is done in love or it is worse than useless. I firmly believe God honors perspiration more than good intentions and the real work and labor of God is just that; work and labor. We are to "labor for the Master" and the work is, preeminently, a labor of Love!

The tragic and pathetic part of all this is, that while there are divisions among believers because of "Phariseeism, etc." the Gospel is brought into disrepute in the eyes of the world and our words are "like tinkling cymbals and sounding brass." (I Corinthians 13:1).

There is a very real distinction between "legalism, Phariseeism" and sound doctrine. The distinction is the love of God in us.

Jesus stressed love in all his teaching and so did the Apostles. It is not difficult to understand Peter's consternation over Jesus' question of Peter's love toward Him. Understanding the love of God enabled Peter and others to eventually lay down their lives for him.

It is only given to those who can willingly give of themselves, absolutely for others, to understand what God means about love being the end of all His hopes and dreams for us. It is only such love that almost paradoxically can often find itself alone with a full understanding and appreciation of the loneliness of God Himself and the necessity of His gift of love to those of us who seek such love.

When we examine the list of rules by which some men attempt to justify themselves we discover that such attempts fail miserably confronted by a logic that dictates all such efforts must fail. We might wonder why, since such failure is an obvious reality, men continue such vanity? The answer is hard.

Love is the end of the law for righteousness. But, love is the highest morality and carries with it the immense responsibility of acting upon its demands and the knowledge it gives us, and, of course, love is supernatural in its extreme sense. The love Jesus spoke of transcends as it fulfills the law. It goes far beyond human comprehension and is known better than understood. It is what I know "In my bones!" It is that part of God Himself in a few that gives so willingly and actually condemns lesser attempts at so-called morality. And, excites hate in those who will not commit themselves without reservation.

Experience has taught that suffering pain and tragedy matures such love. The Scriptures say that even though he was God's Son, he became perfected through the things he suffered. But, having given himself to the suffering established that love and set the motives and goals of our hearts far beyond human understanding.

Such love does have a price in a sense. It demands everything. It encompasses soul, spirit and body. It is easily misunderstood because the world demands order and legality of which this love makes a mockery. The giving which is implicit in such love cannot be held by the boundaries normally set by even good people.

It creates life and happiness while, many times, creating enmity and hatred. Jesus said he did not come to bring peace to the world but a sword. And so, his love does in fact divide. It divides husband and wife, brother and sister, father and son, mother and daughter. But to those who accept it on its terms it is the absolute against which all else must eventually be measured. Anything short of it will be cast aside as unworthy.

Such love often is asked to risk all else of less meaning and sets its own priorities, often at great cost by this world's standards. But the one who loves in this way can give even his life for those he loves least, knowing there is something of far more value than life and a loss to be far more feared than death.

Maybe it would profit all of us to experience something of what our dear brother Richard Wurmbrand did in prison. Such suffering does reduce all to a very elemental level. What strength of unity is possible when only God is the criteria of fellowship and love for one another. Bearing this in mind at all times, nothing less than a serious attempt, in His Love, at unity among the brethren is going to stem the rampant tide of Godlessness which we face. If we continue to "bite and devour one another" simply because we do not baptize the same way, do not understand "election" the same way or practice communion the "right" way, we trample the love of God under foot and make it a hollow hypocrisy.

I am adamantly opposed to the concept of a universal, organized, world church. Such a church, I believe, will be a satanic victory, even as a world government. But, if peripheral points of doctrine keep you from offering me the hand of fellowship, you are acting contrary to the love and Spirit of God.

The body of believers is just that- a body. The hand is distinct from the foot but, they are members of the one body and hurt to one is hurt to the others. Why can't we accept the clear message of God's Word in this? Are you strong where I am weak? Then pray for me and counsel with me but do not cut me off, doing despite to yourself.

Is my liberty judged by you to be sin? What does God warn in this regard? Should my good be evil spoken of just because my collar may be "backwards?"

Beloved brothers and sisters , if there is a sign of the times we may all easily discern as taught in Scripture it is this: that the love of many will wax cold; that they will heap to themselves teachers, having itching ears; above all else, the love of God will be overshadowed by a multifaceted kind of "orthodoxy" that will attempt to supplant the simple Gospel that even the smallest child can comprehend, "Believe on the Lord Jesus Christ and thou shalt be saved." Acts 16:31.

The attempts of false teachers throughout the centuries to place conditions on the free gift of eternal life have only resulted in continued divisiveness among believers. While Satan cannot delude the true believer into thinking God's love may be earned or bought by some righteousness of our own (Isaiah 64:6 & Titus 3:5), he has been vastly successful in deceiving many into thinking a man cannot be a "proper Christian" or used of God if he does not fit some common or peculiar mold.

This is a very roundabout way of coming to a conclusion: All believers need to humble themselves under the mighty hand of God (I Peter 5:6) and repent of any hardness of heart toward other believers. Since whatsoever is not of faith is sin (Romans 14:23) and love is greater than faith (I Corinthians 13:13), how should God judge our unlovingness?

I fear that it may be this unloving self-orthodoxy that will prevent my children's generation from enjoying the liberty my generation has taken so much for granted. This nation was established on the Word of God. The Bible was its textbook and our Constitution, our Declaration of Independence; our very system of law and government was cast in the mold of God's Word. The implicit trust and obedience of our founding fathers was such that little had to be made of their assumptions in this regard. Modern so-called historians have often made the blunder of ascribing simple religiosity or some kind of deism to men like George Washington. But our forefathers' trust in the Word of God was absolute. They, like me, knew that the Bible was the cornerstone of true liberty. They did not need to preach it or write columns about it; it was assumed and not open to question or debate.

God's Word enjoyed a prominence then that is so desperately needed to day. The natural and revealed Word of God both testify to the need of salvation from sin. There is a heaven to gain and a hell to shun. The adversary's most successful attack has always been in getting men to question God's Word. By denying God's Word, by questioning it, by excising portions of it, by twisting it, we are denying our children the freedom, the liberty we enjoyed and our children will pay a terrible price for our so-called convictions and separation.

I realize that time is short and the night seems fast approaching when no man can work. Let us please pray for one another and bear one another's burdens and show the world that there is indeed a balm in Gilead.

There are few issues that deserve the attention of God's people today as much as that of education. Politicians are getting on the bandwagon in droves. America, the Flag, the Home and Education are a "hard money" currency for the astute politico.

I have given many years of my life to the areas of both state and Christian education. By professional experience and academic training, I am an expert in the field. This expertise was gained at tremendous cost.

While God's people have failed in many ways, none has had the impact on this generation that our failure to properly instruct our children has had. We rightly decry the deplorable conditions of our pulpits and seminaries, the decline of Godly scholarship and true worship, the ungodly environment of a culture gone mad with sin of every description.

We wail and lament the foundations being destroyed, the ancient landmarks being moved and all the while we see multiplied hundreds of millions of dollars being spent to enlarge the empires of religious charlatans that prey on the gullible and emotionally immature, whose so-called ministries do nothing to effect positive changes or educate The Lord's people in the building of His Kingdom.

Children "are an heritage of the Lord." We are warned by God what the penalty of not properly instructing our children will be. We have reaped the whirlwind and are more than willing to blame everything and everybody but ourselves for our own failure to follow God's clear instruction for the training of our children. God says that if we train up our children in the way they should go they will not depart there from (Proverbs 22:6). Does God lie? He does not! Men lie.

No one, Jew or Gentile, should mistake the Great Commandment. In Deuteronomy we read, "Hear O Israel, The Lord our God is one Lord: And thou shalt love the Lord thy God with all thy heart and with all thy soul, and with all thy might." Deuteronomy 6:4,5.

Now, we are familiar with this passage and no child of God will find fault with it. But how many clearly understand or even know the significance of God's placing the following in the immediate context of The Great Commandment, and which forms a part thereof? "And these words, which I command thee this day, shall be in thine heart: And thou shalt teach them diligently unto thy children, and shalt talk of them when thou sittest in thine house, and when thou walkest by the way, and when thou liest down, and when thou risest up. And thou shalt bind them upon thine hand, and they shall be as frontlets between thine eyes. And thou shalt write them upon the posts of thy house and on thy gates." Deuteronomy 6:6,9

I have worked with nearly two thousand teenagers in classrooms in eight different school districts. I have worked with pupils from Kindergarten through graduate school but I have spent the bulk of my time with adolescents. I can speak volumes of their cries, fears, frustrations and hopelessness for our present age. The Psalmist could weep that no one seemed to care for his soul and that is the lament of our young people.

I suppose most are aware of the tragic epidemic of suicides among young people today. The reason for this is the fact that they have lost hope and purpose for their lives. The natural consequence of such loss is a turning to drugs, alcohol or anything that will fill the void. Since such things are obviously self-destructive, the person will suffer continuing dissolution.

If, in fact, it is true that God alone can satisfy the longing of our hearts for real purpose in our lives, then it naturally follows that anything less will not take His place. All else will ultimately fail.

I took my Doctorate in the field of Human Behavior. I learned nothing about the nature of man that God's Word did not clearly address. Few positions in our culture bring a person into such intimate contact with the pulse of a generation as does teaching. I can make the categorical statement that the parents that truly believe and live the truth of God's Word need not fear what the world may do to their children.

But how much easier it would be if parents truly knew what God expects of them in this regard. I realize that the majority of believing parents think they know. I can tell you from years of experience that THEY DO NOT! Such a statement invites challenge but if you will bear with me I think you will finally agree that I have not overdrawn the situation.

We have been told that our nation is at risk due to the deplorable condition of our schools. This is not news to someone as familiar with the problem as me although if I were not so intimately acquainted with the situation I would have difficulty believing it is as bad as it is.

To understand the problem, I need to clearly delineate it as it relates to both state and Christian schools. A history of the problem is also necessary for clear understanding followed by its current status and, finally, resolution of the problem. As you can see, this is quite an ambitious task and must be undertaken in parts. For you to understand and, hopefully, accept some of the seemingly outrageous things I may say, I will offer some prefatory material.

First, even as most men reject the Gospel, leaving only a believing remnant, the truth of what I am going to say will only be accepted by a remnant. I tell young people that the answer to life is available only on an individual basis; that there is no reason to be hopeless or live in fear, but only on an individual basis. So, what I am about to say will have to be received in the same manner. It will be far too hard for the majority of even those that call themselves believers. It could not be otherwise if God's Word is to be believed and adhered to.

How many of those we call great in the eyes of God failed with their children beginning with Adam, thence to Aaron, Gideon, Eli, Samuel, David, Solomon, Hezekiah and so many others? How very difficult is this supreme responsibility of rearing our children in the nurture, fear and love of God. How much easier it is to preach, teach others, sing in the choir, do visitation work, drive a Sunday school bus, be a seminary professor or anything else in the name of God than to do the job God requires in our own homes. If some of the greatest men of God failed in this regard, how can we hope to succeed? Where is the wisdom and strength to enable us to see our children saved and walking in the light?

Before you pass these things off as rhetorical questions, search your own heart diligently for specifics rather than a shallow, religious cliché for an answer. I had three treasures of God entrusted of the Lord to my keeping and nurture. While, as a teacher, I dealt with over 150 children on any given day, these were my special, personal responsibility. I learned more, as a parent, from my own children than I did from the hundreds of others I worked with each year. I have lost count of and forgotten most of the books I have read on this subject over the years, both religious and secular. Few, if any, really address the true issues. God has clearly said His Word is the foremost essential to knowledge, true wisdom and proper behavior. To remove this from the area of religious cliché to reality is a monumental task which only the hardiest of the Lord's people can accomplish; the Remnant.

I could, and will, in the fuller body of this work, multiply anecdotes and examples of how difficult the task truly is. Many of you probably already believe you know this but you may not have heard anything yet. Few preachers or teachers either know or have the courage to "tell it like it is." Perhaps I am willing to do it because I have no reputation or empire of which to covet or enviously protect. Perhaps God, in His wisdom, has kept me a lonely plowman for the task. If so, praise God!

I will ease myself and you, dear reader, into the work by calling attention to the fact that so many of you are already aware; the fact of division among the brethren.

Along the way you may believe I have forgotten the theme of this work, Education; but please believe that I have not. Oftentimes a teacher, to make his point indelibly clear, follows a tortured and seemingly circuitous route.

There is little clearly delineated, detailed and consecutive instruction for the people of God today. I cite the following as an example:

We are very knowledgeable of the fact that, "the natural man receiveth not the things of the Spirit of God." It is too sadly true of our age that the True Gospel is so little known and preached. At a time in history when the technological marvels of communication enable us to reach, in an instant, the uttermost parts of our globe, we discover much that is religious, but little that is The Gospel.

What we do have is a cacophony of voices, each proclaiming that The Gospel is only part of a system of philosophy, the adherents of which would immediately repudiate the very term being applied to their own movement or group. On the contrary, most of these latter-day groups are quite sensitive to any criticism that would suggest that they preach anything but "Christ and Him crucified."

Jesus pointed out that the children of this world are wiser in their own way than the children of God. I have no doubt that he was calling direct attention to the fact that the Lord's own seem to be more intent about this world than that which is to come.

Not that the child of God should not be, or is not, vitally concerned about this world or can be excused from the responsibility of being effective in it. But a hell-bound person is readily seen as being wise in getting all from this life that he possibly can by whatever means possible.

A ruthless criminal easily commands more respect from me for the very integrity of living by his system of unbelief than the most moral individual who rejects God. At least there is no veneer of hypocrisy to the man who lies, cheats and steals openly in flagrant disregard of the laws of men and God.

Such a person is easily perceived as lost. But the wolves that ravage the flock are seen as angels of light. "If another comes in his own name, him you will receive." We may express outrage over how people could be deceived by Jim Jones and not even recognize the immensely larger danger of an Oral Roberts, Robert Schuller, et al.

We are not of the same "stuff" as a Jeremiah or Luther. We are guilty of "having men's reputations in regard." We are not willing to stake all on Jesus and forsake homes or lands for the sake of God. We are guilty, not of the seven deadly sins so much as of the seventy times seven deadly "virtues."

John Bunyan would have great difficulty distinguishing the Vanity Faire of his time from its counterpart in organized religion today. No one who knows me would accuse me of being a pietist. But God knows we could use a large dose of the piety practiced by our forefathers (and foremothers). Organized religion, today, is a laughing stock and, largely, a reproach to God.

Within the inner circle, preachers lie about the number of baptisms, professions of faith, listeners to their radio or TV programs, personal and church incomes, missionary involvement etc. HOLY LIARS! but liars nonetheless. The world hears, sees and understands such chicanery and laughs or derides; deservedly so.

The TV spectaculars of some of these "Electronic Churches" put Hollywood to shame. Religionists like Jimmy Swaggart, Rex Humbard, Peter Popof, Oral Roberts, Robert Schuller and a host of lesser "lights" have discovered a market and know what sells. We have traded the coliseum with its lions for a mess of pottage and call ourselves rich and full, not knowing or realizing that we are naked, poor and full of dead men's bones.

As a teacher, I have heard the cry of unsaved young people for the truth, for someone to just not lie to them anymore, to help them to make sense out of a system seemingly designed for their destruction; a system that leaves them without hope in world gone mad (Mutual Assured Destruction included).

How easy it is for me to reach out to these young people and tell them the "Old, old story of Jesus and His Love," but invariably there are those in the group that are tainted by some damnable heresy as outrageous as Mormonism, Jehovah's Witnessism, Romanism, Mooneyism or Charismaticism. More insidious yet are the errors of the Pharisees in the camp of so-called fundamentalists who certainly hold sound doctrine, even as their predecessors did, but insist on adding their peculiar list of "touch not, taste not," rules and regulations. In the ranks of this latter group are to be found those who should know better, but it is here we find some of the greatest dangers and challenges.

It is here that we find those that are called after Paul, or Cephas or Apollos or Christ (I Corinthians 1:12). It is among this group of people that we find those that know the truth but prefer the label and distinctiveness of their group and their interminable and divisive lists of "do's and don'ts" and "holy days" and their own peculiar brand of "true separation."

It is to this group we may assign the blame for being better known for the label of the church rather than the label of God; who give intellectual acquiescence to the truth of God's Word and deny Him by the hardness of their hearts no matter the altar calls, bus ministries, baptisms, decisions, hundreds (yea, thousands) in Sunday School, visitation ministries, Bible schools and colleges.

The announced goal of the National Education Association and virtually every teacher union is state control of education (i.e. control, by proxy, of the "professional" education hierarchy). Federal funds are so much a part of the school picture (tragically, even private schools) that school leaders now say they can no longer function without such support. Yet, Title I funds are almost entirely spent on programs and personnel which have absolutely no merit for a community school.

The State of California is obviously committed to control of schools to the extent that bail-out funds post Proposition 13 are virtually assured and the cry of the schools is that more, ever more, is needed. It is business as usual in spite of the clear desires of taxpayers for real, school reform. I quote a recent article on this very subject:

"Federal aid fails to improve public education. With graduation ceremonies fresh on our minds, it is dismal to read that the Department of Education has estimated there are 24 million functional illiterates in the United States, virtually all of whom have had from eight to twelve years of compulsory public schooling."

The Elementary and Secondary Education Act of 1965 was by far the largest federal aid to education bill ever enacted by Congress. National Education Association consultants helped draw it up. President Johnson heartily endorsed it. The U.S. Treasury gushed forth billions of dollars.

In his book, "New Trojan Horse in American Education," Samuel Blumenfeld tells us the results of those billions of federal dollars spent to improve education: "From 1952 to 1963 the SAT (Student Aptitude Tests) verbal mean score rose a modest two points, from 476 to 478. But three years later, in 1966, it was down a full eleven points to 467. In 1970 it was down another 7 points to 460, and in 1977 it had plummeted to 429, a staggering decline of 48 points from 1963."

In the last 10 years California dropped 58 points in SAT scores, Connecticut 49, New York 59, Massachusetts 46, and Texas 53. Every state experienced a considerable decline.

Federal money obviously did not solve the problem. It appears to have made it worse." (Raymond Wilson).

Because of the inroads made by the adherents of permissive and "innovative" education, test scores naturally began a steep decline. In order to cover up, the educational hierarchy began to denounce tests as irrelevant. It was easy to enlist the aid of educational "quacks" from universities who knew a good thing when they saw it. There were reputations to be made by joining the growing throng jumping on the "education band wagon" and, not incidentally, money.

Some of these "professionals" began to say that tests were not only irrelevant, but also harmful. The utter hypocrisy of such self-serving attitudes can best be understood in a time framework of the early 50's. Because of permissive and altruistic dogmas gaining credence through our universities, the "cure" for failure to learn was to devaluate learning and the "cure" for social failure was to devaluate success. I quote here from Rushdoony:

"Teachers from such universities or colleges become propagandists of the statist creed. Their obvious inferiority has been substantially demonstrated by the Army's draft deferment testing program, which reveals that not only are prospective teachers the LOWEST in intelligence and ability of any group, and by a substantial margin, but that those who are headed for school administration are a RADICALLY INFERIOR group."

In 1956 William Whyte Jr. in THE ORGANIZATION said: "It is now well evident that a large proportion of the younger people who will one day be in charge of our secondary school system are precisely those with the least aptitude for education of ALL Americans attending college."

How very prophetic these words have become. Statist education can only offer, at the very best, a mediocre education, since by virtue of its very being and the essence of its character it is repulsive to individual responsibility and integrity. It cannot call the best to its ranks. This leaves it with those whose primary interests are, in general, self-serving.

A good example of this is a letter to the editor of a large, metropolitan newspaper headlined, "As scores fluctuate, so does Cortines."

I quote the text of the letter:

"Oops! Superintendent Ramon Cortines' slip is showing. On publication of successful California Achievement Program scores for San Jose Unified high school students, Superintendent Cortines credited the increases to the fine reforms going on in his district by administrators and teachers, high expectations for kids, etc. (Mercury News editorial, March 29, 1985).

"However, last November, upon publication of unsuccessful CAP scores for elementary students in San Jose Unified, Cortines criticized CAP as a 'bad test that doesn't test students, not credible, not in the interest of reforming education, not in the interest of business and industry buying into public education,' etc., (Mercury News, November 28, 1984).

"That nasty old Educationese bugaboo raises its ugly head once again: High test scores mean competent educators; low test scores mean inept tests.

"Cortines enjoys so much respect and support in his community. Let's hope he does not blow it on fluctuating test score interpretations."

This Superintendent is no different than most. They are trapped in a failure mode and lack the real educational and experimental expertise to change the situation. The CAP is not a difficult test; it really assures a ninth grade level of achievement at best.

In their attempts to change things, school board members have discovered they are little more than rubber stamps for socialist, union goals and objectives. Any valid attempt at real change is rewarded by utter frustration and the enmity of the educational establishment. I know, personally, of one case where a board president lost his bid for re-election because of illegal electioneering by teachers in their classrooms. This good man tried to get the district to require at least one counselor have actual work experience. Can you imagine a school district requiring a counselor having actually worked out in the real world? Unthinkable! In actuality, anyone with real work skills, especially blue-collar skills, is looked upon with a great deal of suspicion by those who are sole products of the colleges and universities and have no practical skills.

California and New York have resolved the problem of declining test scores by the subterfuge of instituting their own tests that, of course, show "progress" being made. Johnny and Susie are no longer going to be penalized for a poor education. The State will now declare them "adequate."

There is none of the dust of nostalgia for the good old days of the little red schoolhouse in my own view. We must deal with realities, not wishful thinking. The predominate reality for any Christian is that there exists no real motive force for moral behavior and the concomitant discipline necessary for learning apart from God Himself.

I am not speaking of some sophist drivel concerning a universal fatherhood of God and brotherhood of man, but a clearly defined doctrine of the supernatural sovereignty of a just and loving God who has declared Himself in nature and the Bible.

To speak of good for goodness' sake or virtue for virtue's sake is to talk nonsense. To talk of community need, social progress or the "golden rule" apart from God is just so much delusion at best and hypocrisy at worst. We are deceived if we believe that God will bless evil with good, mocking Himself.

The ultimate answer given by God is to know the truth that alone sets free. It is a freedom to choose the good and fight the evil; the freedom to accept personal responsibility and know that our labor in the Lord is not in vain; the freedom of knowing that our lives have directing purpose and meaning through the truth of God.

I make no pretense of being particularly astute, let alone prophetic, in regard to this world's condition or future. We all have available to us the same, general media of information. We all, to varying degrees, possess the ability of reason and deduction. Our mission is to teach children not only English and arithmetic but to affirm the divine trust of the parent-child relationship. We fight, not as those who have no hope, but those whose hope is eternal and absolute.

Well-intentioned individuals have attempted to "enlighten" me on my position in regard to state education. There is no question about my harsh treatment of any Godless system. I can take no other position. The problem is that state school systems have been such sacred cows that anyone who speaks against them is too often treated as though they are part of some radical "down with mother, flag and apple pie" fringe group. I will freely admit that there are far too many who make a lot of noise and have nothing of constructive value to say. But I ask that you consider my personal qualifications and track record before you lump me in such a group.

The present condition of state education is particularly distressing in view of the total, historical framework of the schools in America. We are now told by the bureaucrats and so-called "professionals" that it is required for the good of the state to sacrifice our children on the altar of state education. Thank God this is not yet law but the intent of government and unions is plainly to make it so. Constant vigilance is required to hold such legislation against private education at bay.

The NEA is one of the most powerful lobbies in Congress. It promotes the concept that all education must come under the "guidance" and control of the state. In other words, absorption of all individuals into the collective whole is good and individuality is bad.

The Christian position is to place responsibility on the individual and this does not mesh with the humanistic, socialist goals of a God-denying system. With ex-president Carter's blessing, we witnessed a major advance of this system through the establishment of a separate, Federal level bureaucracy of education. There is no question about the ultimate goal of this Department of Education, in spite of good men's intentions to the contrary. It will become controlled by the teacher unions and directed to Federal control of all education "for the common good of all society."

The most tragic aspect of all of this, to me, can best be represented by a story told by a man I consider to be one of the best and most faithful Bible teachers I have ever personally known; Dr. J. Vernon McGee. As he tells the story, a man was driving through a beautiful part of the country and stopped for gas at a station overlooking a lovely valley with a picturesque little town nestled against the tree-studded hills. A surprising number of church steeples rose above the community. As the attendant was filling the man's car with gas the man remarked, "My, the people in that town must certainly love God!" The attendant, who was a resident of the town, replied, "I don't know about that but I know they sure hate each other."

I offer this little anecdote to point out the obvious fact that unless God's people are willing to surrender to the headship of being true to the true Gospel of love and put aside their petty differences, we will make little impression on the evils of this world's system that is destroying our children and families.

I do not believe the present crop of so-called "evangelists" is helping. I do not believe the doctrine of the tongues, healing, visions, miracles, prosperity, signs and wonders crowd is, in any way, advancing the cause of God. Their cause is largely seen as emotional and money. By decrying good, honest scholarship and trying to shout down those that disagree with them, they are harming and bringing shame to the Gospel. At a time when the Lord's people need desperately to pull together, these "wonder-workers" are deceiving people, at great financial cost, all in the name of Christ. And what, you may be asking by now, does this all have to do with what's wrong with education? More than most people realize, as I will prove. Just bear with me. You will be amazed, I'm sure.

CHAPTER FOUR

THE OKIE INTELLECTUAL

JUNE 1992

Revelation 3:10,11

I walked into a time machine May 29th. I went to the first school reunion I have ever attended and saw a group of people I had not seen in forty years; my special thanks to you Ann, and Arlene for making it most memorable. My thanks to the Malones and so many others for what had to be a Herculean effort to put the whole thing together. While I was only able to attend the function Saturday morning at the park, it was more than worth it.

The past forty years had taken its toll on all of us. It's a good thing we had nametags. But, as we got re-acquainted, the years slipped away and we were all, once more, transported back to an age of innocence in the late forties and early fifties. I could recognize Ann and Arlene but, I have to confess, it took a little while to see, in the mature bodies and faces, the "children" of those bygone years; however, once recognition took hold, the "kids" were there after all.

As a loner way back then, and now, I contented myself with meeting a few of you like Jim, Lee, Bob and Lois, J.L., Ann and Arlene; the rest of the time sitting by myself, watching and listening, and letting my imagination take me back so far in time to the magic of the old Kern Valley and the old schools. I had been in touch with Henry, Tom, Russel and Ted in recent years. I wish they could have been there at the park. In spite of the absence of a few, I was surprised by how well represented my group from that far away time was. I was told Myrtez and Donna were there but I didn't see them. No one seemed to know what became of Ethel.

Of course, the great majority of those that attended were strangers to me. By force of circumstances I removed from the valley in 1953 and lost all contact with you folks. But I never forgot any of you. Because of the construction of the lake, many newcomers were not really known to me at all.

I focused on Ann and Arlene because they, more than anyone, epitomized what changes with time and what doesn't. I was a painfully shy boy during those years of school. It was a fascinating thing to examine my thoughts and emotions as I spoke freely with two girls I would have hidden from back then. Girls were strange and interesting creatures but totally alien to my sphere of abilities. Talk to one? Terrifying thought! Not on your life!

Oh, it wasn't because I didn't want to, I simply couldn't. For only the briefest time, shortly before my departure to the South Bay, was I just beginning to find the courage to even think of speaking to you girls. I would apologize for the many, seeming, slights of that time, but it wasn't that I wasn't interested; I simply lacked the ability to communicate with the opposite sex.

Like many of us, I fell in love with a couple of you but could never say so. The romance of the valley and the music we all shared, the poetry of the time and place, could not have but resulted in all of us being in love at some time in our young lives back then. But, I was a loner because I was not able to communicate those desperate longings and feelings to any but the forest, mountains and creatures with which I felt at ease. While most of you were managing your adolescence in more normal ways, I was hiking the mountains with rifle or shotgun and note pad or fishing Bull Run Creek.

Part of the problem was the fact that I was living with my grandparents and, thus, rose a generation behind times. I was reading Sir Walter Scott, Brett Harte and Cooper while many of you were into literature of much more contemporary usage. The band and orchestra were more my forte and interest than mixing in the more usual interplay between most of you. Thus, self-excluded for the most part, I didn't really get to know many of you as I wished I could.

Even being one of the few kids with his own car and the magnificent job as the old Elementary School's first "Junior Custodian" (remember Guy Schultz?), I still bluffed my way past, denying the fact that I was simply too shy to really communicate my real feelings for some of you. I could deal with the guys, in that I could be "hard as nails," but you girls? Not a chance. Terrifying! I fell apart inside and nothing but confused and twisted verbiage was at my disposal in your presence; totally mortifying.

That is what was so intensely interesting in speaking with Ann and Arlene. The "painfully shy boy" was still trying to think of something to say. The 56-year-old man with a Ph.D. in Human Behavior was discussing and analyzing the situation: Fascinating.

In no time at all, the "boy" saw you girls forty years back. We were all, as with some of you guys, teenagers once more. The years rolled away and the magic of that simple era was there once more. The jarring impact was the talk of children and families. "Not possible!" I thought to myself. We're supposed to be talking about the latest hit song by Rosemary Cloony or some track meet with Johnsondale, not "jobs, careers, husbands, wives and children." No! I wanted to be back at the old schools when we were all young, strong, invincible and so full of hope for the future, excited by the possibilities of life, surrounded by the pristine, majestic mountains filled with wild life, deliciously clean air and water, so far removed from the stress, hatred and strife of the metropolitan areas.

Nostalgia and melancholy may find a voice in the magic recesses of memories, in the longing for those simpler times; but our eyes and faces bear testimony to the fact that we have lived, each one of us, lives that have had to deal with the grief's that come with the passing years, of realities far removed from the simple joys of adolescence spent in our valley.

I tried to share some of the magic we had then with my own children as they were growing. I would often take them camping, shooting and fishing in the area over the years. When I started teaching in the Antelope Valley, I would take many of my students as well. Over the years, I maintained a kind of "presence" in the area. I must confess I did not care for the growth that, little by little, began to restrict and destroy much of what used to be wide, open country. Too many "foreigners" began to invade. I remember when the gate had to be installed at the end of Burlando Road to keep the riff raff out and prevent them from trashing the Bull Run area.

Also, it seemed that real estate agents were breeding like lice everywhere. Now I have always placed real estate agents just a notch above judges and TV "ministers" and a notch below winos and used car salesmen; I haven't met one yet I would trust. They have always seemed a blight on the valley. But how good it was to have a chance to "run away" from the present of a world gone mad to those days of yesteryear, when we all dreamed dreams and all things were possible to those that believed.

One of the things that nagged at the corners of my mind was the fact that we were back then, before the TV generation, readers. Reading was important to all of us regardless of the genre. Our teachers helped make it important. Two things seem to correlate in our present, dismal society, a society that doesn't offer much to the young people of today; seems bent on, rather than offering hope, destroying them. One: Poverty swells; middle class shrinks. Two: "The more students read, the better they read...Unfortunately, our children aren't reading very much." Education Secretary, Lamar Alexander.

I have already made my views of Mr. Alexander known (He should have stuck to the piano) and the utter assininity of his statement only confirms my view of the idiot. Of course our children aren't reading very much you dummy! There isn't much to read on a Playboy Centerfold or watching Murphy Brown. And that, Mr. Alexander, is the Elder Generation's "gift" to the young, the "birthright" to posterity; that and the NEA's exaltation of perverts and perversion with the imprimatur of our Supreme Court, a court that can't seem to decide whether filth and perversion is really filth and perversion.

And there is no discounting the fact that the record 8.6 million "immigrants" to our nation during the 80s mostly wound up on the Dole and the number is exacerbated by the Illegals who have helped to steal the hope of American citizens with impunity. Who can forget them dashing brazenly across the border at Tijuana without restraint. Even now the INS is being censured for chasing one who killed five, innocent people. The bleeding hearts are making it look like the fault of the INS that the S.O.B. killed those people. And just what will our "Leadership" decide? Why of course! It will do just like it did in the Rodney King case, it will make the officers of the INS look like the "bad guys" and more fearful of trying to do their, already, impossible and thankless jobs.

If folks wonder at my affinity for Thoreau, there are a multitude of reasons. I do not admire his pomposity, and he could certainly be pompous, but his arrogance, such as it was, I find more admirable than the phony humility of too many that are so obviously important in their own eyes and do nothing of which I admire in Thoreau.

In speaking of an Irish immigrant of his acquaintance, he wrote that the Irishman came to America so that he could have tea, coffee and meat everyday. "But the true America," Thoreau pointed out, "is that country where you are at liberty to pursue such a mode of life as may enable you to do without these, and where the state does not endeavor to compel you to sustain the slavery and war and other superfluous expenses which directly or indirectly result from the use of such things."

I have written so much about the laws and codes that have made owning your own property and doing with it as you wish impossible that I won't go into it here. Suffice it to say that when a government fails to meet the need for families to own their own homes through criminally restrictive codes and petty tyrants such as building inspectors, such a nation has become a slave-holding nation whose sole function is to protect the rich and powerful and enslave any who cannot afford $100,000 mortgages (not that they get paid off).

Thoreau would be one of the first to challenge, through Civil Disobedience, the unjust laws that prevent a man from building and providing for his family and, thus, circumvent the clear intentions of our founding fathers. It is the same evil system and the worshipers of the Evil One that continue to try to take the guns away from law-abiding citizens. And when my own state senator tells me "Nothing can be done about it," that makes me madder than hell! Is my own senator telling me from his vantage of the "Halls of Power" that I am to belly-up like all the other dead fish and be content to just float downstream, not resisting the evil? Not a chance senator. If you think that, you haven't been reading the essays I send you! And if you won't fight for me and other Americans who recognize this evil for what it is, I'll do the fighting for you!

I just bought a house on a beautiful tree-studded piece of property in the Lake Isabella area for $15,000. With a $1,500 down payment, I will have a $13,500 mortgage and payments of less than $200 per month PITI. This is what is known in the trade as a "Fixer." There is much electrical, plumbing and sundry other repairs to be made. But I can do these things. My total capital outlay for repairs will be about $1,000 for the materials. If I had to hire the work to be done, the labor costs would run around $10,000 (the trick is to get, what is called in the trade, "labor-intensive" houses). But because I know how to do such things, I can anticipate owning a decent house mortgage free.

I have had houses of over a quarter-million dollars value but never with the intention of paying them off. Fortunately, I still enjoy working with my hands and back as well as my mind. There are a lot of "sweat equity" opportunities out there if you have the necessary skills. But far too many people become slaves to a mortgage and general indebtedness, never planning for the future. Such people do not teach their children the necessary skills to meet the challenges of life, do not teach them to accept responsibility and take charge of their lives. The vast majority of parents are selling their children into the very slavery that consumes the parents. Like Thoreau, I would far rather be able to pick up hammer and saw and not let the bankers enslave me. Far better the "critters" as neighbors than the asphalt jungle with its noxious fumes and the attendant sorrows and crime.

Far better to drive an old, but paid for car and live in a small but paid for house. But for people like Thoreau and me, we will continue to interpret "quality of life" as the founding fathers did. I will continue to be free of debt and free to pick and choose where I live and where I go and when to do so. I will not let debt rule over me no matter what happens. Nor will I let a corrupt society dictate what I say concerning the evil system and people that continue to try to enslave my children and me.

I find it curious that Thoreau's simplicity of living and Thomas Wolfe's "Seeker," the hope of America, could sell out so cheaply. And what have we, the people, given in exchange for the highest standard of living in history (according to all the "wage slaves")? Small wonder we have become a nation without a "soul."

Granted, I have yet to find a woman who would live so simply and under the circumstances I have chosen. Not that I have given up hope, I just haven't found one yet. Of course, I haven't found one that could be faithful to one man yet either. Some of my friends have pointed out the fact that I am not trying very hard to find such. I suppose they are right, it just isn't very high on my list of priorities at this time. Sorry about that ladies.

In any event, it is back to living with the dirt and sawdust until I can make the place habitable. But the weather is nice for it and the lake and river are nearby. So is the old mining claim where I can commune with great-grandma, grandma, grandad and Ronnie. I can still visit with those special rocks, trees and hills that were home so long ago. Bull Run Creek with its large trout and magnificent pools is also at hand. I find Kernville very pleasant still except for rowdy, special events like Whisky Flat Days.

When I want to take a break from pulling wire or threading pipe, I can sit out under the oaks or a huge pine tree and let my mind wander in solitude. The nights are glorious and the stars still speak of the excitement of eternity with the Lord.

I still enjoy the drive up and down the canyon, up to Johnsondale and over the pass to the desert. There is still enough "country" in and around the valley to bring back the precious memories.

When I finish this old house, I may rent it out as I have done with others or I may stay awhile. It's nice to have the choice. I have learned not to deal in $1,000 plus a month rental units. Much better to have three or four $300 to $400 rentals, particularly "specialty properties" that are in the country. I won't work in tracts in the cities anymore. People will always need a house to rent, unfortunately, and "low-income housing" is "where the game is" within the present, evil system.

I am doing a lot of traveling to Merced, Bakersfield, Lancaster and Lake Isabella lately. It is tiring and I'm getting a tad old to do the kind of moving and loading I used to do without ill effect. But I have tools and personal items strewn about California because of my Bohemian mode of life. I also have the time to travel and visit my children, especially my "Little Angel," Karen, and friends while they don't have the opportunity to do the same.

While visiting with friends in Bakersfield, I had a "good old boy" come by and offer to buy my '64 Chevy truck. It chanced, because of all the moving about, that I had left my '69 Dodge wagon at their place also. Not long after my fellow Okie had tried to buy the truck, a Negro man offered to buy the Dodge. My buddy, good friend that he is, asked why I didn't sell the vehicles and upgrade my mode of transportation to walking! How sharper than a serpent's tooth, the wounds of a friend.

Seriously, folks, I didn't retire from having to punch a clock for a living some years ago by making car payments and keeping my Master Card maxed out. I did it by planning and working my backside off. I now enjoy the physical activity of working with my hands and back as a needed corollary to preventing the coronary that might be my lot from the solitary and sedentary task of writing. I will always be a man who has to work with hands and mind.

The physical work also keeps me lean and mean. And considering the unholy work I have to do in writing, the meaner the better!

Speaking of "mean," I must respond to James Dobson's latest mailing: "In Defense of a Little Virginity." I wish everyone in America would read this well-documented essay on the risks of AIDS and the multitude of sexually transmitted diseases facing people, particularly teenagers, today. If all the facts were known, a panic would surely ensue.

While the godless in government and education are touting "Safe Sex," they aren't telling you that using a condom is the equivalent of playing Russian Roulette (that's one chance in six, folks). Seems HIV measures .1 micron. That's 1/25th the width of sperm. We know that latex has "channels" of 5 microns. That is the reason that of 800 sexologists at a conference, when asked if they would trust a condom to protect them during intercourse with an HIV infected person, not a one would do so. Yet this same group is telling teenagers to practice "safe sex?" How? Certainly not by relying on condoms, but the "Lie" sells a lot of condoms. The best that can be said about the findings concerning the use of condoms is that at least a bullet is quicker if you want to "play the game."

There is simply no getting around it folks, the only safe sex is commitment and fidelity with one uninfected partner for life just as God planned, and commanded, it should be. Unfortunately, by allowing this nation to go to the Devil, by the elder generation's failure to adhere to the values and The Book that made us a great nation, we have sown the wind and are now reaping the whirlwind. God will not be mocked by either individuals or nations.

The problem with Dr. Dobson's essay is that it ignores the most vital points in the controversy. Not because he is unaware, assuredly, but, because, as I pointed out in my last mailing, men like himself, who are at the mercy of "Tax-exempt" status, cannot tell the whole truth. I can!

While venereal disease and AIDS cuts across all cultural and ethnic boundaries, it is largely the perverts and minorities that are both more at risk and spread the diseases to the general population. If the statistics are to be dealt with honestly, and they cannot by men who are at the mercy of Uncle Sugar's handouts, it would be readily apparent that the largest populations of diseased individuals are perverts, Negroes, and Mexicans. When it comes to drugs and dirty needles, you have the same groups. Caucasians and Asians are a paltry component in the equation. Racist? Homophobic? You bet! When it comes to the threat of a horrible death by the perversion and willful ignorance of those that are destroying my country and expect me to pay the bill and like it, that expect me to accept the risks to my children and grandchildren who are not a party to their sinful wickedness!

We have an interesting portent of the future evolving in Bakersfield. Sheriff Carl Sparks is training "Citizen Patrols" to help because the county can't afford enough deputies to do the needed job. The same day's news tells us that guns are the leading cause of death for Negroes between the ages of 15 and 19 and the numbers are escalating. Take these two things and the heated battle going on to confiscate the law-abiding citizen's guns and what do you have?

L.A. has nearly three times the number of police per 1,000 population as does Kern County; then why do you suppose crime is still worse in L. A County than Kern: simply because Kern County is still, predominantly "Red Neck" country. In spite of the large populations of Negroes and Mexicans, Kern County still maintains more of the Caucasian Ethic than places like mongrel, polyglot L.A.

But we are facing many of the same problems on an escalating scale. For example, the Mexicans want to "cure" the problem of graffiti by painting "murals" on walls and fences. Now my problem with this is that the so-called "murals" being proposed all glorify the Mexican culture. The pictures will portray old cars, low-riders, Aztec temples, Mexican heroes and faces, Mexican language; nothing of "Gringos" will be allowed.

This is nothing more than a blatant attempt to subvert the American Ethic and culture with a foreign one; and one that seems bent on destroying Caucasian America. As I mentioned in an essay some month's ago, since the "leadership" can't seem to stop the graffiti vandals, let's just go ahead and call it "art" and live with it! But, of course, the "art" must be Mexican to win approval of our leaders.

They have a valid point in one respect; if the art were Caucasian Art, it would soon be defaced with graffiti. If it is Mexican Art, it might well be "honored" and left alone. If this proves to be the case, just who is calling the shots? The Mexican criminals of course. Ethnic Blackmail does work, especially when it is aided and abetted by so-called "Hispanic" (a non-sense term) "leaders" and spineless politicians and preachers.

Ray Bradbury visited Delano and gave voice to the very point I have long advocated to others in my writing. To stay young in mind, stay in love with the things you loved when you were young. Thoreau and I agree. I will always draw strength from the mountains, the wide-open spaces of the desert, a starry sky and trout stream. I will always love the music of my youth and the literature of past, great writers. I will always love to apply the skills, mastered at great effort, in using tools of all variety, whether lathe, mill, hammer, wrench or computer. I will always love learning in a great variety of things, of making discoveries in the processes of mind or the activity of hiking and camping in wilderness areas.

The discoveries that are being made in "mapping" the brain are exciting. The idea that the "soul" may be contained in the quarter-inch thick cerebral cortex, that PETs and SQUIDs, pinpointing neural activity in all its huge, electro-chemical complexity, may finally give us insight into the concept of "The brain is the mind" or whether "consciousness" is more than the sum of such material activity, is something of intense interest to me; particularly since so much is still not understood about energy. It is this "phantom" that seems to constantly elude us and makes all areas of physics, particularly astronomy, so fascinating to me.

Believing in God I also believe in the Spirit and Soul of man. But that does not lessen my interest in the intrigue that surrounds such studies. I took my Ph. D. in Human Behavior largely because of my fascination with this last, great, biological frontier that I believe to be far more than mechanistic answers will ever supply.

Two of the men at the forefront of this controversy are Daniel Dennet of Tufts University and John Searle, philosopher and author of "Minds, Brains and Science." The battle is over whether, as per Dennet, the mind is an illusion, the brain is a machine, there is no soul or, as per Searle, such men as Dennet have failed to prove or explain anything and have tried, unsuccessfully, as I accuse theologians, to "explain away" by the simple subterfuge of "labeling" and trying to pass the labels for "explanations." I am of Searle's view that: "I think it is madness to suppose that everything is understandable by us. However, let me say we have to act as if everything were."

It is the inability to see everything in objective terms that makes us so different from the beasts of the field. Whether examining the mechanisms and motives of love and hate or looking at the night sky with the moon and stars beckoning, there is definitely a "something" that defies any attempts to restrain our imaginations. And what, exactly, do you have to offer, Dr. Dennet, by way of "explanation" for that highest of all faculties, the Imagination?

One would think that as long as so many subjective areas remain unexplained by the mechanists, things like love, hate and imagination, they would give up the argument. But, like the blind fools that, in spite of the huge amount of evidence to the contrary, still subscribe to the antiquated idea of "evolution," those that try to "explain away" the hugely complex subjective areas of human thought and behavior would throw in the towel. But "faith," even if misplaced, dies hard; even among scientists, who, after all, are only human also.

Our Declaration of Independence contains these words: "We hold these truths to be self-evident, that all men are created equal, that they are endowed by their Creator with certain unalienable Rights that among these are Life, Liberty, and the pursuit of Happiness."

In nothing that Lincoln did, said or write, could a case for his considering Negroes to be equal to Caucasians be made. Historians have, with equal facility, made Lincoln both racist and humanitarian. To fully appreciate the gravity of the argument, one has to consider the intent of the words of our founding fathers in the Declaration. Did they, in fact, really mean that they believed "... that all men are created equal?" Of course not! If that had been the case, they most assuredly would have heeded Franklin's wise counsel to abolish slavery by the Constitution. The fact that they chose, purposely, not to do so speaks volumes of their ideas of "equality."

Neither did the founding fathers consider women to be equal to men by their very words and actions. Did they, then, purposely denigrate Negroes and women? To weigh the question one must keep an historical perspective. It is the history of the times when these events took place that sheds light on the entire matter, both for the founding fathers and Lincoln.

If we can assume, and we most certainly can, that the founding fathers never intended that this nation countenance homosexuality and pornography, that they would rise up in wrath against "professional politicians," that they, even now, are crying to God to bring His judgment against a nation that has gone whoring after false gods, that has evolved a system that has become the antithesis to the very ideals of liberty that they pledged their lives, sacred honor and all their material possessions, that they would be horrified at the loss of control of our borders, of the Welfare Slavery substituted for the slavery they countenanced, just what, do you suppose, would they say of all this?

Properly interpreted, using all the skills of hermeneutics, you can only come to one conclusion concerning their use of the term "equality." It should be patently obvious that such equality was considered in the Biblical and historical use of the word with which all these great men were so familiar. This was an "equality" directed against a tyrant, King George and his minions, together with all aristocracy.

Such an "equality" did not include women, Negroes, Indians or those that were, by qualification of property ownership, education and other proofs of commitment and responsibility, automatically excluded from exercising the franchise and given authority to rule or lead in both the founding of the nation or the running of its affairs. A very "exclusive" kind of "equality" indeed!

Even by the time of my early, school years, the "propaganda" was in place that had utterly distorted the "equality" of the founding fathers to mean gender and "multi-cultural" equality. Nothing could be further from the truth than to suppose they meant anything but an equality based on ability and means, framed by European, Biblical Christian ideology. But a lying, liberal, revisionist "history" was well planted in the schools and my generation was prepared, propagandized and taught (brain washed), to pass this lie on to the next. It would take J.F.K., the so-called "Civil Rights Movement," NOW and the ACLU to really make a total mess of things.

I have met men of every color and have never considered myself "better" than they because I am Caucasian. Neither did the founding fathers consider themselves, before God, superior because of their color. But they clearly understood the mechanism of the founding of this great nation to be Biblical Christianity and, as such, primarily, according to their own culture, Male, Caucasian authority. Regardless of the "color-blind" quality of the Gospel, no other nations of the world had come close to producing the cultural distinctives that culminated in the race of men who would subdue the vast, North American Continent and bring forth the kind of government envisioned and set in place by the founding fathers.

No one in their right minds would expect a Caucasian American to be able to intrude himself and his culture into the affairs of another nation like Mexico, Africa, Japan, China, India, etc., and demand "equality." Neither did the founding fathers envision or mean such a ridiculous thing by their choice of the term "equality." The founding fathers, I'm sure, had no intention of trying to force their own concept of equality on other nations.

In sum, the use of the term equality in the Declaration was clearly intended to convey the ideal of equality based on the Christian, Biblical model. Such a model had given the European nations a distinct culture that was alien to all others. But it was a model which placed responsibility on the individual to do what was right according to Biblical principles of the Gospel, to have the liberty to choose and do the things necessary to bring forth a great nation and govern it by men who had the highest ideals of personal value, morals, responsibility and liberty and would exercise these noble things for the building of a free nation and the good of their posterity. And, I have to emphasize, it was clearly never their intention, according to the Biblical Imperative, to give women the vote or allow of women exercising authority over men or in government.

Since it was, clearly, never Lincoln's intention to give women or Negroes the franchise, A "Mr. Wills" obviously, as so many others, has his own "agenda" to advance in trying to, as the Chicago Times did, make Lincoln mean something he clearly did not intend. Lincoln obviously, in his quote from the Declaration, intended to convey the equality of those honored dead, both Union and Confederate. An understanding of the antipathy of the press and Lincoln's detractors would have made this clear to Mr. Wills. And, worse, if Mr. Wills is aware of this, just what is he trying to prove by his dishonesty? More "multi-cultural" propaganda of course!

Given the real intent of the founding fathers in the Declaration and our Republican form of government, have we made any real progress in the human condition by departing so far from those ideals? Regardless of how women and minorities may resent the exclusionist mind-set of those great men, are they better off for having demanded an "equality" which they were never intended to have? I think not. But it has allowed a great many evil men to, as Adam, blame God and women for their own spinelessness and failure to lead, for their own failure to be responsible.

Another book caught my attention recently: "Art of the Third Reich." Peter Adam, the author, has done a service by, admittedly left-handedly, he being half Jewish, in focusing attention on this much-neglected era and, even, epochal, form of expression. Whatever Mr. Adam's motives, he has captured much that was of value during Hitler's regime. One can accuse Hitler of not being a good artist but he left a legacy, decried and defamed as it has been, of peculiar treasure in the arts.

Some wit has suggested that welfare reform start from the top with America's ruling elite. With the leadership such as United Way's William Aramony soaking the "little people" and the heads of such august institutions like Stanford University bilking the people and the lawless swamp of Congress sticking it to all of us, the suggestion has merit. Taken with top CEOs who give themselves million-dollar bonuses even as their companies lose money, as the groaning taxpayers shell out for every kind of rip-off imaginable, it isn't any wonder that some are talking outright revolution or anarchy. But, dream on; the top dogs didn't get there by playing by moral rules and they know how to fight dirty to maintain their obscenely decadent life-styles. But a "French Revolution" or another "1917," who knows? If I were among the rich and powerful, I'd sure start getting worried about whom really is minding the store. Wouldn't it be something if Ross Perot...? Nah; he didn't get where he is by being "Mr. Nice."

Why did God name the stars? If you will send me your answers, I will be glad to print them. I find things like this of intense interest; maybe you do also.

Tiny Oildale continues to catch the heat from "interested parties," like Don Laity, the realtor who is trying to save his commission by accusing two county Board of Zoning Adjustments members of racial discrimination. Seems the board members were taped by Mr. Laity and said "unforgivable things" like: "I like Americans to speak American." Imagine that; expecting someone who plans to run a re-hab center to speak American instead of Spanish! Seems that is the only language the so-called "pastor" of an Assembly of God Church, one Zoya Lopez, speaks. He actually needed an interpreter at the zoning hearing. Then a pompous ass, one Richard Prado, the chairman for the Kern County Human Relations Commission, whom Mr. Laity sicced on the Zoning members, says: "American language? What is that? Give me a break."

I'll give you a break Mr. Prado, American language is English, no matter what you and Mr. Laity decide it should be. If you are both that hot to make it Spanish, move to Mexico. You certainly have my enthusiastic encouragement to go. I'll even make a donation for your moving expenses to hasten your departure from my America!

Mr. Laity, you profess to be a Christian but you don't seem to give a damn about your own, and my children's, America. I accuse you of being a traitor to our nation, to God and our founding fathers! It is no accident that your kind aids and abets the Charismatics in being the instrument most likely to lead the churches into the arms of the Pope and a "One World Church." The Charismatics, being steeped in the propaganda of the Devil, being sold out to superstition and lying, are a "natural" for the mystical nonsense of Romish "worship." And it doesn't matter to people like you, Mr. Laity, if they speak "American" or not. At least not as long as you "get yours."

I have to wonder, Mr. Laity, would you be as "conscientious" in standing up for a bunch of perverts in the face of these "rednecks" as you are for Mexican "druggies" and charismatics in order to protect your commission? Just how "liberal" in defense of "rights" and opposed to "discrimination" are you?

Mr. Perot and I certainly see eye-to-eye on the issue of so-called "Special Education." Seems he gained some insight into this huge boondoggle while involved in the Texas educational travesty. I hope he sticks to his guns and doesn't become so political that he fails to carry through on his imminently practical idea that education should encourage the best and brightest and quit aiming at the lowest common denominator; particularly when that "denominator" is largely Negro and Mexican.

It may be a moot point by this time, however. Like Theodore Dreiser, I am in the enviable position of being able to actually say what others, like politicians, can only wish they could say; those things that are so very obvious but nobody dares give voice. So, I will say, if we have traded morality, the belief and fear of God, for purely mechanistic answers to our problems, it only makes sense to adopt FDR's, Hitler's and Stalin's "solutions" to our problems. Apart from God, mechanistic "solutions" are the only workable options.

While Stephen Crane and, later, Dreiser and William James, could initiate a dialogue with the facts of human nature, we will not admit, as a society, that human nature has remained constantly selfish throughout history and is not likely to change to suit a particular culture no matter how "multi-cultural" we, hypocritically, pretend to be.

To that end, I will not be a hypocrite; if Mexicans want to conquer California and Texas by the ruse of "racism," let them give it their best shot. I will oppose them. I am sick of having Spanish forced on me by the government. I am sick of the attendant costs of supporting a foreign, increasingly criminal, culture and language that is intent on supplanting American history, language and ideals.

Think Tanks, pundits, economists and just plain folks have finally gotten the message that the rich are getting richer and poor are getting poorer at an accelerated rate; if Bush seems to be snubbing Rio who can blame him? Given his options, what other choice does he have? Between the utter betrayal of the middle class in this nation and selling our grandchildren into slavery to debt, he has to "make do." If that follows the formula I describe in my books, the "Third Worlders" are going to be made slaves in any event.

By shipping all our middle-level jobs overseas, the only survivors are among the two-tiered society we have evolved through betrayal, the rich and the poor, those with highly specialized and expensive skills or wealth and those on the dole. Now, faced with economic disaster of incalculable proportions, the "leadership" is intent on an agenda of "practical solutions." Sometime before November, we are going to see "signs of the times;" in fact, we are going to have our noses rubbed in them!

It seems the world is on "hold" awaiting November. I have to credit Clinton with the guts (but why did he have to do that sax bit?) to confront Mr. Jessie Jackson about Negro "rap" and, particularly, so-called "Sister Souljah" (wherever do they come up with these names?) calling for the killing of whites; and to think that the riff raff didn't even have Rodney King as an excuse for rioting and looting in Chicago. The Bulldogs won. Big deal! No wonder sociologists and psychologists are worrying about the commonality of "breaking and taking" at any pretext. Now why doesn't Mr. Jackson ask Souljah, as he has Clinton, to practice a little "sensitivity?" Is it any wonder that our own, local riot in the prison at Shafter was "racially motivated?"

But, now, I am left wondering at the curious ruling by the Supreme Court that it is ok for the U.S. to kidnap criminals from other countries and try them in our courts? Mexico, naturally, took the most immediate exception to this ruling. This could have some very interesting ramifications. This leaves other countries, of course, free to come to the same conclusions. Now where should my list of "criminals" that, say, Hussein, should decide to kidnap from here, begin? The mind reels.

I am so very grateful to be returning to the "Forest" where I can work out some of the bad taste all of this leaves in my mouth. The mountains and streams, the trees, rocks and critters are a most welcome relief to what is happening to my America while no one is listening. It may be a lonely occupation but it is far worse to dwell among those that say and do not, that are caught in the trap of "honoring" the Lord with their lips only and let the Evil One have his way in their lives and my country by default! But, of course, most of them "go to church" and that, for such, is enough. I have to admit that Idaho is looking more attractive to me all the time. At least they speak "American" there.

I spent last Sunday and Monday at the old house with kerosene lamp and battery radio. As I sat out back that evening, the stars and moon were beautiful. The slight breeze was enough to make the old pine "sing" and rustle the leaves of the oaks. Magic. Peaceful and quiet. I do miss having someone to share such moments with. We all need them. But, now that I have power and water, the real work begins.

The "missing dimension" in the teaching of history in our schools is, and has been for many decades, the role of religion. I have deplored the fact that the great wisdom and literature of our noble heritage was passing away in the schools even while I was a youngster.

While Bob Jones Sr. or Jr. wouldn't give me the time of day if they saw me smoking or drinking a beer, those worthies have, at least, held on to most of the things that stand for America: Truth, Justice, the Bible. Unlike people like Billy Graham and Jerry Falwell, Bob Jones University and its leadership has never equivocated on the principles upon which it was founded. I have to wonder just how much longer the university can last in the face of things today, particularly in view of the accusations of "racism" being leveled at the university. May God help the folks at Bob Jones stand firm!

I believe in being a faithful witness to the Gospel. I believe in passing out tracts, in preaching on street corners, in personal evangelism. I believe in the teaching of Creationism and having prayer and Bible reading in our so-called public schools. I know the Bible and our witness of God are what our young people desperately need. But it takes teachers who are willing to put it all on the line to do this.

There have been too many times in my life when all I had was God and His Word; and they proved sufficient. My own experience in dealing with thousands of teenagers has proven this need in their own lives as well. It is tragic that there are so few teachers or other roll models of God for our young people to turn to.

In my own "midnights of the soul" when all alone with no one with whom to share the grief's or tragedies in my own life, The Lord has been faithful. He didn't always take the pain away, but He always made it bearable and helped me through those "sloughs of despond." In short, as Jesus said, I was never truly "alone" as long as I had our Father in Heaven to turn to and

His Words to comfort, strengthen and guide me. How our young people need this today as never before.

Many years ago, I was telling students of the "Beehive" communities coming into vogue, cities where automobiles would not be allowed to operate and people would be forced to live in compacted enclaves. Now, from Brussels, Belgium: "Cars are strangling our cities... A car-free city is not 'utopia,'...it is all possible if people become aware that cities are becoming unlivable."

Over the years, as I have tried to keep, as much as possible, my children in tune with nature and learning to work with both hands and minds, I struggled with what I saw coming in our own society. I began to realize they would inherit a society that would be inimical to children and young people, one that would not hold the promise of unlimited possibilities as a reward for thrift and hard work. The G. Gordon Liddy's would become the "heroes," people who would flaunt the laws and morality and come out the "winners."

This decadence was thoroughly evidenced throughout my years of teaching and administering in the schools. As Honig faces felony charges for his part in his nepotistic scheme to enrich the family coffer at the expense of the schools and taxpayers, as the State subpoenas him to answer charges of wasting money as Superintendent while demanding more money to steal and waste, the children have to deal with the lack of morality in the leadership while being asked to "do right" in spite of the utter lack of doing right all about them, from the highest offices to the janitors.

Imagine the impact on society of just one thing: Sears is guilty of ripping off their customers on auto repairs! Now Sears is an American success story, an institution, if you will, of the American Dream. If you can't trust Sears, whom can you trust? The inescapable conclusion, for young people especially, is "No One!"

So, I have spent years with books and education, with wrench, hammers and saw because I early realized that the great institutions of America, beginning with the Church, were failed entities. I have tried to warn young people to learn to do for themselves and have tried to put my "preaching" into practice by never allowing myself to become a helpless victim of an ungodly system.

We have our own version of "Rodney King" going on here in Bakersfield with one Offord Rollins, a Negro, the principal. A new trial was requested and denied. The accusations of racism are rife. The young man has been found guilty of murder and, whether he is actually guilty or not, our system of justice has pronounced his fate. But Negroes know they are imprisoned in disproportionate numbers, they know they don't get the same treatment as a Mr. Liddy or the crooks involved, as Bush's son, in the BCCI and S&L thefts.

But few of us, the great unwashed, do. There is a saying, a great "principle" at work, in the churches and politics: "Money Talks!"

It is no accident of our culture that drugs have made an entire criminal class that didn't exist a few decades ago. Think of the "planning" that had to go into creating this huge cancer in our society. As Washington and Sacramento struggle with an impossible, economic situation, watch carefully as the "leadership" creates more "criminals," those that are going to "steal bread." Will a "higher law," once more, be acknowledged? Not likely. Instead of "Use a gun; go to jail," we will have: "Steal a loaf (or a glass of water); go to jail!" All you "Serfs" get ready for a "New World Order!"

You have to ask yourself how the government expects to fund the hundreds of billions necessary to save the elite and at the same time "struggle" with cutting a requested two billion to less than one billion to help the urban poor! When the leadership is "proving" its "concern" over "fiscal responsibility" by "killing the poor" while making ever more provision for "it's own" you know how it all has to end.

As a child, during WWII, the Manzanars might have been there but they were meaningless to me. The propaganda and the reality of concentration camps in Europe and Japan were not. As an adult student of history and, particularly, the war years, I began to learn, that, while we did what we felt we had to do, we did so with peculiar humanity compared to the Axis powers. That was a result of our Christian heritage.

But another peculiar fact came to light in my studies. Given the circumstances, it became easier to understand why Hitler, Stalin and F.D.R. did what they felt they had to do. The substantive difference was our Christian heritage as per the founding fathers.

This is why I stress the importance of knowing the factual history of our nation rather than the revisionist one that, successfully, excluded the Bible and religion. Apart from God, Hitler and Stalin did the pragmatic and imminently practical thing; they enslaved and murdered millions for the good of the state and the elite; a pure working of the Darwinian ideal. The fact that the world today is neither German nor Russian speaking is entirely a matter of the providence of God, not our own "righteousness."

So I continue to read my Bible and Thoreau, I continue to "eat dirt" working on old houses and taking the time to wander the mountains and desert and study the stars. I continue to live in hope that my children and other children will follow my example to "come apart and be separate ... touch not the unclean thing."

While we watch the crumbling of our society, as the Supreme Court upholds prop 13, as it decides jurors cannot be challenged for racial bias, as Casper Weinberger is indicted, claiming Reagan was "ignorant" (I sure have to leave that word as is), as Quayle is vilified for suggesting Hollywood might be more responsible for decaying values, as Meg Greenfield excuses everything from perverts to divorce, we have to wonder what ever happened to the "myth" of morality? If it's so bad now, was it ever that good? My own answer, based on the changes of the past fifty years and my study of history and literature, is Yes!

Granting that the disciples of Freud have made a simple idea a monstrosity of unmitigated muddiness and license where no standard of right or wrong exists, granting that the Judiciary is unable to distinguish the same, we are left with no alternative but "unthinkable solutions" to "insoluble" problems. With moral "No-fault" firmly entrenched in the modern thinking, every man does what is right in his own sight; hence: anarchy and lawlessness that begs for order no matter the price to liberty.

There is no longer time for the assiduous cultivation of setting neighbor against neighbor; that much has already been accomplished in any event. The gray of Puritan garb and manner has been traded for the garish colors of MTV and degenerate, ruling elite. We "out-grew" the lessons of Adam, Shakespeare, Dickens, Dante, Clemens and Melville and have justly inherited the whirlwind.

So, as McCartney "rocks past 50" and violence continues to erupt at so-called "concerts," as "Killing Cops" become more popular lyrics, as "evil men and seducers wax worse and worse," a society is screaming for "bread and circuses." And such a society will most certainly get the same "meat" that choked the wandering Israelites, as the "Bread of Heaven" goes wanting.

In Poway, a 12-year-old Negro boy is kicked by a group of five boys of other races in a "Rodney King game" to the tune of London Bridge is Falling Down using the new lyrics of "Rodney King is falling down" and other classmates come to watch, the Appeals Court upholds Wilson's cut in welfare for the ballot, the Senate votes, insanely, to extend unemployment benefits again, a guy in Kentucky is arrested for driving an electric wheelchair "under the influence," ... it's all too much for this mere man.

The June issue of the New American has a write-up on Lawrence Monterey's new book: "Our Cultural Self-Destruction!" This is a Must-Read for real Americans. Two points: How is it that Martin Luther King Jr. has his own, special day and George Washington doesn't and a quote: "Multiculturalism should be understood as an attempt...to tear down, discredit and destroy the shared story that has made us a people and impose on us a different story which tells us our civilization and past history are essentially evil. The goal, to put it brutally, is the creation of compliant citizens of a new social order, whose feelings towards the pre-1965 America and its heroes (to the extent that they know anything about them at all) will be contempt, guilt or indifference..."

But take heart, even though Winnie Mandela says: "Burn the cars and schools, burn everything down. Everything which belongs to the whites must be burnt!" even though Israel, with U.S. cooperation, got the wrong "Nazi," Time Warner and Electronic Arts will soon be giving the proletariat "Virtual Reality" TV! Just imagine, you can replace Michael Keaton and do as you wish with Michelle Pfeiffer or take the place of Rhett Butler or Scarlett O'Hara (thanks, Louis Rukeyser). If Lee S. Isgur is anywhere near correct in his prediction on "interactive entertainment," the sky's the limit thanks to entertainment software. Talk about the "opiate of the masses!" The mind reels! Who will opt for the poor, inadequate skin flicks of the dirty bookstore or Playboy when you can put yourself in the picture vicariously? Just wait until the "Tactile-software" and "smell-a-vision" arrive!

Dear Dan, Karen and Michael,

It is hard to write the things I feel compelled to say. I wish I could spend my time in whimsy and tell more of the stories I used to share with you children. But the world you and the grandchildren are inheriting is an evil one and the evil must be confronted. While I long to string gracious words as pearls, where the virtuous throat and bosom upon which such treasure would be suitable adornment? I would far rather write of the tumbling Hawk, gamboling in his ethereal aerie, of critters, mountain streams and the joys of reveling in the Lord's creation.

But, just in case you are worried about Dear, old Dad becoming overly morose through the sober subject matter I must treat, I present you the following:

It was a dark, but not stormy, night. It was, actually, a beautiful and balmy, summer evening when the Indian and grandad decided it would be a good time to "jack-light" some deer. The Indian had a brand new Hudson and was anxious to show what it could do. Thus, nothing would work but to take Jack Ranch Road up into Wagy Flat where the deer were plentiful and the road was a challenge. I would go along as "spotter" in the back seat, my eyes being exceptionally sharp and well suited, almost cat-like, to night vision.

Loading various weapons for the nefarious purpose into the Indian's new car, we were off in a cloud of night-dust. For some reason the only gun I had in the back seat was an H&R .22 nine-shot revolver. I suppose it was for killing a rattler if we spotted one in the road.

For those unaccustomed to the delights of Jack Ranch Road, suffice it to say the Hudson was in for a workout. A dirt track with sudden switchbacks, numerous pot holes and sundry rocks, trees that grew close enough to scratch fenders and steep hills, the road is not to be dignified with the label; rather one should call it a glorified animal track. The Indian was soon cursing a merry tune in his unique dialect (a few Anglo-Saxon, four letter words were easily distinguishable) and wondering at what insanity had brought him to this sorry pass in his new car.

The right, front wheel slammed into a hole and we were treated to the caressing sound of the dirt track screeching against the bottom of the car and impacting with the differential as the rear end was bounced, forcefully, into the air jolting the joints of the occupants. My head hit the roof of the car. The Indian added a couple of lyrics to his tune. Some fun.

Coming around a curve in the track, the headlights picked up a small herd of about half-a-dozen deer lying down against the side of the hill. There was some confusion with the occupants of the front seat trying to stop the car and get one of the guns unlimbered. Not so in the back seat. Its occupant had the window down and was already cracking away with the .22 H&R.

Having made the deer dance to the music of the .22, the deer were scattering all over the hill. One jumped into the road and started up it in some obvious distress from the .22. The Indian began to give chase but grandad still didn't have his gun operating for some reason. It was then that grandad's genius for improvisation came to the fore.

Having a small piece of rope with him, he quickly fashioned a loop at the end. As the Indian pulled alongside the deer, a young forked horn, grandad was able to get the noose of the rope around his horns. Yanking the deer against the side of the Indian's new Hudson, the deer, understandably, began to tap-dance, beating a smartly executed, staccato tattoo with his small, very sharp hooves, against the side of the car. The Indian, adding new lyrics to his music, understandably, expressed some concern about the obvious damage being done by the deer beating the tar out of the side of his new car with his horns and hooves. I have to admit it was considerable noisy and exciting.

Grandad, in some pique at the Indian's lack of sense of humor and good sportsmanship, drew his hunting knife, reached out the window and cut the critter's throat so as to end the spirited exchange between the hapless source of our Bambi Burgers and the hide of Hudson. A profuse amount of blood erupted and sprayed all about and into the car, satisfactorily baptizing the front seat occupants and, incidentally, the Indian's new upholstery. He slammed on the brakes. New lyrics were added. With feeling.

Bailing out of the car, we surveyed the gore and damage. I marveled that the small forked horn could have done so much alteration of the sheet metal and paint with his small hooves and horns. But, alas, such was the case. The Indian was adding a "hunting dance" to his music; obviously one of the native customs to show his "gratitude" to the Great Spirit for a "successful" hunt, though his tone of voice might have been easily misinterpreted by someone not well tutored in the lore of his tribe. In fact, to the unschooled in such ritual, his language and dance might even be misunderstood as anger about the damage to his, used to be, new Hudson. Fortunately, grandad and I knew better and were duly appreciative of the Indian's performance in propitiation of the hunting gods.

The carcass was loaded and transported back to the claim without further incident and the venison was excellent. All's well that ends well. Oddly, the Indian did not volunteer his car for future excursions after meat for our "lodges." The ways of our Native neighbors are somewhat strange to us at times.

CHAPTER FIVE

THE OKIE INTELLECTUAL

SEPTEMBER 1992

Revelation, Chapter 18

"There's A Fire!" The phrase worked very well for the plot of "The Andromeda Strain," one of my favorite SciFi movies. Maybe it will serve equally well to draw people's attention to some of the possibilities our nation faces in its present crisis.

Not that it isn't possible that we, even now, entertain space viruses (we could never trust the "leadership" to tell us the truth in any event, particularly if the military or NASA were responsible) or that AIDS might even be a result of some foreign, "space dust." I mean there's *A Fire* in relationship to the potential for absolute, worldwide catastrophe and particularly in this nation due to the amazing ignorance and greed of world leaders.

For some years now, I have pondered the striking similarity between Babylon the Great of the Apocalypse and the U.S. Is it more than an eerie coincidence? And, if so, the destruction of this great nation may be well under way. And, as portrayed in the Bible, the rest of the nations will most certainly mourn its passing for: "Who will buy their wares; especially the luxury items for which America has such a rapacious appetite and consumption!" (my translation with apologies to King James). More to the point, where else in the world will such a bunch of suckers be found who invite the riff raff from everywhere under the sun to take advantage, like a bunch of hogs, of all Uncle Sugar's freebies? Where else, under the sun, a bunch of suckers who will do more for outright strangers and enemies of our nation than is done for our own citizens? Well may the nations of the world "look and wonder with amazement!"

The euphemistically called "natural disasters" around the world give one pause to think. We just experienced the rash of earthquakes in California and hurricane Andrew, the costliest disaster in U.S. history. For the first time in modern history, a hurricane of force 4 has hit Hawaii. A volcano erupts in Alaska, massive flooding in Iowa and Pakistan. The "Beginning of sorrows?" It would certainly not be surprising to see the most expected catastrophe yet,

81

that of the entire West Coast crashing into the Pacific Ocean when the San Andreas finally lets go. The total effect of such massive loss of life, property (including the loss of the actual land and the resulting, gargantuan tidal wave that will reach, no one knows how far) and economic impact is virtually impossible to calculate. And this is not a "what if" scenario; it is a "when?" one! And any astronomer will tell you of the possibilities of those "rocks," some many miles in diameter, that could, at any time, impact on our planet with incalculable devastation. Yes, all of this is real enough, not science fiction and, yet, no one can miss the reality of such disasters to come in spite of their comparison with Biblical, Apocalyptical dimensions. Those four horsemen and bowls of wrath are real enough to those of us who believe God's Word. But even unbelievers cannot fail to acknowledge the possibilities and, in the case of the San Andreas, the probability.

Recently, in Georgia, 3,000 people lined up for 20 jobs at the Ford plant. And, get this: the jobs weren't even advertised! The news of the openings was by word of mouth only! An acquaintance of mine applied for a job here in California and found out 900 people had applied for the position in just one week. Another acquaintance is traveling to Blythe from Lancaster to work on a prison extension. He sees his family on weekends and is lucky to have employment of any kind. But, prisons, like welfare are a "growth industry."

It seems the world is holding its breath over the global economy. Just what will the economic fallout be as a result of what is happening in the EC? It is my contention that history is against France, Germany and England ever trusting each other; and particularly in regard to economics. But, if Iran really is intent, with the help of China and Pakistan, on having the "bomb," we may have a handle on a "solution" and the administration will be able to provide "full employment."

Well, as the man said: "We ain't dead yet!" But I say: We're sure nuff workin' at it!

Drugs continue to be "international currency" with the additional "benefit" of being a useful device of even the lowliest flatfoot to trap anyone he wishes to "get." The "Feds" have become quite expert in this department. Guns are also useful in this manner (as per Randy Weaver). I am glad I got out of the business before I took up this ministry and became such a target myself. My best protection is my notoriety and education. Poor Randy Weaver didn't have these advantages.

Richard Price in his book "Clockers" says: "The problem is not drugs, the problem is all these people who don't have enough of a reason not to do drugs. Or enough of an alternative not to sell drugs." Senator Ed Davis, then State Superintendent Ryles and a host of others can dust off my writings to them during my tenure at good old David Starr Jordan in Watts in the Sixties and find I beat Price to that conclusion by over 25 years. For all the good it did then or now!

Jack Hamp and his Kentucky Serenaders: I am visiting my son, Daniel, in Lotus Land. Dan lives in Torrance, a "White ghetto," surrounded by encroaching "minorities" which are determined to seize all white culture and destroy any vestige of Caucasian, European derivatives. It sickened and appalled me to see gang graffiti on the freeway signs coming on LAX as I entered L.A. Has law enforcement given up to the gangs? It took time, in plain view of countless motorists, for the riff raff to climb those tall poles and do their dirty work. It is truly sickening.

It seems fitting, after my journey to Dixieland, to come to SoCal and see if there is any thing that still speaks to the poet. Fortunately, Daniel is a chip off the old block when it comes to the things of real value like the music of the Thirties and Forties. He has just treated me to a marvelous rendition of Jack Hamp and the Kentucky Serenaders on his wind-up Victrola. Now that is really choice. The boy has class. He drove a Harley for years and now has a '47 Packard in pristine condition. I'm proud of him for not getting into the "Plastic" scene.

I am indebted to Dan for a great sticker snicker: "I feel much better now that I have given up hope!" Talk about tragi-comedy; and how very suitable to our time.

You can't beat the selection of music in the South Bay. I'm listening to one station and hearing Jan Garber, Vaughn Monroe, Guy Lombardo, Benny Goodman, Wayne King, Paul Whiteman, Mood Indigo and Twilight Time; a turn of the dial and I have Pat Boone and April Love, another turn and I can have the Beatles; and I am hearing this wonderful music on old Atwater's, Philco's and Zenith's of the Twenties and Thirties! It seems that Dan and Gary's roommate, Ray, has been bitten by the old radio "bug." When I walked into the place, I was confronted by no fewer than fifty of the old boxes! They range from old headphone sets to "state of the art" masterpieces of "furniture."

The music and the balmy climate are unbeatable in this "oasis" from the insanity in Long Beach, Wilmington, Carson and L.A. in general and all about California. I am still young here and the girls have never grown old. Dan and I share memories of the "old" Redondo, Hermosa, Manhattan Beach, Venice, Malibu, of the life his mother and I had when he and Dianna were babies. So much has changed; I am thankful for the music that remains.

As our society seems to crumble all about us, I cling to the things that are good, the memories and the music which sustain me in the midst of the ugliness and confusion. Maybe it is characteristic for someone who wouldn't shoot the deer.

I was living on the mining claim at the time. It was a beautiful morning when I shouldered my Savage .30-.30 lever-action and set out to get something for the family pot. I was fourteen years old.

As I trekked further into the hills, I topped a small rise and a large doe came out of the ravine below and started up the opposite side. I quickly threw down on her when, all of a sudden, another movement caught the corner of my eye. Out of the bushes some distance behind the doe, I saw a fawn emerge. For some reason, the "hunter" in me drained away as I silently watched the baby trot quickly to catch up with its mother.

I had killed my share of deer and venison was a staple of our diet while living in the National Forest. But, in spite of the hunting instinct that burned within me, there were some things I couldn't bring myself to do. This was one of those things. So, I watched as the mother and baby crested the hill and disappeared from view.

You must understand that does were fair game since they outnumbered bucks inordinately and, though I had read Bambi and seen the movie as a child, I wasn't confused by emotions contrary to good sense. After all, I love bunnies and squirrels but they were fair game for the table. I love baby duckies also but a Mallard on the wing is good on a platter.

Maybe it was the disenchantment of T.S. Elliot in his Wasteland that is in my "genes" which, even then, with so little real understanding, was at work in making me loath to relinquish innocence in favor of "blood-lust." Whatever it was/is, it enables me to listen, still, to Orrin Tucker and Bonnie Baker with real pleasure.

But, before you class me with those who say: "The old is better," of trying to reach into the past for unrealistic simplicity, self-deceived with the marvelous convenience of psychic memory to which we often resort for sanity's sake, I plead "not guilty." It has to do with the loss of national "innocence." There is the truth of our nation's tragedy and fall from grace.

Now I have not encountered any glaringly obvious interregnum between our age of innocence and our contemporary, raging, rampant materialism and generation of professional, practicing hedonists. And, while my supporters marvel at my great capaciousness for sustained indignation, my detractors, a scurrilous, base lot all, accuse me of carping criticism; the less charitable use other less palatable aphorisms. But, as per judge H. Franklin Waters of Arkansas: "...you should never try to teach a pig to sing. It can't be done, and it annoys the pig." My enemies will never shut me up and I know better than to think they will ever sing my tune. But annoy them in the attempt? Oh my, yes!

Since our lack of leadership is so pronounced that the great majority of voters would choose "None of the above" rather than what we are presented, it would seem the "chickens have come home to roost" for this generation. After all, we only get the kind of leadership we actively support. If the leadership is a greedy bunch of clowns that is the way the majority has voted for a long while to bring us to this sorry pass. If good men cannot be elected because of the "system," it is "We the People" (And I mean those "We the People" that our founding fathers meant, not the mongrel, hyphenated bunch and aliens, "legal" and otherwise) who allowed the system to become the evil thing it is, whether by design or, as in too many cases of my personal knowledge, the apathy of those who handed the Devil the victory by their refusing to vote, by their being "too busy" to insure their children's future by actively involving themselves in the process of supporting good men for office.

I know; where to be found the "good men" who would openly advocate the positions required by God's Word and the values of our founding fathers and mothers to qualify? But I have written so much on this theme, as with education, to do other than refer the reader to those works.

The system now is set on destroying every vestige of personal responsibility and individualism as per Randy Weaver. Now I don't know Mr. Weaver but from what I do know I am assuming he was "set up" and I know his wife and son were killed by the "duly constituted authority" which can do any of us in under the present "rule" of government. I am reminded of the scene where the German officer shoots two of his own men and the elderly sergeant turns to him and says: "Has it come to this, that we are killing our own?"

My next, anticipated, excursion out of California is planned for Idaho. At the invitation of Richard Butler, I hope to get "The rest of the story" on Randy Weaver and the answers to some other questions regarding the so-called White Supremacist Movements. In speaking with Pastor Butler, I found him an intelligent and erudite man. Oddly, Richard Butler and I have lived and worked in Lancaster, California and both of us have worked in Aerospace. I am eagerly looking forward to meeting the folks in Idaho and will report what I learn (where possible) in my next publication. But, as those in "authority" have already learned, I know how to respect a confidence and have never betrayed a trust. But I am also "my own man" in respect to "calling a spade a spade."

It does my "reputation" no good to be able and willing to speak to men like Mr. Butler. But, unlike Pilate, I have the advantage of knowing something of Truth through The Lord, His Word and the guidance of the Holy Spirit. It is my contention that if men do what is right and are earnestly seekers of truth, it may be found.

The necessity of seeking the truth of such matters was just brought home to me in a most vivid manner. I recently met a couple of ladies and their stories have become an all, too-common theme in the tragedy of our nation.

I wish I could describe the occasion and circumstances of our meeting but for their protection (they are in easily identifiable occupations where to simply tell the where and how of our meeting would place them at risk), I will just recount their stories, stories that are increasingly familiar to me and which millions of other women could duplicate.

The younger woman was raped by her stepfather (one of the tragic "benefits" of divorce is this vile, very common occurrence). In spite of the heinous nature of the crime, the man is still living with the family. Because of the nature of the case, the young woman became a "trouble-maker" to the local authorities. This young woman, due to no crime on her part, is followed by the local police, pulled over and questioned at will, and, in general, made to feel like the criminal her step-father, in fact, is. She would like to move out of California.

The older lady is experiencing the "system" as a result of being a single parent and the results of one of her children (as me with my own children) getting caught up in the machinery of the euphemistically called: Juvenile Justice System. In spite of the fact that she has never committed a crime, she has been arrested and charged with "interfering" with an officer who was arresting her son. This woman has a very responsible, professional position. Yet she is discovering the fact, as with the younger lady, that if the so-called "authorities" are "out to get you," you are virtually defenseless. Her case is made all the worst for the fact that, like the younger lady, she had become known as a "trouble maker" because of her pursuing the prosecution of a man who had beaten her severely.

Incredibly, the case was not prosecuted by the D.A. in charge and was dismissed by the local judge in spite of the doctor's report of the beating and required plastic surgery for the victim. Her "mistake" was "making trouble" by going over the "locals" heads and complaining to the "higher-ups."

This was the background of her arrest for "interfering" with the arrest of her son. Her son had his juvenile probation "violated" for not getting "permission" for visiting his mother; a most "dreadful crime!" But, my own experience in such matters devolves on how the "authorities" feel about you, not on any real crime.

The mother was summarily hauled off to jail. She spent four days in confinement, subjected to the most humiliating treatment as only those who have experienced it are qualified to tell, before she was released. This woman who had raised five children, no criminal record, holding a responsible position in the community, had to stand, in jail clothing, manacled by wrists and ankles, before a judge just as if she had been a serial killer!

She is facing trial now and the whole thing has been, as you must be able to imagine, totally devastating to her. The local police follow her and park in places where they know she can see them watching her. Like the younger woman, her concept of "justice" in our nation has taken a real beating. These ladies now know the truth of my statement: They can get you anywhere and for anything! They know, without my having to tell them, that if the "locals" want to plant a "baggie" on them or resort to any of the number of "devices" at their disposal, they have no protection whatsoever. The older lady, understandably, would like to leave California also.

One of the crueler realities of life which both of these ladies have been forced to face in our "enlightened" society is the fact that they are seen as "sexual objects" by the typical "authorities" (please refer to my other publications on this point). But, as I explained to them, and as I have written so much about, the job of law enforcement, in general, attracts all the wrong sort of men (and women). It is a wonder we have as many good policemen as we do and that the whole, corrupt system, like Congress, doesn't "self-destruct." But, I rather think Congress, at least, has a firm leg up on this happening. As to the cops and many police departments, they have made the decision to become "vigilantes" by force of the fact of thoroughgoing corruption throughout the entire system of law enforcement and government, that they have found themselves in a "no-win" situation in society. As I have said before, I can think of no segment of our government that faces such frustration as policemen.

I have referred both of these ladies to their state senator, Don Rogers, a good man of my acquaintance. If I know anything of Mr. Rogers, he will give them a fair hearing and do what he can to redress the evil these ladies are suffering. I can certainly do my part by making their plight known to my readers both as a warning and an object lesson. My essays go out to a good number of powerful men in government. I hope some of them will listen to this "heart-beat of America!"

Those of you that know me well are probably anticipating my further remarks in regard to "women in general." I won't disappoint you. Here goes. Please keep in mind the fact that I love women. In fact, I'm not really meant for "single status" and am always searching for that particular woman who can stand to live with a poet.

I find it of singular curiosity that, like minorities who seek special privilege at the expense of the majority, women, ever since the most blatant extremes of NOW and "libbers," have suffered mounting resentment on the part of men. Nothing on God's green earth can ever justify any man for abusing a woman or a child. Such should be held in the deepest contempt and, in my opinion, summarily shot or hung!

But women, as I have written at length, cannot expect to be treated as anything but "pieces of meat" when they depart from their proper role, when they put such slight value upon themselves as to sell themselves to pornography and prostitution on the one hand, and demand "equality" on the other. It simply won't wash. To paraphrase Sam, their demands for "equality" with men demeans them and as I have said so many times: Men don't write poetry for such creatures. Such tragic loss in exchange for a "mess of potage" and the vote!

While Caucasians have not resorted to rioting and burning their own communities and businesses, while they are treated with increasing contempt by the greedy clowns in "leadership," it would be a grave mistake, as I have said often, for the "leaders" to lose sight of the fact, that with the proper leadership, factions will arise that will place the scoundrels in government in the "crosshairs" of a new age of "Minutemen!" We are over-ripe for a new "Boston Tea-party." The difference is the "fire-power" available and the degree of anger and frustration among honest, hard-working taxpayers. Those that are trying to destroy our country had better quickly note the fact that the vast majority of these are Caucasians.

While I stand accused by evil men and women of excessive use of my own liberty from accepted conventions, so were those accused to whom we now give lip service as our founding fathers. I can't help but be reminded of those Jews who said, if they had lived in the time of the prophets, they wouldn't have been guilty of treating them as their fathers had. But Jesus had their number; he threw it back in their faces that they would probably have done worse, as they proved later when they stood crying out: "Crucify him!" And, one should never discount the curse: "His blood be on us and on our children!" which they called down upon themselves. Wouldn't it be another malevolent twist of history if these same Jews and their goi counterparts used our own system to do us in just as their predecessors used Rome and the lackey, Pilate?

December 30, 1991, Bill Buckley put out a special edition of National Review entitled: "In Search of Anti-Semitism." The special edition was in response to a good deal of heat brought on Bill because of a senior editor, Joseph Sobran, being attacked for anti-Semitism. It is curious indeed that such an expensive venture was felt required by Bill. The 44-page document covers many points that are treated as only a William F. Buckley Jr. can do; you just cannot beat Bill for the turn of a phrase. He and George Will are two of the very few men who might be accused by lesser lights of "committing erudition." Perhaps my counterpoint of, as one colleague so amusingly phrased it: "refreshingly plebeian" writing serves to get the attention of those that don't subscribe to NR.

As I read this issue, it got curiouser and curiouser. Just who are these "Jews" who require such a defense in the face of the truth of Sobran's justifiable concerns? Granting that this peculiar race manages to perform far beyond what their numbers would signify, that they get more "press" than would be thinkable for Blacks, Browns, Reds, Yellows, that they are so very, very quick to "pull the trigger" if the slightest thing strikes them as anti-Semitic, you begin to feel that to render any criticism whatsoever of Israel or Jews is akin to supporting the rebuilding of Treblinka and Auschwitz and hanging out an "Open for business" sign.

The most curious thing of all is Bill Buckley's use of an entire, hugely expensive, special edition of NR to go into such depth on an issue he keeps saying is a "non-issue?" Bill is an extremely intelligent and most erudite man. He is someone I have always taken note of. But my own credentials entitle me to examine the following: "If it looks like a duck, if it walks like a duck, if it quacks like a duck, it probably is a duck." Now any "Okie Intellectual" worth his salt is going to look at this lengthy and expensive piece of Bill's and say: "What's wrong with this picture?" It certainly looks, walks, and quacks like a duck but William F. Buckley is no duck; and since he is not, why all the "feathers?"

It may be that Bill's involvement in "other organizations," like Skull and Bones, his "pedigree" and his excellent sources of information not available to us common folks, has led to casting Sobran, Pat Buchanan, et al. in the anti-Semitic mold for his own purposes. It gives me grave pause to wonder. The darker side that looms before me would only be possible if Bill has joined the "God is dead" crowd; a point I am not yet willing to concede. But I do wonder at the enormous effort he has expended in respect to this very volatile subject, particularly since he cannot count on everyone who has read this epistle to be unable to follow his often convoluted, even, at times, seemingly purposely obfuscated, train of thought. Granting the obvious, that we have become an illiterate nation, there are still a few of us, non-Jewish, who enjoy a well-reasoned "pilpul" and even a handful such as myself who thoroughly enjoy following an expert "wordsmith" through "crest and trough" and are capable of sustained, subtle thought and analysis. Then, too, this may well be only one of those strange enemas of life! (You must forgive my occasional malapropisms. In my defense, I use them most sparingly).

It would help my readers to quote, here, Buckley on Vidal: "At this point, as tends to happen to Vidal, he goes a little banshee." This in reference to Vidal, vis-à-vis: "Joyously they (Norman Podhoretz and Midge Decter) revel in the politics of hate, with plangent attacks on blacks and/or fags and/or liberals, trying, alway, to outdo those moral majoritarians who will, as Armageddon draws near, either convert all the Jews, just as the Good Book says, or kill them."

Now it would be silly of anyone to compare me with Gore Vidal; we are literally poles apart. While it is interesting and informative to watch Bill and Gore go at each other, largely in fun, I assure you (?), there is one point on which Vidal and I are totally agreed- taxing religious organizations (one of my "heresies"). But we couldn't be further apart on the reason. He would do so from a non-Christian perspective, and I, from a Christian. He would correct a social and governmental injustice; I would honor the Lord and make Christians "Men" by eliminating a begging church.

Part of my own "Banshee wail" has to do with the fact that a loving parent will always defer, even abrogate, his or her desires to the happiness and needs of the child. It is the welfare and happiness of the child that takes precedence and makes sacrifice in love meaningful and fulfilling. In short, truly loving parents take the "worst" and give the "best."

A friend and I were, as usual, discussing religion. I brought up a point with him that I may not have expressed in my other writings and will share it with you now; it is the ignorant phrase: Judeo/Christian. I have written about this being an ignorant and contradictory phrase. What I have not done is elaborate on the ignorant and wholly incorrect assumptions people like Jerry Falwell, Pat Robertson, even some really honest Christians and a whole lot of ignorant ones, and a host of politicians make in its regard.

God is the perfect parent. He took the worst element of humanity, the Jews, to accept His responsibility for sin and grief in this world and show His perfect and unchanging love and mercy toward mankind. Jesus came of that despised, idolatrous, prophet-slaying, stiff-necked race. He literally took the shame and penalty of sin on himself on the cross in much more than one respect. There was a "racial" price to pay as well.

Now if The Lord had "chosen" a well-behaved, obedient and loving "child" that would be one thing. But He didn't! He took the most unloving and unlovable, the most disobedient and rebellious one of all humanity! That is something only a truly loving parent will do; one that loves, and keeps on loving, in spite of the lack of anything lovable about the child. The most loving, human parent might give up at some point- not God. He just kept on and keeps on. The Jew exists today, in spite of the historical improbability and to the consternation of all who have persecuted them, as a testimony to God's love and faithfulness, certainly not to that of the Jews!

"Chosen People?" Indeed; but not because they are so "lovable." On the contrary, God chose the worst and in that sense, and that sense alone, are they entitled to the label "Chosen!"

I do not hate Jews. I do not hate Negroes, Mexicans, etc. I do love my country and my Caucasian, European, Christian culture and I will stand against any who try to impose their alien ideologies on me whether by force of law or arms. When they, by these or any other mechanisms, try to subvert or attack my culture and beliefs, they become my enemies and will be treated as such.

A curious footnote in Bill's lengthy "soliloquy:" Compare: If someone had predicted earlier this century that the presidents of Princeton, Dartmouth and Harvard would one day be named Shapiro, Freedman, and Rudenstine (the latter was born half Jewish), he would have been laughed out of town" (quoted by Buckley from Newsweek, October 7, 1991).

Consider as "laughable" if you can: Princeton's incipient beginning with the movement of the Presbyterian Synod of Philadelphia in 1739. Consider John Hamilton, George Washington and John Witherspoon in the context of the university's origins.

Harvard. Begun 16 years after the Pilgrims landed at Plymouth, the oldest institution of higher learning in the United States. Endowed by John Harvard, a Puritan minister, in order to prepare ministers of the Gospel!

Dartmouth. Begun as the outgrowth of the ministry of one Reverend Eleazar Wheelock and was once known as Moor's Indian Charity School.

"Laughable?" I hardly think so. What would be the reaction of the Christian men who gave us these great schools to Jewish leadership of them? Why of course! Their reaction would be, to say the very least, vehemently "Anti-Semitic!" We have certainly come a "long way." It is small wonder that Jews have such a disproportionate say in our government and nation when they dictate the rules of "anti-Semitism, homophobia, intellectualism, morality, racism, bigotry, prejudice in general, etc."

What the Zionists (and the President, Congress and the Supreme Court) seem to be blind to is the fact that if any race or culture gets a stranglehold on people, impoverishing and enslaving them, there will, eventually, be a "French Revolution" and heads will roll. They should note the loss of Capet's; just another historical imperative. In such a case, like the desperate conditions that prevailed in post, WWI Germany and, are beginning to prevail in our own nation, it is only reasonable to expect the "great unwashed" to follow any "Savior" who promises "bread."

Now it has been my experience, and part of my field of expertise, that paranoia is often the result of a guilty conscience. If you shoot someone, you can expect the family members or friends of your victim to seek revenge. That is simply human nature. In the case of the Zionists, they have ample cause to be paranoid and their fanatical, religious intolerance only serves to deepen the paranoia and resulting acts of cruelty toward those that are seen as the "enemy!" And that is everyone who is not a Zionist!

I will presume to take Bill Buckley to task for his statement that Rabbi Kahane's anti-Christianity postulates a complementary anti-Judaism. I don't think you had your eye on the ball on that one, Bill. You just cannot credit

Kahane for "...truer insight into authentic Jewish theology" as a fanatic unless, you yourself, are of equal fanaticism and knowledge of the subject, and experience in "polite anti-Semitism" won't pass. One can say the same of fanatical Muslimism, Catholicism, Baptistism, etc.

One glaring fact which none can possibly deny is the "mongrel" status of the U.S. None can dispute that Japan makes its laws for Japanese, Africa for Africans, Mexico for Mexicans, etc. If our founding fathers had been Portuguese, our whole history would reflect that race and culture. But America became a nation under Caucasian, European, Christian culture and was astoundingly successful far beyond any nation in history under those guidelines. To quote Bill Buckley's most recent letter: "The young in particular need to be reminded that the faith of those who believe in limited government as an acknowledgment of the supremacy of the individual isn't transient stuff, it is based on two millennia of Western history and on the surefooted philosophical intuition that men and women will go to great productive and creative lengths if left free to do so, and confident that they will enjoy the fruit of their work" (please refer to several of my own publications on this same theme, particularly on the part of building codes and building inspectors and the value and values of Western culture).

Our present, polyglot, mongrel status is doomed as a "multi-cultural" experiment by liberal, so-called "social scientists." If our government were all Negroes, I would reasonably expect to have laws passed for Negroes, if Mexican, laws for Mexicans, if Asian, then laws for Asians. The point is that each race and culture reasonably acts for its own benefit; the rights of others, if any, are understandably subordinated. In our case, where there is so much hyphenation of races, each proclaiming its "rights of identification and privilege" from perverts to you name it, where is the case to be made for equity? It simply cannot exist in such an environment. But, our founding fathers would never have believed the insanity of today's conditions could ever possibly exist! The one exception of Franklin's attempt to abolish slavery and prevent Jews from entering the country by Constitution fell on deaf ears.

Even granting that Sobran is an outright anti-Semite, which I do not, he was certainly correct in his assessment of the status of the situation both in this country and in Israel. Of course the Jews of Israel prohibit non-Jews from all the "goodies" of "decent people," the "People of the Book." Israel, like Japan, etc., doesn't have to be overly concerned for the feelings and rights of "mongrels." When you speak of "Civil Rights" for the enemies of your own culture, only the idiotic leaders of America bleat such absolute trash and they do it for the basest of motives; greed, power and money.

It is pointless, and certainly not "politically correct," to call people's attention to the fact that when perverts, abortionists and minorities keep crying for their "rights," they are trading on the blood and honor of the men who gave them the very liberty to set up such a howl and would have had them cast in prison for their perversion of our Constitution, Declaration of Independence and Bill of Rights. Ask yourself, just when did it become a "right" to practice perversion, kill the unborn as a means of contraception and seek special privilege because of your perversion, age, disability, gender or skin color? Ah, the battle has ever been between good and evil and only a perverted government and its perverted courts can fail to distinguish between the two!

Imagine, if you will, the subject of "family values" in the context of the culture that made this nation great. Would you even be discussing the issues of "queer families" abortion and adultery as "acceptable?" Imagine a proven and admitted adulterer actually being considered for President in such a context! What changed? Why, of course! How dense of me! We "grew up" and became "sophisticated." God, the Bible, Jesus and the Gospel, the values of Plymouth Colony and our founding fathers, predicated on their faith in God, became outmoded and passé. That is why we are doing so astoundingly well these days; why we are such a roaring success as a nation and why the world is so much better and safer (Don't worry about China and Russia selling nuclear technology to Iran. The Iranians will, we are assured, only use it for "peaceful purposes" and, after all, business is business). Now if only people could find jobs and didn't have to live in fear it would be virtual utopia!

I am fully aware, through years of experience, that anyone who professes a belief in God and any veracity of the Bible is not likely to be taken very seriously by an evil generation which has turned its back on such "outmoded" and "antiquated" concepts. I am also aware of the fact that much of what I have written has set me against many who profess to believe in the same things. But I will continue to oppose those that bring shame to The Lord, regardless of the numbers such charlatans attract.

And, I am acutely aware, as well, that my academic credentials are a thorn in the side of "colleagues" who view me, at the most charitable, as a misguided misanthrope, harking back to a time when Theology and my belief system was the norm for those of my qualifications (excepting my "heretical" ideas). But what has actually changed in the last two centuries if it hasn't been a turning away from the God? The unregenerate know, better than many who claim "salvation," that the battle may not always go to the strong or the race to the swift but that is still the way to bet! Too bad they don't know the truth of that bromide when applied to God. He's bigger and He will always win!

"Old men plan wars, young men fight them." What is missing, though implied, in this historical truism is: "And the young men die!" In our own national attempt at suicide (The Civil War), it is not politically correct to point out the fact that greedy men in the North were pronouncedly at fault for fomenting rebellion, a rebellion which these bloodsuckers knew had to result in victory for the North. They marked their victim well and, with Lincoln well out of the way, carried out their evil purposes. The issue of slavery, a Trojan Horse, was certainly well suited to the plotters. The issue of State's Rights wasn't a bad drum to beat in view of the pride of Southerners. Not a few "Copperheads" had a hand in fomenting this trait. Pity those poor, deluded "sheep" of the North that, like John Brown, were led of "visions and dreams," precursors of our own "If it feels right, it must be right" crowd (re: particularly the charismatic, shameless fools who holler and spout gibberish in the name of Jesus). Pat Robertson and Paul Crouch: what a pair to draw to for our "salvation!"

Is it "defeatist" to point out the obvious? I think not. The only real hope for our nation, as with Nineveh, is repentance and a genuine turning to God for our salvation. But, notwithstanding the shameless, crowing crowd of TBN, etc., I don't see "Jonah" or "John the Baptist" anywhere on the horizon. That statement alone disqualifies me for consideration as a "true intellectual," let alone my "outmoded" belief system.

But I know what it is to be betrayed. I can empathize with God over this nation's betrayal of Him and I hurt for Him and for our nation, I grieve for the loss my children suffer because of such betrayal by those who have no belief in, or fear of, God. The thinking has been, as with education: "If we set the standards low enough, everyone will pass!" The problem, of course, is that once the standards are low enough, excellence is lost and, with the loss of excellence, every man (and woman) does what is right in his own sight! God says it better but I think you get the point.

I enjoy music of a great variety. I played clarinet and tenor sax for years. I also played guitar (I had a marvelous Gretch; Chet Atkins model). But my preference in Country Western is of the Eddy Arnold, Hank Williams type. Blue Grass and authentic "Hillbilly" has a place in my heart as well. But, I do confess, music of the Ballroom of the Thirties and Forties holds sway overall. Music to fit every mood and the ability to enjoy such a wide variety is something for which I am most grateful.

My taste in literature and art runs a wide gamut as well. It is certainly true that variety is the spice of life and I am well "spiced." One of the rewards of such a wide-ranging interest is being able to discern the shamelessness of a great artist indulging himself as Faulkner did in The Bear. In no other work did he grant himself such utter license and display his fondness for laudanum at the expense of his readers. But, the fun for the reader is sorting through the drug-induced maze of maunderings to reach the scattered gems of real quality. Alas for a writer like myself for whom nicotine and caffeine must suffice.

If fault may be found with writers like Bill Buckley it is to be found here. Bill, like George Will, seems to be addicted to language for the sake of displaying academic intelligence and good breeding. Both gentlemen can wax lyrical on some themes such as Bill's sailing adventures. But neither seems to be able to join the kinship of those whose pleasures are derived from the love of people and God's creation.

For example: I am writing from my place in Lake Isabella. We are experiencing the tag end of summer. The nights have turned cool with marvelously warm days. Last night, a full moonrise cast its silver gleam over the mountains and you could discern every leaf on the trees. I could almost distinguish the colors in the glare. Being an early riser, I was treated to "moon-set" as well. There is an enchantment in such a setting that speaks to a fraternity of writers to which I don't think Bill and George belong. I think they have missed a critical and invaluable part of life in denying themselves an openness to such influence. In short, I don't think they ever "chased butterflies."

But, unlike others of strictly commercial interests, I do discern glimpses of a longing for such knowledge and experiences of the best of the child in these men. And, I sincerely wish it for them. They would be all the better for it and this to the profit of their readers.

Having succeeded, monumentally, in separating myself from "true intellectuals" by taking a stand on the dangers of Zionism, of making an issue of my belief in God and His Word, of speaking out for the values and culture upon which this nation was founded, by confronting the charlatans who pretend to speak for The Lord, I find myself in the unenviable position of the "Loner." Not by choice, but by compulsion; many are the times I have wished I could keep my mouth shut and just "go along to get along."

But if Robertson, et al. wishes to bow to the Zionist plan of "Christianity as the sister religion of the Jews," a kind of "Judaism for the Gentiles," I am adamantly opposed to them. But, as per Buckley's excellently researched, though at times fuzzily gyrating missive (his Roman Catholic turns of mind?) and in spite of Pat Moynihan's "defense," one cannot, in good, semantic conscience, separate the definitions of Zionism and Nazism; the semantic differential simply does not exist!

A point of which the ACLU and Zionists seem in a quandary is why Negroes do not flock to their banner. In fact, if there is a segment of society that expresses "raging anti-Semitism" it is to be found in Negro communities. Why? Negroes do not discriminate between "blood-sucking Koreans" and "blood-sucking Jews." Just ask Mr. Farrakhan; he will tell the truth of it. Don't bother the "Rev." Jackson; as one of my Negro friends said: "He ain't nigger enough."

Now it is obvious that no contradiction can survive indefinitely. And we are living with a host of contradictions. "Why America Doesn't Work" by Chuck Colson and Jack Eckerd is a case in point.

Aside from the bias of the authors (a "bias" of which I am, in large part, in agreement) their point is one that I have written a few thousand words about. Government cannot, by fiat of its courts, etc., ever be permitted to be the arbiters of morality. The recent indictment of the House Post Office and a number of, as yet, unnamed "high officials" of government is symptomatic of the whole diseased and corrupt, and corrupting, system. Joanna G. O'Rourke is just the opening gun. Another woman, who should never have been given the vote, let alone lead in government, bringing double shame to her sex.

But if "Son Neil" can get away with pleading "terminal stupidity" in the S&L fraud, why shouldn't Joanna, et al. in their post office scam? Oh well, maybe "hot-shot" Perot will have an "October Surprise." Somebody better do something. But, again, I've already made my views of all these things too abundantly clear to belabor it further.

If those in government are as blind as they are acting, falling all over each other in search of what? you simply cannot dismiss any scenario no matter how stupid or far-fetched. That is a most sobering thought. Education always serves as a "worst possible" case in greed, ego and stupidity. Seems the Kern County Schools missed their projected enrollment by a considerable factor. This will further increase their bleating for more money. And why did they miss the number by a substantial number? Obviously because they can't read! I know this is the reason because the daily papers and newscasts have been filled with the numbers leaving California due to the catastrophic, economic downturn. With rapidly rising unemployment and reverse migration the schools were anticipating larger enrollments? Come on now!

In respect to that required reading for "foreigners," The Economist, it calls to mind a quote from a recent source: "If Germany reduces interest rates, it will set the stage for harmonious worldwide economic growth." This statement, taken with the forthcoming (as I write) vote in the EC is most alarming! Taken, further, with recent events in Germany, i.e., neo-Nazism attacks on foreigners you do have to wonder?

Note the U.S. does not matter in this equation. Don't you wonder why? Well, I've said it in my books and won't trouble you with the redundancy of further repetition. "Sieg Heil!"

"Bobby Fischer has been told in a Treasury Department letter that playing chess in Serbia-Montenegro would violate U.S. sanctions; conviction on the charge carries a $250,000 fine and up to 10 years in jail. But Fischer, who returned to the chessboard after a 20-year absence for a rematch against his old adversary Boris Spassky, seemed unfazed by the threat. He spit on the government letter and went on with the match." U.S. News and World Report.

I do not see it a very likely thing, in view of world opinion, that the U.S. will do anything to Mr. Fisher. He operates at a higher level than mere U.S. government sanctions; he obeys a "higher law" that says: "Chess is more important than your funny laws." In that respect Fischer deserves applause but what about Randy Weaver?

We all wish reality were as simple as the old "morality plays" we grew up with on the silver screen; I fervently wish I lived with the surrounding integrity of those I knew as a child, with the noble characters portrayed in James Fenimore Cooper, in a time when it didn't take Bill Buckley 44 pages of rambling searching for a non-conclusion about "modern" anti-Semitism. Like most of you, I think I know the difference between right and wrong and I am angry about the injustice and inequity all about me. Like most of you, I am filled with anger and frustration over the betrayal of my country, my children's loss of hope and the hurt done to children all over the world.

It is not in me to ignore the dreams and hopes of those that are of another skin color, of another culture; no caring person does not recognize these things and, whenever possible, try to help others regardless of differences; ethnic, religious, physical. Jesus exemplified the principle of the ideal to which anyone of human compassion bows and recognizes as the best of "God" within His creations; within His "adopted sons and daughters," to "Do unto others as you would have them do unto you!" But, in spite of its numerous failures, even cruel and wicked episodes, to do so, history accurately records the fact that the Gospel has found its most fertile soil in the Caucasian, European culture by the most astounding margin over any other ethnic group.

Who of any sensibility whatsoever would not want "Justice for All!" But: "The wicked walk on every side when what is vile is exalted among men!" Under those circumstances, the circumstances that, tragically, prevail in my country today, there can be no equity, no justice, and, again, tragically, the innocent, largely the children, suffer the results.

The September 14 edition of Newsweek has on its cover: "Gays Under Fire." Far from a denunciation of perversion, the cover story is nothing short of a glorification of sodomy, child abuse and sacrilege (as per Mapplethorpe, et al.). Those of us that hold to God's view of perversion are ridiculed as "homophobes" and guilty of "dark ages thinking." And it is no coincidence that many of the media and entertainment "big guns" propagandizing "acceptability" of perversion are, disproportionately, Jewish. Just read the articles in this edition of Newsweek for an example of the truth of this statement. Meg Greenfield does her usual stint of stabbing Biblical morality in the back along with all the other "selected" writers in this edition. "Ms"

Greenfield, you don't even have to like Pat Buchanan to acknowledge the truth of his comments at the convention. And if public figures that dare to speak plainly opposing perversion are attacked, one must take a careful look at the "attackers" and question their motives and agenda. I, for one, have not failed to notice how the perverts have tried, continuously, to have their "cause" allied with anti-Semitism and minority discrimination and who the persons in the media and "Hollywood" are who are aiding and abetting the effort.

As a man who thinks, not a pat on my own back, just a statement of personality, I find myself, "writing in my mind," various scenarios based on history, knowledge of the Bible, experience and education. One scenario has the "Final Conflict" between a revived Fourth Reich and Zionist control of the U.S. through the same "economic strangulation" that fomented the rise of the Third Reich. Nazism vs. Zionism; some of the scenarios are far more prosaic and not nearly as titillating.

Rather than beat the drum of "racial characteristics," it is far more "socially acceptable" to delve into the raw data of basic, general, human nature and behavior. Further, it is probably much more conducive to real understanding of what is working in geopolitics. But, as Bill Buckley would agree, racial characteristics do play a part, along with cultural distinctives, in why people and nations do the things they do and must be acknowledged and examined factually in order to arrive at any consensus of action.

I have taken a break from the writing to "visit the folks" out at the old mining claim in Boulder Gulch and do my "walkabout." I like to visit the old pines and granite boulders and commune with Grandma, Toady, Grandad and Ronnie. I like to think these departed loved ones hear and see me. I ache for their love and counsel when I don't know what to do or what I should be doing. Whether it's true or not, I find comfort in the thought that they are with me in a way that transcends our limited physical "reality."

I walk up the hill behind where the "main" cabin used to be. Ronnie and I, on one of his infrequent visits with our mother, sled down this slope on barrel-staves one winter when we had a nice snowfall. The old cabin had served as a cook shack until Grandad, with some "help" from me, had added on to it. In the summer, we would move the old, wood cook stove out of doors and cooking and eating took place under the pines.

Great-grandma (always "grandma" to Mom, Ronnie and me) took up residence in the other cabin. How I miss sitting in her lap while she would read to Ronnie and me!

I stand under the tall, old pine where I shot the hawk. I was feeding the chickens and rabbits when I spied the Red-tail land on the very top of the tree. The .22 Remington single shot was, as usual, close at hand. I always kept a gun close in case of Indian uprisings, bear and lion attacks and the usual calamities which were sure to occur to a "pioneer woodsman" in the "wilderness" (Thanks, James Fenimore Cooper).

Unfortunately, the only round I had with me was a "short" already chambered in the gun. Now I know, looking back, that the Red-tail was probably not a threat (unlike owls and the wild donkeys) to our livestock. But it was a real enough "threat" at the time to me as a child and, carefully shouldering the .22, I took aim and fired. The hawk came tumbling down through the branches.

Running up the hill, I saw the hawk. He was standing on his legs, lopsidedly, bracing himself with his right wing on the ground much as one might use a crutch, and breathing heavily. His bright, intelligent eyes pierced me. It was soon obvious that, due to the low velocity round and his natural "bulletproof vest" of feathers, that the small bullet had only knocked him off his perch. The fall had probably done him more hurt than the small slug.

I entertained the thought of doing him in with the butt of the rifle but, for two reasons, did not. One: I might damage the gun and, two: I simply could not bring myself to do violence to such a noble bird when he was so obviously at such a great disadvantage. I won't flatter myself as to which of the two objects of reticence were most objectionable. I'd like to hold to the latter, and nobler, motive.

For some reason, possibly my Choctaw Cherokee heritage, I struck up a conversation with the Red-tail while he huffed and puffed, gathering his strength and getting his wind back. Now those of you not familiar with the ways of a boy in the woods might have cause to wonder about having a conversation with a hawk (or any other critter) that is lacking in the social grace of making small talk. But, for me, it seemed perfectly natural that I would be discussing the nature of his present discomfiture and "explaining" what had happened.

The Red-tail did not seem particularly impressed with my explanation; in fact, he seemed rather in a hurry to terminate the discussion with little regard to the polite niceties of civil conversation. Looking back on the incident though, I'm reasonably sure, had the hawk been able to voice his opinion of the affair, he would have added greatly to my, then, woefully, deficient knowledge of maledicta.

Teetering back and forth, he brought his dragging wing back up into normal position and, taking an experimental hop, began to hop, hop, hop, down the hill, his wings taking a couple of practice flaps. After a few yards of this exercise, he gathered speed enough to make a low-level take-off. Wings now fully distended, he glided downhill slowly a couple of feet off the ground. Then, with a few, slow flaps of his wings he began to gain altitude. Finally, he was high enough to soar over the opposite hill from me and out of sight.

As I stroll the hills among the rocks and trees, the old, familiar sites bring on both the aching melancholy and the precious memories of precious loved-ones. My readers of some years have heard most of the stories and I won't repeat them. I know you understand the state of mind and heart that keeps drawing me back to this site and a few others of like preciousness. These are the "pilgrimages" that help me to maintain a perspective of the "best of the child" in me that nourishes the poet and keeps butterflies and trout streams relevant and essential; most essentially the gentleness of strength to confront evil and to love sacrificially without any sense of sacrifice. How else I often wonder, to love God and one's neighbor as oneself?

When I resolved to go to work on earning my Ph. D., one of the many hurdles (including financial and the Miller's Analogy; what has to be toughest graduate entrance exam ever devised) I confronted was the University's foreign language requirement. U.S.I.U. is one of the few universities that require either two foreign languages or one foreign language and advanced statistics in their program. Since I was proficient in German and my New Testament Greek did not qualify, I had to take the statistics route. I have always been glad of it. There were few classes that have been as utterly absorbing and beneficial as this one. But, it became clear, that, if you are to do real research in any area, such an ability to work with numbers is absolutely essential. Unfortunately, it does presume one has a facility and aptitude for some rather esoteric, mathematical concepts such as random, number tables and their application, not exactly "meat and drink" to most people. (This aside is to warn you of some "number-crunching" and "polling" in the future).

As I contemplate my possible trip to Idaho (yes, in the old, Dodge wagon), I have to wonder if I'm not trying, myself, to get away from the madness here in California? Certainly I look forward to traveling through Western country that I love so much; to re-acquaint myself with the majesty in the wide vistas of grandeur that so speak to my mind, heart and soul. One of my old school chums, J. L., lives in Gooding. I'm sure looking forward to seeing him. He just got back from Alaska and is still an avid hunter and sportsman. I reminded him of the Husqavarna .270 I bought from old Bert James in Kernville so many years ago (by some stroke of luck I still have this fine rifle). I know many others that have left California and opted for Idaho. One fellow who was a neighbor in Isabella left and, with a couple of partners, started a "cuttin' 'n' shootin'" joint in Idaho called "The Westerner." Another, "Duke," left just to get away from "minorities."

Regardless the motivation, people that can get out are getting out, along with businesses. A friend was just relating a perfect, horrible example of the madness of the "economic suicide" in California. Seems he knows of a small business employing about 100 people that is packing it in due to the insane "Workman's Comp" situation. The owner had been paying $2,000 per employee and just got his new bill- for $4,000 each! He is closing the door and calling it quits. Only in California do we see TV commercials by lawyers telling people how to "scam" the state for "job stress" and "kick back" on "disability" payments. Some of these "ambulance chasers" have people picking up folks, largely limited or non-English speaking, from unemployment lines. They are then "rehearsed" as to how to "cooperate" with "certain" doctors to bilk the taxpayers through Workman's Comp and a number of other "debilitating injuries" such as the aforementioned "stress" and "accidents."

There is no longer time for "polite politics." Thanks to a corrupt legislature led by a tax and spend Negro (Willie Brown), Democrat-led body politic, my home state is bankrupt. Danforth was at least honest enough to quote me to congress: "We have spent our children's inheritance!"

So, the attractiveness of leaving California is certainly before me. I can write anywhere and Idaho, as with the South, has many attractions, not the least of which is a dearth of "Spanish" radio stations, "interpreters" in Post Offices, etc. As a poor, "card-carryin'" Okie Intellectual I can, at least, say it like it is without having to suffer the opprobrium's of the "better class" of my conferees, the, largely Jewish, intellectual fraternity. But, in true, Okie Intellectual fashion, I simply reply: "Stick it in your ear!" (Or some other, probably more appropriate, body orifice).

I freely admit that the great majority of academics are justifiably afraid to speak to the issues in plain and unmistakable language and, understandably so. You don't spend years gaining the knowledge and experience to do so and lightly risk it all on an unpopular and, even, risky venture such as the times require. If it were not for my children and my belief that I will face God one day for His judgment of my life, I would most certainly join the "Ostrich" set.

CHAPTER SIX

THE OKIE INTELLECTUAL

OCTOBER, 1992

Matthew 9:36-38

When he saw the crowds, he had compassion on them, because they were harassed and helpless, like sheep without a shepherd. Then he said to his disciples, "The harvest is plentiful but the workers are few. Ask the Lord of the harvest, therefore, to send out workers into his harvest field."

Next month we will be going to the polls and vote on whom we consider to be the lesser of evils. Even the least sanguinary assessment of the situation tells us that we will not be voting in the hope that the candidates will not be crooks, we know they are, or that they will address the hard issues that must be dealt with; we know the candidates will not be "guilty" of moral integrity or have any real sympathy for us, the great unwashed. As for myself, I will vote because, by God's grace, I still have the freedom, responsibility and privilege to exercise a franchise for which so many good men pledged their sacred honor, for which so many good men gave their blood. In this respect I read George Will's comments on Bruce Herschensohn with great interest: "... the Senate will be a much better place if it has a Herschensohn there to give everyone a history lesson and an uneasy conscience almost every day." Mr. Herschensohn, at least, would offer those of us in California a choice in the state that we lack in the White House.

I dream of a time when the electorate will support the Herschensohn's, Dornan's, Rogers' and Richardson's, and, as a result, someday give us a better choice for the Presidency. But this will not happen until people, Real Americans, with genuine concern for our posterity, unite against the evil men and women who have betrayed our nation and begin to actively support good men for office. If you're "too busy" to be involved in supporting good men, you deserve what you get.

In this respect I am reminded of Benjamin Franklin's words to the Constitutional Convention:

"In these Sentiments, Sir, I agree to this Constitution, with all its Faults, if they are such; because I think a General Government necessary for us, and there is no Form of Government but what may be a Blessing to the People if well administered; and I believe farther that this is likely to be well administered for a Course of Years, and can only end in Despotism as other Forms have done before it, when the People shall become so corrupted as to need Despotic Government, being incapable of any other."

When you consider the fact that this great Statesman came to the end of his years, like Thomas Jefferson, wondering if the "species was even worth preserving," when you consider the fact that corruption is the norm at all levels of our government and society, when you consider the "choices" we face in November, is it any wonder I have been harping for so long on what we face "...as to need Despotic Government, being incapable of any other?" (The Hitlerian "solutions" I have long warned and written about).

For real students of history, history that has not been "sanitized" by Jewish Intellectuals and their goy dupes, history as it was taught over 75 years ago, the fact is that Benjamin Franklin, considered the wisest man in the nation at that time, had little hope that the country would survive more than a "Course of Years." He saw too clearly the flaws of men and the flaws of the very document, the Constitution he was the essential cause of supporting and passing. Franklin knew that slavery and Jewry would raise their ugly heads to undermine the resolve of those unique men who gathered in Philadelphia in 1787 to attempt to correct the increasingly obvious weaknesses of the Articles of Confederation.

Benjamin Franklin did not oppose slavery or Jewry on the basis of any emotion or prejudice (neither he nor any of the others, factually and understandably, considered anything but a Caucasian America. History had proven the impossibility of ethnic or religious "mixing" ever succeeding in anything but conflict. As to Jewry, specifically, Franklin had witnessed the devastating work of the Jews abroad), he did so because he firmly believed, and had witnessed, the pragmatic and empirical facts of the evils of both. So it was, tragically for us, that the "wisest man in the nation" failed of his attempts to exclude both by the new "Constitution." One can only wonder what other course of our history might have been possible had Franklin carried just the abolition of slavery? Avoided the Civil War certainly, but might it also have left us a better chance at a moral commitment to the "colonization" of the 1800s in our Westward expansion? Of a certainty, the abolition of slavery and Jewry by the Constitution would have precluded the greatest evils of our early history, evils that we, now, have to face daily!

It was Franklin's failure to carry his sound judgment on these two things that left him supporting this "flawed" document in the face of the reality that no better would be forthcoming and his, by then, fatalistic acceptance, as later with Jefferson, of the equally flawed nature of men. But it also left a document which Jefferson and Lincoln would have to attempt to support with one arm tied behind them, a document that, as Franklin and these men clearly perceived, the evil and corrupt would twist and pervert, as they do the Bible, to their own, wicked intent and advantage.

To truly get a firm grasp of the seeming "dichotomy" of the thinking of our forebear's one must study the other documents of the period. For example: the constitution of North Carolina in 1776. Article 34 of that document forbade the establishment of "any one religious church or denomination... in preference to any other...all persons shall be at liberty to exercise their own mode of worship." But, I note with great interest, Article 32 of the same document: "That no person, who shall deny the being of God or the truth of the Protestant religion, or the divine authority either of the Old or New Testaments, or who shall hold religious principles incompatible with the freedom and safety of the State, shall be capable of holding any office or place of trust or profit in the civil department within this State," unabashed and clearly, incisively, exclusivist language which no one could fail to interpret correctly.

But in 1809, one Jacob Henry, a Jew, was elected to the lower house of the legislature of North Carolina as a representative of Carteret County. After what some describe as a "masterpiece of American oratory (one has to wonder at what their interpretation of American is)," Mr. Henry was allowed to assume the post in direct contradiction to the state's own constitution! He was aided in this by Roman Catholics who were more than willing to aid Henry with a view to their own interests in circumventing the Protestant clause of the state's constitution. Obviously, if a Jew could thwart the constitution, how much easier for Catholics!

Did those early men, the "fathers" of North Carolina, really mean to exclude Jews and Roman Catholics from holding public office? Most decidedly! The seeming contradiction between Articles 32 and 34 were not contradictions to men who were Protestant Christians, the sons and heirs of the founding fathers and men who sincerely believed in Christ and the Bible. It was the maneuvering of unscrupulous and wicked men at the highest level of government and finance who cut the legs from under the clear meaning and intent of their own state constitution for their own evil purposes and cleared a path for the same evil to get a foot-hold in every other state and the nation. It was just such "maneuvering" which Franklin feared and led to Henry Adams' statement that "colonization" of the 1800s lacked the moral purpose of the early colonization of our nation.

In just such a manner was the "public school" movement undermined by wicked men from its intent to teach reading and writing for, first and foremost, the educating of the young to the end that they might be able to read and understand the Scriptures and live moral and productive lives as good and knowledgeable citizens! See the history of what led to the Old Deluder Satan Act of 1647 in Massachusetts. Then read the Act itself. We have certainly come a far distance from the early principles of education to our tragic, dismal and sorry situation today. And, well and correct as men like Copperman and Damerell were they missed the essential point, of which the writers of the Old Deluder Satan Act were acutely aware, that only the fear of, and belief in, God, can motivate morality. Even further than that, such a belief and value system as held by the Puritans and our founding fathers provided the impetus of learning which is utterly absent in the systems we now live with and try to force upon children as "relevant." At least the children, lacking in the developed hypocrisy of their "elders," know better!

A judge has thrown out a plea agreement, clearing the way for a trial for Christopher Drogoul, head architect for the 5.5 billion dollar "loan" to Saddam Hussein. Mr. Drogoul claims Mr. Bush approved the loan. We'll see. But, as with the "missing suitcase," the most incriminating documents implicating Mr. Bush may be "conveniently lost." Should be most interesting; of at least as much interest, to me personally, is the issue of Bill Clinton's trip to Moscow while he was busy "draft dodging." Did he, as an insider claims, go to make a "deal" with the KGB? Did, he, as claimed, even seek information about a change of citizenship "just in case?" Would the "missing pages" help or damn?

But one of the most damning indictments of a Clinton presidency is not his deceitfulness and chicanery, Bush could easily match him here, nor his immaturity, his willingness to make any kind of a deal with whomever will help him, his proven immorality or, even, his brash "wife:" It is his agenda, with the help of an anti-gun congress, of disarming the citizens of America!

Nothing could be more deadly to what shreds of liberty we have left than for the government to take away our guns. To paraphrase Cicero: There is an inborn law which will prevail in the hearts of men to protect themselves, when endangered, by any means possible and the "means" be acceptable as morally right.

In the October edition of the National Rifleman, Robert Corbin, president of the NRA says: "...if gun owners don't unite to defend our freedoms and most fundamental birthright now, America could one day be enslaved to a new tyranny-of crime and violence. Once forged, such chains aren't easily broken." Corbin is absolutely correct.

California has led in the insanity (evil agenda?) of trying to disarm law-abiding citizens. The wicked men who would usurp our right to bear arms, who would annul this Constitutional guarantee, are rightfully fearful, as are all despots and tyrants, of an armed citizenry. I urge all my readers to join the National Rifle Association. I urge all of you to call that number: 1-800-368-5714. And, while you are calling, I strongly urge you to ask for the list of California politicians which the NRA has compiled which are for or against taking away our right to bear arms; it is most enlightening and will help you when you go to the polls next month. Don't delay, call TODAY!

What about this "great trade agreement" with Mexico? Why not give it its correct title: Free Trade Slavery! Just when I am beginning to feel sorry for the beating Mr. Bush is taking he does something so stupid that it belies the intelligence I know he surely has. Mr. Bush, how can you, in any name of conscience, try to say, with a straight face, that this agreement will do anything but drive wages even lower in the U.S., will further the "Dark One's" purpose of making Americans ever more "wage slaves" than they already are? Further, are you willing to "settle" for being the "Emperor of North America?" With so many "conspiracy" theories abounding, you do something so heinous to just add fuel to the fire! In doing something so cold-bloodedly conscienceless you only tell people:

"Yes, I did know about arms for hostages" and "Yes, I did ok the loan to Saddam!" You saved son Neil at the cost of prosecuting crooks in Congress and plunged all us "sheep" in horrible debt to bail them out and now this! Whatever history will be left to us, it will not deal kindly with you! You have not only been callous and unfeeling of the American people, you have betrayed and stained the trust of your high office and neither "Skull and Bones" nor all the "secret signals" of all your Mason "friends," your work at a New World Order with its One World Government and One World Economy (global enslavement) will be able to save you from the judgment of that history and God!

And speaking of your "judgment," don't think people like Schwarzkopf will always "play the game." He knows about the "token Negro," Colin Powell and all America knows about Clarence Thomas. The "best men available?" Why? Simply because "Whitey" wasn't welcome or considered! The utter shame of it!

Mr. Bush, in view of the things coming to light concerning Clinton, Perot's obvious egotism, offensiveness and irascibility, the fact is most of those that cast their ballots in November will be more afraid than angry (at this time!). As a result of this "fear factor," you might retain the presidency but by now I'm beginning to doubt this. And just how does the leader of our nation feel about leading through fear, lies and deceitfulness? What good can possibly come of such "leadership?"

But, Mr. Bush, you will stand as a reminder of the woman I know who is so very, very proud of the fact that no coarse language, no word of profanity would ever escape her lips; but taking the sex organs of men not her husband into them, fornicating with other men! With these things she had not the slightest compunction or conscience, saying, as the infamous Whore of Revelation: "I have done no wrong!" And this adulterous woman will claim to believe in God, even reviling him by taking His very name on her adulterous, whoring lips! In spite of the common knowledge of her shameless actions, even to her own children, she would seek to be an "example" to them and others! Such is the fathomless hypocrisy of those that Jesus called *Blind leaders of the blind*, that infamous society with which you, Mr. Bush, will be remembered unless you change your ways! And God is not fooled by you, anymore than He is by the adulterous woman cited, by your recognition of the need to keep "religion" prominent in politics as the methodology, given the imprimatur of history, by which the poor are kept from killing the rich! Our founding fathers would steadfastly repudiate such hypocrisy should they even stoop to deign to answer such charlatanism at all!

Now why am I reminded by all of this of Jimmy Swaggart's statement that God told him he was the only man God could trust to save the world? Of course, this was before Jimmy's "fall from grace." I doubt Jimmy has changed his mind about his "unique qualifications" to "save the world." But one could hardly blame God for changing His. Of course, cynic that I am, I am a little dubious of God speaking to him at all. Not that I would doubt people like Swaggart, Crouch, Robertson, Roberts, Cerullo, et al. hear "voices." I just refuse to blame God for them.

Dr. Marc Miringoff with his Index of Social Health makes the following points (which I have been making for years):

Social ills are the worse ever recorded

Teen murder rate doubled over the past 21 years

400,000 Teens attempted or committed suicide in 1990

The SAT, in 1990, was 450, the lowest ever recorded

Health costs have escalated beyond the ability to pay

Dr. Miringoff uses the 1990 stats because the information for '91 had not been collated. I can guarantee the figures did not improve in that year and will prove to be much worse for '92.

You may have missed it unless you subscribe to some of the more exotic, religious publications. Herschel Shanks has gone to court over the Dead Sea Scrolls. Seems, as I warned, neither the Jews nor Catholics are anxious to let them see the light of day. Elisha Quimron of Ben-Gurion University in Israel is claiming "copyright" in order to bury the information. Remember the "I told you so!"

A personal note to Mr. Texe Marrs, the so-called "evangelist" in Austin, Texas: Christians need your "Living Truth Ministry" like a drowning man needs more water. You make much (money) by touting "forbidden knowledge" about "Bilderbergers, Illuminati, Secret Brotherhood, etc. But in nothing you have said or written do I find anything new, just another immense ego attempting to titillate the senses of the ignorant and gullible. Do The Lord and His few, remaining people a service: Go earn an honest living and quit the pulpit! You're an embarrassment, not a prophet.

The "Killer Bees" are coming to California, but, "Not to worry" say the experts, "We'll learn to live with them!" Reminds me of the "experts" who keep saying: "AIDS is not an easily, transmitted disease!" Why do I feel uncomfortable in the light of such "assurances?" Maybe because I know too many of these "experts," and, of course, my tastes in media go beyond People Magazine and Murphy Brown.

Have any of the politicos picked up on the fact that C&W is a "Whites Only" phenomena? Can you, my readers, make the connection between this and the T-shirt of a masked Jew in Bonn that has the names Judenwitz, Turkenwitz and Auschwitz crossed out followed by the phrase Nie Wieder (The buzz phrase "legitimizing" the holocaust hoax). Let's go one step further and read Victoria McKernan's essay in Newsweek about the "Drug War" where she says: "It's a scabby little affair where women and children are the foot soldiers...Perhaps if all our policymakers were required to spend a week living in my neighborhood, they would come up with something. Maybe then they would quit pretending that as long as it is only the poor and the dark-skinned of the inner cities that are under siege, it doesn't matter."

My dear Victoria, you simply don't get the "big picture." Drugs are "needed" by the government. They are needed to fund the Balkanization (more specifically, the mongrelization) of America, the clandestine operations of our "keepers," they are needed to help enslave the country in fear, they are needed to keep the undesirables and incapables killing each other, they are needed to make a slave-criminal class who will lie and turn you in to the feds, they are needed to make spies for our "slave-masters," they are needed to frame trouble-makers like myself, they are needed to keep the level of violence at a manageable level and by giving the hopeless a means of burying their hopelessness and so-on.

When drugs, as with our uncontrolled borders, are such an obvious and disastrous condition, you, reasonably, have to ask: "Why isn't something done about it?" Of a certainty, no reasonable person can miss the fact that these things can be dealt with effectively; the answers are too simple to miss. And if the answers are so simple and the magnitude of the problems is so staggering, the only unavoidable conclusion has to be: "Who is profiting by these things?" Since I have written so much on this theme, I won't belabor it further; just remember: "We wrestle not against flesh and blood..." As with all crime, motive and opportunity (position: Bush, Cranston, Keating, Milken, et al.) are the prime factors.

What the rich and powerful always fail to learn, their greed and egos blinding them to it, is that there is an unavoidable "Domino Effect" in their actions. Cause and Effect will, invariably, lead to their destruction. I'm sure Asaph realized this when he entered the Sanctuary of The Lord. Tragically, the results include incalculable suffering and bloodshed in the process and even "Sunshine Patriots" will "pay their dues" then and PIPs and PCPs will suffer together.

"Goodbye, California; Your Dream is Done." I might well have written this article in "California Political Review." I have, in fact, covered all the same points the author, James Schefter, has. I'm surprised at its candidness. He sums up: "As the region sinks into perpetual recession, as its violence bubbles toward that inevitable day of implosion, and oozes back down the scale, I'll be somewhere else, where just getting through the day isn't a full-time chore." Mr. Schefter has left California. He lists all the things I have listed, such as the huge taxes prompted by illegal's and welfare, which, in turn, causes huge increases in government spending which, in a vicious cycle, causes ever more increases in bureaucracy and concomitant tax increases, gang warfare and violence, etc. *ad nauseum*. Quality of life? Who's kidding whom? In California? Why don't Governor Wilson and Willie Brown just hand over the deed for the state to Mexico and have done with it, especially since Mr. Bush has given them a running start on an excuse to do so!

In my travels I have seen our great nation; the clean streams, rivers, lakes, mountains free of smog and nights so clear you know the stars are without number, vast areas free of graffiti, litter, gangs and violence. I know why the James Schefter's and businesses, wholesale, have given up on California. Why do I choose to remain? Because this is where the real battle for the soul of my country is going on! What happens in California is symptomatic of what is wrong with the entire nation and, if possible, I remain to be part of the solution or, at least, to fight the good fight where the warfare rages.

There is still no place like California with its varied geography; I can still, in a very short time, choose the forest, desert or ocean. I can still get to a beautiful trout stream (but I carry a gun with me); I can still mix it up with a host of varied people with varied interests. In other words, I will not give up on my native state without a battle. And, I look to men like Herschensohn and Dornan to give me hope that all is not lost.

I've been going through the box of photos I collected from my mother when I was visiting the folks in Arkansas. Mom was a prolific picture-taker. I'm glad she was. I had no idea she had so many of the old mining claim. One shows Ronnie and me holding deceased ground squirrels, shot with an old

Stevens .22. Another shows Johnny trying to hold onto a recalcitrant rabbit. There are many of Little Oklahoma, the church, house and grocery store which grandad built at the corner of Cottonwood and Padre.

But some of the most intriguing pictures were a "rogue's gallery" of my ex-wives and girlfriends. Mom was dedicated, it seems, to preserving a photo past not unlike her own, in the marrying department. As it stands, I only need one more to catch up with her (6). But I must point out, in defense of my own matrimonial career that the first one, an ill-starred teenage marriage, lasted 3 years; the second, also 3 years. The third, 21 years with a hiatus of a divorce after the first year of this marriage and a re-marriage to the same woman (talk about making the same mistake twice!). The last "marriage" lasted less than one month. By this time (you may have guessed that I'm obviously a slow learner in the marriage department), the fact finally penetrated my thick skull that Solomon really knew whereof he spoke!

Now at first blush this wouldn't seem anything to brag about but I take my defense from Proverbs 31:10 and you must admit Solomon knew a lot about women! I must also admit these were all very attractive females. I must have had something going for me to get so many good looking ones. But, alas, a faithful one was not to be had. Solomon and I certainly shared in that department and could have a good cry on each other's shoulders over the fact.

Ah, nostalgia! It was while reminiscing on the various marriages that it suddenly occurred to me; you can easily unload a husband or wife but the kids? It seems that people can dispose of unwanted mates but the kids just stay there. Now we do have the recent case of a 12 year-old boy "divorcing" his mother in Florida. Seems Emerson's Portable Property, his description of children, is no longer set in stone. It is a little unclear how the judge dealt with the biology in the matter. Is the boy still related to the mother; if so, what of the "rights of inheritance?" If not, how does he cease to be his mother's child (a father is somewhere "out there" but not worthy of mention apparently)?

It takes the laws of men to engage in such insanity. But it does remind me of the "mother" who disinherited her two sons (here too, a father seems not to be in the picture) in favor of a grandson. When pressed on the matter, the sons were informed: "They hadn't 'earned' an inheritance."

Now I don't know about you but it had never crossed my mind that children were to "earn" an inheritance from their parents. Maybe I'm just not "with" the modern sense of inheriting, preferring God's view that parents are to "lay up for their children."

Now my maternal grandparents raised me but I never inherited anything from them. My mother got whatever there was and it never crossed my mind that this was somehow unfair. But, after all, didn't I do all that "toting and carrying" for the grandparents while mom was nowhere to be found? But no! It would have seemed an obscenity for my grandparents to cut their own daughter out of their will in favor of me, their grandson.

Looking back on the whole thing, my grandparents and I were never confused by our relationship. I called them "Grandma" and "Grandad" and so they were. I was never their son. There was a "father" out there somewhere but he ran off when I was three years old. Life with mother was a "sometime" thing and, invariably, I kept winding up with the grandparents. In spite of this less than desirable arrangement, there was, I repeat, never any confusion of the biological facts: Grandson/Grandparents.

Now this Florida judge may have granted a "divorce" for this boy from his mother but we all know the law just can't change the biology. Granting the "mother" was a pretty sore excuse for same, we just can't change the facts: Son/Mother.

This woman who is confused about her sons' "earning" an inheritance and her relationship with her grandson has given me something to think about however. It occurred to me that my own children have come somewhat short of what I would call "earning" an inheritance from me. Now I have grandchildren. Ah, ha! Why not wait a while and see if the grandchildren treat me more like I would have liked my own children to do? Maybe they will prove "worthy," giving me the excuse this woman is using to disinherit her own children!

But, alas, conscience will not hear of it. No matter how my own children may disappointment of my expectations of them, they are still my children, I still love them and the biology and God's Word are still irrefutable in regard to my responsibility. And isn't it a wonderful thing that we don't have to "earn" or "prove our worthiness" to inherit from our Father in heaven! We have been named "Joint heirs with Christ" on the basis of love and the family relationship alone.

It is becoming more and more of a moot point in most circumstances however; if our "keepers" in government have their way, it won't be long till parents have nothing left to pass on to their children; this is too true already. We, our children, and our grand-children have a massive debt "bravely" passed on to the wage-slave-heirs of the great unwashed by the tax-fattened hyenas in congress, the judiciary and the White House while, at the same time, they have ensured criminally fat "retirements" and salaries for themselves. And to think that Benjamin Franklin actually suggested these people should serve Without Salaries!

For those who have expressed some concern over my "venomous, vitriolic pen," my subscription list is inviolate. Further, even those I mail to without a subscription, like politicians and "free-loading leeches," (some, admittedly, equate the two species) remain, largely, nameless for the very reason that they, in some cases, while being sympathetic to my views, feel they cannot afford to have their names associated with mine. Far from being an affront, I'm more than understanding of the need for such "secrecy." I'm the one with nothing to lose.

Another "sign of the times" is counterfeiting. This is happening worldwide and, with the new generation of copying machine technology, few things escape the attention of this class of criminals. This, of course, will make it all the more "necessary" for governments to devise counter-strategy; the "Mark of the Beast" draws ever closer as the "need" for governments to "cooperate" in the effort toward a "secure," methodology of buying and selling grows apace.

I usually sit outside and look at the stars when I'm at my place in Lake Isabella. Last night, I watched as, within 20 minutes six satellites passed overhead, three on a Southerly course and three on a Northerly. "Signs in the sky" I wonder?

A Great Horned Owl flew into the top of the large pine next to my chair. It was a full moon last night and, hearing the slow flap of his wings, I was able to see his approach and landing clearly. He perched for a while, his marvelously keen, efficiently light-gathering eyes searching for his prey. Soon, he launched and with measured flaps of his large wings, took up position in the top of a neighboring pine. After a few minutes, he spread his wings and swooped down from his perch toward the clearing beyond the tree and out of my sight.

Another of my favorite things to do in the area is "visiting the folks" out at the old mining claim. I just returned from such a visit to get away from the dreariness of having to write some of the things you have just read. I sit with my cup of coffee and a cigarette and let my mind wander and wonder amid the familiar rocks, trees and hills. Grandma and Great-grandma died in their sleep in one of the old cabins, long gone to make way for the present campground. They died peacefully in bed without the antiseptic paraphernalia of exotic machines, tubes and hoses with which we now prolong "life" in the dubious notion that bankrupting, "heroic measures" are needed simply because they are available.

I wonder once more at the thought of "Hallowed Ground." Perhaps it is the Cherokee blood, I'm told, that courses through my veins, but if there is such a thing as Hallowed Ground, this is it for me; the site of most cherished, childhood memories and where such precious, loved and loving dear ones lived and departed. I wonder, also, about David and his longing for the water of Bethlehem. He must have felt the same way I feel when I'm at this spot. The bittersweet melancholy and loneliness that often envelopes me in these surroundings is ameliorated and assuaged somewhat by reminding myself that few have such memories to sustain them.

Also, the very freedom to come and go as I choose is something for which I am most grateful and something with which very few people are blessed. And, while far from "rich" in material things, like my kindred soul-brother Thoreau I will opt for such freedom in lieu of the unnecessary and cumbersome "riches and baggage" of those that think mere things are what will make them happy and secure. It is people, not things that make for happiness, and, tragically, grief and misery as well, unfortunately. But the soul of a nation and that of the individual is in the joy and suffering that is God within us, is the express image of Him, and opens our hearts to both. Ah, well: *So ghet's im leben.*

As I sit on a granite boulder beneath an old pine where, as a child, I once had placed boards in the branches for a aerie from which to think, read and survey my wilderness playground in the solitude and imagination of that best part within any child, I'm sensible of the fact that we are too seldom conscious of the things and people, the circumstances which will manufacture memories. How much kinder would we be to others if we only knew how forcefully such things will come, later, in our night visions as haunting, tormenting specters or beloved friends. Tragically, the choice is not always with us, but too often with those whose "self-love" has betrayed the trust of the friend.

The day is getting late and I must leave. Too bad; it seems something is out of joint when I am a "visitor" to what was "home." Somehow, there is something wrong with this. Hearing the noise overhead, I watch a Stealth Bomber and its chase plane making a low level pass, about 1,500 feet AGL I judge, the fascinating form of the bat-like bomber seeming alien and threatening and, strangely out of place. Oh well, back to where I presently "hang my hat;" it isn't "home" but, what is, this side of heaven, for someone like myself?

It has been a life-long habit of mine to read at bedtime, first the Bible and then whatever else piques my interest at the moment. I read very little fiction any more and, as a consequence, I found myself re-reading, after many years, Henry W. Grady's famous (some thought infamous) "New South" speech last night.

Now it is a lot of fun to play with words and expressions of speech. Cultural idiom lends itself to play on words. For example, "Your derriere is bovine provender." It is a tad difficult to visualize some hunk in a bar (unless it's a very high-toned establishment) using such a phrase to announce his intention to clean someone's clock. Under such circumstances, you expect the situation would require, would demand, in fact, the much more common and vulgar expression: "Your ass is grass!" In other words, there is a time for poetic language, even flowery, sublime, exaggerated gems of oratorical rhetoric and erudition just for the sake of the mellifluous flow of words on the lips of men gifted in such a medium. And there are other times, times that require no mincing of words.

It is the circumstances that dictate the mode of expression. I found the language I used to address the Optimist Clubs or church congregations unsuitable for common parlance with my pupils in Watts (and, later, as time went by, in other schools as well). If communication is the goal, the language must, of course, communicate; not obfuscate, be abstruse or obscure.

No one is more appreciative of the English language than me. And, no one enjoys the skill of an excellent Wordsmith, plying his genius, as much as I do. There is that to Mr. Grady's speech to the New England Society of New York in 1866.

The value of the address by Grady is mostly to be found in two things; the marvelous use of words, which so profoundly moved his listeners, and the impact of its ameliorating influence on such men as his distinguished audience represented. To give you some idea of the audience, consider these few names: Dr. DeWitt Talmadge, General William Sherman, J. Pierpont Morgan, Horace Russell, Lyman Abbott, H.M. Flagler, John Inman, Elihu Root, et al, men who held in their hands, in other words, the financial future of the defeated South.

Grady was a young man when he gave this speech. He had not fought in the war but was sensible of the desperate need for the South to come to terms with men such as this assemblage represented. In some ways, the speech was almost obsequious, being saved from such an appellation as much by the genius of the caliber of language as by the few, strong defenses of the Southern Cause.

If the view is held that Grady succeeded in eliciting the help of these powerful men and, as a consequence, aided his native land, he deserves the applause of history. But, if the view is taken, as some did, that he "sold out" to Northern Carpetbaggers- Ah; that is something else entirely. One can easily imagine the reaction in the South to Grady's, seeming, "hat-in-hand," gentle "rebuke" of Sherman's "being a little careless with fire!"

While some find little of any real substance in the speech, I, personally, can easily imagine the impact it must have made on even this most discriminating audience of the rich and powerful. Language moves hearts, even, at times, the hearts of the most cunning and calculating. And Grady proved a master of such language.

Neither Grady nor those of his audience could have been ignorant of the fact that the South had, during the Constitutional Convention, held it "hostage" and sowed the seeds of its own destruction (and perhaps a future

America) upon the insistence that slavery not be abolished. Both Franklin's and Jefferson's attempts at this failed. It is easy to attribute Jefferson's efforts to his study of Locke; this could be said of most of the men at the Convention. But the fact remains that his several drafts of the Declaration of Independence, which included strong language against the slave trade, were, finally, expurgated in its final form. The Northern states could not prevail against the Southern because of profits and the "compromise" allowing slavery to continue became a *fait accompli*. But, had a Jonathan Edwards been present?

Grady did, successfully, use a comparison of the Puritan of the North and the Cavalier of the South to great advantage. This was due, in no small part, to the "character" of his audience. It seems remarkable to me that the "great" Dr. Talmadge, let this pass. But, then, there are Sam Clemens' comments upon the good Dr. to explain his "forbearance." But it would take someone of my credentials to see the "substance" of Grady's most useful device of "marrying the world and the church" which, at this point in history, explains his wide acceptance among what was to become the "liberal" movements of the future.

In spite of Mr. Grady's obvious, and most successful, intentions, if there is a point to my bringing Mr. Grady's speech to the attention of the reader, I suppose it must include the fact that we have lost the tradition and the power of such vocabulary and manner of public speaking; and this to our detriment. We are all the poorer as a nation for its loss. The loss of our innocence and soul as a nation prevents real poets and artists, sincere philosophers, from gaining any ascendancy in public taste. And what can one expect when the ultimate purveyor of such "taste" foists on an increasingly illiterate and ignorant populace such things as the Simpsons and Jeopardy, Madonna and MTV?

Admittedly, it took homes, churches, government and an educational system worthy of the name, a moral nation, to make the King James Bible, Shakespeare and the classics of literature and art meaningful and relevant. All lost to this generation!

It was a long hike from the trout stream, Bull Run Creek, back to where the car was parked. The children were quite young but, due to the circumstances, where I went, they went. It was dark and growing late and Karrie seemed to be having trouble keeping up. I became aggravated with her and asked if she wanted me to carry her. To my surprise, she said "yes." This was not like my "tough" little girl. Even at her age, she could put most older boys to shame in her abilities, and especially, when hiking. And, I can proudly say, all my children have proved to be "tough" in the things that really count. But, at the time, I passed it off as her being in a "mood;" even my "little angel" could have her moods.

We finally reached the car and, driving back toward Lancaster, Karrie was extremely quiet. She was never a "talker," being, like myself, one to keep her own counsel and having difficulty expressing her true feelings. But it soon became apparent that she was actually not feeling well. On arriving at the house, I put her to bed and took her temperature. She had a high fever. I nursed her best I could and, fortunately, the fever broke and she began to sleep restfully. By morning she seemed to be all right. My "little girl" has great stamina and recuperative powers.

I missed one of the most precious opportunities a father could ask for. Karrie virtually never asked for anything. The "greed factor" is entirely missing in her heart and mind. I'll never forget taking her Christmas shopping and having to threaten her to even tell me of anything she would like. I should have carried my little girl that night. I won't get another chance like that one to show how much I love her. When my own sins and failures bear hard upon me, The Lord brings such things to mind to remind me that as long as I do have such love, I'm not an entirely hopeless cause.

It's not unlike the time I had to leave Michael at home, crying, because he had done something terribly wrong and I had to prove I loved him enough to punish him instead of doing what I wanted which was to take him with me. Much more like the time I punished him severely for being disrespectful to his mother. I would certainly "undo" that in retrospect of his mother's later adultery and not even wanting Karrie and Michael whereby I became the single parent.

My point, to finally get to it, is that in spite of the hurt and grief of loving others, I wouldn't trade for the cold-bloodedness of uncaring, unfeeling selfishness I have been forced to witness in some others like Karrie and Michel's mother. Mephistopheles has never been successful in striking a deal with me as yet. And, by God's grace, he never will!

No one has ever been disappointed of time spent with Goethe (or, I imagine, Schiller). T.S. Elliot rightly labeled him Sage more than Poet. Goethe's conscious naiveté fit him like a suit of armor enabling him and Schiller to write the "400 mordant distiches in the manner of Martial" and, at the same time, maintain the essential "soul" of loving in spite of all the evidence to the contrary of the worthiness of men and women who refuse to acknowledge its existence.

If my latest travels North and South, East and West across America, my visits with organizations like the KKK and Aryan Nations, my conversations with "just plain folks" have shown me anything it is this: While politicians and financial betrayers of my country are trying desperately to bring us to ruin, the love some of us have for our children and the honor and duty, the responsibility we feel is the birthright of those of us who know its honorable beginnings will lead us to fight.

The "Randy Weavers" are too much like "shooting fish in a barrel" for our slave-masters and their toadies. It would take hundreds of thousands of Randy Weavers to make a real fight of it, and, more to the point, who would lead them?

As I have pointed out, the weakness of White Supremacist groups is in the leadership category. Not that they lack men who are intelligent, the distinct lack is truly educated leadership. The universities are the primary reason for this. Few, coming through the "sanitized and brain-washed curricula" of today's universities are going to come out with Ph. D. after their names and a genuine knowledge of true history, let alone finding themselves drawn to organizations like "The Order!"

My own alma mater, USIU, is one of the, if not the most, preeminent Humanist universities in the nation. Boasting names like Viktor Frankl and Ashley Montagu, how could it be otherwise? Because of the lack of educated leadership, few in organizations like the KKK will be conversant with the literature in the field such as the classic work of Ashley Montagu: "Man's Most Dangerous Myth: The Fallacy of Race." In a handsomely bound volume of nearly 550 pp, going through constant "updating" revisions, sporting copious citations from "learned colleagues and peers" who are a "Who's Who" of "liberal thinking and science," the work is impressive indeed! The obvious academic credentials, experience, intelligence and erudition of the author is a credit to the university and extremely daunting to those not trained and lacking in expertise in the same areas.

It should be obvious that an Ashley Montague is going to win every time against someone whose vocabulary includes terms like *Niggers, Greasers, Chinks and Slopes*! It is thus most uncommon for someone with the credentials I possess to choose to write as I do. But, I am qualified to do so against the Ashley Montagus and Viktor Frankls who badly need to be refuted and, accordingly, have the qualified compulsion and responsibility to do so when I believe them to be in error.

And it isn't enough to "know how to read." The character of the writer is of utmost importance, even vital, to a real understanding of critical reading and understanding. Only in such a manner can the "spirit of truth and the spirit of error" be discerned. This is especially true of any reading of history. Much of the muddy obfuscation, even contradictions, of those that would "teach" the early history of our own nation can be laid to the lack of such knowledge and understanding. A primary example of this kind of hurtful ignorance is our schools and universities which are filled with those that would "teach" history and literature who have never even read the one Book which has had more influence on these two subjects than all other books combined! It is commonplace to find tenured professors of Shakespeare and Tennyson to attribute Biblical passages to the "genius" of such secular writers.

It is such understanding and knowledge that removes men like Franklin and Jefferson from the grasp of the humanists that speak so "knowledgeably" of men such as these as "deists and children of the enlightenment" in a profane attempt to gain credibility for their own evil agenda. While it is joy to me to engage in philosophical discussion of the merits of the transcendentalists, of the subtle turns of minds and words, there must, at last, be an overriding honesty toward the truth wherever it may lead, especially against your own prejudices and biases, for such discussion to result in any beneficence. The pronounced lack of this, more than anything else, is what has led to my most vitriolic denunciation of the churches; they are utterly lacking in sound scholarship, their pulpits filled with "hirelings" and, as a result, are "spiritual eunuchs" where the word "ICAHBOD" is etched over their "sanctuaries" for the whole world to see their shame openly displayed. Some, particularly on TV, wear the badges of ignorance and fleshly ego so proudly as to make me want to scream! I had thought once to seek a wife in a church, but it seems more and more probable that, to avoid the hypocrisy and to find the honesty I need from a companion the local bars may be more suitable!

It can be said without any fear of contradiction that had the churches exercised real leadership, the problems of a "flawed" Declaration of Independence and Constitution would have never been possible. But flawed as they are, they provided the opportunity for a "government by consent of the governed" which the world before had never seen. The weaknesses in these revered documents are, primarily, the weaknesses of men, who, seizing on what is not said, and twisting and distorting what is, have carried the day to their own wicked interests.

But enough is clearly said to provide a legitimate cause for battle against the enemies of the Republic our founding fathers envisioned and attempted, with no help from the churches, to pass on to their posterity! I would strongly urge all of you to carefully read these great documents and, if you do, you will see very clearly what I mean. In the face of the facts, both contemporary and historical, it can be easily determined that the present "leadership" has no intention of leading us back to the "ancient landmarks." Quite the contrary, it appears that the present leadership is leading us in the path of a "Banana Republic!"

My "Pentagon Pipeline" assures me that a scenario such as "7 Days in May" is not very likely. Note, I do not say "impossible." On the face of it, the trouble in our nation would have to be of such astounding and cataclysmic

118

proportions as to leave virtually no other option for a military coup to ever happen. My own uneasiness in this regard is that I know it could happen!

For years I told people we had nothing to fear in regard to a nuclear exchange between Russia and the U.S. though an "accident" remains a legitimate and deep concern. My reasoning was that both systems of government were such as to exclude a "Mad Man" from ever gaining the necessary control of either. The military, however, is another matter. It was for this reason Stalin himself provided such extraordinary; some would say psychotic, measures for his own security.

Tyrants and Despots have always had a need for the "Loyal Guard," their "Secret Police," And whether the Caesar's, Hitler, Stalin or Hussein the need for spies and enforcers have been a concomitant of ruthless and dictatorial power. This, of course, brings me, once again, to the case of Randy Weaver and our own, present, government (you will note the comma after "present;" it isn't a typo).

Our present leadership has a plethora of "enforcers and spies." Not even a benevolent dictator has ever required the vast number of "Praetorian Guards" our government (our taxes) supports. In fact, if we even had a "benevolent dictator," he would fire the vast majority of these "personnel" as unneeded "leeches" and most certainly not fit to sit at the King's table!

If the battle against the present, despotic government is to be enjoined in any effective manner by "we the governed" it will be done through the proven method of John Locke and Thomas Paine; any other methods will lead to nothing but anarchy. Lacking the "consent of the governed," how can it be otherwise?

Clearly, the present leadership cares nothing about the "governed." A new "Social Contract" (Compact) may well be in order. For example, I am not going to be a "willing participant" in handing over the deed for California to Mexico! Neither am I going to "cooperate" in handing the deed for my country to the UN or any other organization for the sake of "world harmony" (The New World Order)!

The problem is obvious; cooperate or face prison or death. How very like the very same conundrum our founding fathers faced. But: "When in the course of human events, it becomes necessary for one people to dissolve the political bands which have connected them with another, and to assume among the powers of the earth, the separate and equal station to which the Laws of Nature and of Nature's God entitle them, a decent respect to the opinions of mankind requires that they should declare the causes which impel them to the separation..."

It would be most difficult (presumptuous?) to attempt to improve on the wording of Jefferson as he and those great and courageous men took upon themselves the mantle of responsibility of such a Herculean task of disassociating, severing, in fact, their ties from Great Britain. A "Declaration" of intent to the purpose of securing for themselves and their posterity a government by consent of those governed with the goals of "life, liberty and the pursuit of happiness" based on an appeal to God and the witness of reasonable men, that a government which would encourage both the responsibility and privilege of individual self-determinism was wanted, possible and needed.

If such an appeal to reasonable men is to be made on the same basis as that of the founding fathers, it would have to be such as would include their firm belief in God as held by Caucasian, Protestant Christianity. Notwithstanding the ineffectualness (fearfulness?) of the churches at this point in history, the firm convictions of Biblical Christianity permeated virtually every act of the founding fathers as clearly evidenced by the documents they produced and the beliefs espoused as the *cause rationale* of their actions.

Not to make them larger than life, there were the equally obvious self-interests in evidence as well. The point is they worked on certain assumptions that, today, are considered extremely racist and religiously prejudiced in the extreme! The wonder of it is that they did so well under the historical circumstances and restraints.

The question of foremost importance for those that believe as I do is whether they were wrong in some of these critical assumptions and declarations in regard to race and religion. To engage any dialogue that would lead to even seeming support of the contentions of racial and religious superiority is dangerous in our present, mongrelized, society (I do not say "culture" for what is that, exactly, anymore?).

Lacking any contemporary consensus of "culture," where does a society such as we have now look for leadership and guidance? Further, leadership and guidance toward what goal; I fear I have already expressed my thoughts as to such "goals" too clearly for my own good. But, in all good conscience: *"Ich kann nicht anders...hier Ich stande!"* Or, as per Locke: "...Whether men, at the same time that they feel in themselves the imprinted edicts of an Omnipotent Law-maker, can, with assurance and gaiety, slight and trample underfoot his most sacred injunctions?"

It is to those "sacred injunctions" that the founding fathers made their appeal and which those of us, who believe them to have been correct and betrayed, must make our own appeal, not with "force of arms" but with the intelligence, courage and enlightened moral dedication and, yes, education, which they possessed in such large measure. All the time reminding myself and you, that had it not been for the "arms" of the founding fathers and our forefathers, not all the grand and noble sentiments of our Declaration of

Independence or Constitution together would have carried the day or have even been possible.

Those of us who hold with the founding fathers and, especially, to the religious views of Biblical Christianity must take action against those that hold to the contrary. Keeping in mind the fact, proven throughout all of history, that no nation can possibly survive our present, vain attempts at some sort of an "amalgam" of contrary religions and ethnic cultures, a concerted effort must be organized to the end that the intents and views of the founding fathers will prevail.

There is certainly no shame in admitting to the beliefs of those great and honorable men. If not, what has made you ashamed to do so? Only the hugely successful propagandizing of an anti-Christ, revisionist "history" and media! Were "We the People," and by that I mean the same "We the People" our forefathers meant: Caucasian, Anglo-Saxon Protestant, to read the facts of history concerning our nation, were to begin to cry out, in concert for, once more, a "government by the consent of the governed," I can guarantee the lights would begin to burn long and late in Washington, D.C.!

Is it even remotely possible for such a thing to come about? I believe it is. My most recent travels about the country have given me some optimism in this regard. The majority of "just plain folks" in this nation are fed up with being "second class citizens" and pawns in the power plays of the "rich and famous." There is an entire generation of young people out there who need, and are desperate for, leadership that will give them some hope of a future. There is nothing wrong in their hopes that such leadership will be moral.

The lines are being unmistakably drawn between the cultures that are vying for ascendancy and supremacy. Unscrupulous men and women together with a Zionist media are hard at work trying to undermine any vestige of pride in our honorable history and the good and courageous men and women who gave us this "One Nation Under God" who provided the impetus for such.

Now is the time for all good men (and women) to come to the aid of their country! Just who, do you suppose, would make of this some trite and rhetorical cliché? Only those, for their own evil purposes, would make our flag Black, Brown and Yellow instead of Red, White and Blue!

Do I believe in "racial characteristics?" Most decidedly! Do I believe Caucasian, Anglo-Saxon Protestants are not only the intended inheritors of this great nation but have the responsibility to hold such as a beacon of hope and liberty to a darkened world? Most assuredly! And so did the founding fathers! Will all those holding such a view come under the attacks of the enemies of such truth? Absolutely! But, I remind myself, that Jesus said: "The cowardly and unbelieving will not inherit the kingdom of heaven!" How much less anything of real value in this world?

Admittedly, as I have already written, our country may already be too far down the path to Babylon's appointed end. But as long as I have breath and the ability to give a dissenting voice against those who would enslave my children and me to a godless system of vice and corruption and mongrelization I will fight with all the means God gives me. And I will pray for the success of those means, just as God gave success to the "infidel" Tom Paine's efforts.

There is much work to do. And, there is a great need for educated men to join in the warfare. Where are such men to be found? I honestly don't know. But, as God told Elijah, there are those, I believe, who have not bowed the knee to Baal, men who God may have prepared that only lack leadership and direction to enjoin the battle.

But I have little hope that such men will come from the ranks of "institutional religion." The very fractiousness that hampers those of the White Supremacist movements will "hamstring" these also. Success can only come with the help of God and that would begin with, as I have always said, genuine repentance and strict obedience to Him and His Word.

My hope is that God has such men in attendance. After all, if there were 7,000 at the time of Elijah when such evil and hypocrisy prevailed that he asked God to kill him because he felt such loneliness, can't I hope God has His 7,000 in an, at least, equally evil and adulterous nation?

I apologize for, perhaps, overemphasizing the need for all of you to do at least these two things I feel you must do: Call the NRA *Today* and, November 3, *VOTE!*

CHAPTER SEVEN

THE OKIE INTELLECTUAL

DECEMBER, 1992

II Corinthians 9:15
Ecclesiastes 12:9-14

You have to admit it's "Crazy Time" in the good old U.S. of A. The inmates are most definitely running the asylum. Just when I decide to run for the State Senate, the inmates are cooperating in making me look like a paragon of reason. Not that I am about to argue the conclusion; it's well past time someone confronted the idiots who are doing all they can to destroy this nation. They won't take hints so I have decided to use a two-by-four to get their attention. And, no, I don't believe my friends in Arkansas had peanut butter and jelly sandwiches for Thanksgiving because they had sent all the turkeys to Washington.

In spite of all the insanity trying to pass as "reason," there are some people and things that give me hope in the face of seeming hopelessness. God still had His 7,000 when Elijah had thrown in the towel. I will remain hopeful of the 7,000 here in America. But it will take the most ruthless and utterly candid appraisal of the truth and facts of the case to bring about any changes for good. And, at that, it has been my opinion and the consensus of men whom I trust that it must get a whole lot worse before people are ready to face the issues with the needed honesty and candor.

I have also made the point, many times, that it is my generation, you know, the one young people call "greedy geezers," a too-often earned appellation, which has the responsibility of doing what is required to offer hope of a future to our children. We have not only failed to "lay up for our children," my generation, with the assistance of the previous one, seems to have robbed young people of the inheritance, spiritual, educational and material, they had every right to expect from us.

As an Election Special, this issue of OI will confront some of this "craziness." For example the case of the courts deciding that a husband and wife, George and Lillie Siplin, are responsible for the injuries to one Wesley Wilkins. The cause of the injuries? Seems good old George caught Miz Siplin "dallying" with poor old Wesley and did him some hurt. George and Lillie have been ordered to pay Wesley $100,000 apiece. How would you like to collect $200,000 for jumping into the sack with your neighbor's wife? Stud fees are definitely on the increase now that Man's Law has abrogated God's! In plain fact, men and women have turned God's Law 180 degrees around. Insane! To add to the insanity, the court, in its "wisdom" told the Siplins that poor Wesley should have been warned in advance of the adultery that George might take it personal! (Now, having faced the same situation myself a few times, I have never found such women worth all the fuss but I can understand old George's feelings in the matter). Due to this court's decision, I expect, at any time, to see the government require warning labels on guns. I can visualize it: "Firing this gun may result in injury!"

Another example: Governor Kirk Fordice of Mississippi made the ignorant remark that this is a "Christian Nation." Rabbi Steven Engel, head of the largest Jewish congregation in the state demanded that the governor retract his statement and apologize to Jews. He did! And about 20 "leaders" in the Mississippi Religious Leadership Conference called Fordice's comments about America being a Christian Nation "Deeply disturbing and divisive." What, you didn't know a Jew could force a governor to apologize for calling America a Christian Nation? And, even further, be joined in his condemnation by "Christian (?) leaders" and "churches?" You do now! As an aside, if Clinton et al. have their way, next year no one will be able to refer to America as a Christian Nation by force of Federal Law! Stick that in your pipe, if they aren't outlawed by then as well, and smoke it!

Strange, isn't it, that this month the nation (and a good portion of the world) "celebrates" the birth of Christ and at the same time repudiates the concept of a Christian Nation as being "divisive and disturbing!" Even stranger, to those that aren't aware of the truth of the things I have been writing about the churches, that so-called "Christian churches" should join the Jews in such condemnation.

Having departed from the Truth of the Gospel and loving their own sin, it only stands to reason that an adulterous church, as with adulterous people, would encourage others in departing from the Truth of God. Birds of a feather still flock together. The irony of the situation is that such "churches," far from being voices of reason and accepting the responsibility of "salt and light" to a darkened world, have actually abrogated the position God intended and utterly failed in any meaningful attempts at correcting social ills.

Yet, the rationale of such thinking is not lost on me. But God still holds those things of such great value to the unregenerate in contempt while the true riches of heaven are, conversely, held in contempt by the wicked. It was the responsibility of the churches to hold up a standard and beacon of love (tough love, where necessary) and morality, of salvation from sin's dominion, to a sin-darkened world. The price has, apparently, been too high for what attempts to pass as the "work" of the churches today.

Cambridge Mass. joins San Francisco and Sacramento in allowing perverts to "marry." It doesn't take much to imagine how early representatives of this "noble" state, the Puritans, founding fathers, Emerson and Thoreau, would react to this betrayal; this at a time when an elementary school superintendent catches hell for making a point that I have long maintained from personal experience in the schools. Albert Marley had the temerity to point out the fact, as I have done, that too many men seeking jobs as elementary school teachers are "effeminate." Brad Laughlin spokes(man?) for the Los Angeles Gay and Lesbian Community Services (you have to wonder who is getting "serviced?") Center, following "Jewish Intellectualism" and the media in general said: "If he's saying some heterosexual, macho male role model is what's best, I'd say that's an ignorant, homophobic approach."

My readers will recall my point in the past of the school's desperate need of good, male roll models in the schools and the jobs of teaching and administration being so disproportionately impacted by women and "limp-wristed," spineless men, to the detriment of children and young people. The result of women and such "men" having "the rule" in the schools has been to make teaching a "wimp" job that alienates and attempts to emasculate real men. The truth of this is seen in the final results, the destruction of education and the success of perverts gaining entree to their favorite victims, the children.

When male roll models are so utterly lacking in the home, churches and schools, this pervert takes advantage of the courageous and truthful remarks of this superintendent to tell us perverts are to be trusted with children! Insane! Keep in mind the agenda of Jewish Intellectualism to foment "rights" (read: Special Privilege) for perverts. Just reading about the recent agreement of 600 priests and ministers across Los Angeles that have vowed to devote at least one sermon a year about Anti-Semitism and the "holocaust" makes me want to vomit! Small wonder that even some of the oldest Christian publications like "American Baptist" and "Christian Herald" are calling it quits and folding publication; the Herald, by the way, is 189 years old and the Baptist, 115. Such attacks by the enemies of historical American ideals and culture will only result in more cases like Marge Schott, owner of the Cincinnati Reds, making favorable comments about Hitler.

In the same issue of the L.A. Times I'm reading about an Air Force Sergeant who has been arrested on 76 counts of child molestation in California City. And Mr. Clinton and "Mr." Laughlin are telling us perverts in the military and schools are "just fine!" Not for anyone who cares about children and our armed forces! Yet nothing seems to be said about the genuine and reasonable fear of those in the military and the schools over the risk of AIDS that perverts carry with them. Insane!

In Nashville, N.C., four young whites shot a black man and started fires in the hope of starting some California trouble so they could take advantage of the hoped-for riot in order to loot stores. This kind of insanity knows no racial bounds. The German media is trying to resurrect the "dangers of the Left" in its racial troubles. Seems about 25 "Leftists" attacked a restaurant frequented by neo-Nazis. The "program" never changes, only the faces. The Beast may have seemed to have had a "mortal wound" but it is still alive and well in every form of ideological hatred throughout the entire world.

Istvan Csurka, MP of Hungary, is making great "progress" in reviving the Beast. So much so that a local Jewish leader is quoted as saying: "They (Jews) know that exactly the same movie has already been shown in this country before." Seems Mr. Csurka's enemies have resorted to name-calling. The epithets have a very well known Jewish history: Anti-Semite, Irredentist, Xenophobe. (Reason. 12/92) But Mr. Csurka, as Benjamin Franklin and Hitler did, knows something of the history of the enemies of his country. And, historically, Zionists never seem to quite get the message that their "culture" will always be repugnant to others and resisted. Any group that attempts to enslave others whether the master-minding by Zionists of Communism or the nuclear threats of Muslimism will be confronted by men of reason and good will.

As a Christian, I believe it is the sole purview of God to make a regenerate change in the hearts of men and women, that the result is hearts free of prejudice and bigotry. But wisdom and love for children, a sense of fairness and equity, of justice, belongs to all human beings, even the most irreligious. I would far rather trust my own case for justice and fairness to men like Franklin, Jefferson, Adams, Emerson and Thoreau than the Pope's, Pat Robertson's and Rabbi Engels.

As a nation, we have been "seduced" by the "Dark Side of the American Dream." Gangs, mobsterism, perversion of every kind, Jimmy and Tammy and Swaggart and conspiracies of all kinds have made their contributions to this Dark Side. Even now politicians and judges, the CIA, FBI, State and Justice Departments continue to flaunt liberty and justice; we have been cheated and lied to for so long that we take it as the "norm" of "doing business" in America.

My campaign calls attention to the helplessness of the churches to be a force for morality because of tax-exempt status and the fact that they, just like those they condemn, are hugely infected with the sins of divorce and adultery. This failure of the churches to take a moral stand has contributed greatly to the failure of family values and the utter absence of men of moral stature and statesmanship as leaders. Even the so-called "Christian Media" does not dare touch the underlying reason for the failure of the bedrock of our civilization, the Family! The reason, for those who try to avoid and deny the obvious, is Adultery and Divorce working together with their handmaidens of abortion as contraception, pornography and homosexuality. When you have the likes of Baker and Swaggart making a mockery of family values, when you have an admitted adulterer, pervert-coddling draft-dodger as president of the United States, just how is the situation to be redeemed?

If this nation is ready, as it most certainly appears, to accept such "leadership" and "standards" because of its own adulterous sinfulness, we are indeed without hope. Such a society will not have to meet any ethical conundrums as to what to do about a brain-dead child whose welfare parents insist on keeping the child attached to hoses and machinery at an enormous cost to taxpayers and the elderly and infirm will most certainly be hastened "on their way" and get on with the business of dying so we can get on with the business of balancing government budgets!

What do you suppose ever happened to the dreams of such men as John Adams who said: "I always considered the settlement of America with reverence and wonder, as the opening of a grand scene and design in Providence for the illumination of the ignorant, and the emancipation of the slavish part of mankind all over the earth," and if the successor of George Washington, our second president of the United States, could look at the leadership today?

What the Puritans, founding fathers, the Edward's, Mather's and Adams's failed to consider was the need to export an ideology, not import slavery and foreign cultures to our destruction. To that extent, Franklin and Jefferson were absolutely correct in their perceptions of the Constitution as a "flawed document." But there remained the hope that, given time, men would follow through on the clear intent of the founding fathers. Sadly, this has not been the case.

The result has been our own *Kultur Wahr* in vain attempts to re-define American in a historically doomed multi-cultural framework with every faction crying for dominance. You must admit that when the situation is so insane that even perverts are trying to use the mechanism of "civil rights" to legitimize their perversion things are out of control.

I have recently learned of California's following Hitler and Stalin's lead of registering printing presses! Yes, you read that one right; the state is registering printing presses! It will cost printing businesses $700 per press to register them with the state. The ostensible reason for this is for the state to keep track of harmful emissions from some of the chemicals used in printing.

While this is only happening in L.A. County at present, my friends in Kern County see it, rightly, coming our way. And few are deceived by the state's "environmental" concern. Anyone who knows of the historical mechanism of tyrants controlling the print media knows Caesar is far more interested in keeping track of, and destroying, people like me than "clean air." This intent of Caesar to destroy the freedom of the press works together with the plan to take away the guns of American citizens. Caesar knows both of these things have to occur in order to enslave us.

Another, similar thing in California is the list of rules in attempting to sell your home. You are now subject to imprisonment and a $10,000 fine if you use "discriminatory language" in describing your home. Realtors, especially, are at risk in this attempt of Caesar to legislate "morality" and the insane coercion of making people bow to the god of "multiculturalism." There is a long list of words and phrases that Caesar proscribes; for example, you cannot use the phrase "nice neighborhood" or the word "nice" in your advertising. Such language, according to Caesar, is "discriminatory." You can tell prospective buyers which school district your house is in but not the actual school their children would have to attend! Is it any wonder that I have said that I choose to remain in California because this is where the war for liberty and American culture is being fought?

A further word to those churches that consider themselves to be orthodox and "fundamental" in the faith; when you refuse to accept your own responsibility for social failures such as family values, you leave the door wide open for "liberals" and the enemy to justifiably point the finger of shame directly at you! All the "crusades," hand-wringing sermons, Sunday School bussing, hymn-singing, youth grouping, etc. *ad nauseum* will not absolve your guilt for becoming hypocritical eunuchs in the face of the enormous evil that you refuse to confront beginning with spineless "men" in your pulpits and pew-warming hypocrites who live so "delicately" while a God-rejecting nation and its children, without hope, plunges into ultimate slavery and perversion of every description.

But God is not the peculiar "god" of Baptists, Catholics, etc. He is God over all! In my own studies of theology, church history and history in general, it is clear that there no longer exists a "Council of Jerusalem" where reasonable, authoritative and responsible men, in concert with the Holy Spirit, provided the leadership necessary to God's purposes.

In harking back to the origins of our own nation, the lack of such leadership is clearly seen. And how could it be otherwise when men like Calvin, who, in the name of God, burned Servetus at the stake, were held in veneration while the churches denigrated the wisdom of the Franklin's, Pain's and Jefferson's!

Ultimately, it took the cooperation of such men as the Cotton Mather's, Jim Baker's, Jimmy Swaggart's and other false shepherds, hirelings in the pulpits, to lead us, as a nation, to kicking God out of our government, schools and society in general. And, without God, there is no true motive for morality by whatever definition. And if we will not have the God, Caesar stands ready, and is preparing, to demand worship! But with the Zionist agenda succeeding, aided by perverts and an adulterous generation, of kicking God out of the churches, schools, government, the Boy and Girl Scouts, what, exactly, is the choice except Caesar? Even such outspoken critics of organized religion as Franklin and Jefferson understood the need for the churches as a moral force for the common good. But they could not foresee the condition of the churches in today's America! To our shame, what might they have said if they had been able to see such conditions today? I shudder to think.

As a simple country boy, it is hard for me to accept graffiti as part of American culture. Somehow, spray-painting walls and buildings with gang and Mexican slogans still strikes me as vandalism by peoples whose cultures are alien to America and evidence no sense of responsibility or concern for private (or even public) property. Perhaps it is only the vicissitudes of age and changes that I construe as destructive that leads to such a conclusion but I doubt it. Irrespective of age and society, I still believe such activity is criminally destructive vandalism, an attack on my concept of what America should be.

Perhaps, following the lead of the "Prediction" company I mentioned in a previous essay there exists the possibility of a "fusion" process in the field of Human Behavior. As a physics aficionado, I have always recognized some of the weaknesses in our mathematical models. For example, the impossibility of reaching some rational conclusions based on our decimal system.

Physicists, limited by our understanding of some of the anomalies of mathematics, are forced to use what "works" in spite of such things. In just such a manner, we are forced to use what "works" in human behavior whether we understand some of the mechanisms or not.

Not to become incomprehensibly esoteric, the ideas represented by such works as Adler's Great Books could be compressed to a mere handful. The sheer, daunting volume of such a display of the wisdom of men is attributable to the genius of the individual's phraseology, not to any "new" concepts. As with the space between atoms in physical phenomena, the "new ideas" are exceeding sparse, the apparent "structure" immense. But regardless the appearance, such structures are, largely, empty space and, in many cases, verbose fluff, not material substance. (Very much like the mountainous heap of seeming "material" concerning education and religion).

As the Preacher of Ecclesiastes said so succinctly: "There is nothing new under the sun." In the context of his statement, he was absolutely correct. For example, murder and adultery are nothing "new." Neither is the idea of immortality or God's judgment of the wicked. Aristotle, Cato, Socrates and Plato had a pretty fair grasp of what were, even then, ancient concepts of good and evil, justice and injustice, which are as valid today as they were then.

To put it another way, the sheer weight of material available on most subjects is often given credibility as "substance" simply because of the unique personalities involved and the, occasionally, genius of the person's phraseology. For example how many poets and writers of great reputation have described, exactly, the same things; nothing "new," just different ways of saying the same thing.

Unlike the "hard" sciences, theology and philosophy (including education and government) has no on-going building of an empirical database. We are, as a result, lacking new ideas in these areas and suffer a corresponding, hurtful ignorance when new situations and circumstances present themselves.

But "children" must learn or suffer the pains of their ignorance. Great advances in science are always the result of observation and testing. Even some of the most seeming, fortuitous "accidents" of science were still the result of the empirical seeking of data. Why haven't we pursued the same scientific course in human behavior?

Given that mathematics is fundamentally flawed. In 1930 mathematician Kurt Godel made the obvious point that self-consistent rules like those of arithmetic contain statements which cannot be proved either true or false; but they work! "The procedure Fk(n) is true of the number n if and only if there is no number N for which the Nth possible proof in the formal system S is a proof whose Godel number is n." Regardless the genius of the men, whether mathematics was "discovered" or "invented," there are simply no means available in our present systems of mathematics from the simplest to the most advanced forms, to prove certain of the "workable" mechanisms.

Philosophers have always recognized the weakness of the mathematical constructs and have been correspondingly shy of intruding themselves into scientific arenas of "proofs" in human behavior as a result. While physicists continue, in spite of the weaknesses of the mathematical models, to pursue the holy grail of the unification theory, there hope (faith?) that such a thing exists keeps them in pursuit of it.

There is an old saying in science that "Redundancy is the enemy of efficiency." Now when I used to do a lot of flying, I was grateful for the "redundancy" built into, or available for, aircraft. When conditions are VFR and the weather CAVU, you can do quite well with Needle, Ball and Airspeed (a Wet Compass puts you in "fat city"). But when you are suddenly thrust into IFR conditions, you bless the "redundancy" of avionics.

The vast weight of material in the social sciences and religion is, however, not of such redundancy, and, far from promoting safety and knowledge, has only led to ignorance, waste and dreadful inefficiency. It has been well said, for example, that the field of education is terribly flawed by the lack of empirical data. While the hard sciences advance by the rules of observation and testing, social "scientists" tinker. Why haven't we pursued the most logical and reasonable paths of scientists in gaining knowledge of God and human behavior? Simply because of ingrained prejudices and the egos of the leaders in these areas; unlike the mathematician who isn't trying to prove that .3 will ever reach a discernible terminus, such ignorant "leaders" will continue to "explain" the unexplainable and major in pious nonsense. The mathematician has a symbol for infinity but he has sense enough not to try to "explain" it.

Good scientists are gaining knowledge by the very same God-given minds and intellects, the very same natural creation available to all of us. I am not even calling for a search for some kind of "Cold Fusion" of philosophy and religion. I am only asking that the same rigor be applied in seeking answers in theology and human behavior that credible scientists use. Franklin, while assenting to the existence of God, did not let prejudicial ignorance keep him from a theory that lightening was a natural force of electricity. While owning the God of the natural creation, he took silk string, a key and kite and proceeded to advance knowledge in spite of the "professionals" in religion.

Empirical evidence does exist in human behavior. Such evidence is exemplified by God's requirement that men repent of wickedness and prove their genuine turning from sin by showing it in their lives (the fruits of genuine repentance). Another bit of evidence exists in the fact that no matter the amount of empirical material available, you cannot make people care! Organizations such as the Mafia and KKK might well envy the organized churches for obvious reasons but even the churches face this overriding principle.

There is further evidence in the commonality of the beliefs and thought processes of all men and the laws, codes and "taboos" of civilizations. There is, indeed, a "true light that lightens all men;" The Gospel of John, chapter one. And, as stated in Paul's epistle to the Romans, God Himself is clearly revealed in His natural creation so that men are "without excuse" for their ignorance. Our present "blindness" in religion, education and human behavior in general is the failure to apply "string, key and kite" to what is already revealed!

In a corrupt interpretation of Jesus' words, "Blessed are those who have not seen and yet believe," religionists have come up with the hare-brained doctrine of "blind faith" as though that were the excuse of not searching out answers to legitimate and reasonable questions. It's as though there were a "missing" beatitude: "Blessed are the ignorant for they will not seek knowledge!" On the contrary, "they" will, in supreme ignorance and pride, "explain" infinity, eternity, heaven and immortality! Fools that they are they frustrate honest attempts, as did their predecessors, those Jewish leaders whom Jesus condemned, to find the very knowledge of which they themselves are ignorant!

Of course there are things that in our physical environment and mortality are unknowable. My complaint is against the fools who engage in pious platitudes and phraseology as though they understood and offered explanations for things which honest men grant "unknowableness." Tragically such dishonesty and charlatanism seems endemic to professional religionists just as it is to professional educationists.

The failure of the New England saints to set up God's Kingdom in the New World was a failure to recognize God as preeminently pragmatic, practical and reasonable. They, as the churches have done for centuries, insisted on keeping Him unknowable, unreasonable, superstitiously mysterious, and, even, capricious.

Philip Freneau (1752 - 1832) is called "The Father of American Poetry." In the mold of Thoreau to come he wrote:

A hermit's house beside a stream
With forests planted round,
Whatever it to you may seem
More real happiness I deem
Than if I were a monarch crown'd

Reminiscent of Pope's "Ode on Solitude," Freneau did, early, ape his "betters." But, in time, he developed into a very real poet in his own right. For example:

O come the time, and haste the day,
When man shall man no longer crush,
When Reason shall enforce her sway,
Nor these fair regions raise our blush,
Where still the African complains,
And mourns his yet unbroken chains.

Opposed to the veneration of men, Freneau deplored making more of Washington and Franklin than those worthy men would, themselves, have allowed. But he knew the truth of such men; for example in respect to Washington he wrote:

He was no god, ye flattering knaves,
He own'd no world, he ruled no waves;
But-and exalt it, if you can,

He was the upright, HONEST MAN.

Not a bad epitaph for any man, great or humble. Freneau was not held in much esteem by the churches because of his criticism of the very things of which I have found fault, particularly their "confusing" the difference between belief and knowledge.

Among the Connecticut Wits John Trumbull (1750-1831) was considered by many to be the most talented. Regarding religious "knowledge" and "holy offices" he wrote:

Oft dulness flying from disgrace
Finds safety in that sacred place;

. . . . . .

Where scripture sanctifies his strains
And reverence hides the want of brains.
...tries with ease, and unconcern,
To teach what ne'er himself could learn,

. . . . . .

On Sunday, in his best array,
Deals forth the dulness of the day,
And while above he spends his breath,
The yawning audience nods beneath.

And, in my own experience, Trumbull's accusation, "More oaths than words Dick learn'd to speak and studied knavery more than Greek" rings with contemporary truth.

Trumbull's "The Progress of Dulness" should be required study for all seminarians:

'Gainst scripture rail in modern lore,
As thousand fools have railed before.

. . . . . .

Thus 'twixt the taylor and the player,
And Hume, and Tristram, and Voltaire,
Complete in modern trim array'd,
The clockwork gentleman is made.

. . . . . .

In vain may learning fill the head full,
'Tis beauty that's the one thing needful.

This last in regard to Miss Harriet Simper: the certain antidote for Tom Brainless the "cleric" in question.

In attempts to understand my contention that new ideas are exceedingly few and the few we have should be given the gravest study, I will cite the problem of our historic origins as a Nation by asking that you consider the case of Thomas Jefferson and Alexander Hamilton. As many the differences between them, one an espoused Federalist (Hamilton) and the other, a Republican (Jefferson), they exemplify the conditions that led to our form of government, the good and bad.

Jefferson, it is to be remembered, came to the end of his days, as did so many others like he and Franklin, doubting if "the species were worth preserving." It doesn't take that much reading of history, together with our present conditions in the world, to understand their doubt. As Jefferson once said in regard to the question of slavery: "I tremble for my country when I reflect that God is just; that his justice cannot sleep forever; that considering numbers, nature and natural means only, a revolution of the wheel of fortune, an exchange of situation is among possible events; that it may become probable by supernatural interference!" The "wheel of fortune" did, indeed roll over the nation, as he feared.

Jefferson, as many other good men, retained his slaves because he knew they would fare much better under his ownership than they would, as happened, cast to the "winds of fate" to try and make their own way in a nation which would never accept them as equals. Even Franklin, and later, Lincoln, accepted the truth of this dire dictum of historical truth.

Opposing the "early" Jefferson, Hamilton said: "One great error is that we suppose mankind more honest than they are. Our prevailing passions are ambition and interest...Your People is a great beast...It will ever be the duty of a wise government to avail itself of the passions, in order to make them subservient to the public good; for these ever induce us to action...the people commonly intend the public good...but they do not always reason right about the means of promoting it."

This, of course, ran counter to Jefferson's early ideals "that morality, compassion, generosity are innate elements of the human constitution." Hamilton, in contrast, supposed the "vices" of the elevated classes "...are more favorable to the prosperity of the State than those of the indigent, and partake less of moral depravity." He also felt: "The influx of foreigners must...tend to produce a heterogeneous compound; to change and corrupt the national spirit; to complicate and confound public opinion; to introduce foreign propensities."

It was the contrast between the early idealism of Jefferson and the more pragmatic Hamilton that make the Federalist papers the classics of early republicanism that they became. While I still share Jefferson's view of the nobility of working the land and believe such closeness with nature builds more of desirable character than the "manufactures" of Hamilton's view, their ideas were not antagonistic. In reconciling the two views, it needs to be remembered that Europe was spiritually bankrupt. The condemnation of America's "dollar-chasing" was, for the most part, sour grapes. Europe had already, largely, raped its resources. But here in virgin America! The possibilities of gaining wealth, the seemingly endless resources were truly mind-boggling; talk about the kid being let loose in the candy store!

It is obviously impossible in a short essay, even in the heaviest tome, to open the door but a fraction to the understanding which is possible with an in depth study of the views of our founding fathers. My reason, in part, for bringing up Freneau and others is to try to dispel the ignorant supposition that there was some kind of contemporary orgy of adulation for the heroes of our beginning history as a nation. True enough that such men were, in many cases, larger than life. Meeting the exigencies of the times with such perseverance, courage and intelligence made them so. In many cases, men like Hamilton and Jefferson, Hobbes and Rousseau did present the subjects of government and philosophies in needfully fresh terms. The "treasure" is indeed, a mix of the old and the new.

Departing from the ancient landmarks, those "workable" concepts like those of mathematics, in spite of their imperfections, we have reaped a whirlwind of hopelessness and lack of direction, personally and nationally. In my opinion, Jefferson and others were absolutely correct in their condemnation of an "artificial aristocracy" based on birth and wealth. The founding fathers were agreed that an aristocracy of educated, propertied persons who had proven records in their personal and business affairs were the only ones who could be trusted to provide enlightened leadership in government. As to my campaign, I have mentioned "Voter Eligibility Reform" among other points. While there is a desperate need for such, it will be one of the most difficult and thorny issues we must all deal with if there is to be any hope of responsible government.

"We the People" as intended by the founding fathers did not include crooks and welfare deadbeats. Men like Hamilton, Adams and Jefferson, and, later, Lincoln, pointed out the fact that if "special interests" such as the lazy and indigent were allowed the franchise, they would always, as in Caesar's day, demand "Bread and Circuses" without accepting any of the responsibility for payment. Only the most degraded and selfish politician would, as with our own Willie Brown, pander to the cry of such a mob.

They also understood the female psyche of emotions overruling good sense. Apart from the Biblical injunctions concerning the position of men and women in God's scheme of things, the founding fathers knew that if women were to share in government on equal terms with men, the result would be chaotic. And, so it is today. But we have the further problem of those many ignorant, indigent and lazy who, with the urging of the likes of the Willie Brown's, voting a free ride on the backs of those who work and pay the bills for government, a government which can no longer afford, due to the vanishing middle class, all those "freebies."

The founding fathers clearly recognized the weaknesses, both real and potential, of the Constitution. For this reason, Jefferson wrote: "No society can make a perpetual constitution, or even a perpetual law. The earth belongs always to the living generation...The real friends of the constitution in its federal form, if they wish it to be immortal, should be attentive, by amendments, to make it keep pace with the advance of the age in science and experience...A little rebellion now and then is a good thing, and as necessary in the political world as storms in the physical...The tree of liberty must be refreshed from time to time with the blood of patriots and tyrants."

Most assuredly, if an ignorant and selfish electorate continues to vote ignorant and selfish leaders into office, the results are easily predictable and equally catastrophic for a civilization. For example, one of the reforms I would work for, if elected, concerns the so-called "Juvenile Justice System," that system which is so out of control that police and judges are unable to cope with it. I submit this for your consideration. Why shouldn't a child, regardless of age, be held accountable for criminal acts? I would ask for legislation that would hold that child accountable until full restitution is made to the victim of his crime. If some 12-year-old steals a car and wrecks it, why should his parents be held accountable? I would track that child the rest of his life until he, not the parents, made restitution. Further, if such an act should result in incarceration, he should still be held liable for restitution until the debt to the victim is paid in full!

I ask you; why should I have to pay insurance to protect myself from juvenile crime and things like "uninsured motorists?" Why don't we have sensible and reasonable legislation that makes the criminal, regardless of age, responsible for his own acts? And such legislation should not have any statute of limitation. All the states, working in concert, should cooperate in dogging the heels of these criminals until the victim is fully compensated.

In my own experience, which has been substantial, with the Juvenile Justice System, I have found it to be one of the very most frustrating factors in Police work. It is thoroughly demoralizing to police who know these young thugs, if arrested, will often be back on the street in hours. If that young person knows he will never be able to avoid paying his debt, that it will continue to hang over his head until it is paid, he will think twice about "joy-riding" or breaking into your house to steal.

And what of the role of the schools in this scenario; it is substantial-critically so. Schools are in crisis, both educationally and morally. This has been the case for over thirty years! But, as I have often said, unless education becomes a national priority, there is no hope of any improvement. And, to repeat like a broken record, you don't find solutions to problems by asking the very people who created the problems for those solutions! Insane!

Of all our institutions, family, church, industry and government, none have the impact on our society as that of the schools. Our educational system impacts every single child and, correspondingly, our whole nation at every level. As go the schools, so goes the nation.

Because of this fact, we are a demoralized nation without any certain compass heading. We are not only failing to educate our children, we can't even seem to give them a relevant or, even, relative reason for their getting an education! And this is the fault of the failure of an entire society, not just that of the schools. I have often said that education must receive a national priority. Our present, dismal circumstance should make this need all the clearer.

The Greedy Geezer generation too often has the attitude that since it has raised its children it no longer has a vested interest in addressing the problems of the schools. I have made the point to many that this is the single, most difficult hurdle to overcome in my campaign. Somehow it doesn't compute in the mind of such that juvenile crime, as one specific, has its roots in a failed school system that desperately needs all the help it can get from mature citizens. And I don't mean financial help. I mean the kind of help children have a right to expect from the wisdom of mature and caring leadership.

For example, it has come as a surprise to most of those I speak with that memorizing the multiplication tables has not been a requirement in the schools for decades. This seems to be incomprehensible to "Senior Citizens." Yet, that is the fact of the case. This is the reason for "pictures" taking the place of numbers on cash registers used at Burger King, etc.

In teaching math at the high school level, I soon discovered that these teenagers did not know their multiplication tables. This was even true of some of my algebra pupils. Knowing that this most basic and rudimentary skill had to be mastered before anyone can have success in math, I required my pupils to do the required memorization. I would not allow calculators until the student demonstrated mastery of the subject. They whined and growled but soon discovered they were having success instead of failure; math was becoming, for the first time in many cases, comprehensible.

My most antagonistic critics were not the pupils; they were the administrators of the schools. The very people that had no comprehension of the necessity of rote memorization, and that is the only method of learning such things as the multiplication tables, were constantly haranguing me for teaching such a basic and essential skill. I did it in spite of such "experts" and it led to more than one poor evaluation of my classroom teaching. But the kids learned.

In spite of my constant feuds with administration, I was tenured in both the L.A. City Schools and the Antelope Valley U.H.S.D., the only two districts in which I stayed long enough to qualify for tenure. But I stuck it out for the sake of the kids, not because of any help or support on the part of administrators. In the long run, insane as it seems, I became "too educated to be an educator!" Once I had earned my Ph. D., together with my experience in industry, I became too great a threat to the educational hierarchy; as one board member candidly told me: "Don't expect to try for any advancement in this district, they are afraid of you!" He was absolutely right.

There is no more paranoid group in the nation as that of school personnel. Why? Because they know they are incompetent and don't really care about children. They know they have failed and are drawing a paycheck undeservedly, feeding at the public trough without any semblance of accountability.

How does a school district go bankrupt; because there isn't any accountability, if a qualified CPA were to examine the books of any school district the first thing he would discover is the insanity of their accounts. No business would ever survive the book keeping of the schools. Because of this factor, embezzlement is a commonplace.

To compound the matter, there are no qualifications for election to a school board. Board members hire an "expert," at a ridiculously obscene salary, the superintendent, for whom the board becomes a "rubber stamp." This expert is supposed to know school law and codes. To the degree he is ignorant and self-serving; to that degree the entire system suffers his incompetence, greed and ego.

An instance in which this promotes actual theft by such "leadership" is the practice of counting pupils in attendance that don't attend! True story. While I was a teacher in Watts, we were ordered to count pupils in attendance that came to school only sporadically. This provided fraudulent ADA and skewed the actual absentee rate that was horrifically more than the schools would admit. Back in the middle sixties, our dropout rate was an honest 75 per cent, not the 25 per cent the schools were reporting.

We knew in 1954 that the bottom 15 per cent of college students was going into education. It wouldn't have taken much to predict the outcome of such a travesty; exactly the situation we face in the schools today! The question: knowing this, why wasn't the situation faced and rectified; because the schools of education on college campuses were, themselves, staffed by incompetents. This is the reason the schools of education are the laughing stock and embarrassment of colleges and universities.

The worst class of "students" I ever confronted was a graduate class, fresh B.A.'s in hand, of adult, prospective teachers. The class I was teaching was called "Teaching Strategies." The first papers this class submitted to me were not even worthy of college freshmen. But this group of adults had been graduated by their respective colleges and universities and had been led to believe that they had a "college education" which qualified them to become teachers!

When I confronted this class with my feelings about their dismal performance, they set up a howl. They demanded, rightfully, that I prove my criticism to them. I began with the first paper on the stack without naming the individual. Dealing only with syntax and grammar, I hadn't finished the first paragraph of this first example when the class begged me to stop. Tragically, this group of "college graduates" had come through the entire system of college preparation for teaching without ever having anyone confront them on their own educational deficiencies.

From Rushdoony to Copperman to Damerell, the research has proved that we have been moving to a permanent educational underclass in this nation. Fomented by the agenda of Jewish Intellectuals with their Zionist/Marxist theology, the universities and colleges swallowed the Big Lie whole. By little by little, selling the proposition of "equal education and opportunity," the entire system, from top to bottom created an institutional mind-set of the lowest common denominator predominating.

If you doubt this, due to its seeming extremeness, read just one book: "Education's Smoking Gun or How Teachers Colleges Have Destroyed Education in America" by Reginald G. Damerell. This man has paid the price, professionally, for speaking out about a system that, as I have often said, is not as bad as you think, it is far worse!

So it is that education is the focus of my campaign for the State Senate. If our schools do not educate, from kindergarten to graduate studies, we are doomed as a nation. And when the schools and colleges are not staffed by caring and educated people the children and students are doomed. This poison is carried into the classrooms across the nation by those, like the "graduate students" I cited who, in all earnestness, believe they are actually prepared to do the job of teaching. And why shouldn't they believe this lie? Haven't the colleges and universities told them they are qualified and prepared to do the job!

Believe it or not, school personnel are not above breaking the law! I have witnessed teachers politicking in their classrooms, against the law, for a favored issue or candidate for public office. Even as I write, there are employees of the schools and colleges, together with another hefty segment of "public employees" mounting a band wagon called: "Bite 'Em Back." This is an organization of people feeding at the public trough, mostly drones that are attempting a recall of Governor Pete Wilson. This because he is actually trying to do something that needs, desperately, to be done: cut the fat out of these entrenched bureaucracies. The ruse of the organization: that the governor is "picking on" the elderly and disabled!

There are some extremely hard choices to be made here in California. They involve goring just about every ox that has existed on the dole. There simply aren't any more cookies in the jar. The last thing we need are more "Droids" like Willie Brown and the Welfare and Educational "Leadership" telling us to give them more money for failed and prohibitively costly boondoggles. And please, Mr. Dornan, at least spell my name right! Speaking of which, did you know that spelling, grammar and diagramming sentences went the way of the multiplication tables in the schools as well? You do now!

Everyone knows insurance reforms are needed throughout the entire industry and the whole country. It certainly doesn't help when so many lawyers and doctors are involved in so many insurance scams. Is it any wonder, however, that insurance company's red-line when such a disproportionate amount of money is spent on claims in predominantly minority areas where hospitals know they aren't going to get paid and investigators are forbidden to investigate "accident" claims in "certain" geographical areas? The same situation, in fact, exists in California where, not only are insurance investigators forbidden to go, but Welfare investigators are forbidden to check on claims in "certain" geographical areas as well.

Under all this failure of an entire society is still the problem of morality. The schools and government reflect an entire society. If that society genuinely cares for its posterity, this will prove itself in that society's institutions of home, church, school, industry and government. If, in an attempt to re-define America, this generation chooses multiculturalism with its concomitant chaos and lack of morality, there can be no hope for a future for our children regardless of creed or race. If the broken home, ignorant and uncaring schools, corruption in government, failure of churches continue its present course, nothing but destruction awaits us.

This lack of morality carries a death sentence in the AIDS epidemic to which our young people are so susceptible notwithstanding the issue of abortion as contraception that, according to my own belief system, is murder of the innocent. Just how much of this holocaust can be laid at the foot of ignorance and the glorification of sex aided and abetted by the schools? I have written much about women as "victims," what about the fact that the great majority of AIDS sufferers will be women in three to five years?

Neuhaus is a thinking man's thinker. I join him in the hope that Brecht is not correct that food must come before morals, that men and women are better than that. But if our schools continue in their present course, nothing but Hitlerian "solutions" will be possible.

It would be amusing, if it weren't so tragic in its consequences, to see Clinton already waffling on his campaign promises. If he had been honest in his campaign, he could never have won. But he lied! He surely knew he couldn't begin to solve the problems we face in the manner he campaigned but, as with most politicians, all he cared about was getting elected. But he won by lies and deceit, the media, women and minorities and that will become ever more evident as time goes by. On the other hand we weren't given much of a choice as per Bush.

But I do have to wonder why Bush so obviously "shot himself in the foot?" Was he "following orders?" With the proven, undoubted conspiracy of JFK's assassination, was Bush scared? Does a "bullet" await Clinton? Some believe so! Just the most recent events of the MIAs, S&Ls, BCCI, Iran/Contra scams should give him pause to think. He would have much more cause for concern if the real truth of Rudolph Hess, etc. should become common knowledge. And, might it also have to do with the abundant evidence, like the "bullet on the stretcher" which obviously had to be "planted" and the bullet wound in his back, at the time of JFK's assassination? After all, "they" got away with it in killing Lincoln!

Conspiracies do, indeed, abound. But I don't fear any of them. If the enemies of freedom and liberty were really all that well organized, then I would begin to fear. But they are not! This is due to the inherent selfishness and egos of those involved. That is a fact of human nature on which we can always rely.

Were it not for my belief that the light of God is in every human being as per the first chapter of the Gospel of John, I would indeed abandon all hope. But it is that hope, evidenced by men like Aristotle, Socrates, Woolstone, Franklin, Jefferson, Emerson and Thoreau that keeps me from entering, irretrievably, the "slough of despond."

A great part of the national tragedy is that people like myself, blessed in precious memories, who are easily transported in an instant of time with beautiful music in the background and the sunlight brightly glinting off the rocks, trees and mountains, a lake or trout stream, and cause us to lose ourselves in the reverie of what was then and what is now. We know what was lost to our children. We knew there was romance and adventure out there somewhere, somehow, and that there was a "someone" with whom to share our dreams and hopes of the future, a someone that would stand by us and return our love and faithfulness.

It took a very great and grand culture to inculcate such things in its young. Only betrayal on an equally great scale could bring us to our present, dismal state and the loss of all those things that made life worthwhile, those things of such value that transcended the merely material.

Perhaps it is my "Okie" origin in Southeast Bakersfield that makes me think, in respect to politics, of the old story of Zeke and Zeb. Seems they were talking about the closeness of their friendship when they had the following conversation:

Zeb: Zeke, ol' buddy, iffen Ah had'a pint'a corn likker, Ah'd giv'ya half.

Zeke: Zeb, ol' frien', iffen Ah had'a chaw, Ah'd giv'ya half.

Zeb: Zeke, iffen Ah had three dollahs, Ah'd giv'ya half.

Zeke: Now Zeb, thas not far; Yah'll knows Ah've got three dollahs!

God says a man is judged in his giving according to what he has, not what he doesn't have. That seems imminently fair and sensible. But we have to face the fact that people, including politicians who, according to some charitable souls, qualify as such, operate on the Zeke and Zeb principle. I don't think congressmen really started out to become, as per Sam, The only true, Native American criminal class. Nor do I believe Judas was, necessarily, only a premature congressman! But it certainly seems to have worked out that way in practice.

As we watch the shameless and selfish manipulation of children by the teachers and their unions in Los Angeles, we should be taking note of the fact that it is only the utter lack of accountability on the part of the schools and our legislators that has led to this sorry spectacle. And without the requisite accountability, why should you care or accept responsibility? It will not get any better nor will our children receive an education until men like me are elected to confront the "Beast" and work for desperately needed reforms and accountability.

The Nazi flag, not surprisingly, flies alongside Spain's at a rally in Madrid commemorating the dictator Franco's death. The Stars and Bars gets the attention of the media in the South as it is hoisted atop a capitol dome, Malcolm X commercialism is making millions for the promoters of another "alien" culture, Marge Schott is "uninvited" to our Business Conference in Bakersfield, Somalia, Bosnia, Iran, our "help" in promoting Pakistan's building "the Bomb," endemic AIDS in Uganda, and so much more, all of which serves for the on-going full employment of the UN, Interpol and the "Feds." If all this weren't enough, Newsweek devotes a special section to "Doomsday Science," calling attention to, among other scary things, something I have pointed out; that there is probably a huge "rock" out there with our name on it! The rock called "Wormwood" of Revelation? Also, the media is having fun scaring the wits out of Californians with the "impending" catastrophic earthquake I spoke of a while back. In view of all this, I take cold comfort from Midge Decter's comment: "It's the Democrat's Deficit now!"

I hope you will give me your support in the forthcoming campaign. It will be well worth it if we succeed in opening the door to honest and candid discussion of the issues, those things that the entrenched leadership know, but are afraid or too selfish to address. Help me, especially, to deal with the host of "Entitlement" programs that are only financial disasters and empire-building mechanisms for the greedy, selfish egos of the "experts" who have made this mess, so-called "Special Education" being an infamous case in point. We had better get back in the business of spending money for the "Best and Brightest" immediately instead of pouring money down the rat-hole of stroking and feeding "special interests." And let's get rid of alien languages like Spanish on our ballots and in government offices. You won't find this insanity in any other nation and it certainly does not promote American culture and ideals!

H. St. John De Crevecoeur (1735-1813) wrote: "Men are like plants; the goodness and flavor of the fruit proceeds from the peculiar soil and exposition in which they grow. We are nothing but what we derive from the air we breathe, the climate we inhabit, the government we obey, the system of religion we profess, and the nature of our employment."

Of Crevecoeur's "Letters" Abel writes: "The essential theme of the 'Letters' is that self-interest, furnished opportunity, but restrained by law and conscience, has brought about American felicity, and the best attainable, human nature and the world being as they are."

Crevecoeur recognized the huge opportunity America represented. But his conclusions were based on the American Man being a refinement of European culture. He, as so many others, condemned slavery as being anathema to the realization of America's potential for good. But he was absolutely right in prophesying that America: "...will one day cause great changes in the world." We would do well to hearken to such men in their praise and warnings. Our current direction does not bode well!

By the way, I am adamantly opposed to proposed Voucher systems. No one is a stronger proponent of private schools than I am; I wouldn't have started three of them otherwise. But make no mistake about it, the loopholes in such a system beg for every kind of fraud and rip-off to the taxpayers. I am also opposed because of the fact that We the People have paid dearly for an existing system of schools for all children. We have a duty and obligation to make the existing system perform responsibly and sensibly. A voucher system will only undermine efforts for reform in the schools. Do what is needed in the schools, homes, churches, give parents and school personnel authority to exercise discipline, reform the Juvenile Justice System and other related fields and give children the safe, moral, disciplined learning environment they deserve and the job can be done! As a society we must stop making the schools the scapegoat for the failures of so many other institutions of our society. Hold them accountable by all means for the job of educating, but not for being unable to do what only parents and society can do.

CHAPTER EIGHT

CHRISTIAN PERSPECTIVE

FEBRUARY 1992

I Peter 2:7

In 1863, at the Senate's request, President Lincoln set aside a national day of "...fasting, humiliation and prayer" for April 30. The Civil War raged across the Potomac when Lincoln said: "It is the duty of nations as well as of men to own their dependence upon the overruling power of God, to confess their sins and transgressions, in humble sorrow, yet with assured hope that genuine repentance will lead to mercy and pardon; and to recognize the sublime truth, announced in the Holy Scriptures and proven by all history, that those nations only are blessed whose God is the Lord.

"We have been the recipients of the choicest bounties of Heaven. We have been preserved, these many years, in peace and prosperity. We have grown in numbers, wealth and power, as no other nation has ever grown. But we have forgotten God. We have forgotten the gracious hand which preserved us in peace, and multiplied and enriched and strengthened us; and we have vainly imagined, in the deceitfulness of our hearts that all these blessings were produced by some superior wisdom and virtue of our own. Intoxicated with unbroken success, we have become too self-sufficient to feel the necessity of redeeming and preserving grace, too proud to pray to the God that made us!"

At one time Lincoln said to his treasurer, Chittenden: "...I decided a long time ago that it was less difficult to believe that the Bible was what it claimed to be (God's Word) than to disbelieve it." The "Great Emancipator" was called by the "evangelicals" of his day, as was Ben Franklin, an "Infidel." Yet, it was this "infidel" that led a nation to victory over slavery and lost his own life in the process. Of course, as I have pointed out, the so-called "victory," by the machinations of evil and wicked men and women could hardly be seen as such today.

But Lincoln owned his sincere obligation to God and His Word in the keeping of the Union and in the affairs of men and nations, particularly The United States of America. The man was utterly lacking in any taint of hypocrisy and the admission of his "ignorance" of many things "religious" people claimed to "know" led to the accusation of "infidel." I know how he and Franklin must have felt for so it is in my own case.

I have never expressed my thoughts about the assassination of John Kennedy in print before. Like many of you, I will never forget the horror and shock of those days as a nation struggled with the unfolding drama of the loss of our president and the fantastic events of Oswald, Ruby and the wild speculation surrounding the whole affair.

The recent "offer" of a K.G.B. agent to "sell" his story prompts me to comment at this time. First, I have to engage in some background for my conclusion.

I am a qualified gunsmith. In my prime, as an avid shooter, gun enthusiast and handloader, I was an expert marksman and well educated in the manufacture, history and capabilities of small arms. I could nail a leaping jackrabbit with my Single-action Army Colt, my Husqavarna .270 and my Springfield .03-A3. The .270 was mounted with a Weaver 2.5 with a post reticule; a very fast scope with a wide field of vision. The Springfield was National Match with quarter-minute click peep sight; even faster to pull down on a running target.

This is not intended as braggadocio or some kind of phony, "macho" nonsense. Many of my old, shooting buddies can attest to my skills as a marksman and my expertise in firearms. When I was dealing in weapons, I had a large collection. I was most interested in military arms. In my collection was the same type of Carcano Oswald was supposed to have used to kill the president. And there is the fallacy of Oswald being the shooter.

The Carcano Carbine was, without controversy, the worst of all small arms used in the war. Notoriously inaccurate and poorly made, Oswald would have done well to have hit Kennedy's Limo, let alone a moving target as small as a human head at the distance he was supposed to have been shooting from. Coupled with the fact that Oswald was a proven, poor marksman, it would have required nothing less than a miracle of the magnitude of that unnamed marksman whose arrow, at random, smote Ahab, for Oswald to have hit the president.

In the time-span established, 6.2 seconds, for Oswald, an inept shooter, using the poorest of weapons for any distance with any degree of accuracy, to work that bolt and score two out of three shots in such a fashion would be nothing less than miraculous in the fullest meaning of that word. My position: It couldn't have happened the way the Warren Commission would have us believe! The recent movie by Stone, notwithstanding, I have no doubt whatsoever that We the People were either lied to or the Commission did not include a single weapons expert who was allowed to tell the truth.

It would have been a simple matter to take a man like Oswald and, appealing to his vanity as a "small man," use him as a tool. The questions of who "they" were remains to be discovered. The possible "players:" The C.I.A., the K.G.B., Castro, the "Mob," and then vice-president Johnson. All had motive and, because of our "Shadow Government," the Cuban Missile Crisis, the Bay of Pigs fiasco, anything is possible.

General A.I. Gribkov, who was stationed in Cuba at the time in 1962, recently disclosed that the Soviets had given authority to the local commander in Cuba to fire nuclear weapons at the U.S. if Kennedy ordered an invasion. McNamara said he didn't even know about the presence of such weapons until this general disclosed it. "We were absolutely at the brink (of nuclear war)!" said Philip Brenner, a professor at American University, who took part in the recent closed-door conference of Soviet, American and Cuban actions concerning that time.

Just today Frank Ragano, a lawyer in N.Y., said: "Jimmy told me to tell Marcello and Trafficante they had to kill the president. Hoffa said to me, 'This has to be done.'" Two weeks after the assassination Regano said he met Marcello in New Orleans. He said the mob boss "looked like the cat who ate the canary. He had a smug look on his face and said, 'Jimmy owes me and he owes me big.' Quoting a newspaper trying to get more information: "Ragano, 68, didn't return a phone message left Tuesday at his Tampa law office. Trafficante died of natural causes in 1987, and Hoffa has been missing and presumed dead since 1975. There was no answer Tuesday afternoon at the Detroit law offices of Hoffa's son, James Jr." My personal opinion is that Castro, with more freedom of choice, believing it was "him or me," acting on better intelligence and "connected" better than Kennedy, beat him to the draw. Thus, in the minds of the players, a very real threat of WWIII was averted; a patriotic act performed and if a "small profit" was made in the exercise of such a "duty," that was all right too.

The "freakish" murder of Robert Kennedy must also be factored in. The whole matter may help explain Senator Kennedy's self-destructive lifestyle. What we are left with is the distinct possibility, probability, in my opinion, that there was indeed a conspiracy to assassinate the president and it was successful. Since Oswald was obviously not the shooter, since he had to be disposed of, since Ruby was a "natural" for the job, these things make sense. Given the mind-set of the "players," and their motivation, the whole thing comes together. Otherwise, we are left with an inexplicable "miracle."

The problem remains, short of such a "miracle," of the continued actions of the "players" who still believe they must "rule" and guide the destiny of our nation and the world according to their opinion of what is best. And, best for whom? P. J. O'Rourke: "Parliament of Whores." 'Giving money and power to government is like giving whiskey and car keys to teen-age boys.' "

Bush's collapse in Japan was electrifying. For those who like "omens" and looking into chicken entrails, much will be made of it. It is interesting that the most graphic scene, that of the president actually vomiting into the lap of Prime Minister Kiichi Miyazawa, was only aired in Japan; it was edited out for American viewers.

One of the reasons I castigate the churches so much is because I am a Christian, though not orthodox. Because of this fact, whatever shames God makes me angry. The Presbyterian churches, like so many other denominations with noble histories, have fallen on hard times. It seems one of the churches in Rochester N.Y. has appointed an openly lesbian woman as its "pastor." When asked about this abomination, the "Rev." Rose Mitchell, one of three "co-pastors" of the church said: "She was the most qualified!" The "pastor" in question, one Jane Spahr, was ordained in 1974 and has worked in several churches in California and Pennsylvania. When an attempt was made to challenge the appointment, the motion failed by a vote of 105 to 66.

In last month's newsletter I repeated Marilyn Savant's excellent remarks about the "hyphenated American." I repeat: "There is no such thing as a "hyphenated American. A hyphenated American is no American!" I add to this the recent remark of Louis Rukeyser. His father, arriving in this country from Hitler's Germany in the 1930s, said to his daughter: "We are in America now. We will speak English." Louis says, in response to his father's comment: "How contrary to the current view that ethnic pride should take precedence over national patriotism. Yet, as it turned out, how central to his family's quick adaptation to, and ultimate success in, an authentic land of opportunity... Exclusionist, paranoid ethnicity is alien to American instincts. It is the destructive force that is once again rending societies east and west. The American dream of freedom, unity and equality remains the key to our national strength, past and potential." Ruckeyser points out what I have been saying all along. A nation can only survive with a common culture and language dominating.

For some years now, I have been witnessing the disintegration of our nation. During the past few years, I have been writing about it. I used to preach and speak to various groups about my concerns, particularly in the area of education, but a funny thing happened on my way to trying to get people to do something about the situation; nobody cared!

Now, admittedly, I have a peculiar concept about "caring." I think if someone cares about something, they try to do something about it. I think that if someone cares about someone, they do something about it. I have to admit further, I am obviously wrong! Over the years, almost everyone I

147

have spoken to or written to have said they "care" but they have never done anything about it.

For example, if a young man is in love, you can't get him to shut up about the girl; if a person has an intense interest in growing eggplant, he will tell you more than you ever wanted to know about growing the stuff. Of course, the girl may be ugly as a mud fence and people will stop inviting the eggplant expert to parties but you get my drift.

Take church people for instance. Please! Get together with them and all they want to talk about is the excitement of knowing The Lord, His Word and how wonderful Heaven is going to be. Say What!!!

Now you know I'm pulling your leg. For years I have waited in vain to meet some "Christians" who really cared about the things they claimed to believe. In the comfort and safety of their pews, they vilify the Lord in song and so-called "worship services." Whether they go to church or not, the so-called *Christians* I have known had much rather talk about their latest carburetor overhaul or operation than anything real about God in their lives. Of course, the girl and eggplant are real, not God.

But these hypocrites are no different than the people that complain about our government and never vote or even know the name of their local Congressman. All such people are what I call "Two-dimensional, Picture or Mirror-people;" they have no depth. They typically show their real "caring" and "depth" when it's Super Bowl Sunday or they talk about their favorite "Soap." Onward Christian Soldiers must sound, to God, like an Ice Cube "rap song" in its fullest sense of the vilest profanity on the lips of the typical churchgoer.

As a man qualified by the state to teach the subject of psychology in College, having a Ph. D. in Human Behavior, the whole subject of thought processes is of the utmost interest to me. Why do people behave the way they do? What "triggers" psychotic behavior; what is the attraction of evil? What accounts for the differences between men and women in their choices of behavior, likes and dislikes? Why are we attracted to an accident scene; why do we have an insatiable appetite for news, entertainment, TV?

Now I know most of the bio-medical/mechanistic answers to these questions that are current in Academia. I still ask: What about the "Glory of Evil?" For, it is an absolute that the attraction of evil, as Paul the Apostle and Benjamin Franklin noted, is far superior to that of good. Man is a religious creature, and, while I am a "blight" on the "feasts" of "good, church-going" people, I'm well qualified to point out a few things on the subjects of religion and psychology.

It is true that the whole business of good and evil has, historically, been the purview of religionists. We may call it Human Behavior in psychology, but the subject matter is the same.

The basic theme of literature and art is, and throughout history, has been, the subject of good versus evil. And, while we hope the "good guys" will win, the realities of life are that it is evil, more often than good, which attracts. Evil is "strong," exciting and well directed, purposeful while the "good" is often indecisive, hesitating, mild and boring. Hitler, Tojo and Mussolini got things done.

While we couch evil in such terms as "prejudice, bigotry, anti-social behavior, etc.," we fail to acknowledge the fact that these things are only the symptoms of something much larger in human nature per se. Good Calvinists call it the total depravity of the natural man; they just don't know what that means. But, typically, if we can hang a label on it we will make that a substitute for understanding.

The reason for my undertaking this subject at this time is the rise of the "Forth Reich." This is taking place world-wide and much of it is happening under the auspices of organizations calling themselves "churches," remembering that Hitler and many of his supporters were "good Christians."

Evil has its contradictions and its followers often work at cross purposes (no pun or literary allusion intended). Stalin and Hitler had the same motivation and psyche but were hardly agreed on what was best for the other. But both agreed it was "better to reign in hell than serve in heaven."

Undoubtedly, MTV contributes much to our nation's growing "cannon fodder" of those that are willing to follow the "excitement" of violence and the Reich. Eddie Rabbitt is right about the "Heavy Metal Mentality" making young people illiterate and violent. The glorification of pornography and violence by such media as MTV makes fertile soil for the "purification" methodologies of a Hitler.

There are no more David Livingston's to explore and carry the Gospel to our "Dark Continent." But the "White Man's Burden" remains. Further, the "Livingston's" are not as exciting as the "Hitler's." Given the lack of leadership in our nation, the anger, frustration, without defined goals or direction, we face nothing but uncertainty about the future. And there is fear in the land; fear that things are getting, and going to get, worse. Dickens' "Bleak House" looms ahead in most people's thinking.

C.S. Lewis couldn't hold a candle to Melville as a writer but he told the story once of the little, old lady who, perfect in all her ways, had to have her toast "just so!" Dear McGee would often repeat this story because it so well describes the many "dear, old ladies" we have both known. While this old lady could never be accused of using coarse language, engaging in any activity that could be possibly construed as inappropriate, her toast had to be "just so!" If it wasn't, she let the offending party know about it in snide language and her nose would point straight up, her face expressing all the sentiments she would, proudly, never give voice to.

In fact, as Lewis and McGee would point out, she may as well have cursed the offender roundly in the most vulgar, gutter language and have done with it. She certainly never fooled God by her "restraint" and she didn't fool others either. All she succeeded in doing was fooling herself and grow in sinful pride that she was "better" than those that were, obviously, inferior to her "high standards of righteousness" and "godly" behavior.

I have a couple of examples of letters I have received from readers who are, obviously, "good church goers." They take me to task for inserting an occasional, mild expletive in my writing. I mentioned one of these folks in my last letter. Curiously, they say nothing about anything else in the letters. I can only assume they think it more important to reprove me for saying hell or damn than address themselves to the fate of their country or doing anything to help. Curious indeed; it reminds me too much of those folks who had stomping ants down to a science but couldn't be bothered with the elephants rampaging through the village. And, like most of the religious people I know, they don't support my writing or me.

Like Paul the Apostle, I used to "believe many things that were not so." I didn't smoke, cuss or imbibe strong spirits. I was the husband of one wife. I was quicker on the draw with chapter and verse against all "sin" from bob hair to hug dancing than most of my peers. I was "accepted among the beloved." It was obvious to all that the "divine anointing" was upon me and I was "called to preach."

And so it was, that, while I used to be surrounded by such people who would never engage in the coarse language and behavior of "worldly" people, I grew weary of wading in the cesspool of hypocrisy they called "church" and "walking with the Lord." That, together with what was called "worship" and "service," with no regard for actually getting their hands "dirty" in real work, insulating themselves in the safety of their "sanctuaries," led me to accept the fact that the whole thing was a sham.

Little by little, I found myself joining those worthies, Franklin, Emerson, and Thoreau, whose sentiments I shared, and in the words of that good philosopher of the Pond: "...through the liberalizing influence of all the worthies, with Jesus Christ Himself...let 'our church' go by the board."

My regard for The Lord and His Word has never changed. On the contrary, it is only my firm conviction that the Spirit of God wends its way throughout the Bible and leads me to such condemnation of the merely "religious." What tries to pass itself off today as "church" has altered considerably from its history in this nation. I'll have none of it. There are many more worthy "clubs" that are doing the work the churches are "too good for." As my mother often pointed out, "If the churches were as friendly as the bars, they would be crowded!" My work in the churches certainly confirmed the truth of her criticism.

Do not misunderstand me; any friend of God is a friend of mine. The problem is that Jesus set the criteria of friendship. He said: "You are my friends if you do what I command you... and my commandments are not grievous." The primary commandments of Jesus were that we were to love God and one another. As with my "odd" belief concerning "caring" I also believe if someone says they are a "friend" of God, they will evidence that friendship in the reality of their lives, in the way they deal with others and not some phony hymn-singing and church-going. As a result of this "fruit inspection," I have very few "church-going" friends.

The point of this "tirade" is that such things not only lead to the founding of organizations like Fundamentalists Anonymous, they lead to the Glory of Evil. The suspicion and paranoia common in the churches leads people to seek a better and more "real" environment. But too often it is difficult for the person, persuaded as he is, that he is "godly," and truly "seeking" to find a suitable substitute. Lacking real conversion, he is easily led to any organization that promises to do the things the "churches" are failing in. The success of the charismatic churches, particularly, is founded on this precept.

So, with the abject failure of the churches to be relevant except as cushy social clubs, deceiving themselves that they are "serving God," people are looking for leadership that promises real action and involvement in real issues. And there's the rub.

What constitutes "real" issues? The churches, too confused, and too busy fighting with one another, stealing and money-grubbing, "struggling with the powers of darkness" over ordaining perverts and women, or, as Franklin pointed out, "trying to make Presbyterians instead of Patriots and good citizens," have given up the command of Jesus to go out into the world and do what they were intended to do. The "Salt" has indeed "lost its savor."

Our nation, leaderless, rife with corruption in all our institutions, a ship without a rudder, leaves people seeking something, someone that will make sense and set a course of action that promises hope. The high "morality," the pseudo-religious trappings, the "purity" of a Fourth Reich makes a compelling and appealing case for itself. It attracts the young who want strong leadership and a "just cause" to give themselves to. Being young, they crave action. MTV, etc. has done a good job preparing the young for just such a thing as a new "Hitler" youth movement. High unemployment, the loss of hope in our future, loss of hope in our institutions and government, all these and more have made this nation, among others, the logical breeding ground for the movement.

I have attempted to warn politicians, as well as churches, that, unless they get their act together, a Fourth Reich is a probability. All that is lacking to make it a reality is the right leadership. Given that leadership and the continued, dismal economy, the probability becomes reality. This is a historical imperative. It will not be denied.

I have warned in the past that Hitler had his Jews; we have a broad range, a plethora of choices including the Jews. Being a polyglot, mongrel nation, with each minority, including perverts making itself a target for the "movement" by stressing its "ethnicity" or "freedom" to practice perversion rather than its "Americanism," they become the "enemy" for the Reich's work of "purification."

Continued erosion of the economy by unfair, foreign trade, particularly by Oriental nations, is grist for the Reich's mill. It is a simple matter to engender hatred toward the Japanese. We were easily propagandized during WWII to hate the "rotten Japs and Knocksies." But a curious thing has happened. "Histories" are being taught that reveal the Germans, and Hitler particularly, were really the good guys. You can guess how easy it is now to see ourselves allied with Germany in the "new" war against the "Yellow Peril" and other "ethnicities."

Recent TV airing of old movies is especially interesting; particularly those old propaganda flicks that enforce the brutality of the Japanese during the war. The recent airing of injustices against some of the Nazi war criminals is equally interesting. Seems there were a lot of "mistakes" against some of these men at Nuremberg! I have studied German history and literature. With two years of college German language studies under my belt (which helped qualify me for doctoral studies), I can make my way, still, through a German newspaper or Bible. I have the utmost regard for what German culture and science represents; it is praiseworthy. But to say there can never be a revival of Nazism, of a Fourth Reich, is to talk nonsense.

The "string" is stretched near the breaking point worldwide. Old, historical hatreds are being re-kindled and those that have never abated, as with Arabs and Jews, gaining new fuel. It would be a simple matter for me, with my Biblical knowledge, to draw a "Doomsday, Armageddon" scenario ala Hal Lindsey from all of this. And, it may well be that God has had enough and is going to, shortly, call an end to this age. But that is in His hands; that is His job. Mine is to continue to try to do the best I can to confront evil, resist it and do battle against it- daily!

Civil disobedience is a requirement, a duty, spelled out in the words of our own Founding Fathers. If you doubt this, you haven't read our own

Declaration of Independence, Constitution or Bill of Rights. It is unmistakably clear from the view of these men that *The Rights of Man* take precedence over any act of government and that any unjust law is to be opposed. But we lack the advantage of these early heroes; they believed in God. It was that, above all else, that motivated them and caused them to cry out and act as they did in their own rebellion against unjust laws of their time. Endowed by our Creator with certain, unalienable rights among which are life, liberty and the pursuit of happiness are hollow words to the ungodly.

We no longer have a leadership that has the advantage of the reverential "awe" of God that fears His judgment of their acts, which seeks His approval and blessing before they make decisions. And, lacking that, the attraction of the Glory of Evil fills the resulting, moral void.

Legitimized in the panoply of uniforms, oaths, symbols of power like the Swastika, and with leadership that has the authority to reward or punish (unlike the churches), with a body of literature both historical and contemporary, the New Reich is ready to do business. Ironically, the charismatic movement and MTV have performed the identical service in preparing people to accept this New Reich, both preying on the emotions rather than rational thought.

Since a belief in God no longer holds sway in our nation, particularly among the churches, people are easily led into movements that will give them a "cause" and justify their existence, something that will promise to make sense, and bring "order" out of the present chaos. Given my "credentials," I could easily start such a movement myself.

But that is unnecessary; "Seven Days In May" though implausible together with all the other implausible movements like the Aryan Nations may get the job done with the same facility that dispatched the "threat" of Kennedy. If it were not for my "radical" position concerning The Lord and the noble history of our nation, I would be meeting many more of the "interesting" people I presently know and getting more of the "interesting" phone calls and "literature" of present, "interesting" leaders (players). I must point out the fact that most of these "leaders" will do their work in the name of God and they will use His name a lot! Historically, the "crusade, inquisition" and "jihad" has always invoked the name of God. It hardly needs to be mentioned that the greatest crimes against humanity have been committed in the name of God and our present, and potential "leaders" are fully aware of the need of His "imprimatur" for the success of their schemes.

As to the "literature" it is replete with everything from the "Protocols" to the "Mud People" and building all the time. It seems that, unlike the "good people" I know, the "power of the pen" is not lost on the New Reich. Their presses are running day and night. And they deal with "real" issues, not "pie in the sky by and by." The very impotence, frustration, hopelessness, anger and rage of this time will cause people to flock to "Champions" which promise action. The "Champions" of the "Mud People" like Rangel, Brown, Jackson, Farrakhan, will play into the hands of the militant factions advocating racial "purification."

The so-called "leadership" of minorities, making themselves targets by their insistence on special privilege at the cost of over-burdened taxpayers, largely Caucasian, will discover that they lack the power and authority to carry through since such power and authority rests with Caucasian leadership.

200,000 people in this country now have AIDS. D.C. Comics glorifies homosexuality with its "Flash" character and Marvel Comics does it with "Northstar" in its Alpha Flight series saying, "They are only keeping in tune with the times." Tragically, such perversion only adds fuel to the fear and anger of people who, sensibly, refuse to accept such trash as a "legitimate" danger to our well being as a nation. The perverts, minorities and their "enlightened" supporters, like Rangel et al., don't think in terms of the danger to themselves. They have lulled themselves into thinking the danger is only from a few "kooks" that shouldn't be taken seriously. They are victims of a mind-set that sealed the fate of so many Jews: "It can't happen here!" I repeat: "Oh No?"

Jack Anderson: "What we need is a moral resurgence. We need to produce more, consume less, and get back to the basic principles of our founding fathers." The John Birch Society, Louis Rukeyser, George Will, Pat Buchanan, David Duke, myself all agree. George Bush, I'm sure, agrees. If I were to list the names of the people, many rich and powerful, who agree with such a pronouncement, the time would fail me. But what a disparity of agendas and methodologies would be woven into such a tapestry.

Speaking of Anderson, he recently said in a speech in Bakersfield (yes, Bakersfield): "This is a crucial year!" He was referring to the need of our nation to get its act together. He is right, of course. This is a crucial year. We will choose a president. None of the contenders has said anything specifically about how the nation is to "get its act together." We hear about welfare reform, changes in doing business abroad, the need for a "moral resurgence," the need for better leadership, the need for jobs, the need etc. A few specifics such as Governor Wilson's are met with cries of "racism" or "uncaring of the poor." It is, indeed, a crucial year. We are a bankrupt nation, financially and morally.

It is left to people like me to call a spade a spade; people who have nothing to lose by saying it like it is, and, "It" is ugly and brutal in its stark reality, so ugly and brutal, in fact, that a "Glorious Reich" is far preferable to multiplied millions. While we must contend with the fanatics of other cultures and lack, because of our European mind-set, the legions of "falling, cherry blossoms," we will have "Elijah's" who will, rather than blowing themselves up, call on blowing up others.

The fact that in this nation we now have only an illusion of freedom and liberty, it will be a simple matter to stir up the hoards and rally them to a siren call of "Glory" and "Death to the Infidel!" As to my cruel statement of the "illusion of freedom and liberty," I mean: You are no longer "free" when you are bankrupt because you cannot afford to pay a speeding ticket or get that muffler or taillight replaced to satisfy a mechanical. You are no longer "free" when you lose your home for failure to pay exorbitant taxes. You are no longer "free" when you cannot afford medical insurance and the "incapables" and "illegals" get it "free." You are no longer "free" when a building inspector tells you to either tear your cabin down, even though you own the land, or go to jail. You are no longer "free" when unjust laws dictate how you must live and try to provide for your family. You are no longer "free" when you live in a society that dictates you must be a more successful thief and scoundrel just to keep up with the other thieves and scoundrels. You are no longer "free" when the only elective choices are between bad and worse. You are no longer "free" when you can only get three dollars an hour jobs in a six dollars an hour country. You are no longer "free" when the choice is between paying the rent, taking a sick child to a doctor, buying groceries or having the gas or electricity cut off. You are not "free" when children are not safe in your schools, when women and children are raped, molested and abused, when you are afraid to walk the streets of your own neighborhood, when crime and drugs destroy millions and the rich and powerful line their pockets by inflicting misery on others. This grievously tragic list is endless and prepares the way for untold millions to "Sieg Heil!" any "Fuhrer" with the charisma and dynamism to grab hold of the circumstances.

A good friend just shared with me a sign that was posted in his workplace: "Due to the current budget constraints, the light at the end of the tunnel has been turned off until further notice!" Not funny, is it?

I have warned repeatedly and for years that the "organized imbecility," the "bunch of Clowns," the "thieves and scoundrels," the "tax-fattened hyenas," that constitute our "leadership" should change their ways or make way for the Fourth Reich. I ask you, the "great unwashed," the hopelessly over-burdened, taxpaying public, to consider the following:

"Joe" sits down to figure his family budget. He decides to give over half his earnings to an organization that promises to use the money to bankrupt him and put him out on the street. This organization also promises to ship his job overseas and provide food, housing and medical expenses to illegal aliens and millions who refuse to work. The organization also promises to prevent his children from getting an education or ever going to college. It promises him no hope and no future no matter how hard he tries to get ahead. Joe, of course, gratefully hands over more than half his wages to support such an organization because if he doesn't, he will go to prison. But Joe is no fool. He knows this is wrong, evil, and unjust. How long, do you suppose, will all the "Joes" wait before they decide they can't be any worse off if they get a gun and "fix" such an organization? And, with the right leadership, they will easily be persuaded this must be done as the "patriotic" and necessary thing to do!

You "Fat Cats" in your "insulated, high offices" that can't be touched by the cries of the farmer who lost his land, the waitress that is surviving on tips, the auto worker or welder who can't get a job, the multiplied millions who are, gradually, being led to believe in "revolution" because you won't listen, you would do well to start listening. I speak for those millions and what you won't do because it is the right and sane thing to do, you will do when your lives are in the balance. Your "Let them eat cake" mentality will bring you down just as surely as the "Jehus" are there, no matter how you "do your hair and paint your eyes," together with the servants who threw Jezebel to the dogs.

It is obvious that, if I should choose to do so, I could easily play the "Goebbels" for the New Reich. While you "leaders" are intent on ignoring the cries of "Joe" and, patronizingly, telling him that he just can't comprehend the "essential need" of a *Weltanschauung*," and he must pay "dues" for a "*Weltschmerz*," you ignore the grim reality of his understanding the cry of a baby for whom he can't afford medicine or a doctor, of his inability to provide for his family while you pay yourselves fat salaries to give his money to the dogs and finance the 141st study on "How drugs affect traffic accidents (this is a fact by the way)." Joe understands the loss of his dignity as a man, the dignity you have stolen from him by your insane and greedy laws. He understands the betrayal of his country and his hopes and dreams for his children. Maybe he doesn't "see the big picture" but you better believe he understands that someone, YOU, are to blame for this betrayal.

Since we are a bankrupt nation, it follows that whatever is done must be at the cost of those that cannot afford any further erosion economically, those largely black and brown people who are the greatest drain on social welfare programs. We can no longer afford to "keep those people in their place" through government handouts. The New Reich has an answer to that conundrum. But, since I deal with this in my book, I won't belabor it now in this short space. Suffice it to say, the answer is imperative, expedient and historical. It will not be denied. Our "Caesar," our "Fuhrer" will recognize his "call of destiny" and act accordingly.

Since the media is setting the "stage" for all of this, it is interesting that so much attention has been focused on single issues like the insanity of "instant citizenship" being conferred on the babies of criminal, illegal aliens.

Pregnant women in droves come across the border illegally to have their babies, all at taxpayer expense, just so the babies can have all the rights and privileges of more "American" welfare recipients and produce more, probably, criminal, non-productive mouths; the "human weeds" to feed. This in spite of the fact that rightful citizens in the same communities can't afford such care for themselves! Insane! And what is Congress doing about this insanity? Nothing!

Since Bush touted himself as the "Education President" as well as lying about "No New Taxes," he can at least take some comfort in the fact that he has certainly "taught" us something; he obviously wasn't sincere about his "campaign promises" going into the job and he sure can't be trusted to do any better a second time. The tragic problem confronting us is who is going to do any better? I think Quayle, like David Duke, if he were older, might be a better option. Buchanan? Certainly the best choice but will he have the courage of his convictions once in office; will he, in fact, close our borders to illegal aliens, press the battle to eliminate abortion on demand as means of contraception, level the "playing field" in foreign trade, etc.? But when we look on the Democratic side? Nothing.

There hasn't been a time in our history since the Revolutionary War that so cried out for leadership, that has had such a void to be filled by an organization and men of conviction that promise, to stand and deliver, the things that made this nation great.

Before you simply write this off as the ravings of a man taken leave of his senses, I ask you to consider the facts. Founded in 1865 by six young men as a social fraternity for idle war veterans, the Klan has had many "ups and downs" because of a lack of consistent and cohesive leadership. In its beginnings, there was no threat of violence and its leadership concentrated on attacking the post war evils of Northern "Carpetbaggers" intent on "punishing" Confederate states. Unfortunately, the shortsighted oppression of Northern laws and lawmakers provided an atmosphere of prejudice and hatred that resulted in some Southerners resorting to violence in retaliation.

There have been some horrendous crimes committed by Klan members. Again, the lack of educated, enlightened leadership, the lack of centralized goals and objectives, methodology, resulted in splinter groups, not unlike the churches, where "every man did what was right in his own sight." But there have been some men, Republicans and Democrats, since the time of General Nathan Bedford Forrest, the KKK's first Grand Wizard, that have lent legitimacy to the organization, men like Harry Truman, Justice Hugo Black and Senator Robert Byrd.

Right now, at this point in time, if the KKK could resolve its "image" by a campaign of, intelligently, presenting its programs, it could easily become a political force to be reckoned with. It has a lot going for it in its organizational structure, its historical goals, and its insistence on God-fearing, moral leadership. The truth of it is many people would now be Klan members if it weren't for the stigma of "racism." But, that "stigma" is becoming a forced issue that Americans must deal with. And, ironically, it is becoming a forced issue by the very minorities and "liberals" that decry the Klan.

David Duke honestly pointed out the fact that the majority of Americans, himself included, agree with the "platform" of the Klan. "America First" is not a four-letter word. Neither is "Americans First!" If "ethnicity" is to be advocated as taking precedence over Americanism, those "advocates" are bound to lose. And, to the degree such "advocates" call attention to themselves by their own prejudice and bigotry, the resulting violence will come down on their own heads. "Smart" politicians will feel the pulse of the "people" and act accordingly. These are not stupid men. As I have said many times, they are educated and wealthy; they will read the "handwriting" and see that it is still "White Power" that will decide our future no matter how the scoundrels talk.

Media distortions of "racism" can be clearly discerned by anyone who cares to consider the fact. Invariably, the media that, selectively, tries to paint it in the worst possible fashion pillories anyone who espouses the Klan or its beliefs. No organization or person can escape such "tarring." But, given the facts, one has to, as I have warned, wonder at the media's own agenda?

For a thumbnail sketch of the Klan's history, I would refer you to the excellent article in the December issue of The New American published by the John Birch Society. It will surprise you. If the Klan would take a page from other, successful organizations like the Mormons, etc., it would found a university, tie its goals in with the founding fathers, promote educated men in its leadership and start a broad-based campaign to overcome its image problem; in short, do the things needful to address the real issues confronting this nation. As crazy as it sounds, wouldn't it be something if the Klan turned out to be the one organization, if it does these things, which could offer a sensible solution to the problems of, and hope for, minorities? Not impossible. Particularly since it is the only organization I know of that seems to have a sense of "The White Man's Burden."

A troubling factor is the lack of factual information about the Klan. For example, you won't find it in your local, yellow pages. I have called several congressional offices and newspapers and none seem to have access to an actual, living, breathing Klansman. Now I am not naive enough to think that here on the West Coast it's all that easy to make contact. A couple of membership applications are reputed to have been circulated in Merced but I can't get specific information about any Klan activity in the area. This is counter-productive to the Klan but its secrecy can easily be understood in light of the attacks by the media and organizations like the NAACP. It is even easier to understand here on the West Coast due to the large minority populations to whom the Klan is synonymous to "devil-worship."

But, speaking of propaganda, the recent films like New Jack City that portray Blacks as fools, incapable and interested in nothing but crime, drugs and sex, play into the hands of those that are forcing Americans to make hard choices about who is deserving of help. The schools in metropolitan areas are "War Zones," due, largely, to their minority populations, with metal detectors used to check for weapons. We should have had them at Jordan High in Watts and Yerba Buena in the barrio of East San Jose where I used to teach. Propaganda films portraying the "gangs" as desirable where the money, sex and drugs flow like water are accomplishing their desired end of targeting the "enemies" of the "State."

America is "choosing up sides." Like it or not, each and every one of us is going to be on one side or the other even if it is by default; that is, by doing nothing. Remarks like those of a top Japanese politician, a Mr. Sakurauchi, that Americans are in trouble because they are "lazy" just adds additional fuel to the fires of racism. He went on to make the dire pronouncement that: "If America doesn't watch out, it is going to be judged as finished by the world." Racism aside, Mr. Sakurauchi's remarks are easy enough to understand. As a "Welfare Society," it is simple to make such a forecast based on our present lack of leadership and the utter lack of hope brought about by a government that has presided over the demise of our middle class, the group of people, largely white, of responsible, tax-paying workers who have been paying the bill for greedy, incompetent, criminal politicians who have betrayed our nation and its posterity.

But, as I have said many times, the great majority of nations are far more racist than America has ever been. Most nations have the advantage of single culture and single race. Those that do not, those like Russia, have constant conflict and internal fighting. That most deadly of conflicts; that which is over religious prejudices is rampant in many parts of the world even between those of a common heritage.

America has a host of devils, demons, bent on our destruction. As long as we legitimize abortion as contraception, homosexuality, pornography, and like perversions, we cannot hope to survive, let alone seek God's help. A group of perverts called NAMBLA, North American Man-Boy Love Association, meets openly at a public library in San Francisco (where else, one might say?). This group of "pedophiles," a polite term for the perverts that prey on children, says opposition to the group is a "witch hunt!" A spokes-"man?" for the group, a "Mr." Bill Andriette, is quoted as saying: "NAMBLA is an open, public organization with nothing to hide." He is right of course; it seems we have molded a society where anything goes and the most outrageous flaunting of perversion of every description is openly displayed- TV being the medium of choice along with slick, glossy magazines; small wonder that Walt Whitman had no real sense of history and his writing suffered as a consequence. Perverts because of their perverted minds, cannot have a sense of history and have no interest in a future that does not promise to promote their depredations.

I mentioned years ago that we could expect every kind of evil to pervade when we have a Supreme Court that cannot distinguish between just plain filth and legitimate art- that cannot identify what is of redeeming value and what is plainly perversion. A society that has such a "Court" deciding its mores, even legitimizing its moral decay, cannot survive. Nor should it!

Earlier in this letter and others, I have called attention to the fact that people are being "destroyed" in the lower courts, like the traffic courts. Some have asked me about this. I give you an example. If you get a speeding ticket for going 72mph in a 55 zone (and on Highway 99 and others, the signs are the same and you seldom know for sure which zone you are in), your fine will be $240. Now California supports a panoply of so-called "services" including judges and police by such exorbitant fines. If you are poor, unemployed, such a fine can break you. But, Ah, hah! The "system" gives you an option. Since a moving violation works additional hardship by an increase in auto insurance, which most poor and irresponsible go without, you, a solid citizen, may "go to traffic school" and the violation will be "forgiven."

"Good deal!" you say. But, when you arrange for traffic school, you discover that the fine has been reduced to "only" $144. Not only that, but you must give an entire day to the "school" together with an additional $23 in "fees." Your net "saving" not counting your whole day in "school:" $73. If the only options were pay the $240, go to jail or pay the $167 and go to traffic school, what would you do? This with the fact that Chippys know where their bread is buttered and state and local governments hurting for more income, you can find yourself in just such a situation whether you were actually speeding or not. CHP officers lied about my speeding three times and I had no recourse but to pay for their lies in court. Mark my words traffic citations, like our onerous DMV fees and exorbitant insurance costs that have to make up for half the drivers going without, are on the increase if only for the reason of squeezing more money out of John Q. Public; factor in the illegal aliens driving without either license or insurance.

As a simple Okie I sometimes have a little trouble figuring out the insanity of the majority of our Janus-faced "leaders." It might be easier if I was crazy but I'm only weird and that don't help much. The inmates are, indeed, running the Asylum. Just had a delightful chat with a Congressional Aide, a fine lady who said she would pray for me. I really appreciate that. We shared a good laugh that we both needed. Its folks like her that gives me any hope at all.

I'm writing from Merced and the weather has not been conducive to my "sunshine" mentality. Tule fog does not make me a happy camper. I'm an inveterate desert rat and need the sun to keep me in good spirit. The constant overcast so typical of the San Joaquin Valley at this time of year is gloomy to me. On the other hand, the weather certainly is commensurate with the "news of the day." Gloom is the name of the game these days.

My lovely daughter, Karen, lives here in Merced otherwise I probably wouldn't be here. But, Merced is fairly typical of areas of California that have large welfare populations with the attendant, large crime statistics. Our governor, Pete Wilson, certainly has his work cut out for him. I wonder if he longs for the days when he was a simple senator and didn't have to face the budget crisis personally? He, together with all the governors and legislators across our nation, faces some hard choices. But they better get off the "kick" of making choices, like the helmet and seatbelt laws, that make sensible and responsible people angry over unnecessary and unwarranted intrusion by government into our personal lives. This kind of "Big-brotherism" always has the vaunted "seal" of "saving lives" or some such rhetoric but if "safety" is the goal of such laws, the "lawyers" in charge of the legislature better turn their attention to making our schools, streets and neighborhoods safe before dabbling with our freedom of choice about whether to ride a motorcycle bare-headed. Such legislation only plays into the hands of those that are actively at work trying to destroy any vestige of personal liberty. The Patrick Henry's are still out there in the land and such slaps in the face of personal choice will only lead to civil disobedience on an ever-increasing scale.

It is easy for the greedy, lazy, incompetent lawyers in the legislature and congress to pick on things like seatbelts and helmets because they can do these things with relative impunity. But the problems of crime and social service handouts, the problems of the homeless and veterans, medical care, in short, the problems that really need to be addressed, these the scoundrels cannot handle.

I cannot help thinking that, if our society were a literate one, if the focus of our schools had continued to emphasize learning of value, if young people had been led to study the histories and literature of our noble past, of the great wisdom of great men throughout history, the great ideas which provided the guiding light of civilizations, things would undoubtedly be better. But even our leadership has become such of a caliber of those that, in the words of Thoreau, are addicted to "...Easy Reading, the primers and class-books, and when (they) leave school, the 'Little Reading' and story-books, which are for boys and beginners; and our reading, our conversation and thinking, are all on a very low level, worthy only of pygmies and manikins." And, perhaps, the leadership would have found purpose in the inevitable lessons of history.

Where, then, is the "Heroic Epic" of our generation? Without it, what is there to lead the younger? Hence, the New Reich is given an opportunity to fill the void. In all the grandeur and heroic glory of promises of renewed greatness, of calls to sacrifice for a noble cause, the leadership of the New Reich will reach out and take in the disenfranchised of the present, evil system of impotence, greed, graft and corruption and substitute its own "pure, moral, goal-directed" one.

"Words, Words, Words," fit a pretty melody by Audrey Hepburn in "My Fair Lady" but they are "Drawn Swords" when applied to ideas. The crying need for the mythic hero, the "gunslinger," the Wayne's, Bronson's, Norris's, Rambo's, who will "clean up the town" and make "Dodge City" safe for women and children, churches and schools, will not be denied. The "Paul Reveres" have been warning us of the "Red Coats" (read: Bureaucrats) for over a hundred years. Millions are now prepared to hearken to the call. But, now, our "Redcoats," the Building Inspectors, Judges, etc., will not get off with a beating; they will be shot and hung in the name of renewed "patriotism."

Where does this poor "Okie" get off making such dire predictions; because I have eaten more than my own share of the "dirt" of the present, evil system; I have gotten more than my share of grease under my fingernails; I have lived and worked long enough as one of the "great unwashed" to know whereof I speak. Further, as I have said many times, I am the bane, the worst nightmare of greedy, incompetent, unscrupulous "preachers, educators and politicians," a truly educated, literate and erudite man who knows how to do for himself.

While I no longer "wear my collar backwards," I am still a "preacher." But, finding myself, more and more, cast in the roll of an Elijah and John the Baptist, warning an "untoward generation of the wrath to come," I take no pleasure whatsoever in the "calling." It is a thankless task at best and no "prophet" ever expected to "eat the fruit" of his labors in his lifetime. I "do" for the sake of my children and grandchildren, for the sake of hope, for them, of a future. A "prophet" that has such a "calling" is not to be silenced by any means short of killing him.

I do not suffer a Martyr complex. I work and write from compelling conviction and I find myself helpless to keep from speaking out, to keep from writing and warning in the miraculous hope that it will accomplish some good; some desired end.

Much of the time I'm like the guy who bought a new suit with two pair of pants and burned a hole in the coat. Given a fifty-fifty choice, I'll choose the wrong card every time. That's why I'm not a gambler. Having learned at an early age that games of chance were not my long suit, I became very conservative in religion and politics. I should have exercised such discretion in women as well. It is a vile calumny that I do not like women! On the contrary, I love women. This is proven by the fact that I married so many of them. But, like Solomon, I never chose a "virtuous" one. Unlike the "Music Man," I wasn't looking for a "Hester" to "win one more 'A';" it just seems to have been my lot.

It may be a fine, philosophical point but perhaps our own "Parliament Of Whores" is the way it is because, like most women, they are easily "seduced" and find a thousand ways to rationalize their adulteries. And, like a marriage that is destroyed by an adulterous wife or husband, the trust and commitment, the adulterer despises the "rock" upon which a successful marriage is built. Tragically, it is the children that suffer the worst consequences of such a supreme act of utter selfishness. In the "murder" of the innocent, the adulterer always finds a "reason" for his or her sin.

The attitude of the present "leadership," that we, the great unwashed, are to be treated as "children," really, more like sheep to be fleeced, can only wreak destruction on the whole "family." It is past time to cut through the phony, selfish "rationales" of the "adulterers," the enemies of our nation and get to the real issues.

Stark honesty compels me to include the host of people that support the adulterers by their very lack of effort, their disinterest in anything but their six-pack and TV, their "too-busyness" to be involved in the elective process. Burke's "All that is necessary for evil to overcome is for good men to do nothing!" haunts our whole society. Can such even be considered "good" by any definition? I think not.

It is a simple matter to understand the thinking of the Cranston's, Keating's, Rangel's, Willie Brown's, as they look over an immoral and Godless society, that they feel they can loot and "deal" as they please. Such people prey on the very greed and complacency that enable them to act the way they do. But their "blind spot" is their ignorance or denial of historical imperatives. Such activity must, always, result in chaos and upheaval of the whole structure of a society. That society, in turn, will hunt out and destroy those considered to be the cause of so much of its woes and injustice; a lynch-mob on a national scale.

Sam called Judas a "premature congressman," a "good one" someone that "hadn't time enough to sell out." One can only guess at what he would have called a Cranston, Willie Brown or Rangel! In spite of this it is my privilege to know some good ones, men like Senator Don Rogers. Such men do offer a degree of hope but they are lonely voices.

I can only wish men like Norman Mailer had put their "hand to the plough" in using their talents in the right direction during my generation. I mention Mailer specifically because of Sam's and my position on the franchise: "We should never have given them the vote!" I need only mention Gloria Steinem to make my point. There is no question in my mind that the whole question of who should have voting privileges should be a matter of national priority. It was, obviously, never the intention of our founding fathers to have the franchise cater, as our schools do, to the lowest, common denominator. An enlightened electorate will only be possible when voting becomes, once more, a serious and knowledgeable activity by responsible people. One example: No one receiving government "assistance" i.e. welfare, should be eligible to vote. It is, obviously, this population that keeps many of the scoundrels in office. In fact, it is this population that voted a known crook, gambler and womanizer into the governorship of Louisiana; it is this population that has a vested interest in staying on the dole no matter what it does to destroy our nation. And what can one possibly say about the Tennessee State Senate opening its legislative session with an ISLAMIC PRAYER!!! Talk about playing into the hands of the New Reich; the "new" World Order! Tom Wicker tells us the personal lives of candidates for office should not be a factor in elections that the trust, commitment and fidelity of marriage has nothing to do with political leadership and responsibility. Once more, the scoundrels, looking at one another, say adultery is of no concern.

Bush wants to spend $30 billion on Space Station Freedom. He is going to make a name for himself in history no matter how much you have to pay for it. His sense of priorities is mind-boggling! Spike Lee is now the "expert" on Apartheid in South Africa. We, as a nation, have a lot to answer for in our inexcusably, hypocritical treatment of that country. We have just "worshiped" as a nation at our "Super Bowl" and I will wait till later to comment on this extraordinary "religious experience."

I miss those loved ones gone on before me who I could rely on for counsel and, simply, "being there." I wish, fervently, that I could find a Brewster, Washington, Franklin, or Emerson who would offer the solace of sincere wisdom, honorable reverence with which to deal with the horrors of this age. Were it not for the unavoidable responsibility of knowledge, of caring for our nation and its young, I could easily escape to the "sanctuary" of "Academia" or my trout stream. But the admonition of: "Knowing what we know, what manner of men ought we to be?" dogs my life as surely as the "Hound of Heaven" my soul.

Will Good Men come to the fore or will the New Reich, with all the enticement, excitement and "glory of evil" with the "noble" goals and high-sounding rhetoric and phraseology of its historical successes be the inevitable destiny of our nation; brought on by the very expediency of need to "fairly" answer insoluble problems, with its promise of "Final Solutions?" God help us then for no one else will be able to.

CHAPTER NINE

CHRISTIAN PERSPECTIVE

MARCH 1992

Psalm 37:1-5

I envy the guy in Colorado that is making a business of sucking prairie dogs out of their holes with a large vacuum device and releasing them on federal lands. "The little guy doesn't know what happens to him...he's a little dazed but otherwise ok," says Mr. Balfour, the genius who came up with this scheme.

Some years ago, I went to Colorado to start a private, Christian school for a group of folks in Wiggins. When it came time to return to California, the family flew back but I was left with the task of driving the largest rental truck available and towing the family station wagon behind; a big, Chevy Kingswood Estate. Since this occurred in January, I called for weather conditions and was assured they were ok. Wrong! I was only a few hours on the road and hit a blizzard that remained with me all the way to California. At times I was creeping through blinding snow at five mph. When I began to see big rigs that had slid off the road, I knew I was in trouble. If the "pros" were "losing it," what were my chances, especially with that big wagon pushing me down the long grades?

I knew, in many instances, that just one push on my brakes would be the end of it. Ice formed on the windshield and, freezing my backside off, I was forced to keep my head out the window at times to see where the road was, as I would creep down the steep hills.

The trip was made more interesting by the fact that I was transporting a Colorado Cottontail rabbit my daughter, Karen, had caught shortly before our departure together with a cage of parakeets and a white momma cat. I was able to keep the birds warm by placing the cage on the floor in front of the heater when I had to have the window open. The Cottontail proved no problem because when I put it in the truck and took off; he ricocheted around the cab like a ping-pong ball for a minute then disappeared under the seat not to be seen again till I reached my destination in California. The momma cat didn't seem to care about anything but sleeping and eating.

But a funny thing occurred on my way that still brings a smile to my face. I reached Boomtown the second night, dead tired and ready to crash in bed. I hadn't shaved or bathed for two days and looked like death warmed over. Bundled in my overcoat, gloves, muffler and stocking cap, birdcage with its inhabitants and a grocery bag in arm, I entered the motel-casino to get a room for the night.

I know I had to have made quite an impression in the splendor of the gaming establishment. There were all those "high rollers," dressed to the nines, and this "desperado" appears in their midst. Security guards abounded and I attracted no little interest from them. It didn't occur to me until I, dead tired, was sitting on a stool, birdcage at my feet, waiting for the clerk to do the paper work for my room, that the bag I was holding contained five pistols (airlines being sensitive about such things carried on board) that I instinctively didn't leave in the truck. Tired as I was, the humor of the situation impressed me. If those guards only knew I was armed to the teeth! Suppose one asked to check my bag? What a stir that would make; another opportunity to make "film at eleven." By God's grace (and sense of humor) no one checked me out, though I am certain no more disreputable looking character had ever appeared in their glittering midst, and I got the needed night's rest.

In my last "epistle" I promised to share some of Dee Dee's and my experiences in the Dust Bowl labor camps when we, as children, traveled across the country. While we had the luxury of going to Cleveland Ohio by train, our mother and stepdad decided to make the return trip to California by car.

The current stepfather, Dan Pospieszynski, was a mechanic and it was decided, with the grandparent's help, to set up shop in Little Oklahoma (Southeast Bakersfield). The trip occurred in the summer of 1946. We were packed into a venerable Terraplane, we now had a baby half-brother, Johnny, to accompany and "amuse" us and off we went- Westward HO!

The Terraplane had a disconcerting habit of breaking down in every state we passed through. Somehow, our stepdad managed to get it fired back up each time but it did pose problems. One breakdown occurred in the Arizona desert. I still attribute our mother's dislike of the desert to this particular episode of "adventures in travel." I know we "baked" for a while to the accompaniment of our baby brother's cries of discontent and malodorous diapers. Perhaps my brother and I added some to the experience but memory, being so kind in such matters I don't recall our doing anything, as with any well-mannered little boys, but exercising great forbearance and patience in the situation. Our mother may remember it differently.

Anyhow, I do recall a truck stopping, an empty car-carrier rig, and the driver and our stepdad trying to get the Terraplane onto it without success.

My childhood memory includes a few vultures circling overhead and someone making a threat about "there was going to be one more death in Death Valley" during these pleasant hours in this Big Empty which may just be fanciful. But every time I think about the incident, the vultures are there.

The car wound up in some town where our stepdad could make the necessary repairs throughout the night and, the next day; "On the road again!" The "road" was good old route 66 with its fascinating "Old West museums" and their displays of rattlesnakes, Gila monsters, meteorites and other desert memorabilia; one even had a "mummified bandit" complete with rope around his neck and rusted, iron "bracelets" hanging from one withered wrist: Fascinating to childish imagination. I remember one exhibit with two Gila monsters in a "circle of death," each with the other's tail chomped in its jaws. I have never lost my fondness for lizards and horny toads. Still shoot rattlesnakes.

I marveled at the Painted Desert with its magnificent, splendid vista and grand array of subtle shades of colors. I so very badly wanted one of the glass jars which were filled with layers of the colored sands but the folks couldn't afford souvenirs.

It was, undoubtedly, this early, nomadic life that helped prepare me, as a child, for the loss of my family and the fact that I have had no "home" or certain dwelling place these past few years and learn the hard lesson of "abased and abound." Still, I would not have chosen such a life. I will always be a family man at heart but not many women would be able to stand for such a life as I now lead. And, too, on those occasions when I have had to eat dirt and coexist with cockroaches, I found that it was worse being considered "inconvenient" or "tiresome" to "friends." The cockroaches have proven to be better company, even preferable, on some occasions.

There have been times, though, when I needed a blanket and floor space in lieu of the "road." I am properly grateful for such and never considered it being for my benefit alone. People have needed my company and visits many times that they weren't even aware of. I have also learned the luxury of being able to close a door for privacy; something I will never again take for granted.

It was in our travels throughout the South that brought us into contact with the labor camps and the people that Steinbeck and Guthrie immortalized. The simple living conditions and the simple ways of the people touched me as a child as did those early Okies and Arkies of our neighborhood of Little Oklahoma.

As I have said several times, these folks didn't know they were "underprivileged" and "culturally deprived" because there didn't exist, then, the host of bureaucrats and officials telling them they were underprivileged and culturally deprived; there didn't exist a host of "social services" that catered to the "poor" in order to build their own bureaucratic empires, keep scoundrels in office and fill their pockets at the expense of the working middle class. Certainly, without the demonic instrumentation of television, we had no idea of what we were being "deprived" of.

It seemed reasonable to me, as a child that "Santa" only came at Christmas. You worked for anything you wanted the rest of the year. I will never forget selling Cloverine Salve, garden and flower seeds door to door to earn my Red Ryder BB carbine. Of what great value such a noble possession when I had earned it by my own industry!

The real "tyranny" of poverty is accomplished, not by being poor, but by a society's emphasis upon what constitutes "poor." And, while, as Topol so well put it: "It's no disgrace to be poor, but it isn't any great honor either!" it took the bureaucrats and the welfare state to make being poor a disgrace and dishonor humble living and, even the opportunity, freedom and liberty to choose such a lifestyle. The "streets," ghettos and barrios are a poor substitute- a cruel trade.

There have been times in my life when a dollar in my pocket or a can of peaches was "wealth." But it took the "government" to make me feel "poor" and "underprivileged," to make me feel that, in some ephemeral and disquieting, vague way that I was being "cheated" of something that I hadn't earned by the sweat of my own brow.

It is just such "misanthropic, dinosaur" thinking that makes the "new" generation consign me to the "elephant's graveyard" of those "old world" values where things like honor, duty, integrity, commitment and a man's word and name had relevance. But it seems characteristic of a man who has a complete collection of "Pogo" books, loves opera, Thoreau, and disdains affectations by freely admitting that he can't stand ballet.

The camps of the forties couldn't have been too different from those of a few years past. Certainly they were peopled by the same kind of folks. The war had left its impress and much talk surrounded this great event of American history. We children still played "war games" along with cowboys and Indians. Cap and rubber band guns were equal to both occasions. The conversations were still held by grownups with the ubiquitous "chew" or snuff doing good service in punctuating speech. There were even a few "Mammy Yokums" complete with corncob pipes.

Some camps had running water, some didn't. Some had cabins, some had tents or "half-tents," a floor and board structure halfway up and topped by tent material. A few had wood stoves. One of the best was nestled in a grove of magnificent trees. Being summer time, I was entranced by the huge, marvelously colored moths, along with June bugs and other assorted insects that would be attracted to the camp lights at night. I had never seen such amazing behemoths of mothdom. Some were the size of hummingbirds.

One of the great inventions of civilization is the Mason Jar. They were obviously designed for children to keep a variety of insects and lizards with which to keep such treasures for the handy and close inspection of budding, inquiring, prospective scientists; the future entomologists and herpetologists; also, you could, if you had a mind to, get some interesting reactions from assorted mothers and little girls with some such collection of varied arachnids, moths, flies, etc. The occasional lizard or small garter snake served admirably in such experimentation of human behavior, especially if the incarcerant(s?) somehow, inexplicably, got loose in a bedroom (your mother's or a sister's, if you played your cards right and the "fates" cooperated).

A parent with such a child is helped in their own growth processes by finding an empty jar and stimulated in their minds by having to imagine what might have been set loose in the house. I am convinced that one of the major obligations of children toward their parents is just such activity. It keeps the grownups on their toes.

Speaking of lizards reminds me of Bob Mahoney, our second stepdad who served in the Army Carrier Pigeon Corps, my mother says, during WWII. Bob was a good guy. It was during one of his visits to our place in Little Oklahoma that he decided to help Dee Dee and I catch lizards.

The place at Cottonwood and Padre, in those days, was surrounded by an alkali wasteland; great for the inhabitant lizards and assorted reptiles. Bob's plan was simple. He took a length of material like a fishing rod and, making "eyes" of thin, copper wire along its length and passing a copper line through them fashioned a "noose" at the other end. The idea was to get this noose over the hapless creature's head and jerk it tight, thus capturing the poor thing. Fortunately, like putting salt on a bird's tail feathers, no lizard was to be had that exhibited the necessary degree of cooperation in the procedure. Looking back on it, I still wonder why it didn't occur to Mahoney that had we ever gotten such a device over a lizard's head, the contraption would have successfully garroted or, even, decapitated the little varmint. Maybe Bob didn't really like lizards?

The subject always reminds me of the heady days of my Iguana ranch and bronzed bullfrog schemes, raising gnus for fun and profit and the time I dropped the mouse down the back of the dress of one of mom's friends while they were talking. Seemed like a good idea at the time but I lost the small, white rodent amidst the confusion, ear-rending shrieks and what has to be a world's record for the "Shimmy." Since I was raising the little creatures at the time, the mouse was easily replaced. Don't know about mom's friend. Don't recall any further visits though.

To my dear and somewhat aberrant son, Daniel (it's in the genes): Though I greatly admire Faulkner I do not come up with these things with the help of laudanum and I await becoming a street person to avail myself of Muscatel or Thunderbird in a paper bag. It is due, entirely, to my gift of being a gate with one hinge missing. "To each his own" as the old lady said when she kissed the cow (My apology to my dear old friend and "spiritual uncle" Charles L. Feinberg, Th. D., Ph. D. for my occasional lack of "couth").

But I'm not so weird that I wouldn't rather laugh than cry and with all that I have had to write about lately, we all need a laugh; me most of all. I remain normal enough to still hate being a landlord, not being "into pain," and I still bleed when I'm cut.

I do feel sorry for our own "King George" not having a sense of humor. How do I know he doesn't? Simple; anyone who thinks, as President, that buying a pair of socks at Penny's is making a statement about improving the economy and fails to laugh just doesn't know what's funny, let alone hilarious. Maybe he gets a laugh out of the stupidity of those that are still going to vote for him?

Do I consider myself a serious contender for elective office many have asked? No. The Truth doesn't pay. I, as some have been honest enough to point out, frighten people. The Truth and its prophets have a way of doing that. Far better the "noble lies" and "fairy tales" that lead, inevitably, to destruction than the Truth which forces us to look deep within our own vile hearts. Also, if I am to be the Thomas Paine of rebellion to an evil system of government rather than the Goebbels of the New Reich, the "leadership" isn't too likely to encourage me.

My distinct advantage, as someone with nothing to lose or an empire to protect, is being able to deal with Truth. Over the years, because of my education and writing, I have come to know many wealthy and powerful men. Many of these, while agreeing with much that I write about, would never be able to put their own thoughts into print as I do. For that reason, these men, many good men, would never put in writing what they share with me in confidence verbally. I understand this and have never betrayed their confidences. But there was a time not long ago when honorable men were able to freely express their minds; when political candidates were not "one dimensional players in a schlock drama."

One thing leads to another and I can't resist sharing another episode; a real "leg-slapper." It happened when my college "roomie" was the Black Irishman, Mike McEvoy, the vilest human being it has ever been my privilege to know.

I was "courting" the kid's mother at the time. She worked as a cashier for the old Roxie Theater in downtown Whittier. Nixon's birthplace, if you know anything about it, was a lily-white, staid, conservative town of upper class folk; boutiqueish shops and manicured lawns; Rodeo Drive environment.

It was a warm, summer evening when I decided, with McEvoy's encouragement in evil, to pull this stunt. I had a straw sombrero that I had adorned with the spike from a German, WWI helmet. Putting on a pair of ragged Levis, a weathered and corrupt flannel shirt and a pair of Firestone, radial sandals (no socks) and draping a large, polka dotted bandanna around my neck together with a heavy necklace of large beads, and a scroungy serape over my shoulder, a two-days growth of dark beard and sporting a pair of dark sunglasses, I would have been the envy of Pancho Villa. McEvoy managed to make up an outfit that is best described as a lumberjack down on his luck. Thus it was, properly attired to terrorize, or, at the very least properly offend the locals in all our sartorial splendor; we assayed the evening stroll through downtown Whittier- destination: The Roxie!

With the polite citizens of the town crossing the street to avoid contact with us (McEvoy had the presence of mind to carry a tin cup in case we got close enough to anyone to "panhandle"), we made our inexorable way to the theater. As luck would have it, we made it all the way without encountering the local constabulary and being detained from our quest. It was only the recognition of McEvoy that kept, I'm sure, the kid's mother from fainting, screaming at our sudden appearance at the front of her box. I don't think Whittier ever forgot us. No, we didn't get to see the movie that night.

It's a tragedy in our society that women sell out so cheaply. With nothing going for them but their sex, once youth is gone, they have nothing left with which to trade in our culture. Buying into the Devil's game of adultery, with no sense of family, commitment and fidelity, with divorce so simple to obtain, poor, foolish women, lacking a sense of self-worth, fail to comprehend the end of such foolishness. Statistically, a single woman over 40 can kiss off marriage. For those that find a man willing to take the chance, the "prenuptial agreement" makes it sum-come-nothing game. "Spreading themselves around" in their youth, they discover, too late, that men aren't interested in "used" and wrinkled "merchandise" when it comes to legal entanglements.

Harsh and cruel as this truth is, it is still women who have brought this upon themselves. Their willful and, often, ignorant actions against men and God's commands have brought this to pass. I will never excuse the men who use this foolishness of women to excuse their own failure as leaders, who use this silliness of women to fulfill their own lust, but it is still the woman's responsibility to accept the truth that she simply cannot save her cake and eat it too. As with men, it is still God's way or shipwreck and destruction. The historical imperative of virtue is not heartening: "One man among a thousand have I found, but never a woman!"

Women, not recognizing that God, the Apostle Paul and I, are not the "enemy" in failing to give in to their ridiculous claims to "equality" mistaking this for "value" should pay more attention to the fact that they, not us, make the decisions that lead to their being undervalued in our culture. It is women who sell out to Playboy and Penthouse, the strip joints and jumping into one bed after another and so on. Tragically, I don't see any man of stature in the religious or political leadership that women can trust who would provide the motive for doing other. And, as MacArthur so well said: "The problem is, basically, theological!"

There are many men of history, some of great genius, whom I admire in spite of our disagreement on some particulars, even some, who, in their persons, I find perverted and despicable. Some have found me so as well saving the perversion.

One of my mentors, Walt Kelly, portrayed in cartoon format, the mouse that wanted to be an elephant. Coming upon a fairy godmother, he was granted his wish. He should have noticed something amiss when the godmother was found living in an alley as a street person. Sure enough, the mouse soon found being an elephant not all it was cracked up to be. Tearfully and fearfully, he was able to get the godmother to change him back into a mouse. So it is with women that itch for a "something" that will make them "better" than they think of themselves. Even finding a "man" that will allow them to "rule" doesn't relieve the "itch." God's way is the only way of relief even though obedience to Him doesn't guarantee total satisfaction in everything we think we want. Sadly, it often takes being an elephant for a while to appreciate being a mouse. Or, as Erma Bombeck said: "The Grass Is Always Greener Over The Septic Tank."

Admittedly, my relationships with women have too often been that of "armed neutrality." I have had some unusual pets. I once had a skunk and, at another time, a porcupine. Both had some endearing characteristics but required a large degree of accommodation to their natures and were hard to live with. Not impossible- hard. Some, more easily daunted souls, would say it isn't worth the effort. I disagree. But I'm admittedly strange in some ways, though not so much so that I ever tried to cuddle the porcupine or aggravate the skunk.

Vice is a monster of so frightful mien
As to be hated needs but to be seen;
Yet seen too oft, familiar with her face,
We first endure, then pity, then embrace.
Alexander Pope

"Woe unto them that call evil good, and good evil; that put darkness for light, and light for darkness; that put bitter for sweet, and sweet for bitter!" Isaiah 5:20

Sometimes I get a call or note from someone that takes something I have written personally. I tell them all the same thing; if I didn't name you personally and the shoe fits, wear it. If not, look to your own heart for the cause of your concern.

I mentioned a while back that you cannot publicly, and that means from pulpits, read portions of God's own Word in Canada without breaking the law. And, I ask, when is that going to happen to her neighbor in the South? The feelings are so strong against God's Word and Caucasians that a copy of one of my books mailed to David Duke was defaced through the postal department. The torn wrapper was returned to me with the imprint of somebody's boot heavily stomped on it. I am keeping it as a reminder and souvenir of battle. Minorities should learn that they are only the puppets of a satanic ACLU which presents the "liberal" face of evil in duping them into thinking they are on the "same side." The ACLU and JDL have only one face: Zionism. The pathetic NAACP and other such organizations dangle and jiggle by their strings. When the "agenda" is met, Negroes and Mexicans will find their throats cut along with all others who oppose Islam and Zionism.

It is certainly a commonplace befitting our human condition to, lacking position in the higher classes; make a virtue of the lower. It has somewhat to do with my own, professedly tongue-in-cheek, appellation of an "Okie Intellectual." But it serves me well in getting the goats, if not the attention otherwise, of my self-assumed "betters."

Reminds me of my own kin; my brother didn't write much because he was proud but couldn't spell his way through a book of cigarette papers. It is a tragic loss because he could have helped so much in putting some things of interest to his own children in print and helping me in much of my own writing. It is sad to me that our great-grandmother, grandparents and mom didn't write down many of the stories they shared with us as children. I determined, years ago, that I wasn't going to let that happen, for better or for worse, to my own children. So it is that many of the incidents I describe in my own life are for their benefit. Sadly, there are some things, like what really counts in life, that are only appreciated with age and wisdom.

If I, to any degree, heed the wisdom of those that have served as the poets, the "makers" that encourage both the "doing" and the "dream," I will have served well. I hope I write for my posterity, not only my own children, but all my "children." The vicissitudes of life too often prevailing over the desired ends and ambitions, it still remains to workers like me to do all we can to help children dream dreams and live in hope.

The seeming disparity between Andrew Johnson and Abraham Lincoln is easily resolved in the reading of recent histories. It is for that reason I encourage you to read Bowers' The Tragic Era (the so-called "Reconstruction"). If people would only read this account they would certainly have a better understanding of what was really working in the Civil Rights movement and why the resentment is so deeply entrenched in the South toward the hypocritical government that nearly destroyed it. There had never been a time when the Constitution was so used as a "door mat" for the unscrupulous, the "Carpetbaggers" and "Scalawags," that profited by the misery of others and created such hatred and prejudice where they didn't exist before.

It was the government's excess, in spite of Johnson's efforts, in punishing the South that left the door open to what our "leadership" has become. Once the ideals of our founding fathers were totally abrogated, the twistings and distortions of our Constitution were set in place. It was such machinations of evil and wicked men that led Clemens to call Judas Iscariot a "premature congressman."

I have caught some "flack" in my observation that the franchise should only be for those that are responsible citizens; that no one on the public dole should be able to vote. It will surprise some that the Great Emancipator did not intend that Negroes should be given the franchise. It was Lincoln's enemies that encouraged this fiasco for political reasons alone, promising the Negroes that they would become the "new Massas" and be given the lands of their former owners. Thus it was, through political promises, that the Negroes first became the innocent slaves of a far more cruel system of bondage.

It took men like the nefarious Chief Justice, Salmon P. Chase and his "Boswell," Whitelaw Reid, the Union Leagues and a subverted Northern Press to make the Negro, from the very first day of his "Emancipation," a slave to expectations of being "taken care of" by government largess. A further, most cruel misconception was fostered; that of the idea that "Freedom" meant no longer having to work.

While historians are quick to point out that the Civil War was not really fought over the issue of slavery, notwithstanding the effectiveness of Stowe, the Abolitionists, John Brown and the Underground railways, that the issue was State's rights, it was, in fact, slavery that became the focal point. It is argued, rightly, that the North had advanced the idea of "Bigger is Better" in respect to federal government to such an extent that the South felt it had to take a stand. It was this situation that led to historians trying to make the war a "State's Rights" issue while ignoring the fact that, had slavery not been an issue, the differences might have been worked out in the political arena instead of on the battlefield. But "State's Rights" makes "better history" and paints a more "civilized" picture of fratricide.

In justice to the strictest interpretation of the affair, had the Northern politicians kept to the Constitution and the ideals of our founding fathers for limited federal government and the sovereignty of State's Rights, slavery would have never been a point of conflict or any justification to wage war on fellow citizens. Whatever one's point of view on the subject, the assassination of Lincoln and the following rape and pillage of the South after the war proves beyond doubt the causes of the South's genuine fears that led to an attempt at secession. In sum, however, it is a tragedy that the framers of the Constitution did not heed Franklin's advice to abolish slavery.

Thus it was, as I have often said, good men who, we might think, should have known better sowed the seeds of the following destruction. To their defense, however, like the issue of religion, they could not have known, given the historical circumstances, what evil the future held for America. Further, slavery was an established institution in the history of the world and the Bible nowhere speaks against it. The Apostle Paul even returned Onesimus to his owner. God does, however, make a distinction concerning "cruel bondage" and "harsh taskmasters" and how slaves are to be treated. And who can deny that we, in this nation, have become "wage slaves," even those "tame and abject slaves" that Washington warned of? It also remains my conviction that sin, not God's will, fostered slavery. This may be in the category of Jesus' comment on divorce being granted on the basis of the hardness of hearts, not on what God wanted or intended.

It is ever thus that it takes an emotional issue to rally the passions. Politicians (and religionists) have this, always, in view. The most recent being: "We're going to kick Hussein's ass!"

It takes the historian of the soul and appreciation of the poet to do justice to history. For this reason, our most ancient historians were, literally, poets. The mythic of some of the "histories" had more to them than a simple embellishment of facts. The exaggeration of truth is not always with the intent of passing a lie. It is not always for the purpose of making the teller more important than he really is. The Indian acting out the hunt serves to provide, not just the bald facts, but also a "story" that will be remembered.

It seems that evil men have assigned the intent, even the very words, of our founding fathers to the category of "myths and legends." For example, the very first Article of our Bill of Rights: "Congress shall make no law respecting an establishment of religion, or prohibiting the free exercise thereof..." Being Caucasian, Western-European Christians the Founding Fathers could have never foreseen the distortion of this Article to protect the many religions and cultures that are utterly alien, even maliciously antagonistic, to Christianity. Franklin, being wise in business and world affairs, tried to have Zionism, as well as slavery, specifically excluded by the Constitution.

To force any other interpretation on the clear intent of Article One was to open to door to every kind of evil. Our founding fathers knew full well that the only operant of the values and morals of a society and its government is religion, in this case, Christianity. They had to try to keep this in focus that is the reason God and Jesus figure prominently in all their writings. But, since all they had in view was Christianity, can they be blamed for their "failure" to address the issues of foreign religions and cultures? I think not. All future actions of the government and its Supreme Court to open the door to alien religions and anti-Christian cultures are a betrayal of the clear intent of the founding fathers and our Constitution, a betrayal of the Revolution, our nation and our posterity.

We now live, thanks in large part to the infamous "Tragic Era," in a society that makes those that try to live by the rules the victims of those that deem themselves "above" the law. Not just those that openly rob and steal, but our judges, building inspectors and such like bureaucrats and their "good old boy" networks, the CIA and the scoundrels, scalawags and carpetbaggers that support their lavish lifestyles on the backs of working people. The "rules" are for the great unwashed, the taxpayers, who have lost any voice in how they are to be ruled. "Government of the people, by the people and for the people" sounds good but it doesn't make good "policy" for liars, cheats and thieves, i.e., Washington D.C. and present government in general.

It has been my privilege to spend years working for an honest living, to work with the folks that have kept this nation going, the mechanics, machinists, laborers, construction workers as well as the doctors, lawyers and teachers, a few of which I have found to be honest. But my heart is still, largely, with those poor folks of my Dust Bowl era like my grandad whose philosophies of life, as with Thoreau, were based on such simple verities but proved so profound in the working out.

One of the earliest jobs I had that paid a wage was on a rock crusher in Old, Lake Isabella. The rig had been set up along a stretch of the river where the rock and sand could be processed for building materials. I was about fifteen years old and was paid a whole dollar an hour for lubing the machinery, keeping the ditch clear for the shovel and tossing boulders into the crusher' jaws. Being summer time, a 55-gallon steel drum was available to immerse my body when the heat got to me.

It was marvelous to watch what those iron jaws would do to the rocks I threw to them, slamming, busting and chewing into the various parts of aggregate that would drop through the screens for sizing. The long shovel, dragged by cables, would reach out and drag a mammoth mouthful of material up to the crusher and spill it into its jaws, there to be hammered unmercifully to pieces.

Once, while clearing the ditch for the shovel, the operator not paying attention to the fact that I was still in the ditch shoved the contraption into gear. The slack, steel cables suddenly whipped tight and caught me in the chest flinging me bodily out of the ditch. I was fortunate enough to escape with no more grievous injury than the loss of my shirt and a full-chest cable burn oozing blood droplets. A dunk in the water drum and I was back at work. A slight mishap was not going to deprive me of the opportunity of a dollar an hour.

If such a thing were to happen in today's society, some lawyer would have had me owning the rig. Not to mention the possibility of some kind of Workman's Compensation scam, apart from my age. Why, I might have wound up one of those forty five percent getting some form of government "assistance." Of course, where would a fifteen year old get a chance to do such work today? No insurance! In spite of the potential for accidents, I mourn the loss of opportunities for young people to do the kinds of work that were open to my generation due to the exhaustive "controls" government has placed on jobs; another case of government "overkill." It's not that workers do not need protection in the workplace, but excessive, bureaucratic intrusion with its attendant litigation has emasculated industry. They have "protected" (read: Enslaved!) us to death.

I do not, however, suffer the delusion of a William Ellery Channing, a champion of The Elevation of the Laboring Class: "There are men who, in the face of all history, of the great changes wrought in men's condition, and of the new principles which are now acting on society, maintain that the future is to be a copy of the past, and probably a faded rather than bright copy (as per George Will)." I am far more the "weekday preacher" of Thackeray, the "Harlequin" who, filled with sorrow for the human condition, nevertheless, knows the absolute need for humor.

In keeping with a balanced perspective, I am Thoreau's "Saunterer." Like he, I don't "take walks," I saunter. The word, derived from the French, *Sainte-Terrer*, a Holy-Lander, meant in the Middle Ages one on pilgrimage. Casting aside the more base meaning of the word, Thoreau and I do not "take walks;" each walk is a pilgrimage. Our walks are more of his choice of *sans terre*, without land or home, for, although we may, at times, have a bed for a while, we know it is not our "home."

A further condition to "Sauntering" is the freedom of Thoreau's caution: "A man is rich in proportion to the number of things which he can afford to let alone." Therefore, like Thoreau, I draw strength from familiar commune with the mountains, rocks, trees and streams of God's creation and being thus "wild," pity those "wage slaves" who, because of tyrants and their own greed in "wanting ever more and more," all suffer, more or less, the tyranny of poverty no matter what their material possessions and wonder, as Thoreau, that they have not all committed suicide long ago; but we are willing to credit them with some fortitude, even heroism that they remain by their lasts and anvils.

Thackeray described Swift as: "Wild, witty and poor." I have suffered somewhat the same description of my own choice of lifestyle the past few years. But, though the "lengthening shadows of the evening of life approach," as long as I can saunter, I will continue to draw my strength from commune with my friends of the Book, and others like Thoreau and Cooper; together with the pines and rocks of the mountains and the fenceless, "cleanness" of a desert panorama.

I still find comfort and joy in examining the skin of an old pine and the lichen, mica-mottled, shape and strength of a huge, granite boulder; of staring up through the branches of a tree to a clear, blue sky. There is joy and the sense that we are not alone, that there is eternal purpose, when staring at the star-studded canopy of the night, listening to the flutter and scratchings of night creatures or in the blazing heat and light of Midsummer Day in the middle of the Mojave. I still thrill to the sun and a full, moonrise; I'm still moved at their setting. A good thunderstorm is a delicious joy to my soul. Though the "scars of battle," those "life-lines," etch ever more deeply into my face, I have never lost or "traded" the "wonder of it all." These things I share with all such men irrespective of "color."

Men owe it to women and children to never lose the best part of the child in them. It is the wonder and magic of childhood that, retained in the man, evokes the tenderness and understanding, even the strength, so necessary to those "weaker." It is that best part of man, in God's image, that becomes the poet and artist. That which began with lying on the grass or sandy loam watching the ants in their fascinating industry or, if you were fortunate, a "doodle bug" working his way into the soil creating a marvelous cone in the process. Looking at the sun and your surroundings through a piece of colored glass or clear, colored marble, a "purie," of believing anything is possible if you are honest and true, of believing in a world of adventure that would reward thrift and honest toil.

My life in Little Oklahoma and on the mining claim in Sequoia National Forest, my reading the classics of Cooper and others, forever and indelibly molded the values and ideals I carry with me today. No amount of betrayal of them has alloyed them, only tempered them by the ugly realities of the baser natures of men and women.

Thus it is that my need of "Walkabouts" in what I can find here in America of that great, empty, Australian Outback keeps my mind in tune and the real issues and values of life in perspective and the best part of the "child" alive. This helps keep me from the mere sentimentality of "Meet John Doe" and the overly simplistic "fixes" of hugely, complex problems that only lead, ultimately, to Hitlerian "solutions" while, at the same time, able to enjoy Nelson Eddy and Jeannette MacDonald and grieve over much of what children choose to listen to.

It is not that age and experience has left me bereft of the social needs or graces. I know which is the salad fork. But I thoroughly enjoy, along with opera, Cigareets 'n' Whusky 'n' Wile,' Wile' Wimmin with its lilting melody and profound psychology. Frankie and Johnny still stirs a kind of melancholy in my soul and the rooty toot toot of the crescendo of the drama still rings of true romance; an American, tragic, mini-opera of profound simplicity.

You "ladies;" why aren't you working as hard at getting "your own" to stop "selling their selves" and pandering to the things you profess to hate in men as you are on the ruse of "equality" all the while mistaking this for "value." When will men ever take your mock cries seriously when it is your own kind that foments the concept of women as "objects," as "things?" The Truth is that men see you in the light of how you truly are, not what you claim to be. As long as you live a lie, your brand of "truth" will not fly. You are whipping a dead horse. You cannot have both "Gloria Steinam" and "Penthouse." Neither can you have a truly good man and rebel against God's commands no matter what you see on TV or read in trashy novels. Your claims for "equality" can only become legitimate when all the rape laws are removed from the books, when every cry for "special handling" and consideration are done away. Of course, this is not "logical" to women and would be a tragedy for America.

From where the "mythic" of "mother love?" Since when did a father's love fall into decadence and "mother" become a legend? From the same source that denies the Roman Catholic Church insurance against molestation of children, from the same source that sold "reality" to the state schools in "Catcher In The Rye" and now that same "reality" is on the lips of children every day; weak men bowing to rebellious women in their own sinful desires. Far too many women attempting to do jobs men were intended to do and, consequently, failing miserably in leadership.

There is a definite need for extremes. The Truth is only recognized as such when the balance of extremes is at both ends of the equation. Jesus used this in his teaching. We now know that the cosmos is not "chaos." This is the reason for vain attempts at "randomness" in mathematics. Genuine randomness is impossible to achieve and we settle for what will work in the circumstances. But the impossibility should have been a clue, long ago, that there is purpose in all things.

As paradoxical of my opinions as it may seem, I am going to intrude a word of sympathy for politicians (religious charlatans will never get one). In far too many cases, the pols themselves are "victims" of the evil system as are we, the great unwashed. The best-intentioned politician must confront the fact that he is dealing with a mass of humanity that is ill equipped to accept or understand the problems of government. Too many of the electorate are of the same category of those newly "freed" Negroes of Reconstruction that are non-readers and utterly ignorant of the price of freedom. Too many who should know better choose to be self- disenfranchised and ignorant of either the issues or what is needed to correct the abuses of unchecked governmental constraints on liberty.

Political leadership knows that only an informed, enlightened, educated and property-owning electorate can result in enlightened government. They cannot say, as I can, that we have forsaken the Republican form of government of our founding fathers and exchanged it for a mongrel, "democratic" form where the "majority," no matter how low the common denominator, decides law. Forced thus to accommodate such an "electorate," we lose the statesmanship of the long view for our posterity and cater to the short-term greed of something for nothing, the dwindling "republicans," the middle class, forced to pay for the indolent, "incapables" and illegals together with lavish salaries for those that have the "rule."

It may well be that only revolution, as it has historically done, can "fix" the situation. But keep in mind that revolution is only seen as such when placed in the extreme of one dimension. When the extremes of both ends of the equation are clearly seen, a revolution may be the sensible balance, the Truth. Whether by design or seeming circumstances, "Nations will rise and nations will fall and every nation which forgets and forsakes God shall go down." And, faced with a generation for whom Pascal is no match for MTV or the destructive noise that passes for "music, "how will they be "saved?"

A "class war" is already ongoing. The fact that this, necessarily, includes the issue of "race" is a given. Politicians know this. Consider how this is happening in other countries and the attendant threat to the world this poses, particularly in Russia and the Middle East! How, short of revolution, are they to be extricated from this conundrum? As I have said, we needn't hope, uselessly, for a revival of God's way for our nation; there is no hope on the horizon for the kind of leadership which would have the moral integrity to call for national repentance, prayer and fasting. The "remnant," forsaken by government and church, must seek its own way through the evil days and stand the best it can. My ministry is in my writing, to do what I can to help in this stand. Admittedly, my reward, even a word of thanks, from the "faithful" is near zero ("that which costs little, my time and effort, is lightly esteemed") and I must fight the battle of facing each empty page (screen) every day I sit and attempt to fill it with something of value, something relevant that will help those that need such help.

But I learned years ago the truth of that saying: "I would like to do business with "Christians;" I just can't afford to!" Too many times I have faced the fact that the Truth does not pay, particularly among the "religious."

A "good Christian friend's" car had broken down. He called me and, not being able to affect the needed repairs in the parking lot where he was, I pushed his vehicle over to my place. It was a hot, summer day and, sweating profusely, I spent about three hours fixing his car. His handshake and the words "Thanks, but you would do better being paid" was typical of my dealings with the "saints" over many years. I have spent too much of my years "casting my pearls before swine" and "giving that which is holy to the dogs" to excuse any further laxity or naiveté in this regard. I'm sure politicians feel the same way and have experienced the same things. That "Pearl of great price" continues to go without bidders while the World; the Flesh and the Devil do a brisk business.

At the same time the leadership has to deal with foreign affairs such as the Zionist's displacing Arabs in Jerusalem. By not allowing Arabs to work on their homes, denying them the necessary "permits," Jews are forcing Arabs to sell out to them. The situation in Jerusalem is fast becoming a focal point of Biblical proportions in world affairs, especially as Jews threaten Al-Asqsa Mosque and the Dome of the Rock.

We are being subjected to a barrage of material designed to foment racial strife. The recent airing of "Blood In The Face" by the Discovery channel is a case in point. It was obvious that the media was quite "selective" in painting the Caucasians as the "enemy." People like George Lincoln Rockwell make good "straw men." In using the worst elements of those that put on a sheet or wear a Nazi armband as "typical" of such feelings among Caucasians, the real enemies of our nation are playing with a stacked deck. Oddly, they don't seem to realize that what they are doing is going to come down on their own heads.

It is vain to hope for a moderate voice of conciliation to prevail in the midst of world turmoil. Action is demanded and those that are making themselves targets by their demands for "special privilege" are going to be the hardest-hit victims of their own greed, selfishness and bigotry.

I am indeed fortunate that I can "escape" to the mountains occasionally. I fervently wish I could remain in my cabin among the pines and the critters. This kind of "ministry," the writing, is a great, emotional drain on my physical resources; it's hard work. Far better to seek the wily trout or simply sit on my screen porch and listen to the music of the wind sighing through the pine needles and rustling through the leaves of the oaks; to watch the lizards sunning themselves on the granite boulders and listen to the call of the quail and the barking of the squirrels. But, the old Dodge wagon needs a tuneup and you folks need stirring up. So, I'll keep at the work a while longer as much as this "tent of clay" will stand it. I always have Spike Jones and Tom Lehr when it becomes too much for me. But I have to admit that much of what I am constrained to write is about as much fun as my motorcycle accident or the time I dumped a cup of coffee on my computer keyboard.

For a few of my newest readers who have expressed some wonder at what they think is a "new tack," in regard to Zionism I'll explain. As far back as the early sixties I was beginning to learn, especially through my work in the schools and the ghetto, about this threat and try to warn others. Many of my intimates, particularly in the early seventies, will remember my continued warnings. It is part of the Zionist agenda to, not only vilify Christians, but to take away our Constitution by the actions of government and the Supreme Court, to take away our right to bear arms, to get women abortion and divorce on demand and other such "rights," to foster a bankrupting welfare system and mentality, to "preach" a message of "forced equality," to foster pervert "rights," to force a larger national debt thus putting us entirely in the hands of Zionist bankers, to encourage the disastrous course of "equal" education for all regardless of ability which has resulted in our shameful schools, to strip men of their ability to lead by using women through pornography and unjust laws that emasculate men.

Aimed like a knife-thrust at every institution of our nation, the Zionists and their puppets, the minorities and perverts and women in general together with the jellyfish in our pulpits, they are succeeding in destroying every vestige of the dream of our founding fathers and spitting in the face of God Himself! Such are the enemies of God and those who will, at last, imprison and kill people like me saying: "We do God a service," and all this in the high-sounding rhetoric of "civilized" behavior, "equality" and "fairness!"

"So," God says, the "signs of the time" will be. Some of you will remember my words of caution concerning the United States in Biblical prophecy; is it possible that that "Great City," that "Whore of Babylon," is being set up by Satan? I have never said the U.S. is that "city," but I have said, and say again, especially in light of all that is happening, you do have to wonder.

All the efforts of the Zionist leadership of present Israel and organizations like the ACLU and JDL in this nation are directed at making our laws meaningless or counterproductive (like our drug laws) or hateful like our inability to meet out justice to the likes of an Alton Harris. All of these things make a citizenry angry and frustrated, wanting to lash out at those that they feel are the instruments of their anger and frustration. It is in just such a climate of anger and fear that the devil plans to bring about his own grand design. But, because of successful brainwashing by "religionists," the professing churches have sold the oxymoron of "Judeo-Christian" to millions and any legitimate warnings of Zionism are treated as Anti- Semitic. "Woe to that nation that calls evil good!"

Another reason I feel some sympathy for the pols is that they don't seem to realize that God is the only answer this poor, old world is ever going to have. He is the only answer to selfishness, greed, prejudice and bigotry. Admittedly, religionists, as Franklin so well pointed out, have obscured the spirit and intent of the Bible and replaced them with their own peculiar notions. As a result, politicians lack moral leadership ever as much as the electorate. I have to wonder; what do you suppose they would do if we had some real men in the pulpits of America instead of the mealy-mouthed, spineless hypocrites that hold sway?

As it is, the mainline churches can't even seem to come to terms with the fact that perversion and adultery are just as much a stench in the nostrils of God as they have ever been. It is an historical absolute that the leadership of government can be no better than a nation's religious values and the active support of leaders in both areas by an enlightened, informed and moral citizenry.

This is what our government leaders face; chaos in the churches, a Billy Graham that has never had anything but "half a gospel," the Jimmy Swaggart's, Jim Baker's and snake-oil salesmen like the Schuller's and the "Oh, so polite" Kennedy's; but nowhere to be found the Elijah's, John the Baptist's who, by their lives and the message, have credibility. I cannot help believing that if the churches could get their act together, there are good men in government that would listen and even be joyful to pursue righteous courses of action. In other words, our leaders desperately need leaders themselves. Makes you kind of wonder what would happen if President Bush had a believable church leader?

But tragically as with Israel our religious leaders have gone "whoring" after other gods; even the "good" people I know, for the most part, only give lip-service to what they profess they believe, their lives giving the lie to their profession of "faith." The godly man "ceaseth" and "who will show us the way" let alone any "good?"

I can only hope that what I did in love for my children will become clear to them as they grow older. I know they will, when, in those immortal words: "They have children of their own!" I know God must feel just as we do in disciplining and judging His children. There is more hurt in the heart of the loving parent than any suffering the child endures. But, sadly, it takes "growing up" to realize this. No "child" ever would while his own hiney is burning. The lone parent who loves his children enough to prove that he cares about how they will grow up thus often finds himself consigned to the children's department of "deep doo doo." But, I repeat, to a chorus of "Amen's," only until they have children of their own!

The propaganda war is really heating up. The old, WWII flicks and things like the Hitler era in Germany getting more frequent exposure on PBS, the Discovery channel, etc. Then there is the "propaganda" of buying and selling that makes the U.S. look like one, big commercial (Babylon) or the movies and "entertainment" that portrays a nation sinking in a cesspool of sex, violence, crime and drugs; the "glorification of evil!" The escalating violence in our schools that I saw beginning in the early sixties and no one would listen. Administrators protecting their "backsides" in an attempt to maintain the "status quo" with thieves and fools like Honig "leading," and a recent, one-hour, prime time special on David Duke; and a not very flattering portrayal.

Is it any wonder that when, given the option between "urbane and domesticated" I would choose the "wild and untamed?" But I am of the same conviction of Thoreau and London that a man draws his real values and strength from the "Garden of pines and mountains," the desert and the sea, rather than from the neatly manicured lawns and shrubs of his comfortable "prisons." It is natural in our hearts to admire the wild that excites and equate the "tame" with "dull." I concede the need of being with people and my own proclivity for "musty" books. I open a book and stick my nose, literally, into it and breathe its perfume of the printer and binder's craft before I even begin reading. I draw strength from such a "wild" source as well as that of naturally and unrestricted flowing streams and rivers. Admittedly, it makes a man like me a challenge (threat?) to any woman, politician or religionist. I won't be "tamed and domesticated."

I never think of God's judgment but what the discipline of my own children comes to mind. God says that "foolishness is bound up in the heart of a child but the rod and reproof will drive it far from him," that "He that spares the rod hates his own child" to "not spare our own hearts" in the chastening.

No one could love their children more than I do mine. Before God, I lie not, if He should ask me what, in this life, was the hardest thing I ever had to do, I would immediately reply: "Not sparing the rod!" Many are the nights that I had to go to bed hating myself for what I had to do in disciplining my children, particularly my son Michael. I had to leave him at home once when I went fishing due to a very malicious thing he had done. I can't describe my own hurt at leaving him crying because he could not go with me. My heart was certainly not in the trip without him. I had to go, nonetheless, or the point couldn't have been made.

The major problem in my family was the fact that the children and I were cursed with a "mother" who would not cooperate in their discipline. She was a "yeller" and "screamer," one of those people who would make bizarre and totally irrational threats against misbehavior but would never carry out any punishment. Worse, she would never support my own efforts, arguing in front of the children about my own "unreasonableness" and, as a consequence undo my own efforts at discipline. Children respond in the worst possible way when parents are not in agreement and consistent on what is best for them. And, if a woman is not in agreement on God's command of a man's leadership, disaster is the inevitable result. I, thus, became the "heavy" when it came to the area of disciplining our children. I can only hope that what I did in love will become clear to them, as they grow older. I know they will, when, in those immortal words: "They have children of their own!"

CHAPTER TEN

CHRISTIAN PERSPECTIVE

APRIL, 1992

Proverbs 17:17

My verifiability for "Kookdom" has always included my insistence that God expects us to take His Word at face value and believe all He has said, that people who do so cannot help but evidence it in their lives. This has always alienated me from all "pretenders to the faith."

For those that continue to express an interest in my political views, I have to include a word about H. Ross Perot. I stated in a previous letter that the election of Perot wouldn't change things. I meant, as with the other "choices" with which we are being presented, that it wouldn't change things for the better. You will be able to see, from the following, what I mean. I believe you will find my comments of interest. I preface my remarks by stating categorically that I am not "prophesying." I am simply presenting these comments for conjecture alone. If God is bringing this nation into judgment, if the "great falling away" is occurring, if this nation is "Babylon, that great city" of Revelation, my comments may have merit.

Maybe you read or heard that tests have confirmed the bones of Dr. Mengele, the infamous doctor of Hitler's time. The path is now clear for the doctor's "shrine."

Most Negro students at Olivet College have packed their bags and left, many electing to finish classes by mail rather than suffer more racial strife.

Gambling has reached the astronomical high of $50,000,000,000 in this country. People are looking for a way "out" and Vegas, Atlantic City and lotteries offer hope, no matter the odds, of a "quick fix." It is a certain criteria of the depth of the desperation of people, particularly the poor.

Because of the present climate economically, religiously, politically we have "point men," men whose ground was "plowed" by David Duke with the help of the greedy vandals, past and present Congressmen, Justices and Presidents with their creed o "let the public be damned." As a result, men like Duke become the voice of the great unwashed, the anemic tax paying, responsible, hard-working middle class for whom there is no hope but a

187

"lynching" of the scoundrels who robbed them and their children of a future. The "scapegoats" are being prepared for "slaughter."

None of this is because David Duke may be, in fact, an evil man. I know some really good men in the various legislatures that are honestly trying to do a good job. But the hopelessness of our circumstances doesn't allow of any easy answers. They don't even allow, in most cases anymore, of even fair ones. As a nation, we are too far past the point of answers without great sacrifice and, because of so much evil, it seems to be a matter of who will make, and be, those "sacrifices."

In the present, political atmosphere of "get the rascals out," the "anti-incumbent" groundswell brought about by the greed, avarice, selfish, "public be damned" attitude of the fools in D.C. and state governments, a man like Perot is a "Godsend." A "White Knight," a self-made man, a business giant who has proven he knows how to "get the job done."

It takes Mr. Bush's "Team 100," a group of about 250 people giving $100,000 apiece, buying for themselves, among other things, ambassadorships, to generate a "soft-money" war chest of $25,000,000 for his campaign. Perot, by himself, has pledged $100,000,000 from his own pocket and for Perot this is "pocket-change." He needs no other contributors and is, thus, free from the "special interest" crowd. If the presidency can be bought, Perot can easily afford the price.

A self-made man who knows the "score," who has proven he can get the "job" done, the ultimate "rags to riches" success story. The allure is positively enchanting, or, possibly, "bewitching?" Is Perot a "Dark Horse" seen as a "White Knight" but in actuality quite the opposite?

As a pragmatic businessman, Perot knows what is wrong with the present system of government. If what a senator recently shared with me, that electing enough good men to change things for the better "...isn't going to happen in two hundred years," a Perot is definitely the answer because we don't have even a few years, let alone two hundred or more.

Perot favors abortion. While he has not said so directly to my knowledge, I presume he also favors euthanasia. He, thus far, has refused to answer the question posed by reporters as to whether he is a racist? But, he has said the things about the poor and minorities that are usually construed to be racist comments. He knows something has to be done to eliminate the problem of the "incapables" and other non-productive elements of society that are bleeding our economy dry. He would close our borders to immigration and take a firm stand against foreign aid, he would enact the tariffs that would protect, and isolate, the American economy.

Perot is a man who is used to giving orders; he is not a politician, schooled in the art of compromise or diplomacy. He did not become successful through compromise or flexibility. He did so by being pragmatically ruthless. He is uniquely qualified to demand congress obey him. Not a one of that body would dare to defy a man who could, easily, destroy any of them. Being completely his own man, owing no favors to PACs or special interests of any kind, he would be a virtual Caesar, an emperor who could rule with an iron fist.

So it is that the circumstances are such that a "strong man" is on the scene and the electorate is ready to "Sieg Heil" him, a man who is ready and willing to implement all those "Hitlerian Solutions" that are necessary for the country to survive without God. For those few of us that really believe God's Word, the result is described, graphically, in the Bible. But I don't think Perot really has a chance.

CHAPTER ELEVEN

CHRISTIAN PERSPECTIVE

MAY 1992

Jeremiah 29:11 N.I.V.

Because of the Rodney King decision, you have been watching the truth of the things I have been writing and warning of. It's an ugly portent of the future for this nation in its ungodliness. It's far past time for the churches to "get real." Will they? Not unless God's Word is obeyed.

It is a hard thing to watch what is happening in our cities but it is not going to get better until our leadership turns to God. But I will address this topic in the next edition of O.I. along with some of the things a few of our congressmen have been telling me. This issue of CP is going to go back to its original purpose of speaking to Christians and the churches. But I feel I must say a couple of things in view of what has happened recently.

I have been talking with some of our legislators as usual and the picture is pretty grim. Since I live in California, it is particularly grim here. The Thursday before Easter, I chatted with our U.S. State Senator, John Seymour (I wouldn't give the "other one," Alan Cranston, the time of day. That crook only deserves a hard time. Maybe he should be "doing hard time).

Well, I wanted the Senator to know, as I try to let other good men know, that I am solely interested in helping them in trying to do an impossible job. I wanted to let them know that my vitriol was reserved for the crooks and charlatans that are robbing us blind and did not want to step on the toes of those that are sincerely trying to do a good job for our country or make their task more impossible.

The Senator thanked me for my concern and asked that I remind the voters that he comes from a background of seventeen years experience in business and has a better sense than most of what is wrong with the business climate in our state. He, as I have done, stressed the importance of making California attractive for business and, as I have written in the past, get rid of the scoundrels who have the "tax and spend" and the "public be damned" ruinous philosophy of state and federal government that is destroying us.

While I applaud the stand Governor Wilson took in respect to Alton Harris and some other things, his increasing taxes is definitely not the answer. And, I would caution John also that, unless he gains a more conservative overview, a good man, Bill Dannemeyer, is going to unseat him. Bill is speaking to the issues without sugarcoating. And we are far past the time when we can afford "comfortable" and "liberal" so-called "solutions" to the problems that are killing off the middle class. So it is that come election time, I, as well as other conservatives, are going to be lining up behind Bill. We could all wish there was an easy way to deal with the problems we have had our noses rubbed in these past, few days. But there aren't. The "cultures" are poles apart and will never become "multi-cultural."

It is all too obvious that we, in this state, are fast losing our tax base, chasing businesses out of the state by prohibitive taxes and cutting our own throats in the process. Our state "leadership" better get their act together before all hell breaks loose. There aren't any easy answers to the problems, like those of welfare, but the sacrifices better be made fast that are necessary while any choices remain before those "Hitlerian" ones are the only alternatives. But, in most cases, our local representatives need the input of the electorate and too many people are out there grousing and complaining about the dismal state of affairs and don't even know who their local representative or congressman is. Even worse, many are not even registered to vote! This is utterly inexcusable!

It is my good fortune to have a man like State Senator Don Rogers representing me in this district. Don is a levelheaded and pragmatic man who knows what to do but needs all the help he can get in doing it. Unlike many others, Don is working for the best for his constituents and our nation, and not "special interests." All you folks on my mailing list should get involved; know your representatives, help and encourage the good ones and vote the bad ones out! If enough good people get involved, it doesn't have to be the Devil's game all the time. Politics is an essential of our liberty; it's only a dirty word when dirty people are in the saddle. We all face the ugly and pernicious fact that if "Carpetbaggers and Scoundrels" are running things, who voted them in and keeps them in?

When things are tough, the slightest things provide fertile soil for the root of bitterness. A small cancer cell will eventually destroy the body. I used to tell people, years ago, that the schools were not as bad as they thought, they were far worse. But no one listened.

Wealth is concentrating at an accelerated rate to the top one percent of our population- all in the hands of a few. Pat Robertson made a cool $96,000,000 from an initial investment of about $150,000. This is really what is known as "doing well by doing good!" And this from the man who tells people the sky is falling? Is he that much of a "prophet" or could such a "saintly" man have insider information?

What is needed and true on a national level is just as needed and true on the personal. You and I personify this need. There's enough paranoia to go around. If you think you don't have your share, you are probably not reading a paper or watching the news.

I started writing Christian Perspective about ten years ago. It was my intention that the work would have a Christian emphasis. With this edition, that will be the case henceforth. Not that I have lost my sense of humor, but with the advent of BitterSweet Publishing (my brainstorm), I can now devote the Okie Intellectual, Okie Poet and Weedpatcher to other things like politics and start using CP for it's original, intended purpose.

Testimonies, where we share with others, the things the Lord has done in our lives, often fail of their intended use because of dramatization. Brother J. Vernon McGee used to tell of the young man who gave a stirring testimony that really moved McGee's heart. The problem was, that, when he heard the fellow a couple of years later, the "testimony" had grown quite elaborately in the process of time. I have written about such "testimonies" in my books and won't belabor it further. Suffice it to say that charlatans like Swaggart and Baker used this device with telling effect.

The Lord and life itself are too real to need embellishment. The bare facts are usually enough to dramatize God's and the Devil's work in our lives. A truthful witness of God's work in our lives is intended to provide hope and understanding to others. Keep this in mind if you do send something to share with us.

We all have a story to tell. Too often we think we are alone and unique in the problems we face. This leads, sometimes, to an issue I address further along: Suicide. The "Beast" sometimes becomes too much to bear, and few can face him alone.

I suggest to all of you, if depression or loneliness becomes too much, write out your angers and frustrations; above all, I hope you have a trusted friend who will bear with you through such episodes.

There is a "greater work" that transcends the love of a man for a woman that is only an extension of that love. But leave it to a woman to be jealous anyhow. Before you that know me say, "There he goes again!" I warn you that what follows will cause you to reconsider.

Women are "prey," they are the "hunted," victims of the "beast" that dwells in the wicked hearts of men. Recent studies show one out of eight women are raped in our country. As with homosexuality, this is one of the most somber indictments of an entire society.

I am often accused, as with the Apostle Paul, of having a jaundiced view of women; understandably so. I have written much on the subject and have not recanted anything I have said. This is not an attempt at recanting. I will always maintain a Biblical perspective of the relationship between men and women and the position of women in the churches and society. But I am not blind to the facts. While it is true that women are guilty of spawning pornography, of using the law to bash men, of a host of things for which men are the victims, it is a historical truth that women are prey, victims of the lust of men and pay a heavy price for undervaluing themselves.

Tragically, a destructive, double standard has existed that dictates women are to keep themselves pure and chaste while men are to be "experienced" at the cost of women. It still remains true that women betray men at a factor of better than two to one, that "A virtuous woman who can find for her price is far above rubies," that men are more forgiving in many instances of infidelity (a rather pathetic euphemism for the utter betrayal of love, commitment and trust, the defiling of the marriage bed and utterly, selfish destruction of others) than women and often show more concern for keeping a marriage intact; this in spite of the common, but untrue, misconception to the contrary. It is the double standard and men's victimization of women that is to blame for this thinking.

Perhaps it is because the Biblical standard of "the two shall be one" being virtually ignored in our society that women suffer so much. When a man and woman "come together," they become one in God's sight and according to his Word, they are a "marriage unit" no matter what kind of ceremony or "piece of paper" may or may not be invoked. "A quaint anachronism" you might say. But consider the cost to a society and its children by thinking and acting differently. Further, since God has said categorically, that means unmistakably, that any "relationship" apart from marriage is defiled, fornication, men and women choose, wholesale, to try to justify themselves in their adulteries by twisting and distorting God's Word in the matter or, in most cases, ignoring it entirely or labeling it with the Godless epithet: "Relationship" as if such a label made it approved in God's eyes. It doesn't!

It is curious to many that God has used the phrase, "An adulterous generation" so many times in the Bible. Jesus uses it to describe the generation that will portend the "last age." Adulterers are classed right along with murderers as those that will not enter into the kingdom of Heaven.

Perhaps it is because my children and I have suffered so much at the hands of adulterous women that I feel so strongly about the subject. Nothing takes the place of first-hand experience. But it is a great deal more than that. If the Biblical standards of righteousness and purity can so easily be set aside by women, can they blame men for not taking it seriously? How can women expect men to value something that women, by their own actions, treat as of no consequence?

Men, to their everlasting discredit and shame, are quick to take advantage of such undervaluing of something that God Himself places such a high value and priority upon; the marriage bed. These "defilers" are going to hell! God says it and that settles it!

With the majority ignoring God's Word on the subject, with the majority viewing the subject of sex as a "roll in the hay," is it any wonder that our children have the warped view of the sexual relationship between men and women that they do; that they grow up knowing nothing of fidelity, commitment, honor, dignity, truth, the values God places on marriage and trust? And, since marriage and family is of the highest priority to God and the moral integrity of a nation and its leadership, of success and hope for a future, is it any wonder that we face the virtual holocaust of destruction across the board in our nation? I think not!

No matter what construction men and women place on their choices to ignore God, He will not be mocked and His Word will stand regardless of the "laws" and "mores" of a society. Fortunately, there is forgiveness of sin for those that genuinely repent and, wherever possible, make restitution. Justice and mercy meet and kiss at the throne of God. While "To err is human, to forgive divine," it is only that "divinity" in men and women which can take advantage of such love and, tragically, that is most often lacking.

With a Ph. D. in Human Behavior, being credentialed by the State to teach the subject in college, I have the best of training that qualifies me to pass some judgment on the reasons people do the things they do. But there exists the "Beast," the "Monsters of the Id," that neither Freud nor his disciples would intrude into. We will write our books on the subject of "Abnormal Psychology" and make guesses as to the nature of the Beast. We will put "labels" on things and attempt to pass them off as "understanding." But none will intrude too far into that Dark where the Beast and his demons, those "unclean spirits," dwell. No one truly wishes to behold the face and true nature of Evil. Therefore, a Jeffrey Dahmer remains an inexplicable aberration of "humanity."

But I have not encountered any of my colleagues who are giving attention to the Beast. My religious colleagues will talk about the Devil and demons in the usual ephemeral and nebulous phraseology that, as with my colleagues in psychology, they think, "explains." But any woman who has been attacked and raped knows, experientially, that none of these "explanations" suffice. Every child who has been molested knows, experientially, that the Beast remains unknown and unexplained. But these women and children do know he exists and is there, waiting, waiting, to come roaring back at them.

In my story, some time ago, about fishing as a "religious experience" among men, I made the point that, while I know many women enjoy the wilderness, they have to face the Beast if they find themselves alone at some remote area and see three, strange men approaching. Men do not have to face the Beast in this way and are woefully ignorant of what women have to suffer throughout their lives because of it; of the sacrifices women are forced to make all their lives to protect themselves. I am forced to conclude that men, in such ignorance, if they could only put themselves in that position for only a moment, would find it a living hell. Yet women, throughout history, have to learn to "live" with it as a fact of their existence.

This is one of the reasons women learn to "use" sex as a weapon in an attempt to make the best "deal" they can with men. In too many cases, particularly among young women, children really, and lacking the maturity of thinking, they mistakenly trade their most precious resource for what they think is love. Boys, and men in general, take advantage of this need and lack of correct thinking and the girl or woman is left with the miserable fact that she made a tragic mistake. And this "mistake" too often leaves her with a child that will be born into the most miserable conditions and repeat the same vicious, tragic cycle.

I almost have to laugh, sardonically, as many will, when I think about the whole subject being written about in the climate of our present society. With both men and women hopping into bed with whomever, the medium of TV and films making the whole thing of morality an antiquated concept of Victorian stricture, of people laughing at God's Word on the subject, the whole thing takes on an aura of unreality. But we live with the ugliness of the reality of the consequences of such wickedness and sin every moment of every day, we read of it and have our noses rubbed in it on every newscast, we look at it in the faces of our children and others who are betrayed of any hope of real love because of it. And the Beast wins!

A woman is to be cherished by a man. She has a need to see the flower placed at her bedside, the man coming and putting his arms around her and saying, "I love you," to find in the countless, seemingly small ways, that she has great value to that man she has chosen to give herself to. But, and here is where the Beast lurks, if that woman or girl thinks, deludedly, that a man will cherish something she places little value upon, she is tragically mistaken. If she has "given" herself to a number of men in the misguided, even selfish, search for such value, she needn't deceive herself that she will ever have such a value to any man. The two of them may even succeed, for a time, to hold on to such delusion but, sooner or later, the Beast will come roaring in and leave destruction in his wake. And what woman can ever trust the man who has, like herself, betrayed that trust to others?

A woman needs, desperately, a man who has never lost the best of the child within him, the sensitivity of the poet and lover, the strength of goodness that she has every right to expect from him. But the best of both can only succeed; flourish, in the mutual forgiveness of wrongs, real or perceived, that are bound to occur between any man and woman. The nursing of grudges, the coldness of "He or she has to make it up first," all such thinking can only lead to the destruction of the things that brought them together in the first place. When such things begin to take place, when the two stop talking and trying, when there is no time for the stars and sharing of the beauty of love in all its many facets which, like a diamond, refracts the glory of the light in resplendent arrays of colors and brilliance, from the most sublime to simply washing the dishes, all is lost.

Both must be conscious of each other's needs and strengths. A man needs a woman to cherish and live for. His heart, like Adam's, finds its reason for being in loving, protecting and caring for the object of his heart's desire. Her reason for being is in responding to that best of God in man and nurturing it, helping it to grow and thrive by being receptive to it and encouraging it according to God's commands and desire for the best for each of them.

Jesus said the Kingdom of God is within us. This is only comprehensible in the human experience of love. This requires the divine love that risks it all and does so repeatedly in spite of the number of betrayals it may suffer. It forgives, repents of any wrong, seeks and freely forgives others, makes restitution, endures all things, hopes in the face of any failures and never stops hoping and trying.

Adam committed himself to Eve. Her betrayal of that commitment led to his betrayal of God. But, while the serpent deceived Eve, Adam knowingly allied himself to Eve. In this first act of betrayal by Adam and Eve, their "eyes were opened" and they knew "good and evil." It took an act of redemption by God to restore the relationship. This is known as the "Gospel." But, until you have risked it all in love, the whole thing is incomprehensible. But the Beast knows nothing of real love, forgiveness and redemption. I am saying that God has given us the capacity to love but few are saved because few will take such a risk. They will only see bits and pieces of the Beast in others because they refuse to see him in themselves in his entirety. In the vast majority of cases, a single act of betrayal becomes the justification to never love and trust again. Why? Because we have betraying hearts, unredeemed by love, and are only looking for a way to get away with our own acts of continuing betrayal of others. It never seems to come into conscious thought that all such betrayal starts with the betrayal of ourselves, the betrayal of our own ideals and standards of doing for others what we demand they do for us "or else."

As to the kinds of things that too often lead men and women into a bitter spirit, there is the trap of "intuiting." Here is how it works:

She: "If he really loved me, he would be more sensitive, he would have known I needed him to..." You can find a hundred things to fill in the blanks.

He: "If she really loved me, she would be more sensitive, she would have known I needed her to..." You can, again, fill in the blanks. The obvious point? Both have the same needs but both expect the other to "intuit" the needs!

Since it is reasonable to intuit at some times and about some things as a man and woman get to know one another, it is not reasonable to expect either to be "mind readers."

"Missed Cues!" That is what this is all about. Of the women I have loved and married, it comes down to this more than anything else. The caring begins to show itself, too many times, in fixing the car or washing machine, of sewing buttons or baking a cake. The flowers, the clouds in an azure sky, the stars to watch side by side with that "One," and, unless you are very careful to nurture it, the first thing you know, the cares of this world have been substituted for romance and the things that you used to share together as "Heart's Companions."

If the women I have known and loved had any idea of the debt I have to them in understanding they would be surprised. Too often, the bitterness of betrayal becomes a bitter root of hatred. I thank God that has not been the case or I would have been devoured long ago. I learned, among other things, through them by God, that repentance and forgiveness are the healing mechanisms of injured or grieved love. Where these are not achieved, love withers and dies. Only by this path can there be any hope of recapturing what was lost to the "cares and concerns of this world" that "choke" and, finally, betrays. Love "risks it all," and not just once or twice, but time after time; it doesn't give up. It seeks an object of its love, to give and try to be worthy of receiving. But the Devil has well learned that men and women sell out cheap. He gets by with exchanging trinkets for pure gold.

Did Job's wife really love him? If so, her "Curse God and die!" may have been in response to her not any longer being able to endure his suffering. No commentator of my knowledge has credited her with such a thing. But, consider, apart from the physical attack on his body by Satan, didn't Job's wife endure the same losses and grief as he?

Further, by loving and responding to love, we learn to forgive and, when wrong, repent and seek forgiveness and restitution. Genuine love that Jesus speaks of grieves over any breach between loved ones and seeks with all its strength to heal the breach in any way possible. Ultimately, we begin to know what the love of God is really all about; it leads to an understanding of what

God expects of us and enables us to practice the truth of it in our lives with others, those things that are nearest to His own heart. "Practicing" on others is, in fact, that "Royal Law" that is "God in us," His "Kingdom within us" that is a "working out" of our salvation.

It is this kind of understanding, forgiving love that makes sense of the Holy Spirit making intercession for us with groanings which cannot be uttered. Words at their best are poor substitutes for the most deeply felt emotions and longing of the soul, both in grievous suffering, profound loneliness and love. So it is that the love of God brings these things into being in the individual's heart and this "New Creation" begins the long path to understanding and wisdom.

I would suggest to the "brethren" that they try the "Positive Gospel!" Begin with John 3:16 instead of Romans 3:23. People already know they are sinners; they don't know God really loves them.

A Hallmark of the end of the age is the lack of love in the world. And, because of this lack, people are prepared to believe the "Strong Delusion" and accept the "Lie" at the end.

Too many people have prostituted the love of God, thinking within themselves that something else will substitute for risking it all on Him. Failing in that, they never risk it all on another. Folks, unless you take that risk, you are none of His!

This leads me to the dark and tragic subject of suicide. Like homosexuality, which often leads to taking one's life, this is a subject that most Christians don't like to hear, preach or write about. But it is one that must be confronted on an ever-increasing scale.

First, I do not consider the suicide a coward. I say this as a qualified expert on the subject, both academically and experientially. There is not a single person who has not, to one degree or another, confronted the thought in themselves. The Beast is there.

Not many are knowledgeable of the Psychosis of Grief. I have confronted it through death and divorce, the most common sources of depression and psychotic behavior. The degree of depression and psychotic behavior is contingent on the depth of the love for the lost one or, in the case of divorce, "ones" if children are involved.

My most recent encounter with the Beast was over the loss of my brother, which, in turn, led to the loss of "another." No one can possibly tell how he or she will react under such conditions. Nor, when such a thing takes place, can they recognize the depth of the grief or the changes in behavior that are certain to occur. It is absolutely essential to regaining your mental equilibrium that a very close friend or loved one be there for you at such times. If such is not the case, suicide becomes the seductive alternative to living with such grief and pain of loss.

During this particular episode, I couldn't possibly be aware of how profound the grief truly was over my loss. I wrote about it later but, even in the writing, which was largely cathartic, I was still in a psychotic state, unable to truly grasp the depth of my despair.

Previous experience and academic training were, to some degree, helpful, but it remains impossible to analyze your own emotions let alone explain them to someone else. Words cannot articulate profound grief and you react in irrational ways in an attempt to deal with the situation.

The one I needed most at this time, I only succeeded in alienating because she was perceived as cold and uncaring of my great need and distress. And I couldn't articulate it to her in a rational manner. But she was not a trained psychologist and couldn't possibly be expected to understand. In time, death of a loved one comes into the experience of all of us and that more than any academic training, teaches the required empathy and understanding. All I can say at this time is that had I been able to respond rationally and she had been able to recognize the symptoms of my grief, how differently things may have turned out. Tragically, as in too many cases, a breach occurred that I can only hope time and the Lord will heal.

Did I actually "change" because of this? She perceived that I had. Of course I had "changed." But, in time, that great healer of wounds and suffering, my "compass" returned to its true heading once more; the Lord was, once more, sufficient for my life.

How many, I wonder, do take their lives through such "misunderstandings?" Few are qualified to recognize the Beast in all his destructive manifestations. When the suffering reaches a certain point, he is perceived as a "friend" and not the "... roaring lion, seeking whom he may devour." A great deal of study by Christian scholars still needs to be directed at this subject together with a host of other things that has justified my call for a New Systematic Theology.

I am encountering the subject of suicide all too frequently these past few years. I am hearing the topic brought up in, what would have been in the past, unthinkable areas of society. Recently, I learned the pastor of a Lutheran Church where I used to attend that killed himself in his church study. A short time ago I wrote of an acquaintance, Bill, who killed himself because of divorce and the loss of any reason for living. I placed myself, in that instance, in the position of a "heretic" by calling attention to the fact, for which I am qualified to give an opinion, academically, experientially and religiously, that God must allow of the pain and grief of living to become too much for a human being to endure, where the taking of his life becomes such an overwhelmingly attractive alternative to the pain that it is, in fact, the most reasonable course of action.

A man of my acquaintance recently tried to "gas" himself only to wake up, surprised, and, perhaps disappointed, to find himself still alive. Over the years I have encountered too many who have confessed to the attractiveness of such a "way out" to be surprised at so many choosing this alternative to living with pain, grief and hopelessness.

It is, as I have written previously, not the loss of mere material possessions that leads to such a desperate act. It is, as simply put as possible, and not with the thought that it "explains," that death becomes the viable alternative when a person loses the reason for living. In far too many cases, the "reason" for living is bound up in the hopes and aspirations for love and affection, for justification and hope that living is a worthwhile exercise- that continued existence has relevance and meaning. When that justification is tied to others and they fail, suicide becomes a seductively attractive option. I caution my Christian brethren to be extremely sensitive in how they deal with this whole subject. It is very complex and there is no room for a "mistake" in counseling here, as John McArthur and others are now aware.

As those who know me and those who subscribe to the newsletters are aware, I spent many years in education. My first position as a freshman teacher was at Jordan High School in the Watts District of South Central L.A. in 1966. This was shortly after the Watts Riots and I gained first-hand insight into the troubles of the inner city and the tragic problems the young people faced in such an environment. My conclusion after nearly four years at the school- There was not going to be any change for the better. Not then, not now, not ever.

It will take the book I have threatened to write to explain and document the reasons for such an absolutely negative, doomsday conclusion. I have written so much, beginning with my Ph. D. dissertation, on the subject that it leaves me wondering if anybody will bother, at last, to heed the warnings I have sounded for nearly thirty years. It was what I saw happening in state schools that led me to the founding of private schools. But, in many instances, even private schools are no answer and, in fact, militate against answers in many instances.

It was only by God's grace that I was in Colorado when the leadership of that state tried to take over private schools and I sounded the alarm. With the help of Paul Kienel and his organization, we were able to confront the governor's "Gestapo agents" at the capitol and defeat the measure. But had I not been there and skilled in the Enemy's "art," had I not been well-educated and experienced in being able to discern the subtleties of government intrusion into education and the language of "Educationese" and bureaucratic "legalize," Colorado's private schools would now be under the direct control of the state and state schools. Christian schools would have had to cease to operate as religious institutions.

Has the threat lessened in the past years? Of course not. As I wrote some months ago, have things gotten better for Negroes since the Watts riots? Not only have they not gotten better, they are far worse. Are they ever likely to get better? No! So-called "multiculturalism" may make good "liberal" propaganda but it flies in the face of a grim, historical reality that will grind it to powder.

Christians say: "Christ is the Answer!" But the churches, so misguided and ignorant of any true reality of the Lord, have lost the power and authority of the Gospel in its nature and all its ramifications and, as a result, they have been, as I have said many times, "Stomping ants while the elephants are rampaging through the village, playing at church while cruel men and unjust laws make a mockery of the very truths we claim to hold so dear."

As Christians, we are called to warfare. "Soldiers of the Cross" makes no sense while we atrophy in the safety and comfort of our pews, listening to euphemistic nonsense that is supposed to "equip us for service and do battle with the adversary."

But, as long as we refuse to face the evil in ourselves, as long as hard, unloving and unforgiving, unclean spirits remain in us, so long will we be impotent to confront the evil around us. Consider the damage done by the "Gehazis" that run after Naaman and claim what God has refused. Small wonder the world laughs at the ridiculous posturing that attempts to pass itself off as "worship" in the churches.

Beloved, it is far past time to rouse ourselves to the fact that the warfare is real; that people get hurt and killed in battle. But it remains what God has called His people to do and if you are not getting the attention of the Enemy, you are simply not listening to Him! Believe me when I say there is more than enough evil to go around and if you are not confronting your share you are none of His. Yet, at no time in history has it seemed so true that "...the laborers are few."

A recent, full-page advertisement in the L.A. Times proclaimed the Gospel. This ad was taken out by a group of people in South Africa! The heading of the article said in large, bold letters, "URGENT ANNOUNCEMENT!" Now I know nothing of this group but I suspect that since the source was South Africa, since Christians there are more aware of the reality of the warfare (though I am fully aware that there may be more to it than that) they may have been moved to try to stir the complacency of Christians in this country. To me, it seems, as I have said many times, that other nations see America as the "Mission Field." That should speak volumes to those that claim to be children of God!

I don't think the importance of education can be overemphasized in regard to the troubles this nation and, particularly, Christians, face in the time ahead. With that in mind, I hope to renew a series I began years ago on the problems of education in this country. With the abysmal failure of our schools and another generation of illiterates on the horizon, something must be done and done quickly. Are people ready to listen? They haven't been so far and Rushdoony, Damerell, and I have been voices in the wilderness. But I have an obligation to try though no one heeds the words.

It is a given that answers are impossible from the same people who created the problems. As long as the "experts," those with worthless "doctorates" in education, are the main source of such "expertise," no progress will be made. These are the people that "gutted" practical and vocational education; that gave us "New Math" and decided that "Johnny" didn't need to learn to read, write and compute but needed to "express himself." The educational establishment, the colleges of education that are an embarrassment and laughing stock on university campuses, the empire builders of so-called "Special Education," all these and so much more need to be dealt with.

Why is there virtually no accountability in the schools? Why do superintendents draw enormous salaries and, when the schools find themselves facing huge deficits, are they allowed to cry "more money" as if it were someone's else's fault they are broke? Folks, as I have said for thirty years, "Things aren't as bad as you think, they are far worse!" One of the reasons for this is the local school board. Too often a place where egotists get "stroked" or budding politicians begin their careers, the local school board is a tragic joke. Just ask yourself what the "qualifications" are to run for a seat on a school board and you will get the "joke." But who are the real experts and where will we find them? I will be addressing this question along with a host of others in future essays.

For years, as I worked in various districts and accumulated the evidence and experience that proves how we got to this dismal state, I hoped someone, somehow, would finally get the message and begin to act. No one has. Now, girding my loins and blowing the dust off this vast amount of information, I am going to start to do battle. Going back to Superintendent Ryles and his refusal to heed the damning indictment of my dissertation on accountability, the refusal for the local school board to act on the recommendations the study proved were needed and much more, I will name names and let the chips fly.

Pray that I will be able to get the writings into the hands of our leaders and people that need the help and encouragement, the knowledge that will equip for the warfare. Too many good people are fighting as those that "beat the air" because, as the Lord points out, there is a lack of knowledge. "Where there is no vision, the people perish." But there can be no vision without knowledge and ignorance is a killer that leads into ever increasing darkness.

I recently visited with my friends in Lancaster. The drive was marvelous as the fields are covered with wildflowers. I am not a "winter" person. I love the beginning heat of summer and its warmth felt good to my bones as I drove and simply enjoyed all God has provided in His marvelous creation. I only wished I had someone with whom to share it. Before leaving Merced, I was able to encourage and pray with my lovely daughter Karen. I had talked with my son, Michael, on the phone and he seems to be getting a better grip on what his dad is trying to do.

In visiting with some of my friends at their local church, it was good to fellowship and join in the singing and just enjoy the camaraderie but the preacher was a disappointment. A good man, he was telling us how obedient we were all to be to those in authority. Folks, Civil Disobedience is often the way of the cross and Thoreau has the better message for the times than many churches. The way of the cross has always confronted evil and, as I have pointed out, if this man's simplistic interpretation had been followed by our founding fathers, there would have never been a United States of America. And, as bad as it has become, there is still enough liberty to confront evil before the night wholly overtakes us. But we better start getting "grease under our fingernails" before it *is* too late!

CHAPTER TWELVE

CHRISTIAN PERSPECTIVE

JUNE, 1992B

Ephesians 6:12

I am a well-educated, ignorant man. As the applause and "Amen's" die down among my detractors I will explain the bodacious statement. At the outset though, I have to say, in response to some of these critics that it was never my intention to become the Stephen King or H.L. Mencken of Christian writing. It just seems to have worked out that way.

It took a good education to make me appreciate how ignorant I am. But, being a good student, I have had a life-long love affair with learning. Festus said to Paul: "Much learning doth make thee mad!"

Now I know Festus meant "mad" like in "crazy." But, in my case, the learning has not only opened my mind to my ignorance but also made me most definitely mad as in "angry" at the abysmal ignorance among those that profess to be wise.

As with some of you, I have my share of "friends" who, with no qualifications, experience or credentials to do so, never miss a chance to "teach" me the "errors of my way." They range from the silliness of some of the youngsters I used to teach to Gary North and other assorted religious, educational and political "experts."

I have written about such people and won't belabor it here. Suffice it to say that I am too old now to suffer fools gladly. One of the fringe benefits of gaining "elder" status is to become cranky and cantankerous to the extent that I no longer have to put up with the ignorance others try to force upon me. I have enough of my own that is legitimate to deal with without their "presumed expertise."

Maybe that is one of the reasons I love children so much. Their world is still one of enchantment, mystery and amazement. That is, provided they are fortunate enough to have loving parents and grandparents.

They retain the expertise I try to hold on to in that best part of the man, the child within. My children are grown. But they are still my "children" and I pray they never get too "grown-up" to lose the legacy of their father's "childishness."

Granted; Dan, Karrie, and Michael are too old and grown to allow me to grab them and roll on the floor, tickling and laughing. But, I am still doing that in my mind when I see them. I still want to grab them and kiss, hug, tickle and tease them.

I use THE OKIE INTELLECTUAL, OKIE POET and THE WEEDPATCHER as publications to speak to the broadest, possible conditions of our nation and the world. C.P. was always intended to speak, specifically, to professing Christians and the churches. The others are too "raw" for the delicate tastes of most religious palates. Such writing is the "dirty work" only a Billy Sunday might appreciate.

Speaking of Billy, his was a most unique ministry. He was a man for the times. While ignorant of many of the things a seminary education might have improved, he spoke to the masses and they, the "common people," heard him gladly. Whatever might have been said about him, and a lot was said, he made the Gospel plain to millions for whom the churches had failed. It is profitable to our own age to quote William T. Ellis from his book:

"Billy Sunday, The Man And His Message. ...Men's ears are dulled by the 'shop talk' of the pulpit. They are weary of the worn platitudes of professional piety. Nobody cares for the language of Canaan, in which ministers, with reverence for the dead past, have tried to enswathe the living truths of the Gospel, as if they were mummies...."

There is a reality, humanness, to Jesus that the churches have failed, miserably, to convey. A Billy Sunday is needed to bring Him into focus and make real, once more, the never-changing Gospel message. Putting aside all the baloney, all the pious platitudes and phraseology, the only dimension in which a human being, created in God's image, can possibly relate to and understand is the very humanity of our selves. The swinging censers of incense, liturgies, arm-waving hysteria, visions and prophecies are religious nonsense and the world rightly perceives it to be so.

Nor can the "Easy-believism" of a Billy Sunday, Dwight Moody or Billy Graham be lightly dismissed either. But these worthy men did the best they could with what little intelligence of the reality of the Beast they had to work with. Billy Sunday's forte was Booze. He had a clear perception of his time and the enemy was clear. Liquor was an easy and well-defined target. It was his inability, as with so many other good men, to clearly recognize the Beast in his many manifestations that led to Billy's decline as an important voice in American evangelism.

The Beast is not a simple being. He is hugely complex. The Gospel, in contrast, as per John 3:16 and Acts 16:31, is so simple a child easily understands it. Ignorance, once more, is the downfall of any who try to do battle with evil. Christians are just not being adequately prepared by the churches to engage the Enemy.

Paul's statement that we battle "...not against flesh and blood but principalities and powers..." has been "spiritualized away" to meaninglessness. Paul fought with "beasts" in Ephesus. The failure to recognize those same "beasts" as the wicked that bear the rule in our own society is to give the Devil the victory. The emphasis being distorted to mean something meaningless, assigning it to some ethereal realm for which we accept no responsibility either as Christians or good citizens, is to deny the very words and intent of God Himself. The Beast is real and so are the vile men and women who serve him. They are the real targets of God's judgment and our weapons are the very real one's God has gifted us with like His Word and the Gospel. Those, together with whatever gifts He has given us individually and collectively through the churches and our system of government are all to be used in the warfare. If it requires Civil Disobedience in obeying God rather than men, so be it.

There is a spiritual dimension, every bit as real as the physical, to the Evil. There is the spiritual dimension, every bit as real as the physical, to our heavenly calling and life as children of God.

I pray "in the Spirit." It is the Spirit that gives life and understanding. It is in the spirit that men perceive and act out the evil that plagues our world. It is the "inner man" that responds to gentleness and love or evil and hatred.

In my studies of psychology and my experience as a human being I, like you, confront the same things Paul writes about. The realities of the warfare and our lives as children of God are manifested in our actions as physical beings with physical needs and desires.

To try to separate the two, spirit and body, is impossible. God surely knew we would need "food" for both. In His gifts to men, He supplied His Word and the Holy Spirit. But He also gave the genius of great art and literature to men as well. He supplied the genius for men to build and create things that not only supply physical needs, but spiritual.

One of the greatest of these "spiritual" things is being able to love others. When I can look at my own children and other children with love and longing for their welfare, the "gift" of God is operant in my soul. When a friend is in need and I hurt for him and do all I can to help, God's gift is working in my heart. That love is spiritual in the fullest sense of the word, non-physical, but the working out of that love has to meet the physical need of the object of that love in a variety of ways. It may be a bed for the night, a meal, a hug, the loan of money, or being a good, caring, patient "listener." As James points out, it does no good, is hypocrisy in fact, if you know of someone in real need and fail to help, having the means to do so, and, instead, pronounce some meaningless, religious garbage in place of meeting the real, physical need.

So we meet the hypocrisy of the churches in pronouncing religious garbage from pulpit and pew trying to pass itself off as "preparing" the saints to meet the evil of the Beast. We are not hearing "sermons" that lead to direct action against evil, we are not hearing sermons that encourage good citizenship and electing good men to office, we are not hearing sermons or teaching that equip us to carry the sword to the real battlefield of the World, the Flesh and the Devil. We are subjected to pious phraseology that is trying to pass itself off as "relevant" in the face of real warfare!

As we watch Pat Robertson and T.B.N., Schuller et al., some are very smug in the attitude that "They" (those "sinners") are going to "get theirs" and all they have to do is "enjoy the show!" How very wickedly foolish. Are such "saints" really going to be prepared for the coming Bridegroom? Can such people really expect to hear: "Well done, thou good and faithful servant!"? I think not.

Senator John Seymour favors abortion and caters to the liberal "tax and spend, welfare-mentality" crowd. I like John but I have come to despise his "politics." I will pray, campaign, and hope for the elections of Bill Dannemeyer and Bruce Herschensohn. I pray for good men like Don Rogers who represent honestly the people who elected him.

I am writing a series of articles about education in my other publications. As a professing Christian, do you know anything about the silence of the churches during the Constitutional Convention? Do you know why, when our founding fathers grappled with the issue of slavery, they did not have the counsel of the churches and failed to heed Franklin's sound advice concerning this and the threat of Zionism?

Do you know the historical basis of the failure of the churches to address, in concert, such evil early on that led to the disaster of the Civil War, Scopes Trial and, more recently, the successes of O'Hare and the A.C.L.U.?

Folks, professing Christians are an abysmally, ignorant lot. It is an ignorance of such horrible dimensions and mien that it has led to the evils we live with today; including the evil of "racism." The churches; toothless, paper Tigers that engender scorn and ridicule rather than respect, let alone, the fear of the ungodly. Where now even those few that threatened great, imperial Rome that "turned the world upside down?"

A recent article by Ann Landers referred to the pronounced disrespect for the elderly in our society. I ask you, why are they deserving of respect; just because they have accomplished the tremendous feat of getting old? Of course not! As I wrote a short while back if there ever was a generation that could be justly accused of selling out the younger generation it that one that is now the "elderly." It is this new, elderly generation that invited the Beast in wholesale that is living off the inheritance of the former generation while refusing to provide for the new, have, in fact, spent the inheritance of its own children and grand-children.

God says that those that do not provide for their families are worse than infidels. What, do you suppose, does He have to say to this generation of elderly? What do you suppose they have to say to Him: "We went to church and did our best!" I don't think that is going to "fly."

Reaching back to the days of F.D.R. and before that, we can read of the failure, little by little, of the "elderly" to provide for the coming generation. What we have today is a generation that is sponging off a godly heritage and delivering, wholesale, our nation to the Devil and refusing to accept its own accountability. Respect for such elderly? Not on your life!

Schools, including Seminaries, reflect their societies and their values; if a younger generation knows neither "Joseph nor the God of Joseph" who is to blame? I know too many people who claim to be "Christian" who aren't even registered to vote! I know far too many who can quote Scripture who don't even know the name of their local congressman. If evil men in positions of leadership and authority think God is asleep or non-existent, that there is no one to confront their wickedness in any meaningful, realistic fashion, who is to blame? I would, once more, direct your attention to the pulpits of America and the failure of preceding "religious leadership."

We will gather in "worship," sing our hymns and listen to our pious, innocuous sermons, hearing, for the umpteenth time about the "spiritual" implications of some dusty tale of Old Testament glory, shake hands and go our ways deceiving ourselves with Noble Lies and Fairy-tales.

"Successful" religious authors will proliferate books on fund and membership raising, "How To" books on a variety of imagined spiritual warfare such as "Overcoming Stress in a Wicked World" all the while deluding ourselves that God's "magic wand" will accomplish His purpose in such a world without the same sacrifices and knowledge that the same "world" recognizes as needed for success in material matters.

God is far more practical and pragmatic than "professional religionists" give Him credit. He needs men and women to accomplish His work. But He needs men and women that are willing to pay the price, just as He has always shown to be the case. If you think for one moment we are going to sing and sermonize our way to victory, you are already under that "Strong Delusion!"

It's far past time to give an account, to admit our failure and get our hands "dirty" in real work, not religiosity. If John Seymour thinks he can countenance the murder of babies through abortion as a means of contraception and you don't write to him, you have been a party to murder. If you don't let your local congressman know you despise the new "Adult" bookstore that just opened up, you are aiding the enemy. In short, if you aren't even doing the little that you can do, just what is your excuse before God for letting your own nation, your own children, "go to the Devil?" All the hymn-singing, arm-waving and religious rhetoric in the world is not going to allow you to escape the judgment of God.

Bible-believing Christians are supposed to be the "Light and Salt" to an unbelieving world. Look at your own case and decide, ruthlessly, just what you are doing to deserve such a phrase being applied to you as an individual? If the New Reich is successful in our nation, will you blame others rather than accepting your part of the guilt? You know, if you know anything of God's Word, such an excuse will not do.

If necessary, confront the leaders of your church with the hypocrisy of not being actively involved with the real warfare. Ask your pastor to take an active stand against the real Devil, not the make-believe one of "religious, polite respectability." Ask him to take a stand with the real Jesus that pronounced such scathing words against the religious hypocrites of His time, the real Jesus that whipped the moneychangers and shamed those that "say and do not."

No real man or woman of God can be easy in their minds at simply "attending church" while a Godless generation is going to hell. None such can rest easy in their conscience while the vile and wicked walk on every side with impunity. "Stand up for Jesus?" Why the average churchgoer won't even stand up against pornography and an adulterous politician or neighbor effectively. In fact, divorce is so common in the churches today, one wonders if preachers even take Jesus' words about the vile thing seriously at all?

In over thirty years of church and religious work, I cannot even recall a single sermon preached, without compromise, against this evil that God says, categorically, He hates! We will tune in TV and radio "ministries" and deceive ourselves that, as long as the words and music are "religious," we are "feeding our souls." This trash only feeds lazy egos and the flesh and shames the same God we profess to "worship!" And Jesus made it pointedly clear the real prophets of God do not wear soft clothing and live in kings' palaces. Nor in my opinion do they try to be an imitation of Broadway and Hollywood!

Just how are the "saints" to get the dust off their Bibles, souls and minds and get into the real warfare? Simply by really believing the very things to which they give lip service. Jesus is real; He did real things like driving the moneychangers from the Temple and getting angry with hypocrites. He called real men to Himself who were not afraid to call a spade a spade.

His favorite expression of Himself as Son of Man should speak to our own hearts. He was a real man. He was not ashamed of His humanity and, in fact, boasted of it. If God Himself chose to do battle in the flesh, that is our calling. That, above all else, we should be able to relate to and if you cannot, just how do you perceive Him? Is He real to you or is He some "misty, religious, seeming profundity" that allows you an easy conscience in not doing real battle against real enemies in an all too real world of evil?

Go into the religious bookstores and see what is "selling." The great majority will have to do with "experiences." This is the charismatic trash that appeals to our desire for "reality." But it is a reality that denies the very evil we are called to expose and fight against. It denies the real face of the Beast that is in the very midst of the people of God.

God is not fooled by the gibberish-spouting, hand waving shameful exhibitions of "religious enthusiasm" any more than He is by the sedate, ever so respectful, meaningless, dead, formal piety of the "high churches" or "social correctness" of good Baptists.

Folks, it is going to take some educated Billy Sundays and Moodys to call God's people to repentance of their wickedness and "blind orthodoxy." But where are such men to be found? Can we sit idly by, deluded by the false sense that somewhere, somehow, He has the 7,000 standing by while we do nothing to hasten the day? I think not!

Next Sunday, as you gather to "worship," you ask yourself: "Is my church doing what God requires to confront real evil with an uncompromising Gospel? Is my church preparing real "Soldiers of the Cross" or are we "playing at church? Is there any real threat to me or mine in obeying God being represented by the leader in that pulpit or my "brethren" in these pews? Am I being prepared for a real battle against real evil or am I deluding myself in the comfort and safety of hypocritical pretense?" If you are truly honest before God, please let me know of your conclusion.

"Oh, politics is dirty; good Christians just shouldn't get involved with such a business. Can you imagine the trouble it would cause if our pastor was active in trying to get the scoundrels out of government and if we, as a congregation, were actually to support some good man for office? Why Rome might come and take away our nation (church)!"

Well, folks, just what kind of church do you want? One that is so intent on "playing it safe" that no one is at risk or one that gets the attention of the Devil and his crowd? You don't have to answer that; the answer is so obvious that it cries for God's judgment to begin at "His House."

Can you imagine the howls of the enemy's crowd if you put up a sign in front of your church: "Vote for -----!" Of course, you might lose your tax-exempt status. Bottom line: When the churches cannot stand for good men in government there is something wrong, not so much with that government, but with the churches.

That is one of the primary reasons that I openly advocate the removal of tax-exempt status for all religious enterprises. And that is just what they have become: Enterprises. It has made eunuchs of preachers and lay people alike. It has cost the churches credibility as they portray God and His Church as begging. It has married the churches to a system of evil that they should be actively opposing. Just what, do you suppose, will the cost be to regain that credibility? And just who, do you suppose, is willing to pay that cost? You? Your local church?

Now just suppose that I should decide to start circulating petitions to remove tax-exempt status for religious organizations. Suppose I take placard in hand and start a march on Washington or Sacramento to carry the message to the Halls of Power. Who would be the most likely to shoot me on the way? Those in the "world" or some "good Christian?" Sinclair Lewis knew.

Is this kind of thing necessary to expose the "wolves in sheep's clothing" that are clogging the pulpits and pews of America? YES! You might as well try to tell yourself that God doesn't really mean what He says about the righteous entering into life through much tribulation; deny the truth of what is required to get the job done He expects us to do as "Salt and Light." "Let others suffer for righteousness" is what you are really saying if you would only be honest before God.

You know, we are cursed with hundreds of churches where the following is a commonplace: A woman is unhappy with her husband. He just doesn't measure up to her expectations. Oh, he doesn't beat her or get drunk but she just isn't "happy" with her choice of a mate anymore. So, she sues for divorce. Her home church, if it expresses any disapproval, gets her nose out of joint and she goes down the block and finds one that will happily accept her as a qualified member in good standing. Why, they will even have special classes for those poor women (or men) who just couldn't get their marriages to "work." Finding such sympathy and understanding in large supply, why burden yourself unnecessarily with what God has to say about it?

The Enemy and his "churches" are readily available to any who think God doesn't mean what He says; that the wages of sin are, at worst, a slap on the wrist, not Death! So the murder of the innocent through adultery, divorce on demand, abortion as contraception together with homosexuality, lying, cheating, stealing, corrupt politicians find the "consolations of religion" readily available to them. But "good" Baptists and Presbyterians are so busy making "good" Baptists and Presbyterians that they just can't seem to find the time or mechanisms or means to confront "social problems." God help us!

Now it is patently and painfully obvious that the President, Willie Brown, John Seymour, Cranston, Keating, et al. have no reality of God or His Word in their lives. There isn't the slightest fear of God in them. And just how, do you suppose, is this situation to be turned around? By sitting comfortably and safely in our pews, listening to the fourth in a series on why God doesn't care for rude drivers or drinking hard liquor and smoking? Small wonder indeed that we are having our noses rubbed in every form of abomination and the churches have become a crude joke.

For those few of you who have the kind of faith that serves the real Gospel and believe God's Word, do you really want to see something done to regain what this nation has lost? Are you ready to pay the price of confronting the evil in your own church and home? Then get to work! The laborers are very few. But if enough get busy in doing what needs, desperately, to be done, I know it can happen. Unlike my friend Gary North, I don't believe God is reluctant or waiting for some "magic" moment to move men's hearts. It is the preaching of the Whole Gospel that moves men's hearts. The evil all about us testifies to the failure of the churches to confront that evil and tell the Truth!

Where were the churches, for example, when Anita Bryant was trying to stand against homosexuals as teachers; conspicuous by their absence. Why don't the politicians from Bush on down seem to realize that to talk about "morals, values, home and families" means a clear and uncompromising stand against perversion in order to be more than political rhetoric? Because the churches themselves are in such disarray and lack any clear, moral imperatives themselves!

The church leadership doesn't seem to realize that the battle is, largely, in the very political arena that they are "too good" to soil their hands with. The Church of Jesus Christ is supposed to represent God's view and Word on our lives; both individually and collectively as a nation.

Must the Church confront the evil of racial prejudice? Yes! But in order to do so, it must have a credible leadership. It doesn't. The Gospel cuts across racial lines and is the only thing that does so successfully. But the churches need the kind of leadership that can point out the kinds of evil, largely legislative, that promotes racial hatred, things like racial quotas in hiring, so-called "affirmative action" and many such like evils that only engender strife.

For example, I am an American and thank God for the fact. By "accident of birth" I am a Caucasian American and imbued with a Caucasian European culture. I don't want another culture forced down my throat by fiat of law. I want to choose my neighborhood and those with whom I associate as neighbors and friends.

If so-called "Mexican-Americans" want another culture imported to my America, I will resist that intrusion into my neighborhood. But if MAPA and others of Mexican ethnicity will band together to fight against illegal immigration of their "kind" I will begin to think of them as Americans. But not until they stop trying, largely by criminal means, to force me to bow to their unscrupulous, non-American, non-Christian, anti-white crusades to force me to dilute my own ideals and hopes for my children, to force "another gospel" on me that has only led to the kind of violence and crime we have just witnessed in L.A.

Can you see the churches taking a stand on this kind of issue? Neither can I. They will wring their hands and "pray" and let my nation go to hell by refusing to be accountable, and thus, credible, concerning real evil! But: "This is a hard saying, who can hear it?"

Before you jump on me with the cry of "Racist" you better consider the fact that the Gospel is not racist. It ignores the designation of "Jew or Gentile" and the preaching of the cross is not a "cultural distinctive." But, if a culture is antagonistic to the Truth of the Gospel, and most assuredly are, then conflict is bound to ensue; Mexican "Christianity" whether imbued with Roman Catholicism and superstitions of the Mexican culture or of the Satanic Charismatic variety is most definitely anti-Christ. Zionism and the Jewish religion is anti-Christ ever bit as much as Mormonism, Jehovah's Witnessism or Christian Science and the World Wide Church of God and Moonyism. The charismatics and their TV "shows" and radio "ministries" are largely to blame for inviting every kook and hair-brained scheme that calls itself "Christian" into the fold wholesale. In most cases it looks like the old show: "Can You Top This" as they vie against one another to see who can come up with the biggest lie or "experience." Utterly shameful! And God is going to judge this practice that makes a mockery of the Gospel, His Word, the Holy Spirit and Jesus!

I want to thank John MacArthur, Jr. of Grace Community Church in Sun Valley. John and I were at Biola/Talbot at the same time. I'm sure "Uncle Charles" Feinberg remembers us well. My personal thanks to John for his book: CHARISMATIC CHAOS. I strongly urge all of you to get a copy. You will be amazed and not a little angry at what is going on in charismatic "churches" in the name of God that you may not be aware of. I have been fighting the battle so long against this damnable, satanic heresy that I feared I was alone. It is a tremendous relief for someone of John's stature in the Christian community to say the things someone beside me is willing to say. My heartfelt gratitude to you John MacArthur and my applause for having the courage to do what needed, desperately, to be done in confronting this evil, particularly as portrayed by Paul Crouch and his "hitmen" on T.B.N. If only his viewers knew the vile language Crouch and his cohorts use against those that disagree with their heresy they might stop supporting this charlatan and his network. But we have to keep in mind the fact that Pat Robertson, Jimmy Swaggart, Jim Baker, et al. are all cut from this same, heretical and shameful cloth.

Is it any wonder the world ridicules and laughs at what represents itself as "Gospel Ministries?" The ridiculous, shameful antics and fairy-tales of the likes of Oral & Son, Copeland, Hagan and the oily, smooth Schullers and Hayfords, the whole, damned, lying bunch. And I don't mean "damned" as in epithet, I mean Damned as in liars with their part in the Lake of Fire. And what of the Bible translators of the NIV who perpetuate heresy by dishonestly translating the word for "languages" as "tongues" just to sell more of their Bibles as an accommodation to the charismatics?

With a Ph. D. in Human Behavior I can easily discern hysteria and understand both its need and manifestations. It is altogether too easy to dismiss the silliness of the charismatics as simple, ego-stroking and bad "acting." If their lying shenanigans were for that purpose only, that would be one thing. But, since they are blaming God the Holy Spirit for such outrageousness, bringing shame to my Lord, I am their implacable foe!

I also want to thank John for his book: THE GOSPEL ACCORDING TO JESUS which helped so much in combating the heresy of "Easy Believism" which I have also been attacking for so many years. But it remains for good men to address themselves to the hard issue of women in the churches. I deal with this in my books but, so far, others seem fearful of it; and, for good reason. You simply cannot take the subject up without agreeing with me that we desperately need a New Systematic Theology, a "New Council of Jerusalem."

The "fundamental" problem is "Fundamentalism." I am a Fundamentalist in the sense that I believe the Spirit of God moves throughout Scripture and what is true speaks to my heart and spirit. Believing this, I read that women are to keep silent in ALL the congregations of the saints; that it is DISGRACEFUL for a woman to speak in the church, no woman is to be ordained to the ministry or as deacons or elders, that if they have questions they are to ask their husbands and be in submission to them. I Corinthians chapter 14. I Timothy chapters 2 and 3. Titus chapters 1 and 2.

I know of no fundamental church where the Word of God is followed in this respect. The excuses for not believing God means what He says in this regard are legion. But, invariably, it comes down to this: Spineless Men!

Whether the excuse is to promote one's own wife in a leadership role, to make "peace" in the family or the church, to accommodate yourself to the customs and mores of the culture it all amounts to the same thing; flagrant disregard for God's Word on the subject.

It was said early on of the "tongues" movement that if the women would cease doing it, the movement would soon cease to move. Too true! If women play a prominent role beyond the will and express Word of God in the churches they do so at the cost of obedience to God and to the shame of spineless men.

In view of the foregoing, it is not surprising that the Apostle Paul and I don't enjoy the friendship of the churches today, particularly the women and those hirelings in the pulpits. People don't pay good money for having their noses rubbed in their sins or for "philosophical" treatises that are easily discounted as the ravings of a madman; but if I speak the truth? If God really does mean what He says?

Just consider the childishness of the whole charismatic movement and its adherents and dervish-like devotees. *Sola Scriptura* has never been enough for such fruitcakes. It has to be the Bible and "something else" to satisfy their egos and fleshly desires. "Plain Manna" will never suffice for these people any more than it did for those that died in the wilderness because of their rebellion against God and His Word.

You would think such childishness would have passed away with the complete canon of Scripture. Founding of the Church was miraculous in every sense of the word. But it WAS founded and the greater work of carrying the Gospel to the ends of the earth, discipling and training others in the work was to begin. The churches were to teach, preach, disciple, help, encourage, give hope, confront evil and prepare the saints to do battle, to take care of widows and orphans. The churches were to be the "Light and Salt" to a darkened world.

What do we have in stead? The Vineyard and Third Wave Movements, Pat Robertson, the 700 Club, Paul Crouch and T.B.N., inspired and enabled by Satan and his evil servants, all paving the way for the Man of Sin with his lying delusions and "miracles (lying wonders)!" Just what is it, you have to ask yourself, that these lying charlatans are asking us to believe in- God or themselves? The answer is so obvious it stinks to high heaven!

It is no accident that the multiplying of these false "gospels" is accompanied with so much bad news around the world and in this country. Just today I read in the papers what I have been saying for years, California is bankrupt! But I have carried the bad news further by saying our nation is bankrupt, both financially and morally.

Can it be so surprising that God must send His judgment against such an evil and adulterous generation? You wonder at the utter blindness of the leadership that is ushering in this time of evil to come upon us. Talk about closing the barn door after the horse is stolen! Now the polls are showing the closing of our borders to be a good idea. Cutting welfare is a good idea. Just when, do you suppose, will all those "Hitlerian Solutions" I have been warning about for years will all become "good" ideas? God help us!

The main problem, folks, goes back to the Garden and all that was involved in God's judgments and commands in regard to original sin. If this were understood, the path of the churches would be plain once more. Since I cover this in my books, I won't go into it here. Suffice it to say, the "saints" are impotent due to ignorance and the failure to believe ALL that God has said. If they really believed and understood, could any of them rest easy in their pews in the face of such evil as that which confronts us today? I think not!

Bottom line: Professing "Christians," lacking any reality of the Lord and His Word in their lives, chase after the World, the Flesh, and the Devil. These unholy three will give them all the "experiences" their foolish, darkened hearts could desire. All the legitimate facts in the world will not convince someone who has had an "experience" of "tongues, healings, and miracles" will convince them it is of anything but the Lord. The alternative would be to confess their sinful actions and delusions and for that, they lack the character and sincere faith in the Lord that would be required.

I have to wonder if there are any leaders in California that can equate what has bankrupted our state with the situation confronting tiny Oildale; probably not. Maybe they should read the article in April's Reader's Digest: "California: Paradise Lost?" You don't have to be a "Rocket Scientist" to figure this one out. If so-called "minorities" are to dictate terms to Americans, and the so-called "leadership" seems to be intent on this, all is most certainly lost and there is no hope of any kind of revival- religious, moral, industrial or political!

Dan Quayle was absolutely right. Murphy Brown cannot be allowed to dictate our values if there is any hope of survival. But if we think for one moment we can preach "values" without confronting perversion we are doomed. Perverts aren't acceptable in the military but it is ok for Cheney to say they are acceptable in the population at large? Just who is kidding whom here?

Make no mistake; the perverts are not acceptable with God, with me or with anyone else who has any decency about them. They destroy all decent values; they destroy children and are an outright blight and abomination to any nation or culture! The flaunting of their perversion and attempts at legislative "protection" and "equality" are a stench in the nostrils of God Almighty and no nation has ever escaped God's judgment against this abomination. We are no exception and I will fight this stench till I die!

Neither can we mock God in our attitude toward fornication, adultery and divorce. There can be no legitimate attempts at regaining our values as a nation, to redeeming the "Family," as long as these things continue to be treated lightly, of no consequence. As long as they are, so long is our nation at peril of God's judgment. We have no future hope until a genuine revival, led by repentant leaders in the churches and government takes place! It is a Strong Delusion of Satan to think there is any other "road" to our salvation as a nation!

AN OPEN LETTER TO PEROT AND BUSH

I have been writing for some time about the circumstances that are leading our nation to disaster. In such a short time, the people of America are aroused to the possibility that a "White Knight" may be on the horizon. The things that have angered and frustrated the middle class, largely Caucasian, make them culpable of believing anything that seems to promise a "way out" of our present, miserable conditions.

Mr. President, you have lied to us and, seemingly, ignored the conditions that have led us to this place. You seem insulated from the things that Americans are suffering. Our nation is in grave peril and you don't seem to notice. You and you alone, bear the brunt for this. Instead of acting in America's interests, you have appeared aloof and more concerned for other nations than ours.

Mr. Bush, you are a well educated and intelligent man, politically "seasoned," I must, therefore, credit you for some plan to keep from becoming a one-term president; your connections as the head of the single most powerful position in the world leads to some interesting possibilities.

Your part in the Reagan/Hostage drama, the Iran/Contra scam, your ties to the Trilateral Commission, the S&L bail-out, BCCI, your lying about raising taxes and so much more we probably don't even know about make you, in my opinion, a very dangerous man if you feel pressed to, in your own words, "Do all that is necessary to be re-elected!"

Could you possibly mean by this statement that you purposely did not "get" Hussein- leaving him in power to use him at a later date?

Is it better, in your plans, to let the poor and minorities kill each other off and tax them and the vanishing middle class to the point of virtual slavery so you and your "kind" can assume your "rightful" place as "divinely appointed" dictators?

Quite frankly, Mr. President, by your own words and actions, I have to believe you capable of any actions that will preserve your presidency. There are historical precedents aplenty for such things. Power does things to even those that might begin with noble character and motives. As the most powerful leader in the world, head of the most powerful nation in the world, just what "rabbit" do you plan to pull out of the hat to preserve your position?

Mr. Perot; you have made quite a "splash" on the American scene. You are in the enviable position of appearing in the right place, at the right time and in the right circumstances. Pundits from George Will to you name them have already posed the possibilities of your presidency. I have brought up a few in previous essays that I won't belabor further.

If the election were held today, you might now be president. The American people are more than ready for a change in government and your policy statements and past actions seem to indicate that you know the mood of the people.

As a "self-made man" who pulled himself up by his bootstraps you idealize the American Dream of personal responsibility and "doing it yourself." But any American who knows the "system" knows you had to step over a lot of "bodies" to get where you are!

You know how to be ruthless in obtaining a goal. Will you practice the same ruthlessness in gaining your goals for America? You are expert in "dictatorship" tactics but what of our Republican form of government, our Constitution and Bill of Rights; are you ready to twist these to the concept of what needs to be done to regain America's place in history? Can you, like Hitler and Stalin, do what seems to be needed to bring "order" to America?

Somehow, your background, philosophy and tactics lead me to believe that you, like Mr. Bush, will do what you think is best and "To Hell" with us, the "great unwashed!" When men like you and Mr. Bush "know" what is so "obviously best" for the people, you are not likely to let the niceties of "rights" get in your way. Granting that you would have to break a few eggs in making your omelet, such as encouraging abortion, sealing off our national borders and "troublesome" areas and doing house-to-house searches for drugs, etc., are you willing to bring "order" at the cost of Constitutional rights? I think you are. Realistically, and you are a preeminent realist in obtaining your goals; I don't think you will see any other alternative.

As a "maverick" Christian, I am not naive enough to think we are going to have any thing like a "national revival" since that would take our leaders turning to God in repentance first. Given the condition of religion in American, chaos in the churches and an utter lack of credibility on their part, my heart goes out to anyone in government who earnestly tries to do what is right.

No matter who is at the "helm," I foresee that people like me will have to engage in Civil Disobedience in facing the injustices rampant throughout our nation. As with Thoreau I may wind up saying: "I might have resisted forcibly with more or less effect, might have run 'amok' against society; but I preferred that society should run 'amok' against me, it being the desperate party."

I have chosen to face the evil and confront those that would constrain me to belong to their "odd fellow's society" rather than retire to my trout stream and tell the whole gutless lot to "go to hell!" But, again, as Thoreau so well pointed out: "...wherever a man goes, men will pursue and paw him with their dirty institutions..."

The "dirtiest" by far are those institutions which would enslave us to the present system of evil and make us criminals because men like myself would rather die for the liberty our forefathers sacrificed for rather than bow to any system that would mock those ideals which are the only hope for our children.

I am pledged to those ideals of personal liberty and responsibility for which this nation, once, stood so proudly, giving light and hope to all other nations and which has been so shamefully betrayed by the past, few generations.

Lacking any "crystal ball" and not given to examining "chicken entrails" or offering up incense, I can only work and pray for the best.

But it doesn't take a crystal ball to figure out the future of our planet if the present growth of population, especially third world, continues, if we continue to pollute our environment, if we continue to eliminate forests and despoil and subvert water resources. An Apocalypse Now is just around the corner for our earth.

The greater part of the June issue of Newsweek is devoted to these problems; the "Earth Summit" in Rio, sponsored by the UN, will spell out the rape of our planet. The conspicuous "users," America, Russia, China and the ECC, will be singled out for "special" attention. And what will the consensus show? Why, of course! The "user" nations are to give all the help they can to those poor "third-worlders" who are raping their own nations, who will not practice birth control, who have no choice, it seems, but to continue like human weeds to breed at an ever increasing scale, more "needy" mouths to feed and destroy the environment.

Since I talk about this scenario in my books, I will only point out the obvious fact that it is becoming increasingly clear, to even the most obtuse, that "Strong Medicine" is needed to "correct" these other nations. Is the UN going to tell the U.S., Russia, China and the ECC what to do? Not on your life! The most practical solution, which I am sure Mr. Bush and Mr. Perot would agree, is to direct our energies at enslaving these "abusing" and ignorant nations. A preliminary might be to kill a couple of billion off in "nice little wars." The "saviors" can agree on the division of real estate, just as Hitler and Stalin did, and wait their chance to do one another in at a future date.

It will take great strength of will for the kind of leadership that is "necessary" to "save the world." But, somehow, I can't help but believe that such leadership is already waiting to fulfill its destiny. For a fuller explanation of this doomsday picture, get my books. Will our nation's new "leader" have such "strength of will?" I think so! Apart from Christ, what other choice is there to Anti-Christ?

Sam Clemens had an irreverent genius for truth: "God made idiots for practice and then he made school boards!" Sam could, and did, add politicians to that list. Will the "idiots" prevail? As long as "We the People" don't vote and confront the evil all around us, yes! Are you registered to vote? If not, why not? Those that don't vote have automatically given the Devil their ballot.

CHAPTER THIRTEEN

CHRISTIAN PERSPECTIVE

JULY 1992

Psalm 9:19,20

Its laws, art, music and literature define a nation. It was my privilege to know a kinder, gentler America. The past fifty years has been a time of destruction of those romantic sentiments that shaped my character and hopes for my children.

Music and literature have been so much a part of my life that it is only with an effort of will that I can force myself to examine this theme objectively. For example, the old musicals of Rogers and Hammerstein like "Oklahoma" did not force me to confront the ugliness of "reality," did not force me to a distinction between the grim reality of human nature and the romantic ideals with which I spent my youth. I play the sound track albums of Oklahoma, Showboat, The Sound of Music, Camelot, My Fair Lady and I am still transported to those ideals of romance that such music and plots shaped in my own character.

When I am feeling low and depressed, I can select from a multitude of musical offerings that will renew my faith in love and romance, of people that can be loving and do for one another. The magic of such music cannot be overemphasized in its mood-altering capability. One of the great tragedies of our young people is the loss of such musical poetry and the gentleness and hope it inspired.

There is so much that is noble in our literature of times past that it often is joy to simply reflect on some of the masterpieces it has been my good fortune to know. The intimacy that comes with heart meeting heart's needs in good and sensitive writers is a blessing of God. Such a writer was Richard Henry Dana.

Dana had all the privileges of the "to the manor born;" his grandfather had been the first American minister to Russia and, later, became Chief Justice of the Supreme Court of Massachusetts. His father was a noted man of letters. Dana himself was Harvard graduated and, under Lincoln, was appointed U.S. District Attorney for Massachusetts. He made a meritorious reputation in international law, particularly maritime law. After the war, not approving of Johnson's "Reconstruction," he returned to private practice.

But, as you may have guessed, praiseworthy as his accomplishments in these areas were, they are not what bring this most fair-minded man before my store of precious memories. It was his masterpiece: "Two Years Before the Mast."

Incredibly, none of my professors had recommended Dana to me. I can't even recall how, so many years ago, I came to read this classic. But I was always finding things to read that seemed to have escaped the priorities of Litt. 502, etc.

Once in a while you chance across something in reading of the classics that focuses your attention on the peculiar circumstances of your own, contemporary problems, something that ignites a slumbering spark of recognition and you exclaim: "That's the Truth!" And, in many cases, the discovery is of such a nature you find that most sought and precious pearl of heart speaking to heart, of the genius of that elder's phraseology that with the magic of language, transcends the intervening years with the freshness of new discovery of old treasure. Such was this most worthy man's gift to me.

Dana, while a very young man, took time and interrupted his studies to make a sea voyage. But, with the idealism of youth, decided to do so as a common seaman. It is his vivid description of these two years, refusing the privileges of his station in life, as a working, ordinary sailor, that so speaks to the hearts and minds of all those that aspire to good character, fairness and wisdom as well as adventure.

There is no question that his choice shaped all that character of Dana that was of so much importance in his pleading for the causes of the oppressed before the courts of Massachusetts and the U.S. Supreme Court that led to his reputation in the courts of England as well. Here was no "lawyer," but, rather, a man who "sold out" to those "Higher Laws" so eloquently stated in our own Declaration of Independence, of the hopes and aspirations of all men regardless of the most humble circumstances of their lives due to accident of birth.

I could wish that all men were of the nobility and lofty purpose of Dana, that our leadership was of the same "stuff" that molded the character of such a man but, unhappily, we have moral "pygmies" on every hand. However, indeed, such a judgment may be, perhaps, too harsh in respect to what such men have been cheated of in opportunity to mold such character.

During the eighteen hundreds, it was still possible to "Go West," still possible to wrest opportunity from an often grudging soil whose rewards were still given those of fierce independence and determined perseverance. We still had enough of a moral nation and heritage, enough of unspoiled wilderness, to present the kind of challenges that produce men like Dana.

In nothing do our children suffer such tragic loss as in the stupid, greedy blunderings of Big Brotherism which has betrayed them, robbed them of any hope of making their own way by doing for themselves, by government's stealing of personal property; The Land. In too many areas, you have to get a "building permit" to put up a simple patio cover. In some areas, you can't plant a tree without the "blessing" of government. "Own your own home," even if you had any hope of paying off the mortgage, is a cruel joke. You don't own the property- the government and the bank owns it.

Fragmented Russia is now having to deal with our own harsh reality; without a fair, disciplined and organized system of government, one that provides for its posterity the young people are dropping out of school to go to work. When jobs are not available, they are turning to gangs and crime. Like us, the Russians are losing an entire generation of young people, the "terminally ill" generation who are choosing guns over school, who bring their guns to school. And why not; schools are now in the business of turning out criminals, not educating the young.

We're going to "teach" economics to people who can't afford insurance for their cars?

The hunter is always better prepared than his "prey."

Our "growth industries," as I warned some years ago, are welfare and prisons. Medical and Social Security are going to be "dealt with!" What are we going to do with our elderly? Are we going to kill them?

California, a bankrupt state, will pay its bills with IOUs. But the taxpayers are going to "ante up" to rebuild (reward) Watts?

Auto insurance is 80 billion dollars a year. You can only wonder what the price tag would be if half the California drivers (mostly Black and Brown) were not going without. The 400 billion dollar Federal deficit could be cleared up by each state giving 10 billion dollars. But California is already behind by over 10 billion. And what state could possibly afford the extra 10 billion?

We can't pay the bill by taxing the wealthy. This is only political rhetoric. They could, at best, only contribute about two per cent of what would be needed. It is the preponderance of people like those Pete Wilson just "hired" at enormous salaries, making his own unique contribution to an already exorbitantly bloated bureaucracy, together with social services, medical care, insurance, taxes, social security that are eating us alive. Caring for the elderly, the poor and incapables together with the services they have been given on the backs of taxpayers, illegals, lawyers, these, not the wealthy, are the problem.

Cross burnings, abortion and Swastikas are ok but prayer and Bible reading in schools are not? The Supreme Court has rendered a "kind of" decision on abortion. Even the Court seems to realize, like Pete Wilson, Perot and Clinton, that abortion is one of the key elements of controlling unwanted, largely Negro and Mexican, population. Murdering babies by giving women "choice" is the obvious answer rather than court mandated birth control for human weeds. Why should the kind of High Court and Congress we have do any different than Hitler and Stalin? The "leadership" certainly knows they can count on the women. They depend on the inherent selfishness of women who "want their cake and eat it too!" Far be it to ask women to be responsible for the part they play in the "breeding process." So much for the nonsense of "Mother Love!"

I do not wax as eloquent as Philip Wylie on the subject of "Momism" (his word), and I certainly believe he was exceedingly handicapped by his egocentrism and extreme prejudices. But if his point is taken for the germ of truth it represented, it has to be admitted that his rancor was not without foundation on the subject. Unhappily, his vanity precluded a more objective view and brought, with no little justification, the appellation of misogynist. I have to attribute his lack of a continued following on both his exalted opinion of himself and his vilification of Jesus.

But the Court's decision that a wife need not inform her husband of an intended abortion? Well, men, you already know the term "marriage" means she gets the "gold" and you get the "shaft;" now the highest court of the land pounds another nail into the coffin of marriage. You have no rights at all in the "little woman's" decision to murder your baby! In fact, she legally doesn't even have to tell you about it, let alone let you take part in the decision. For whatever cold comfort men can derive from the court's decision it is oriented toward "genocide," not intended, even though that is one of the "practical" results, of further "sticking it" to men.

Men already have gotten the message, thanks to the "equality" movement, that they are some unmentionable substance on the end of a stick when it comes to women. But, historically, since women typically don't know what they want anyhow, once they get what they think they wanted, they will blame men for not giving them more of it, whatever it is, or their not being satisfied with the results. Men learn rapidly, in such circumstances, the old adage: "There is no pleasing a woman!"

But I reserve my most caustic remarks and loathing for those adulterers who sneak in the back door to another man's wife. Not being man enough to find their own woman, they prey on the easy seduction of silly women who are easily flattered by any man's attentions to their "charms." I have had enough experience with others "plowing with my heifer" to know whereof I speak. Such "men" will always be guilty of the greater sin and deserve God's judgment of such evil. AIDS is just another reminder of God's attitude toward immorality in any form. And, whether due to prostitution, adultery or perversion in some other form, as God says in Romans, they get what they deserve and I have no pity for them. But the children, the innocent that pay an undeserved price for the filthy selfishness of the flesh, for divorce and other perversions, they are the ones that will rise in judgment against the pervert, against an adulterous generation!

I applaud Dan Quayle's attack on the immorality of our nation and, particularly, the extreme immorality of the so-called "Entertainment" media. It takes the satanic "news" media to make so much of an incorrect spelling of "potato" while an entire society is going to hell in a basket. I like Dan Quayle. I began liking him when he took a stand for reform among his "own;" Lawyers. That took real guts. I have to admit, of the poor choices presented, if Quayle were running, I would vote for him. But, Mr. Quayle, do you know your history well enough to act on the inescapable fact that no nation in history has ever survived the moral holocaust of the combination of Homosexuality, Divorce, Adultery and Abortion? Yet, that is the "approved" status of our own government and Supreme Court!

It's fascinating to watch as a man opens fire on a court in Texas because of a divorce action. Expect this scene to be re-enacted at an accelerating rate. This guy was a lawyer. He knew what the score was and gave vent to the feelings of multiplied millions who haven't, yet, picked up their ropes, bombs or guns against an Evil Empire. But they will! I have warned you greedy, incompetent, selfish bureaucrats repeatedly that you are going to find yourselves in the crosshairs of the "New Minutemen" and this is only a foretaste of what is to come. You can only betray and steal the hopes of the people for so long before the natural cause and effect law that always comes to pass comes down on your own heads. And, there is no hole deep enough for you to hide, not even your plush "bomb shelter" so close to the seat of our nation's betrayal. It may yet be years in the coming, but God's judgment is not slack as men count slackness. When it comes it will be swift and final.

The Lord continues to remind us He is in charge. The recent earthquakes are a good example of our limitations and His power. There are few things that put this in perspective like the earth heaving up and down under your feet, when that which we take so for granted as being Terra Firma becomes Jell-O instead of Firma.

Of the many lies being spread by the enemies of my America, one of the worst revolves around so-called "Bilingual Education." Invariably, bilingual education means Spanish. The lie is that Americans are supposed to put up with foreigners coming into our country and we are expected to learn their language, not them learning ours! In what other nation would such a stupid thing be tolerated? You can bet your life that if I wanted to live in

Mexico, I would have to learn Mexican. English is the language of Commerce. The lie says that Americans should be multi-lingual (meaning Spanish, of course) because foreign language is so important in most other nations (except Mexico).

You will find no stronger advocate of teaching foreign language than me. In few other disciplines is there such opportunity for real challenges to learning. Learning a foreign language builds self-esteem, it teaches you much of the grammatical mechanics of your native tongue. If it were up to me, it would still be a requirement for a high school diploma.

The lie is that such teaching should be in Spanish! If it were not for welfare and illegal immigration, there would not be such emphasis on this language. Every time I see a help-wanted add that says: "Bilingual preferred," I want to throw up because I know they mean Spanish and I know why; more of our tax dollars "at work!"

It is interesting to note, now that "Incumbent" has reached the status of a four-letter word, how folks are viewing politics and politicians. There is nothing like death or poverty to focus your attention on priorities. If Ice T and Souljah had any integrity they would be rapping: "Dust the fat cats (Time Warner) and politicians," not policemen. But, Negroes and Mexicans know, taught by the Carpetbaggers, Scalawags, Copperheads and other Rascals, that politicians like Willie Brown, Rangel and a host of others are their "friends." Who else is making the decisions that allow minorities and illegals to live off the backs, sweat and labor of the taxpayers? At least Mr. Bush and a few others are taking exception to such lyrics.

My old school chum, Russell, came over with his tractor and cleared the weeds and provided a channel so I won't flood out when the Lord does send rain. California is entering its sixth year of draught. So far, 1992 is proving to be the worst year on record for disasters: Flooding, Riots, Earthquakes, Draught and Bankruptcy. Imagine the State paying its bills with IOUs!

Yet, Russ and I, exemplifying the true "Can Do" Americanism that still thrives in some of us good ol' boys, loaded the cabin and moved it ourselves to my new location in Bodfish; proving we are still not too old to cut the mustard. In this spot, I can still watch as the fading twilight turns the trees and hills into soft, then sharp, silhouettes in the clear air and I begin looking for our earliest and most easily discernible constellation, Ursa Major (Big Dipper), to appear overhead.

My first night in the place, I was sitting and reading by kerosene lamp when a mouse strolled in the door as if he owned the place. In my surprise I said, "Get out of here!" He got. Some of these little varmints, like government, once they get their snouts in the trough, eat and destroy more than they are worth. Too bad it's so much trouble to get a hunting license for them (the bureaucrats, not the mouse).

Firing up the water heater was interesting. The place had been abandoned for about a year and when I lit off the heater, assorted spiders and two lizards came bailing out of the contraption. I squashed the spiders, black widows, and caught the lizards for relocation to a more suitable environment.

That evening, the largest cricket I have seen in some time came in to keep me company while I was reading. Him, I left alone. I enjoy cricket music and they don't eat much. Had a heck of a time with the stove; the resident black widows gave me a run for the money but I finally managed to discomfit them. Woke up the next morning to find one had kept company with me in the corner of the bedroom; squashed the uppity bugger proper. Lest you take exception to my crusade against black widows, ground squirrels and rattlesnakes, what can you expect from someone for whom having a flush toilet and padded toilet seat is "having it all!"

A curious thing; the Planning Department tells me that if I saw the cabin in half, I can keep both halves on the property without a permit or prohibitively expensive foundations? Seems there is a ten by twelve roof area limit on auxiliary structures. The cabin, with the attached screen porch, is ten by twenty. So I'll wind up with two ten by tens instead of a ten by twenty. Ah, the infinite "wisdom" of the government. There are times when I'm tempted to eat a kit fox or spotted owl just to get even.

Have you heard the one about Tyler Texas experimenting with "No Plea-bargain" courts? Now that should be really interesting. I'll keep you all posted on this noble attempt.

And here's a really good one! It seems Kern County may lead the nation in Civil Disobedience (it's sure about time some county did)! Because of the insane "Entitlement Programs" which the state is forcing on the counties, Kern leaders are telling the state to "shove it" and "take us to court! There just aren't any more cookies in the jar!" Go for it Kern County. I take my hat off to you; makes me proud to be a Kern Countian. When "geldings" in government surround us, the schools and churches, it is a breath of fresh air when someone behaves like they have some manhood left. Keep up the good work, Dan Quayle. I'm for you!

Judges are finally saying what I have been saying about traffic tickets; they are being used to help close the budget gap for cities and counties. The paramount problem is that this "system" preys, primarily, on those that can least afford it- the poor. The poor drive old cars that need repair and are easy targets for the cops. Whether a "Conspiracy" or not, the phasing out of leaded fuel with no satisfactory substitute dooms the old cars in any event. Remember my warning about an evil system that is directed at putting the poor afoot? They cannot afford insurance or repairs. The exorbitantly high cost of tickets is forcing more and more of them to opt for jail time in lieu of payment. This is really insane! This forces the taxpayer to support those that don't pay the citation. More evidence of our two-tiered society and one that will have an ever-burgeoning "criminal" population, like marijuana smokers, based not on actual crime but on the inability to pay registration, insurance, repairs and traffic tickets! The "success" of this methodology is to force more and more of the poor to "stay in their place," the crime-ridden ghettos and barrios. And get this! The EPA is going to make it impossible to get the old cars "smogged." In California, the cost is going to go up to $450 for "repairs" to meet certification. But all you poor folks that are going to give up the cars, like my '69 Dodge, take heart; walking is good for you and builds character! Just ask the people who are making these decisions, like the seatbelt and helmet laws, for our own "good."

One of the "Big Lies" of the system is the "poor teacher." I have written so much on this subject that I won't belabor it here. Suffice it to say, in sum, teachers are grossly over-paid! Having spent some twenty years in education I know whereof I speak. The typical teacher works about six hours a day, 7 months per year. He gets ten, paid "sick days," ten days assorted holidays, two weeks Christmas vacation, one weak Easter vacation and a smattering of "in-service" days. The typical California teacher gets a benefit, retirement and insurance package many doctors would envy. Medical insurance covers everything from a hangnail to you name it together with dental and eye care. The average salary of a California teacher, including benefits, comes to about $65,000 per year and his hourly rate figures about $175 per hour. Not bad for a mere B.A. and basket-weaving courses. Teachers, thus, are the most scandalously over-paid "baby sitters" in our nation. And in nothing is this so scandalously true as in the area of so-called "Special Education," what I have been calling Education's equivalent of the S&L gravy train.

My last year as a "contract employee" of education, I was a Resource Specialist for Stanislaus County. One of my schools was Robert's Ferry. A small, rural school, the setting seemed idyllic. When I first arrived at the school, I discovered the principal had hired a Filipino Aide for the Resource program. The problem was that this aide, while fluent in English, had trouble with some pronunciations. This was a disastrous thing for the very young children who already had problems that had led to their placement in the program.

Now you would have thought that the principal would have recognized this fact before he hired this young man. Not so. He just needed a "warm body" to fulfill his "obligation" to the county. Even after I arrived and pointed this out to the principal, he was unable to fire the aide and the resulting storm of attempting to do so fractured the whole community, leading to picketing parents and news camera crews. Being in charge of the program, I caught all the resulting flack from the county Big Wigs who thought I should have kept out of it. Silly me. Imagine my making a fuss about an aide who should never have been hired to begin with because of his confusing the children due to his accent and improper pronunciations. The crowning indignity was the principal's attempt to enlist my aid in, not only trying to correct his mistake, but, trying to fire a teacher who came to the defense of the aide! It made for a disastrous year.

Thus, I can easily commiserate with the people in Westfield Massachusetts who are facing the cries of "racism" in attempting to point out the obvious fact that a teacher who has trouble with a foreign accent should not be trying to teach young children the intricacies of the English language. "Stupid" you say! And I strongly agree. Yet I have encountered this stupidity throughout my education career. It is not unlike having the coach teach math and biology, an all too common fact in the schools. Why? Because the schools cannot get credentialed teachers in the sciences so they simply plug in a warm body and call it "education." Fewer than 25 percent of our teachers in the hard science areas are actually credentialed for these classes.

It is most gratifying to see Honig indicted and ordered to stand trial. The judge has rightly defined it as a "...significant and complex case." If only some legislator had the guts to use some of my own experiences in education, he could cut to the heart of the matter and make public the extreme abuses in the system that has robbed our state of an education for our children. But, such is not likely to happen. Will they ever see the obvious fallacy that continuing to ask the same people who created the problems, those with worthless Ed. D.'s and other assorted "experts" in education, for solutions, they are fighting a losing battle?

One of the gravest problems in the schools is the preponderance of women in the job (note I do not call it a "profession." There is nothing professional about education). It is estimated that women make up about 83 percent of the total school staffing. I have written about this and point out, once more, that teaching is an emasculating job for men. Hence, not many want the job. The problem is that children thusly lack male roll models, particularly in the inner cities, where they are desperately needed.

But teaching is a "wimp" job. It has catered for so long to those that have become drones, sucking on the public tit, that very few self-respecting men who thinks like a man will have anything to do with it. Confronting this "woman-dominated, limp-wristed" approach to so-called education always brought about my greatest difficulties in the schools. I fought this battle for years. Invariably, the men who became administrators in the schools where

I worked would work out their frustrations by attacking those like me who refused to knuckle under and "put on an apron."

The school boards are no better. Again, they are female dominated and suffer accordingly. Hence, the opprobrium of Clemens that God made idiots for practice then He made school boards (together with school administrators and building inspectors). This, together with the fact that there are no sensible qualifications for the task of being on the board makes them susceptible to the kinds of abuses we are constantly reading about. They are "rubber stamps" for all the mischief done by useless, embezzling superintendents who haven't the haziest idea, like Honig, of what the real world is all about! But they know the "system" well enough to steal the money.

Are women really so silly as to expect to be treated like "one of the guys" in the military? I can't believe it. Yet, if the "Tail Hook" scandal is any example, they continue to want their cake and eat it too. Of course there is no excuse for men to treat women in such a shameful manner. But, as I have warned repeatedly, the nature of the "Beast" in both men and women is not going to change. If you try to force an unnatural environment on the role of men and women, expect an impossible problem with only "solutions" that will paralyze the function of each. The insanity of "equality" rather than "value and compatibility of differences" will continue to be evidenced in every attempt to circumvent God's order.

Isn't it a shame that those Iraqi soldiers refused to treat those two women like soldiers instead of women? But, without the uniform, it was altogether too obvious that they were women! Ladies, if you insist on "talking the talk," you better be prepared to "walk the walk!" No Moslem is going to treat you like anything but a woman according to their culture and religion; only the emasculated, American male is subject to such nonsense as a thoroughly emasculating "equality!" And yet, women complain everywhere I go that "real" men are hard to find. Another case of their not being satisfied and the impossibility of trying to satisfy a demand that is completely contrary to God's Word. God plainly says that men are to RULE their families, not put it to a vote! Of course, our national doom was sealed when women were given the vote by hirelings in the pulpit and other assorted, spineless men who put the sword in their hands. But men deserve in many cases the pain women have caused men that have treated women as nothing but "objects."

Speaking of the obvious, when will we give the President the Line Item Veto so he can be held accountable for his roll in economics and when will we freeze immigration and kick the illegals out?

Imagine my delighted surprise that Stephen Hawking's book: "A Brief History of Time" has outlasted any other book on the British best-seller list! While I disagree on some of his conclusions, Hawking remains one of my heroes because of his superb, creative gift of imagination. I have enthusiastically followed his career and consider him one of the greatest thinkers of our age. It boggles my mind to think of what might have been possible for him if it were not for his disability. No one can ever be disappointed who takes the time to make serious inquiry into the nature and creations of God. It is of consuming interest and awesome to the maximum that so much can be done with only three things: Space, Matter, and Time! And, yes Daniel, I will give due consideration to Vidal's book, "Creation." But it takes a Hawking to attempt answers to the best questions.

What an outstanding example of the pioneer spirit Hawking represents! In spite of a decimated body, in his mind he travels the universe and sticks his inquisitive nose into God's very business- such men founded our own nation. It is a tragedy that we lost such great leaders who combined all that is best in adventure, risk-taking and perseverance. Of course, my years of experience in classrooms and the "machinery" of so-called "education" explained a great deal about this loss. And, I must credit those great men, Whitefield, Asbury and Wesley as well. It was these men, no matter, as with Hawking, their peculiarities or weaknesses, according to an English Statesman, who canceled the debt of Great Britain to the Colonies. Only the Christian historian can think that one through. But consider the gifts of Bishop Ryle, Alexander MacClaren, Henry Alford, Matthew Henry and so many others (and my old friend Gary North deludes himself that his books are going to be of use? Good thing you inherited the money to print them Gary, no one else would have wasted the money. Donating them is the only way you could get them out because it's for sure that no one will buy them. But as an exercise in stroking your ego, you really did a job).

Time would fail me to list the names of the great men God used to explain and promote the liberty we have in Christ. It goes without saying that had not such men "salted" England with Gospel tracts and preaching, that mighty nation would have suffered the same fate as France and there would not have been a July 4th to celebrate in this nation!

Surely I acknowledge my debt to Jung, May, Pearls, Pavlov and Skinner; but the debt to Strong, Ellicott, Checkov, Steinbeck and Faulkner is far greater. It is one thing to study Human Behavior as a classroom exercise, quite another to engage the subtleties of "East of Eden." And who can ever feel they owe nothing to "Death Takes a Holiday?" In regard to the movie versions, Frederic March and the music of Rudolph Friml, James Dean and Burl Ives demand respect for the kind of artistry that commands our emotions and intellect to strive for compatibility. In truth, the selling out of our national soul to hedonism, greed and envy, may have left it to an Italian romantic to capture the essence of love, taking captive the Grim One himself and making him a "friend."

I have to ask myself if a nation that has 70 percent of the world's lawyers can ever regain its soul and self-respect? Not when that nation runs up a 300 billion dollar a year litigation bill! Not when there is an annual 18 million lawsuits! And when these self-seeking leeches do so in the name of "equality, fairness, racial equity and justice for the poor" it makes me want to vomit! It is the lawyers in and out of politics that have betrayed us all! But what have these abominable, leprous spots on our nation to fear from a man who can sit for three hours at the Huntington, simply staring at The Blue Boy and Pinky, who finds better converse with owls and squirrels than most men?

We have "celebrated" our so-called "Independence" once more. Independence from what? The shysters that are destroying our nation have sold us out. "Taxation without representation!" That was the rallying cry of far better men than the abominable and shameless slavers, murderers and thieves that now lead us to national destruction and all the while fatten their already bloated pockets and faces with their disgraceful cries of "Public Service" while taking extraordinary care that their own "retirements" are large enough to feed thousands of the poor they have robbed blind.

Peter Drucker wrote many years ago: "There is a straight line from Rousseau to Hitler - a line that takes in Robespierre, Marx and Stalin." In regard to the "religion" of our educational system, Humanism, it doesn't take a scholar to recognize the end result. The costs for our Criminal Justice System is running at four times the amount spent on education. As I have said repeatedly, when a nation's "growth industries" are welfare and prisons, the end is upon that nation.

Douglas MacArthur wrote: "History fails to record a single precedent in which nations subject to moral decay have not passed into political and economic decline. There has been either a spiritual awakening to overcome the moral lapse, or a progressive deterioration leading to ultimate national disaster."

I warned all of you that the banks were going to go the way of the S&Ls. Just now the news is being "leaked" that Bush is trying to keep the lid on this crisis until after the election. He may be able to for now, but it is bound to come back with a roar in the future.

Of the many periodicals I read, the "Reader's Digest" has been one of the constants. In spite of its "commonness" and its disfavor among my "colleagues," few others are so well oriented to the common people and taste. In 1989, there was an article by Eugene Methvin entitled: "Crusader For Peru's Have-Nots." The story has to do with the discovery by one Hernando de Soto that the people of Peru, when they were able to actually own their own land

and do with it as they pleased, prospered mightily, worked more diligently, had less crime and were morally superior compared with those that did not. Incredible, isn't it, that De Soto found, as a "revelation," the principle that made America an historic success story unparalleled in history.

The lack of this principle, more than any other, led to the USSR's downfall. But, in the case of America, the backbone of our nation's success was its thorough grounding in Biblical Christianity that led from the founding of the colonies to the forming of our government. Tim LaHaye wrote an excellent little volume on this subject in 1976. I wish everyone had a copy.

Napoleon said: "It is religion alone that keeps the poor from killing the rich." You fat cats in government would do well to heed his warning. The poor of our nation are no longer, thanks, in large part, to the charismatics, under the "constraints" of religion.

If "My Prisons" were but a single night in jail, that would be one thing. But, unlike Thoreau, I am beset by a multitude of evils he did not have to contend with, evils like building inspectors and women and "feminine" men in positions of leadership. At least in Thoreau's time women still held, for the most part, to the Biblically honored exalted position of homemaker.

But, as with politicians who have been cheated, like our children, of the opportunity to learn from working with their hands and backs, women have long since left the woodstove, hand laundry, flatirons and ironing boards. Surrounded with the accouterments of "time and labor-saving" devices, and that most onerous, mind stultifying and evil aggrandizing medium, TV, women are bored to death. It may well be called a modern and technological age but human beings are still, by nature, geared to subduing the earth, tilling the soil and honest labor. As I have often pointed out, having the kids do the dishes (where a dishwasher is wanting), taking out the trash or washing the car simply does not do the job of teaching children responsibility.

Dust is a reminder of our own mortality. But it is also a reminder of the need for constant work and imperfection. No matter how often you wipe off the furniture, the next day it needs it again. You can't beat dust for consistency. Howard Hughes tried to no avail.

It is a reminder of the lack of perfection in that "itch" we can't scratch. When I was dealing in guns, I had a high regard for the best weapons and the artistry of the finest gun makers like Browning. When I resolved to get out of the business, it helped to remember that even the finest results of the gunsmith's art had its flaws and imperfections. As a machinist and tool and die maker, I knew that no matter how "perfect" the gun, if I looked carefully enough, I would find that scratch of the reamer or the slip of a Swiss file.

So it is that between dust and the finest workmanship the artisan can produce, the flaws are there. God says that we are His workmanship, created to do good work. But work, in spite of flaws and failures, can be, nevertheless, rewarding. Those Brownings were still works of art and fulfilled their primary function, to shoot well, regardless of imperfections. It was in such thinking that I have begun to look at the Bible as a "Primer" and not the finished and ultimate "Text."

It may be that men are the ultimate text of God. I, as I am sure, you also, have wondered at God's long silence. Almost two thousand years of silence. Throughout the Biblical era, it seemed that God had a lot to say. Then, after the canon of Scripture was closed, nothing!

Now before my Fundamentalist "friends" go off on a rip, I am fully conversant with all of your arguments. I am well grounded in the fundamentals of the Faith. I know the apologetic that in "these last days He has spoken to us by His Son," I know the warning, and I heed it, of adding or subtracting to His Word, etc.

In teaching mathematics, I soon discovered a basic truth of which the schools had lost sight. Children were doomed to failure in understanding math if they had not memorized their multiplication tables. The lack of this most basic tool doomed them to math failure the rest of their lives!

I encountered this in every form from "bonehead" classes to college algebra, from fractions and decimals through geometry and trig. So it was that I began to insist on competence in the multiplication tables before attempting any further procedures. Not a few of the older students resented this "elementary" exercise. But they soon discovered its merit. I would begin with a lecture on the fact that, regardless of the form of math, there are only four things you can do with numbers: you can add, subtract, multiply or divide them. That's it! Whether a basic math class in simple arithmetic or the most advanced course in theoretical physics, that is all you can do with the information. And, these four procedures are paired: Add/Subtract-Multiply/Divide.

Once the multiplication tables are mastered and, by that, I mean when the answers are instinctive, you don't have to stop and think of the answer, you are on your way to math proficiency and not until. So it is that I began to think of the Bible as our "multiplication tables."

Perhaps God has given us enough information that He has a reasonable expectation of our being able to do the job from what He has provided. While I constantly express my gratitude for the great scholars He gave the Church, I knew there was something missing, something these great men were not answering to. There are too many legitimate questions not addressed, too much chaos and chicanery (as per the charismatics and other cults) that insisted they were following the Bible.

But if God has provided a "Primer" and expects us to apply its basic function to success in the "higher math," it might help explain the pathetic condition of the churches today. There is no "Royal Path" to knowledge and you will never be "math proficient" by attempting short cuts such as not memorizing those multiplication tables. The best do so and go on to perfection according to their several abilities. Perhaps this explains so much illiteracy and infantilism in the churches. The members are childish, spoiled brats lacking in the self-discipline that is required for serious accomplishment and further study.

I will never tire of reading and studying God's Word. Like the old "Hymns of Zion" I grew up with, there will always be the comfort and consolation of the old stories of God's dealings with men through the Biblical epochs. I still thrill to David's triumph over Goliath, the deliverance of Israel from Egypt and Paul's defense before Felix and Festus. I still draw strength and understanding from a daily look into the Perfect Law of Liberty, and know that Jesus intended all of this for our good. The Bible is far more than a "primer" in the usual sense of the word. What I am trying to say is that there is a time, as God says, to go on from the basics of the Way and get on with the work; and part of the work is to become "living epistles, living sacrifices" of our time, resources and living like God's children, and expected to grow up. He expects us to get on with it. The Bible, as a primer in the sense that it supplies all the basic tools of the work, is intended to provide all we need to "work out our salvation" in our lives. And, while I never tire of reading Romans and Genesis, I am weary of tired sermons that keep "converting the converted" and continue to be directed at infants instead of men of God.

How I long for a sermon that would address the real issues with which we have to deal. But what do we get? Pap and strained bananas; small wonder the conversations of most of the "saints" and the "leadership" gives me spiritual diarrhea! I'm a man, made in God's image and these silly idiots want to force-feed me spiritual mush! And you silly idiots in the pews seem to not want anything better? I suppose most of you would choke on the "meat" of God, presuming a real man could be found in a pulpit that isn't afraid to confront your lukewarmness! So it is that God says: "I hate, I despise your religious feasts; I cannot stand your assemblies...Away with the noise of your songs! I will not listen to the music of your harps." Amos 5:21-23.

We are seeing the results of God's warning: "The wicked freely strut about when what is vile is honored among men." Psalm 11:8. No wonder Philip Wylie dedicated his blasphemous chapter on The Lord to: "... sixteen million Christians who belong to churches and to hell." The number would, of course, be geometrically higher today.

235

One of the things I learned as a teacher is that children are not, by nature, enamored of school and the discipline of learning (like the "church-goers" and "pew-warmers" I referred to). In fact, it is the loss of the necessary discipline and authority, as much as anything, that has doomed our children in the schools. Remember that it is men, not women, who represent authority to children. They are smarter than their elders in this respect. So it is that, because of the hugely, disproportionate number of women in education, children are seldom confronted with any real authority or discipline in the schools. Put this with the fact that so many children are the product of broken homes and welfare slavery, not to mention the perverts in the job, and you have a genuine and unbeatable recipe for national disaster. This, together with so-called "marriage vows" that don't have the snowball's chance of outlasting a mortgage, spells disaster for children.

Chlorine and fluoridation; now we are told they cause cancer but the risk is "minimal." Should make us sleep easier. But, just in case you still suffer some degree of insomnia, here's a good one; it's a description by Boris Yeltsin's attorney, Sergei Shakhrai of the Communist Party: "The party was all-controlling, all-permeating, and ruthless. Having destroyed private property, swallowed civil society and eliminated any notion of human rights, the Bolsheviks for 70 years hid behind a phantom government, legal system and popular rule." Now, hold a mirror up to this statement and see a reflection of our own nation! But in 1776 it was a reflection of the system our founding fathers rebelled against!

To make the point indelibly clear, Clinton and Gore, reflecting the mind-set of the welfare state, promise to "Take from the haves and give it to the have-nots!" Isn't that what Marx promised would bring in the "Millennium?" Current conditions in "Utopian Russia" makes you wonder why Clinton and Gore just don't cut out the middleman and run on the platform of "Benedict Arnold Was Right!" Treason is treason; let's call a spade a spade. But "breeding will tell" and Clinton is only reflecting the lack of good breeding in his own childhood. He has an actual prejudice, if not outright hatred, of the rich and desperately wants to "get even" and put those "aristocrats" in their place! Vote for Clinton and have our own Sarajevo! But, in all fairness, we are going to have our "Sarajevo's" with or without Clinton.

As it is, the most conservative estimate of the situation tells us that within five to eight years fully one half of the population will be living off the other half. That's right folks, one half living off the working and taxpaying other half! Makes you want to run right out and open a savings account doesn't it! Some of you lazy bums who are only working one job better start moonlighting. There's a long line forming of, largely Negro and Mexican (legal and illegal), "poor" along with all those "greedy geezers" soaking up the hope of their children and grandchildren through medical and social security that are depending on you to quit being so stingy. Your wife ought to at least be taking in washing to help these "deserving" people to continue drawing their government checks.

After all, when you consider the fact that the New York and L.A. riots are really caused by us "tight-fisted" and "stingy," working taxpayers, we really should be ashamed; and the rapidly rising numbers of children (mostly black and brown) living in poverty! Shame on us (mostly white) "gluttons," no wonder Clinton and Gore want to redress this heinous "wrong" by increasing taxes (of those that "have")!

But just look at Perot stealing Bush's line: "I'll do whatever is necessary to be re-elected!" Seems Perot appointed openly lesbian Beverly Hills mortgage broker Deborah Olson as his California civil rights coordinator. She will also serve as national gay and lesbian liaison to the Perot campaign! So much for "Mr. Clean" and his so-called "family values."

It is a given that, with increasing age, one becomes more and more concerned with the bowels. Why a recent trip with a young friend and his motor home brings this to mind is worthy of a comment. Have you ever tried using one of the "facilities" mounted over the rear axle of a moving vehicle on a rough highway sans padded seat? It gives one pause to wonder and reminds me of a recent article by Robert Samuelson.

Seems he thinks, and I agree, that we suffer a lot of technology in reverse; his example of trying to replace books with computer-read discs in a good case in point. With mega-storage now so cheap, technology is, as usual, trying to find uses where the need for none exists. Unlike the marvelous old M1 Garands, try dragging your computer through the mud or sand and calling up "For Whom The Bell Tolls." But, anachronists die hard. I didn't think I needed a microwave until I had one. Now, however did I live without one (admittedly, my Bohemian, bachelor status has found it a godsend)?

But it must be confessed that technology does have a way of making mountains of molehills. The new machines like fax, cellular phones etc., have a way of snowballing. The nice thing about books is their portability and they never develop electrical glitches or require a VCR. Perhaps the survivability of much technology will be attributed to simple ego; if "Jack" or "Jane" has one, I need one!

My fight with building inspectors and silly codes together with thieving taxes that rob a man of the dignity of working and providing for his family on his own land is a point well made. No one seems to realize how devastating this has been to our vaunted "rights" as Americans. If ever a technology has run amok to ruin the American Dream of owning one's home, it is in the building trades. And make no mistake about it; the trade unions bear the brunt of the blame here. Like the NEA (National Education Association) builder and manufacturer's unions have pounded their fair share of spikes in the coffin of home ownership through greed. In the case of the NEA, it spelled the end of meaningful attempts at reform in education. For housing, the unions and manufacturers did the same thing. So the old, Biblical prophecy: "You will build houses but you won't live in them."

The Lord knows that I would far rather live in a ten by ten cabin on my own land and live as I please than owe my soul to Big Brother. I will, like Thoreau, always be willing to exchange the flush toilet and microwave for the liberty that makes a man a man. But, again, such thinking is evidenced by the natural affinity of the kind of man for which a good book, clear air, water, mountains, trees, rocks and the critters are more important than how quickly the defrost setting works for Tater-tots.

I'm enjoying the Convention. I like a "Broadway Play" as well as the next. I'm also an aficionado of cartoons and fairy tales. It is proving an "interesting" year for political junkies, surrounded with an embarrassment of riches as the contenders square off. My greatest fear is that we will get the kind of "leadership" we deserve! Does Perot dropping out surprise me? Of course not; whether the things I have pointed out prompted his decision, the success of Democratic Party solidarity behind Clinton or Perot's avowal of not wanting to promote "gridlock," it remains, given his nature, that he still holds a sword and has his own agenda. The dark side of the Beast is still very much alive and just as cunning as ever.

Shall we ban the "Super Soaker?" Shootings everywhere and the best the "leadership" can come up with is the insanity of trying to take away the guns of the law-abiding citizen. Don't let them do it! I'm a member of the NRA and you should be also. It is the single, most important organization that stands between us and the Devil in regard to our Constitutional right to bear arms as Americans. If you are not a member, you are casting your vote by default to give up this right.

But, then, I wish everyone was reading widely; it takes a wide range of reading to have any hope of having anything close to the "whole picture." Just reading the National Geographic, Reader's Digest, Kiplinger's, morning paper and Newsweek simply doesn't cut it. Valuable as all these are, it takes the outspokenness of the others to balance the picture.

I have said, and now it is repeated in many circles, that a great many young people have it better in jail than their "homes." It was a given while I was teaching in Watts and the barrio of East San Jose that the kids were often at school just to get away from their living conditions. The schools offered the only neat and structured environment they knew. Now that the gangs have taken over, however, the social function of such schools has become an ever more dangerous one. It isn't the Super Soaker that is to blame; it is an entire society that has gone to hell.

The schools may well become the "killing fields." If young people really knew how vulnerable the schools truly are, and all they would have to do is read the things I have written about, they would be in charge. That is why I could make the statement I made a long while back, that, if I sincerely wished to do so, I could personally have a "youth organization" that would be my "army" for anarchy. All young people need to bring this to pass is the "right" leader to pull it off. No, Jaime Escalante could not hope to do this job. The leader would have to be truly tough.

Another legend comes to an end: Goodbye, Eric Sevareid.

Is nothing too low for the "Halls of Ivy?" I can't fathom the seriousness with which the "educated elite" takes some of the hogwash they often bow to. Imagine the utter asininity of some "educated fool," one Shelley Fisher Fishkin, being taken seriously as a "discoverer" of the fact that Sam Clemens was so thoroughly schooled in the dialect of the South that the same dialect was to be found in the voices of both Jim and Huck?

Now while it is true that the term "nigger" averages at least once a page in the novel, the historical setting justifies Clemens' use of it. It was not a racist epithet in Clemens' time or mind. No one is more acquainted with the crazy twists and turns of Academics than me. I am quite conversant with the esoterica with which small-minded people like Fishkin have to attempt to justify (like bureaucrats) their posh stations in life. The "thinking" goes like this: "I am a super-brilliant and very important person. My mission in life is to convince others of, what should be this obvious fact!" Nothing is sacred or too silly to contemplate in this "quest" to justify such a person's opinion of himself or herself.

It would stupefy the average person to read even a partial list of the subjects the Ivory Tower inhabitants, like their cousins, the bureaucrats, attempt to "study" in order to justify their existences. Knowing the mean diameter of a certain species of ant's rectum may be of consuming "need to know" but I can live without the knowledge. To try to prove how academically superior you are by such a "study" gives you a hint of how the "system" operates. "Mz." Fishkin, you can take your so-called "discovery" and forcibly intrude it up your nasal orifice or some like accommodation where the sun never shines. Jimmy doesn't sound like Huck and Huck talks just like any other white, Southern boy of his time and circumstances. Go "fish."

Well, I have succeeded in separating the screen porch from the cabin and, with the help of floor jacks and ten-feet of two-inch pipe, moving the structures the required five-feet apart. Now I have to build the wall at the end of the used-to-be screen porch and I am done. Sure looks weird compared to what was a pretty little cabin. But, it satisfies my need for storage space and the county bureaucrat's need to justify their government checks. While I didn't get the hernia my body was threatening me with, it was close. A come-along would have been the cat's whiskers but, thanks to a thief, mine was not to be had.

A glorious thunderstorm and a beautiful, full moon facilitated the work last night. I sat and watched for nearly an hour as a tremendous thunder cell delivered nearly three hundred lightening strikes to a small area of the Greenhorn range. If anyone was living in the middle of that, they surely must have thought the Lord had finally had enough and was calling an end to this age. He didn't; but He will!

I often amuse myself by thinking about the things men and women consider important and how they differ. Now, personally, I have never understood the full implications of the need for some men to memorize sport's statistics. And, when it comes to conversation, I would rather be held captive to someone's enthusiastic and lengthy discussion of their gall bladder operation than be subjected to some duffer's description of his play on the seventeenth hole or how the league standings are affected by the latest game of the Mets, etc. *ad nauseum*. Ladies, I suffer with you if association with such a man who thinks the world revolves around some football team curses you.

On the other hand, it is fascinating to discover what the ladies think of such import. A woman's magazine is filled with such "delights" as "who is doing what to whom" and why it is so vital to well-being to know who all the entertainment "stars" are and if they really are guilty of biting their nails. Amazing! Perhaps women are so jaded with their lives that they, in desperation, reach out for some kind of vicarious experience through the phony lives of Hollywood. Come to think of it, maybe that's why men are so enamored of sports figures.

Granting the fact that we have become an illiterate nation, a nation of non-readers, a nation of couch potatoes and non-thinkers, it may be that such people settle for letting other people in sports and on TV live their lives for them. A pathetic trade considering the fact that life still offers much to those with the courage and know-how to do things of real value.

Here's a follow-up for those of you that have read my books. It seems that women, because of their physiognomy, are ten times more likely to contract AIDS than men. This has come to light through Asian countries where women are still treated as "things" and prostitution is rife, particularly in places like Thailand. It is estimated that fully one-half of all the women in that nation will have the virus by the turn of the century. One has to wonder how Hillary Clinton's "iron-busted feminism" would fly in that environment. Only in America...! She has succeeded, at least, in making me feel somewhat sorry for what has to be a very frustrated husband. Just imagine, maybe Bill is the epitome of sublimation, seeking the Presidency through sexual frustration! Makes you wonder how far he would go to "prove" his "manhood?" If Bush needed Desert Storm to do this, what do you suppose Clinton would need?

If the Popol Vuh of the Quiche Maya is all that Dennis Tedlock claims, why is Columbia dealing drugs and murdering all those that oppose the cartels? Just another example of the corruption of mere religion as opposed the Truth of God's Word. And it won't do to try to provide a cop-out by attempting to smear "European Values" and "culture." Historically, these nations have become, no matter how corrupt, the custodians of the most valuable aspects of civilization. But, as with Biblical Israel, the stakes increase dramatically with the betrayal of The Truth.

Go for it Berkeley. I would love to see religious organizations taxed and you just may have the guts to do the job.

CHAPTER FOURTEEN

CHRISTIAN PERSPECTIVE

AUGUST, 1992

II Corinthians 2:6-16

Well, I'm working on the cabin and it's over 100 degrees. Good thing I'm a desert rat at heart. The heat just brings out the lizard in me. Stopped on my way to Bakersfield and took a swim in the Kern River. Marvelous! The water was just the tonic I needed. I chose a large, long pool where the water moves slowly toward the boulder-strewn rapids and the banks are beautifully shaded, tree-lined with leafy branches hanging into the river.

The mornings and evenings in Lake Isabella are marvelous. Reminds me of the times on the mining claim when, as a young boy, I would move my bed outside under the pines and fall asleep to the music of the breeze through the pine needles and watching the stars overhead. Sheer magic! I still take time to watch the stars at night and thrill to the occasional, shooting star. I wonder what purpose they serve? Is this the detritus of God's housekeeping or are they simply for our enjoyment of stellar magnificence?

I'm taking a break right now just to share some thoughts. This old house I'm working on shows a lot of promise. The trees provide good shade and I haven't needed a fan or air-conditioner; not even a swamp-cooler. Good thing since the old house doesn't have such refinements. Hard to believe we used to live without such things. Hard to believe we used to drive old route 66 in the summer without auto air conditioning. Of course, I drove and hiked the Mojave for years without it and survived.

I suppose I got on this tack because of the fact that so many people are so spoiled and have taken such things as artificially cooled air for granted. As I write in these new "digs," it's about 90 degrees in the house; it's 105 outside and I'm having to do some "idiot-stick" (shovel) work to locate the old septic system for repairs hence, in the house to do some writing until the heat abates somewhat. I'm wondering if the temperature will affect the computer? But it is quiet and peaceful, the trees are beautiful through the windows and I have some marvelous music from the big bands interlaced with the Ink Spots playing in the background; as old McGee would say, "All this and heaven too!"

When the sun hits the yardarm, I'll go back outside and start digging and swinging my hammer again. Only mad dogs and Englishmen go out in the noonday sun; but I'm very grateful that I can do what I please, when I please and where I please.

There are a good many of you that should be doing something of like value if for no other reason than to break out of your "comfortable prisons." Too many of you have gotten into the mind-set that the only thing in life is go to work, eat, sleep and watch TV. I can never fathom such a waste of one's life. You're dead and they just haven't gotten around to burying you yet. It would profit many of you to pay me just to let you come and help me with the work! That is not meant as a Tom Sawyer ploy.

But, too many of you would complain of cruel and unjust treatment if you simply had to go to Bakersfield for supplies in my old '64, window-cooled Chevy pickup; reminds me of the Baptist who hit his thumb with a 24 ounce framing hammer. No, he didn't say it; he only thought it and that doesn't count!

Being single, I, infrequently, have to "shop." I recently saw a box of dry cereal for $5.19! Ritz crackers were on "sale" for "only" $3.50. Milk is $2.65 a gallon and a loaf of bread of fair quality is over $2.00. The face of famine and the increasing incapability of people to afford common groceries is here now! I'm still able to do for myself and I thank God for the fact. But I can easily understand why dry dog food and the jails and prisons are becoming an increasingly needed option for many!

Seems there is a new strain of AIDS that is undetectable by present tests. Scientists now have the problem of determining whether other germs or conditions that result in the suppression of the immune system may in fact transmit AIDS. The beat goes on. If true, many may have the disease and not even know it; yet! And how about that Asian mosquito found in Florida that has brought the dread "sleeping sickness" to the shores of America? Cholera on the beaches of Malibu; say it isn't so!

Yes, the jails and prisons are becoming attractive to many who have given up. A man, one Donald Whitehead sums it up: "It's not what I want to be (in jail). Circumstances dictate that I be here." Mr. Whitehead robbed a bank and then promptly turned himself in to the police so he could get three squares a day and shelter at the taxpayer's expense; nothing new in that, only the increasing frequency of it and the better caliber of felons doing "business" with our "penal" institutions. The "Institutional Man" is becoming more cognizant and erudite, finding better "opportunities" by incarceration than the government and society offers in traditional pursuits. The young, especially, are discovering this in droves.

When did "I'll Be Seeing You" become an old song? Lord, why has the music gone out of people's lives? Perhaps too many never even knew the music. I know how difficult it is to find anyone who is interested in discussing good literature or even engaging in the fun of whimsy.

Now the fact that houses are built to suit women, not men, is evidenced by the lack of urinals in them. Nothing would make more sense and save more water than to include such sensible devices in bathrooms. Why aren't they? Women! Like the present "styling" of automobiles. As one trained in psychology, I know the shape of present autos is oriented toward women.

Remember my warning about the Scrolls? The opening "gun" seems to be Eisenman's contention that "inconsistencies" in the Genesis account arose because it was pieced together from two sources. This, of course, is a familiar argument to those of us who are well schooled in Biblical Criticism. But, Eisenman and his helpers are going to "reconcile" the 40-day cycles with the 364-day calendar and insert the day of the week on which each event took place. Expect many such changes to come from the "historical re-interpretation" of Biblical texts.

"Lazy" so-called "Christians" will take the attitude: "I believe the Bible and don't care what these men try to do!" As with politics and a host of other things with which an American citizen should be active and concerned, the physically and intellectually lazy will keep "whistling through the graveyard" and wipe their lips, like the Great Whore, and say: "I have done no wrong." My battle with the churches, too many Satan's allies, is due to this kind of lie and selfishness. That these ignorant, lazy louts are content to let the Enemy have a clear field by default is something they will have to answer to at the Judgment.

Have I ignored Willa Cather? No, I love her writing and she had a genuine gift. Her descriptions of the Plains States and life such as "Little House" are a great contribution to our literature. She believed America's promise would endure: "We come and go, but the land is always here. And the people who love it and understand it are the people who own it - for a little while." Cather's gift was to paint the marvelous word-pictures of life on the prairies, to see beauty in the flat, grass covered vistas and make that beauty real to others. But, as she would agree, it would take being born and bred to such to enter the real joy of it.

I do not denigrate Cather's gift by not joining literary colleagues in according her the same merit as that of Faulkner or Hemingway. She wrote as a woman and that, by itself, is a worthy and needed enough contribution to the rich American field of literature of times past. But make no mistake;

it took a Steinbeck to bring the "Okies" to life in our heritage of heroes of the land. And, how could Cather (or Steinbeck, for that matter) know the full extent of the government's betrayal of the people by stealing the land wholesale?

It was not Cather's gift to delve into the psyche of dark motives and cruelty. Her writing was elegiac only to the point of melancholy or vivid geographical, flora and fauna description. Had she married, I'm sure there would have been more realism to her characters. But, psychologically, men, not women, are the adepts at sounding the depths of both love and degradation and making these stir the soul and mind in the most profound manner.

But, among men, the differences are equally profound. I mentioned Dana in my last essay but need to point out, in answer to some questions from my readers, that Dana did not make the spray of saltwater crust your hair, form rime around your mouth or leave the taste of brine on your lips as much as Melville and London do. No, Dana made the life of a Tar real; he had you picking the interminable oakum and breaking your back furling and unfurling sails. Dana's genius was taking the ordinary and making it extraordinary, heroic- a not inconsiderable feat of extreme sensitivity and artistry.

There was a time when ladies were known to be feminine and demureness was a virtue, when they dressed in such a manner that conveyed chastity and the allure of proper behavior. Men knew how to act in the presence of such ladies; poor benighted things, to stick a cigarette in your mouth, a glass of whisky in your hand and take a curse on your lips all in the name of equality. What a poor trade. Men no longer write poetry for such creatures.

"I'm yours. Now you have the privilege and obligation of caring for and cherishing me!" Used to be- no more. You wanted "equality?" You got it Babe! Go to work and pull equal weight! I know that when you get the itch, you'll dump me anyhow so you sure better put an equal amount in the pot in the meantime. Want a kid? Why? Just so when you do dump me I get the "privilege" of child-support while you sleep with another guy? Madness! As a matter of personal experience, I had this "privilege" for fifteen years and at no time was I given an opportunity to have anything to do with the raising of my two children by this woman and her new men. Quite the contrary, it was made very clear that my input was unwanted and of no consequence; but my weekly checks were most welcome for those fifteen years. Unhappily, and tragically for children, this is the "system" and is the rule, not the exception.

I've been asked why I don't invest in stocks or bonds. Now I have nothing against such investing but when a man can do the kinds of things I can, and, further, enjoys doing them, it would be foolish. As one man whose expertise in investment is international said: "There is no 'Black Box' in the stock market!"

Further, you don't really have much of a chance against the "insiders." And, as Mr. Keating, et al. can tell you short cuts can be nasty.

Let me pose you this question. Suppose I told you I could invest $30,000 for you and guarantee you a $750 per month income on the capital? Not only that, your capital would appreciate at least yearly at the rate of inflation and without any risk?

You would ask: "What's the catch?" I would say: You have to be a landlord because I am talking about investing in low-cost rentals. Folks, no matter how you slice it, there is no "magic" to real estate. It's hard work and aggravation but it is still the method with which all wealth is made and upon which all wealth is based. In spite of its simplicity, most don't take advantage of it because they are, in truth, simply lazy and would rather be wage-slaves the rest of their lives than make the necessary sacrifices to gain the investment capital and do the hard work required. It really is just that simple!

If you doubt me, just ask any ten people you know what they would do if they suddenly had $10,000 cash? Not a one would say: "Buy a couple of old houses, fix them up and rent them out." Case closed. Yet it is this simple formula by which I live mortgage and debt free under bondage to no man. And virtually anyone could do the same thing if they were willing to pay the price of self-discipline, hard work, simple living and sacrifice of luxuries such as car payments. No secret there, just hard work and self-discipline.

Speaking of laziness, physical and intellectual, a good many of you may wonder, a few have asked, why I don't do more to justify my academic credentials in the field of psychology? Say no more- here it is!

"Inchoate" is a very nice word. I like this word. It conveys a precise meaning and, like most nice words of its genre, saves much unnecessary verbiage. The problem of this nice word and so many like it is that you just don't hear, or read, it many places. Good old George Will can try to use it but, in most cases, I have to pass because I try to write using words in common parlance and currency. Also, a really nice word like "Adumbrate" can become a pitfall in writing. Scofield in his notes was addicted to this word and it jars somewhat in its repetitiveness; in short, a very nice and serviceable word might only be not understood it can become overused.

What one fellow was actually trying to tell me, and he is "guilty" of the same thing, is that we are trying to express "ideas." These, of course, being the most dangerous things to work with and, in most cases, give people a "headache," are "over the heads" of most. I've been a teacher for too many years not to understand that critical thinking is a learned discipline; it is not "instinctual." But, as with Melville, to write otherwise, I cannot altogether do.

In reading my latest copy of National Review, I came across this little gem: "... Mr. Bush is embracing a presidential Existentialism - he will run on his record." Now I don't know about you but "zingers" like that really give me cerrebelic unction; I really get a kick out of them. But, admittedly, you have to get past TV as your cultural "high" of the day to enjoy the benefits of such things.

First and foremost, I have never "hung out my shingle," though I am qualified to do so and, in fact, am credentialed to teach the subject in the colleges, for the very simple reason that I have a "pastor's heart" and could never deal with people's emotional and mental problems on a paid-professional basis. Secondly, my studies in Human Behavior served to reinforce many of the things I had learned from studying literature, history, the churches and the Bible. There are some other reasons which I will explain as I get into this essay.

Freud, as the Father of Psychoanalysis, has been misconstrued as seeing sexual dominance in all human behavior. That is not to say that he was necessarily wrong, but the emphasis was distorted. He did try to make too much of dreams and, due to the nature of the study, was struggling in the darkness. This is not condemnatory. The subject of the interpretation of dreams is still an area of much dispute and, as I wrote some time ago in regard to present studies of brain functions, one that is likely to remain so indefinitely.

I will begin by saying that people, by and large, are stymied in their lives by varying degrees of hysteria leading to suppression of desired goals and the necessary actions to achieve them. You must understand that I use the word "hysteria" in the clinical sense, not the popular one.

Clinically, hysteria prevents one from acting as he should and leads to various degrees of dysfunctional behavior. If the peculiar form of hysteria does not find socially acceptable means of sublimation or catharsis, it can lead to neurosis or, in extreme cases, psychosis.

Those that have read my books are, largely, unaware that much of what I have written has a basis in psychology because I have purposely not appended such an interpretive parameter. For those of you who have some knowledge of the practice and study of psychology, the signposts are unmistakable; for example, my comments on the fact that no one does anything without a reason, conscious or unconscious.

The most popular and titillating areas of psychology are, indeed, sexual and, even, bizarre forms of expression; the catch-all area often referred to as Abnormal Psychology popularized by movies like "Silence Of The Lambs" and "Bedlam."

Freud found himself on most dangerous ground as he intruded into those "monsters of the Id" in sexual deviation and repression. As a Jew, he lacked the insight of an objective study of Christian church history that could have helped him immensely and, as a result, had to "second-guess" much of the behavior of his patients who had church backgrounds. Genius that he was, he did recognize some of the hurtful influences of religion on mental health, but he was at too great a disadvantage through his Jewishness to benefit from a detached study of Christian religious ignorance, bigotry, prejudices, taboos and repression.

Admittedly, even today, we who are studied in psychology have to admit that we do not know what "mental disease" is and attempt, through "labels," to deal with it in its infinite degrees of expression. I have an opinion that some of the casting out of demons in the New Testament was a manifestation of what we call, today, mental disease.

Am I saying that psychologists and psychiatrists today are practicing a kind of "Respectable Witchcraft?" No more than what passes for most "counseling," particularly by ministers, priests and rabbis who, for the most part, are themselves the victims of being in the dark in regard to the things Freud began to discover.

It is not coincidental, that the Scopes Trial got the attention of the churches. It was a most successful "feint" by the Enemy to divert attention from the really dangerous area with which Freud was involved. The churches had no excuse in being "suckered" into a losing battle, particularly when their "champion," good a man as Bryan was, was far from being a qualified theologian. I am convinced this ill-fated and ill-fought confrontation brought about the broken death shortly thereafter of this "Peerless Leader" of the Democratic Party. He was neither the first nor the last that would be broken on fighting the wrong battle and for all the wrong reasons, just like Billy Sunday.

In this regard, Philip Wylie was correct. Booze and evolution are not where the Enemy is doing his most successful work. The Volstead Act was a tragedy and resulted in the organized crime we now live with. The Scopes Trial only legitimized and popularized the Enemy's lie. But the churches have long given up much of their credibility against evil and, this, due in no small part to their refusal to confront the real battle, which I broached in my first book that began way back there in the Garden.

As soon as the churches in America began to cater to the demands of women to be granted "equality," even ordaining them to church offices, and climbing on the temperance band-wagons, etc., the churches lost any claim to Biblical Truth; they became guilty of denying the most salient, historical fact of God's judgment and command in regard to the most basic of all God's Truth, that men should bear the responsibility of ruling over women.

Once the churches began to depart from this most basic of God's positions, all was lost. We now live with what can be clinically called a "terminal generation," a society that is clinically "sick" in the extreme and admits of no plausible cure.

By refusing God's mandate, the churches became ever more involved with "social issues" such as temperance and "women's lib." Unable to confront the real issues with which Freud was leading the way, church leaders bogged down in a wide array of things that enabled them to escape, temporarily, becoming involved in the main issue; SEX.

As a result, the churches today are in the deplorable situation of not being able to sensibly address the subject and must "talk around it." Even professionals in the field of psychology, because of the twisted and distorted attempts at "equality," are unable to confront the Truth of the matter.

For example, most people are not "beautiful." Most people are ordinary, plain or downright ugly. Just how profound is the fact that a man or woman has no sexual desirability? Just how profound is sexual abuse of children, especially incest?

When a woman never had, or loses, sexual attractiveness, she is not only of little or no value in our society; she must find means of sublimation or a viable methodology which permits her to make a life without such an asset. The lack of urinals in a home and the styling of automobiles are cases in point. These and many other such things are attempts to make women of continued importance, even dominance, though they lose or lack the one thing men find of value in them; their sexual desirability of which, though women, by and large, are trying every way they can to rid our society of it, their submissiveness must be an attendant part.

It is, therefore, no coincidence that most of the women in the forefront of organizations like NOW and favor abortions are, frankly, lacking in sexual attractiveness or are perverts. The sexual frustration of the men who espouse these points of view is quite obvious to the trained psychologist as well.

While the early pioneers in psychoanalysis like Freud, Jung, James and Adler could not, due to the times in which they practiced, have either known or predicted the degree to which women would be willing to pervert those things which made them of value to men, they rendered an invaluable dimension of understanding the rudiments of behavior and opened the door of examination to many of the taboos that had invested such study.

The churches had much to do with the wall of ignorance that confronted, and still does, the earnest study of human behavior. More contemporary scholars like Kierkegaard, Van Til, Rushdoony and others helped get the door of understanding ajar among the religious communities but even they could not, due to their own prejudices and taboos, either understand or acknowledge the full range of sexual power in regard to behavior. And, of course, even men like James Dobson and most "pop" psychologists will not, or cannot, intrude too far into this "forbidden zone."

Menninger tried to pry the door open but faced a society that would have nothing to do with the whole truth of the matter. For this reason, much of what passes for the study of psychology to the present time suffers a "sameness" of such magnitude that when you have read one book on the theories, you have read them all for they all agree on the tame, and "safe," commonalities of which most people are agreed. Whether Rollo May, Reich or Frankl, the "sameness" attends.

Blake's Tyger and Clemens' Huck Finn come closer to understanding the Beast than Ashley Montague or Fritz Pearls. It is for that reason that great literature, art and music, are of greater value than contemporary studies in psychology in arriving at an understanding of human behavior.

In the very commonness of every day living so well described by the great writers like Dana one finds the nature of the Beast. If you take the time to observe the ordinary manner of living of people, you will discover things of significant import. If you have a desire to understand the rationale of people in their attempts to make their lives of significance, of purpose, it is intriguing to note the commonalities regardless of their stations in life.

For example, it is common for most people to engage in acquisitiveness. They will fill their houses with all manner of bric-a-brac, hang pictures on walls and try to consume all the floor space available with "things." This serves many purposes. It gives them "opportunity" to get through the day by "meaningful" activities like cleaning, dusting, washing, repairing, building, re-modeling, mowing, pruning, planting, etc. Hobbies, sports and avocations are extensive mechanisms by which men and women sublimate their unconscious failures and hysterias. America has become a nation of neurotics in its extreme materialism, all in a vain attempt to escape the Truth of what is known by the subconscious: "Things will never bring happiness or fulfillment" together with the unpalatable fact that men are to subjugate, lead and rule.

The vicarious nature of films and TV are other mechanisms with which modern society tries to escape the incessant demands of the Id and subconscious. In the acquisition and entertainment areas, there is virtually no discernible difference of "kind" between those that claim to be religious and those that profess no religious affiliation; only a difference in some, few cases of "degree." The "Rich Fool" of Jesus' story is the inherent nature of men and women regardless of church or no church.

Perhaps it has been my own loss of family and possessions so many times that I am able to have a more objective view of mere "things." I have lost too much and have had to "start over again" too many times to take material possessions too seriously, to fail to appreciate the very transitory nature of "things." But it is an "objectivity" that is purchased at a very dear price. I don't recommend the process to any one else. But, more than that, my early childhood on the mountain mining claim and my nativity in Weedpatch and move to Southeast Bakersfield as a child made their unique contribution together with being raised by grandparents who had so much of the pioneer spirit. In short, almost paradoxically, it seems you have to lose much to gain the freedom and liberty of understanding and appreciating the very ephemeral nature of material possessions. The death of loved ones and divorce teach lessons that don't seem to be learnable in softer fashion.

Why do marriage partners so quickly tire of the very thing, sex, which brought them together to begin with? Certainly they are not tired of sex. They are bored, actually, with sex with the same partner. Hence the burgeoning explosion of books on "What She Wants" and "What He Wants," the "simplicity" of divorce, wide-spread and "socially acceptable" adultery or "serial monogamy" and other types of fornication glorified by an immoral media and abortion on demand. Simply put, what "he or she wants" is something other than what they have! It is answering that conundrum that escapes people while they waste their time and money following the latest fads and quacks that peddle "answers" that only confound the problem further.

Honestly and frankly, if the taboos were removed, men would opt for harems of subjugated females and women would rule the world. Faced with that fact, the problem is discernible in the proper proportion of magnitude. But it is an inescapable imperative that any society allowed complete, sexual license, will collapse; hence, the need for marriage and the, at least, appearance of sexual faithfulness. But the nature of the Beast remains unchanged regardless of the cultural restraints and mores of a society. Therefore, sublimation and catharsis are, typically, neurotic and hysterical. Examples are the thief who refuses to steal, the rapist who does not rape and the murderer who does not kill.

To deny unacceptable oedipal impulses must result in other, more socially acceptable, activity. But the denial still results in repressive hysteria. The alternative may be as innocuous as an inordinate passion for bowling or flower arranging but the Beast is still there. In extreme instances, we find the serial or "thrill" killer, the torturer, the sado-masochist and, even, those who would lead in anarchy. Hitler and Stalin prove prime examples.

Man is the "subjugator" and woman the "submitter." That is the natural order. Nothing has ever changed that fact. The natural creation displays this lesson remarkably well in the animal kingdom. A report on hunting in America serves to make the point.

U.S. hunting is in jeopardy. A recent symposium on the subject in Bozeman Montana was particularly marked by the attendee's average age and maleness - most were white, middle-aged and male. "The changing face of America - more fatherless families, increasing urbanization; declining numbers of hunters - is jeopardizing the future of hunting." That was the conclusion of those present.

Regardless your sentiment on the subject, what was lacking at the meeting was the obvious fact that in a female-dominated society, hunting, the purview of men, is bound to decline. The greatest momentum behind "gun control" is female and homosexual. That is the psychology of it. The political interest is, of course, that an armed populace is the only detriment to the fulfilling of their grand designs to rule a slave population. But, here again, the motivating influence is, largely, sexual. Man the subjugator needs the fulfillment of command and authority.

Some may have found fault with my comment on Clinton's seeking the presidency as a means of relieving sexual frustration. In truth, men are constantly trying different ways, since childhood, of "proving" their "manhood." Why? To whom is such "proof" necessary?

Not understanding or even realizing these motivating influences and their power to control behavior, men are too often silly in the outward manifestations of them. For example, the silliness of a Playboy key chain or the female silhouettes on the mud flaps of trucks. These are only manifestations of sexually immature aggressiveness.

Philip Wylie's sexual frustration led him to make many disparaging, even ignorant, assertions against men and women. While seeming a devotee of Freud, Jung and Adler, even arguing that such men and psychology in general was the only hope of mankind, his distorted, sexual frustration led him a false path.

Jesus evidenced the fact of psychological truths in his own teaching and the examples he used. The preeminent use of "light and darkness" is an example of his understanding of the human condition and nature. One fact alone, the unwillingness of people to look at the truth objectively, from the time of Adam and Eve being ashamed and aware of their nakedness gives a hoary history of the dilemma that has faced mankind throughout history. Archaeology finds most ancient civilizations caught in the same web as evidenced by the preponderance of sexually oriented cultures and their religions and sexual totems.

The fact, as Jesus pointed out, that people are afraid of the "light" lest their evil desires be made manifest is sound psychology. People, in general, are not willing to risk exposure to the truth of those dark thoughts that incessantly intrude. The societal problem has always been to accommodate the Beast and, at the same time, live socially acceptable lives in the face of mounting frustration and hysteria. Civilized good manners are a method of our keeping from coming to blows with one another.

Delving into this murky region, Freud discovered that men and women were, in actuality, captive to sexual thoughts almost eighty percent of their waking lives. That fact has been confirmed over and over by later researchers. This gives more import to the statement by Jesus that unless one became as a little child, he cannot enter into the kingdom of heaven. Only a little child is free of the Beast, and that, for only a moment of time because even before puberty, a society confronts the child with the inordinate demands of the sexually dominated world of men and women. The characterization of those that inherit eternal life, that they will be free of the constraints of the Beast since they are like the angels and neither marry or are given in marriage, is worthy of much examination.

But, not only does religion keep the poor from killing the rich, in the majority of cases it keeps people from acting on the very impulses that result in neurosis and hysteria. In most cases, religion and church going for professing Christian, Jew or Moslem is no more than a "Talisman" or "Rabbit's Foot," a "Totem" of acceptable behavior. Reinforced with the "traditions of the elders," a "manual," whether Bible, Koran or Torah, the "saint" goes forth to do battle against those baser impulses and the monsters of the Id, the Beast.

In our own society, we provide an embarrassment of riches with which to sublimate sexual frustration. Social clubs (including churches), gangs, the Rotary, sports, various and sundry clubs and organizations that cater to men and women respectively or together, charities, etc., provide a plethora of means of evading the sexual question. The host of "Taboos" gives vent to an, at least, equal number of socially acceptable methodologies of evading the truth of repression.

So it is that few will "risk it all" on love, which, would be, ideally, the ultimate answer that men and women give lip-service to and upon which so many "professions of faith" are based. But, rather than risk it all, they will join clubs and "build models" rather than make the necessary sacrifices to find the real thing. What man or woman would descend into hell to light their torch from the Devil? Yet, either misunderstanding or willfully blind, they will refuse the light that is within them at a far greater cost.

Those that are able to conquer their fears to the degree that they are able to look to the stars with longing and unafraid become the pioneers and risk-takers, the adventurers who are unafraid of testing their faith in the crucibles of knowledge. They do not fear the unknown and will conquer the darkness finding, even in that velvet pavilion, an uncommon friendship, never becoming victims of their own despair. Whence come the Leif Ericsson's, Columbus', Vespucci's and Cabot's? They are, typically, men who have overcome the fears so common to men who, invariably, find their roots in sexual frustration and taboos. Men like the Apostle Paul, for whom these things hold no fear or anxiety are, accordingly, rare indeed. And, it must be added, to what degree was the success of such men predicated on the working out of their own God-created sexuality?

How do women become "bitches" and men become "wimps?" History is replete with examples. To separate the diabolical from the divine, you have to have an understanding of both. Hitler's Germany is an outstanding example of an entire system built on sexual fantasy and frustration. Yet, I have yet to come across any study that devotes itself to this root cause of such success. Why not: simply because "modern" civilizations, particularly Western ones, are caught up in the "equality" factor.

Hitler, unconsciously, hit on the winning combination of subjugation and submission. He did not, assuredly, consciously realize that his whole theme of conquest and the structuring of the Third Reich was intensely sexual in all its mechanisms from architecture to blitzkrieg. This, of course, explains much of the continuing fascination for Hitler and his regime. Weapons are phallic, "manly." War is a sexual "high." Therefore, the most unreasonable act of man, war, must be, can only be, understood in its sexual context; the ultimate "You show me yours and I'll show you mine!"

The contrary of this dark side is marriage and parenting. When that baby becomes a life, a genuinely helpless responsibility, it is designed to evoke the tenderest emotions of our heart and soul. In marriage, the woman, in submitting, is to evoke the same emotion and finest sensibility of the man. She is, ideally, saying: "My life is in your hands. If you are a real man, you will deal with me responsibly and tenderly." And, a real man will respond to that so long as the woman remains in submission and never takes advantage of it.

Even an unattractive woman or man overcomes much of this disadvantage in accepting the normal role of each. The "Face that launched a thousand ships" as opposed to the ugly ones that, lacking power through attractiveness or sexual desirability, attempt usurpation through devious means such as "equality," will always prevail. Our "terminal" generation cannot, regardless of the laws passed, make an ugly woman beautiful or desirable, cannot make her "valued." And even the most beautiful woman becomes only a "thing" when she prostitutes her beauty to "selling out" in attempts to dominate.

An ugly man of our terminal generation will often act out his frustration in ugly acts, trying in even criminal ways, to "redeem" himself. Many rapists, homosexuals and child abusers exemplify this.

In sum, notwithstanding Freud, Jung, Adler and all those that followed in their footsteps, unless the sickness of "equality" confused for "value" is confronted, the "disease" will admit of no "cure." It is for this reason that analysis has such a poor "cure-rate," estimated at no more than three (3) percent! It is also for this reason that psychological "experts" are as often wrong as they are right (50/50) in giving testimony as expert witnesses in court; as one judge of my acquaintance pointed out: "You would do as well flipping a coin!"

A non-debatable fact in our culture is the roll the schools play in fomenting neuroses in both children and adults. The "leadership" in the schools is continually sending "mixed signals" and constantly confusing children. For the Insomniac, I heartily endorse such publications as Mr. Honig's "Caught In The Middle: Educational reform for young adolescents in California public schools." At taxpayer expense, of course, you are treated to a handsomely bound (i.e. expensive) lengthy volume of deadly boring "Educationese." The contributing "experts," largely women, in education have, as usual, extolled, using all the familiar concepts and words like "matrix," the marvelous methodologies with which, if the stingy taxpayers would only cough up the dough, they could "fix" all the problems in the middle schools.

This entire, weighty volume could, if any of them had any practical sense and weren't so intent on stroking their own egos, be summed up in no more than two pages. Unhappily, even these two pages would have, as a bottom line: "Give us more money!"

"Have museums and opera houses replaced churches in the moral imagination of our betters?" Richard Grenier.

Closets. Much as we will crowd our souls in the same fashion.

To paraphrase Milton Friedman, the value of money cannot be successfully dictated by the whims of politicians and central bankers.

Clinton-Gore: Never will win an oratory contest but they have brought dullness and political lying to an unprecedented perfection.

Governor Ann Richards exemplifies all I have said about women in general. She was guaranteed applause from her Democratic Party cohorts by extolling abortion as means of contraception. Shame for Texas!

Faulkner to the Nobel Committee in 1949: "The only subject worth the agony and sweat of the artist is the human heart in conflict with itself."

We are all aware of "Media Distortion." Those of you that witnessed what was done with Dan Quayle's remarks about the hypothetical question posed to him concerning abortion witnessed such a flagrant abuse of media power. I have daughters. I love them without reservation. As I watched and listened to the interview with Mr. Quayle, I realized, as a father, what he was actually trying to say. Unfortunately, his literal words were badly, even purposefully, misconstrued.

So, I will say what I know he was trying to say. If one of my daughters were to have an abortion, they know The Lord's and my opinion on the subject. They know the burden of guilt they would have before God. But would I love them less because of their sin? Absolutely Not!

As with Mr. Quayle, if they were to seek my counsel, I would do my utmost to persuade them to honor God and not abort the baby. But no matter what any of my children do in their lives, I will continue to love them, continue to pray for them, continue to try to help them and, in no case, cut them off from that love. It is because of that unconditional love that I will never allow my children to think, at any time, that either God or I would ever condone sin in their lives. But the love remains, and, with true repentance, the forgiveness of sin as well.

There are very few periodicals that I read from cover to cover; National Review is one of the few. This is not because everything that is covered is of such a magnitude that it commands such of my time, it is because of the thoughtfulness and erudition with which the subjects are treated.

It seems almost more than coincidental that NR has an excellent article in the August issue by Joseph Adelson about E. Fuller Torrey's latest book: "Freudian Fraud." Those of us who are familiar with the tack of people like Torrey are not surprised that Freud continues to "stir the juices" of American psychologists.

Professor Adelson does a good job of pulling things together in his criticism of Torrey; many of the familiar names are here; Wilhelm Reich (Listen Little Man) and his "orgone theory," Lionel Trilling, Margaret Mead, Ruth Benedict, Benjamine Spock, Karl Menninger (the adulterer), Hayek, Frank Sulloway, Ernest Jones and, even, Rousseau. I'm not sure how Adelson failed to mention Tom Paine with Rousseau since so much of Paine is seen in both he and Freud.

The professor is correct in his concept that Americans, in general, have taken a real roller coaster ride in regard to psychology. As per Wylie, the "great hope" seems to have been that psychology, and the social sciences in general, would, with the hard sciences, usher in utopia. The dismal fact is that neither psychology nor the social sciences have ever been "scientific." The issues are far too large and, as pertaining to the mind, far too little understood, to ever admit of the criteria of true science.

But the false hope of the social sciences has produced a mind-set that has tried, unsuccessfully, to use the force of political power to try to change human nature. The studied Christian theologian could easily disabuse any of such a notion.

It's a little like Paul West's advice to would-be writers: "Go to those who have no hope!" Once you have entered this arena, whether through personal grief and tragedy or sharing a loved one's, you begin to understand the magnitude of the problem. Suffering does indeed open the "well of the soul" in a way that nothing else does.

Fortunately for us, as human beings, there is the glory and joy of love and God's creation to balance the grief and tragedy. In nothing does psychology hold so much promise, yet have such a dismal record, as in its attempts to translate this composite paradox of human nature and imagination. It is psychology's "unification theory," the "grail" that eludes but offers such tantalizing hints of its existence that the "crusade" must, it is thought, be successful.

So-called "experts" in education are the "poor trash" that attempts to force meaning through psychology that simply isn't there; doesn't, in fact, exist! That is why education has become the joke of the universities. Some benighted Ed. D. will read a book and steal the jargon of psychology, throw in a few buzz words or phrases and voila! He, more probably, she, has a new "theory" that will help students learn. So it was with Dewey and his pathetic and altogether destructive "psychology of learning." Thousands in the universities followed this "snake oil salesman" to the lasting shame of true academics and learning and, in the end, a terminal generation that not only doesn't think, but has no desire to do so!

I would be ever so hopeful if children were even reading Sir Arthur Conan Doyle, Edgar Rice Borroughs and Rex Stout in lieu of Stephen King and the covers of rock, record albums or CDs (presuming, of course, that they are reading at all). But when I consider the fact that education leadership is offering such trash as Honig's "study," which is the equivalent of the young people's mind-stultifying and destructive reading, listening and viewing, it isn't too hard to understand how we have come to such a sorry pass in our nation.

There is one flaw in National Review; it is written to the educated, conservative elite. I know, Mr. Buckley, this is not really a "flaw." Further, I know of the need for such information and the need to have it presented in its admirable format. Allow me to explain my use of the term "flaw."

As I and the contributors to the magazine have said themselves we have become an illiterate and ignorant nation. As such, magazines like National Review can only have a very limited readership. Granting that it is such readership that formulates the ideas and carries them through that determine much of the policy that directs a nation, my use of the term "flaw" is used to draw attention to a most important point, one that is too often lost to those of Mr. Buckley's and George Will's perspective; the fact that no matter how admirable and needed Tchaikovsky may be to our finer senses, to the advancement of a better civilization, Frank Sinatra, Spike Jones and Phil Harris are a part of a workable whole.

Neither Mr. Buckley nor Mr. Will have ever, in all probability, reamed their own septic system or done a valve job on their cars. Why should they? They can well afford to have others do such nasty jobs for them. But, as with Freud, what may they be missing in communicating to the masses of men by the lack of such experiences and knowledge?

As a "commoner," I still delight in "Cocktails For Two" and "Fietelbaum" and a beer will do me as well as the finest vintage. In fact, the "better things" are, doubtless, wasted on a man of my plebeian tastes. But I know the heart's desires of those that struggle day after tedious day to just make ends meet, the heartache of those that are, daily, losing ground no matter how hard they try.

As I was returning from Merced some while back, the old Dodge suddenly lost a cylinder. I got into Bakersfield on seven cylinders. As a mechanic, I knew what the possibilities were and some were simple; some were disagreeably nasty. I did the usual, simple things such as changing the plugs and wires (I had isolated the bad cylinder). No change. Obviously the problem was going to involve hot, greasy, hard work. So, I put it off as long as possible.

Now I knew the problem was not going to go away; it wasn't going to get better or correct itself. Since there was no one whom I could call on to do the work for me, I was going to have to roll up my sleeves, gather my courage and fix the problem.

As it turned out, a rocker arm had broken and "killed" the cylinder. The fix was simple but, hard, greasy and thoroughly disagreeable- particularly in the 100 plus degree heat of the Bakersfield Summer. While I was up to my elbows in sweat, sludge and grease, I changed a leaky exhaust manifold gasket and crawled under the car to fix a cracked vapor-recovery line, things I had been meaning to "get around to." I also charged the A/C, and did a major tune-up on the old car.

Now I did not enjoy any of this. Absolutely not! I may be dumb but I ain't nuts. Could I have afforded to have someone else do the job? Yes. Why didn't I? Because I could do it myself and I would not have to worry about getting ripped-off by Sears or someone else. I know the auto repair business too well not to be sensible of the choices.

There was also something else involved here. I needed to do the work just as I need to fix up old houses and other disagreeable tasks. I am a worker as well as an author and philosopher-poet. I need my children to always know that Dad will never be "too good" to get grease under his fingernails and that it will always be vital that people be able to do such things for themselves.

We have not "fixed" government or education by "throwing money at the problems." We never will fix these institutions in such a manner. They can only be fixed by people that not only care, but are able to "do." Bryan's "Cross Of Gold" speech did not "fix" anything no matter how erudite and persuasive; and if he could now examine his stand on the Income Tax and Farm Subsidies?

Last night, I had a Praying Mantis doing service in one of my windowsills. These insects do good work and I left it undisturbed. As I was sitting out in evening's fading light, the sky overhead was a pastel blue, turning to platinum, copper and, finally, a pastel, rose-gold at the ridge of the mountains; awesome beauty! The clear air and fading light returned the silhouettes of the mountains in such clarity that the individual trees stood out in sharp outline as they marched along the ridges.

The stars made their accustomed entrance. Incredibly, two "smokers" passed overhead within five minutes of each other. These are "shooting stars" that leave a long contrail of smoke as they burn through the atmosphere. It is unusual to see these, let alone, two of them at nearly the same time. Oddly, one traversed a Northerly path and the other a Southerly. Just then, something hit my shoulder and bounced behind my back. I got up and discovered a huge moth on the back of my chair. I sent him on his way. A few bats could be seen, flitting and darting in their, seeming, erratic fashion as they hunted.

I have just finished painting the bathroom in the old house; another thoroughly disagreeable chore. I hate painting almost as much as roofing. But the tiredness that consumes me is from honest work and I am grateful to be able to do it.

Politicians lack the "common touch." This is what I meant by their being "deprived," just as children are, in the opportunities to do honest work that places things in their true perspective. And, lacking this, they do not know what is important or how to "fix" what is wrong. Our forefathers knew. Faulkner still knew as he showed so well in "The Bear." Stephen Crane and a host of others knew also.

I just had an enjoyable visit with my old friend, the Episcopal Priest. I don't name him in deference to not wanting him "tarred" with my brush (I have the same policy in regard to many I know in a host of other organizations). I pointed out to him the fact that Tom Paine could only be understood in light of the appalling condition of religion in his time.

Presuming they "knew," the churches had long since stopped trying to build on the foundation of Jesus Christ and the Bible and had continued to scrabble around the playpen as though a foundation did not need a structure to justify itself. Just so, politicians "know" even though they have never worked up a sweat with hammer and saw. Yet it is such "leaders" that have betrayed, as much through ignorance as through greed, the founding principles of America.

To my good friend, State Senator Don Rogers: Don't give up the battle. As a pilot myself, I really bemoan the potential loss of that great, old Mooney. Better you should give it to me. I had a friend in Texas who had a franchise for this marvelous plane. The IRS has to be made accountable for the horrorific economic conditions in our nation. Like you, I also suffer from the so-called "tax reform" of 1986. People don't generally realize how the Congress itself precipitated the S&L fiasco by this legislation. This does not excuse those, like Bush, who tried to cover up and protect those, like his own son, from early action on the problem and prosecution of the greedy guilty.

Keep fighting the good fight, Don. A host of others and I are in your corner on this issue. And, while the F.B.I. no longer sends agents to visit me personally, I know they are keeping watch as well. I wait each year for the accustomed "invitation" to audit and always find the meetings "educational."

Unlike Senator Rogers, the "system" has a problem with a man who drives an old '64 Chevy pickup with a wet rag around his neck to keep cool and lives on a net income of about $400 a month. The problem is being "rich on paper" and still living far below the government's "poverty level." I would, as a friend pointed out, be a nightmare to some poor eligibility worker if I, as I am qualified to do, applied for welfare, medical and food stamps.

While I am on the subject, let's talk about another group of "second class citizens," the Smoker! Now I am not Andy Rooney. I gave up on Andy when he caved in to the perverts due to the media pressure. But, I do have a streak of "Rooneyism" in me. It really comes out in regard to smoking.

I have been addicted to tobacco since a young child. I grew up in an environment in which tobacco was a given in our culture. It was the patriotic thing to do to send cigarettes to our "boys overseas." Doctors would give their views on which cigarette was best and tobacco companies sponsored our favorite radio shows.

This is not a commendation of using tobacco. It is harmful and does no one any good. It is more of a curse than a blessing. Yet, it was tobacco that, more than any other crop, helped establish the early economies of the colonies. Tobacco continues to be a mainstay of some states. But, again, this is not to say we wouldn't be far better off if the stuff had never been "invented."

Given the facts, the truth, that tobacco is harmful, even deadly; I am talking about the fact that it has become another tool in the hands of government and the liberals to force their will on a slave population. It is one thing that even the poorest dupe can get on the bandwagon about. Nowhere has this "phony war" against a "vice" been more abused than among religious people.

I will be saying much more about Thomas Paine in a future essay. But I will say this of him now. History accurately records the monumental part this much-maligned man had in both the beginnings and the success of the founding of this nation. It was his theological position, like Mencken's, that got him in so much trouble. But Paine was far too accurate in his assessment of "priest craft" to let it go by the board.

As a Christian, though a heterodox one and one who smokes I recognize the point of Paine's apologetic against organized religion. I have suffered more from "good Christians" than from any other segment of our society. And in few things do such "good people" lord it over us "weaker brethren" than in the use of tobacco. The fact, as Paine accurately pointed out, that these "Pharisees" never seemed to have learned the lesson of Jesus in this regard has made them mean-spirited and, looking at only the "outside of their cups," the "judges" of what is "spiritual."

Unlike Paine and Mencken, however, I honestly pity such people. I have yet to meet such a one who takes real pleasure in God's love and creation. So intent are they in preaching their own brand of "righteousness," the only pleasure in life they seem to have is their self-appointed task of condemning all those that don't subscribe to their own peculiar ideologies and smacking their lips in satisfaction with the Pharisee's Prayer: "Lord, I'm not like this sinful 'Publican!'" If only they could be honest enough to say what they really mean it would be this: "Lord, You sure are lucky to have such a pure person as myself to put these sinners in their place!"

As a smoker I have never treated the world as my personal ashtray. I have always tried to be considerate of those that do not smoke and find it, rightfully, objectionable. When I am visiting with friends or others who do not smoke, I will go outside to indulge the habit. In other words, I am sensitive to others in this regard.

My ire is directed toward those, particularly those of religious persuasion that would attempt to justify their own sins by relegating me to second-class citizenship spiritually because of such a silly thing. The most charitable construction I can place on such an attitude is "childishness." Oddly, such people don't see sin in their own lives; they are too busy judging my "sin." They don't see, for example, the sin in shaming God by supporting charlatans like Oral Roberts, Pat Robertson, Mario Cerullo, Schuller, Crouch, and the host of others of their ilk who actually shame The Lord and The Gospel by their Hollywood antics. Of course, such people don't see it as sin to simply "watch" these idiots on TV. It is a sad commentary on such that simply "watching" these shameless beggars and phony "gospel peddlers" is not the "same thing" as agreeing with them and supporting them.

My point is the amazement that such people can so "easily discern sin" in such things as smoking but never realize the sin of such greater magnitude of aiding and abetting the Enemy by giving any time or credence to those that are the real enemies of the Gospel. But here again, the fault of such childishness goes directly to the leadership in the churches. As I said, religious people are still in the business of "re-converting the converted," not building people up in the faith. The churches are "play-pens," not "schools of love, moral discipline and righteousness." It's as if the foundation needed no structure, no on-going learning and discipline, no word of commission except "Go out and play!"

I plan a trip back to Arkansas and North Carolina. I hope to see folks in Texas and Missouri also. There is a need to travel and feel the pulse of my country, to speak to the truckers and waitresses, to fellow travelers and business people. There is a need to not get so involved with the problems of California that I lose sight of the fact that there is a whole nation out there that is in trouble. I'll look forward to sharing what I learn on my return.

CHAPTER FIFTEEN

CHRISTIAN PERSPECTIVE

SEPTEMBER, 1992

ACTS 13:41

I'm writing this essay from my folk's place in Fort Smith, Arkansas.

Leaving Bakersfield about 7 p.m. Friday, I arrived here about 4 p.m. Sunday. It is an historic city with many, old, fascinating structures. The Arkansas River flows through it and they celebrated the city's 150th anniversary some while back.

The folk's house is an old Victorian; two-story with gables, widow's walk and a beautiful, turn of the century facade and thirteen rooms. There is the exquisite charm of old-South decadence, a respectable graying, of assuming the mantle of old age gracefully in civilized style- thoroughly comfortable. It has an interesting history and they have done a great deal of work in renovating. It has all the charm from a South that is, rightfully, proud of its history and civilized manners. The house is filled, top to bottom, with antiques and the accumulation of decades of travel and living. Many of the mementos of my childhood are in evidence. The old pictures are my main interest along with the histories of ancestors from all over the South.

One of the fascinating things about the architecture here is the great number of brick and stone buildings. No fear of earthquakes, obviously. Also, many of the old homes are built in the Victorian manner with an abundance of filigree, gingerbread, scrimshaw and turned columns, widow-walks and turrets. Ancient gum trees and oaks abound and, with the wisteria, ivy and magnolia, many homes are park-like.

I left Lake Isabella Friday, August 7. I stopped in Bakersfield and had dinner with some friends, and pointed the disreputable-looking Dodge East on highway 58 toward Tehachapi. Hitting highway 14, I went through Mojave, hung a left on 58 again toward Barstow. It was evening and quite warm, but not as warm as if I had been driving during the desert heat of daytime.

The closest I came to disaster was two near head-ons before I got through Barstow. The combination of bad roads and bad (drunk?) drivers nearly got me. But, I made it through and, safely on Interstate 40, started following

263

the old Dodge's radiator cap east. Just shy of Flagstaff, I pulled into a rest stop and crawled into the back of the old wagon for some much needed sleep about 3 a.m.

As an aside, I was amazed at the crowded conditions of the rest stops. For example, the one in Flagstaff was so crowded that vehicles were parked on the roads leading into and out of the place. I had to squeeze in between two tractor-trailers for the night. This was evidence of the large number of people getting out of California. On the return trip, the rest stops were virtually empty! No one was coming to California, except illegal aliens and they sneak through the porous borders.

Up early, I was on the road again into the rising sun. Sometime about 10 a.m., the needle for the alternator took a dive to the left and the temperature gauge started climbing fast. I knew I had lost the belt. Now you can drive a long way without an alternator in the daytime but you aren't going far without a functioning water pump.

So, coasting to a stop alongside the highway, I got out and, sure enough, the pulleys were empty. Well, no one drives these old junkers without the requisite "emergency" repair equipment. Hauling out my sockets and wrenches, I soon had the A/C and power steering belts off. Then, getting a length of the nylon rope which all us knowledgeable types always have handy, I fashioned the necessary "belt" and got it hung on the pump and damper pulleys. No point in even trying to get the alternator going with such an arrangement.

Cranking up the old car, "Casa Dodge" for the next few weeks, I was back on my way at about twenty mph max. But that was fast enough to keep water circulating through the engine and slow enough to keep the crude "belt" on. It was now about noon and the desert had heated up pretty well by the time I made it the twelve miles to a place where I could buy the replacement belt. Eight bucks and about an hour of profusely hot and sweaty labor later I was on my way again without any further incident.

I spent the next night at a rest stop just shy of Amarillo. Because of the "torture" seat in the old Dodge, I stopped frequently to stretch my back and legs. This gave me ample opportunity to visit with fellow travelers and talk to people at the roadside restaurants and gas stations.

There is an "Exodus" from California. One fellow, "Bob," typified the new "Reverse, Dust-Bowl migrants." He had left Long Beach and was moving to Georgia. The crime and violence, high housing costs and taxes, lack of employment, alien cultures and graffiti, an impotent state government, these are the common reasons for the exodus of those that have a choice.

Bob had relatives in the South. As he explained, if you have to live poor, better to do so among your own kind than with, as he put it, "...niggers and Mexicans!" Oddly, he didn't seem aware of the fact that many of our fellow travelers were Negroes; and they were leaving for the same reasons! And, it would have been pointless to mention the preponderance of Negroes in Georgia. He would have pointed out, correctly, that they wouldn't be of the Watts variety and, also correctly, the welfare Mexicans, legal or illegal, wouldn't be in attendance.

It left me with a sense of history. All of us who are students of the great migration of the twenties and thirties that settled so much of California, particularly the San Joaquin Valley, can't help but be impressed with a sense of what the road and rest stops, filled with these families, represents. But, unlike their ancestors from the Grapes of Wrath, they are returning to their roots, to lives that began in the South somewhere back then. "Déjà vu all over again" as some wit said.

As I drive, I notice that state troopers pull up behind me, look me over, reading my bumper stickers (National Rifle Association, AAA and American Flag) then pull alongside, notice I'm Caucasian, and sail on by. I never speed but I know the old Dodge attracts their attention. In all the miles across our nation and back, I could count the number of old cars on the highway on the fingers of both hands. One filling station attendant in New Mexico, as I was returning to California, summed it up neatly. He asked me where I was coming from and I told him I had been to North Carolina and Arkansas and was returning to California. He looked at me and the old Dodge in amazement and said: "In this!"

Here in Fort Smith, the kind of poverty in evidence is considerably different; I might as well call it a better "quality" of poverty. As in many places in the rest of the country, California included, there is a mix of the "old and the new." It is sad to see so many of the historic, old houses, falling into decay. Fort Smith has many of these old, historic homes. Also, I must mention the catfishing. The confluence of the Three Rivers Area offers some of the best catfishing to be found in the nation. This accounts to me, as a fisherman, as one of the better "qualities" of poverty as opposed to California and other places not blessed with Arkansas' abundance of water. No man, in my opinion, can call himself truly poor when he has access to a bit of water with bass and catfish.

Also, the trees are worth mentioning. Arkansas, like most of the South, is green! Trees and grass everywhere; I do confess I love the wide expanses of the desert and ocean, the majesty of the mountain ranges. But it is a treat to the eyes, after six years of drought in California, to see such an abundance of water and greenery. If there is, as I believe, a difference in the quality of poverty, better to be poor in Arkansas than California. Even the road kill is better quality, Armadillos and Possums, not scrawny jackrabbits and flea-ridden ground squirrels.

Clinton has not been good for Arkansas. Most of the natives are quick to point this out to me. It is most interesting to get the "home folk's" view of their Governor. He has been particularly bad in the one area he boasts of: Education! Talk to the "grunts" in the schools, rather than listening to the political hype out of the Governor's and Superintendent's offices, and you get a better perspective of the true situation. And, if there is one thing I am expert in ferreting out, it is the real situation in schools rather than the one "advertised."

Every time I get on the topic of education I am reminded of the old lady who wrote the following letter to her state, agriculture expert:

"Dear Sir;

"I went out to my chicken yard this morning and found every one of my chickens on their back with their feet sticking straight up in the air. What's wrong with my chickens?"

The public servant wrote back:

"Dear Madam:

"Your chickens are dead!"

Now there are two sides to this story. One: If so-called public servants are going to get questions like this, you can hardly blame them for the low opinion they have of the "great unwashed." Two: It is unusual to get the kind of expertise and quick response from government this lady received. Of a certainty, most politicians don't know yet that the chickens are dead or, for that matter, would even be able to diagnose what killed them.

The status of education in Arkansas is deplorable and not likely to get any better. Of course, I could say the same thing of any state in the union at this time. But it is particularly acute here in Arkansas. As with most states, one of the prime reasons for such miserable conditions is Special Education and Federally mandated programs; just another case of spending $40,000 for one "special" child while spending $2,000 for one who might contribute to the general welfare of society. And the kids themselves know this is insane! Why don't the bureaucrats? But it is an easy "gimme" for politicians to trumpet their "concern" for the "poor disabled" and "equal opportunity!" The problem, as Californians are finding out, is that the money has run out; the "family budget" is "busted" due to trying to do everything for everybody. And the taxpayers are sick of getting the bill for a failed system of "do-gooding!"- Mostly do-gooding for the Willie Browns and Paul Honigs in politics.

The convention in Houston was led off by two, excellent speeches by Pat Buchanan and Ronald Reagan. I am amazed by Reagan's erudition at his age. If I live to be that old, I hope I will be able to sustain a coherent thought, let alone give such speeches.

But, as to the political atmosphere from D.C. to California, it reminds me a bit of the fellow who came up with a marvelous device to double your gas mileage. It was sheer genius in its simplicity. Once attached to your gas tank gauge, when the needle came down to the half-full mark, it reversed the polarity of the sending unit and the needle would start up to the full mark. The only bug in the device was that no matter what he did and no matter what the gauge said the car would still run out of gas! Even when the gauge said you had a full tank!

As far as I know, the guy never did get the danged thing to work right. The device showed a full tank but there wasn't any way for it to make gas! California has discovered this simple fact of physics: 0 = 0. Nothing remains nothing no matter how much you might wish it otherwise. When the last cookie is gone, you can lick the crumbs. When they are gone, you face the empty jar and the memory of the cookies. Wishful thinking won't put any more cookies in the jar or gas in the tank.

Pete Wilson and Willie Brown know the tank is empty. But neither, understandably, wants to go down in history, any more than Mr. Hoover did, as the one to tell people the facts, let alone, act on those ugly facts! Mr. Bush, and members of Congress, knows the facts also. None of them wants to deal with the ugly reality of the situation either.

But history is rather unforgiving of the facts, particularly when those "facts" are truthful. None of the present leadership can avoid the dim pronouncement of the history being currently written of our nation and its leadership; they are a greedy, egotistical, selfish bunch of clowns without enough backbone or moral integrity to make the hard decisions that are the only alternatives to slavery for all of us. But history will record those decisions and they will, as I have often warned, be made, with or without the "consent of Congress."

I left Fort Smith on Tuesday, passing through cities with magical names like Memphis, through the Smoky Mountains and arrived in North Carolina Wednesday to see friends there. It has been a real treat to see the country. Driving through Tennessee, Kentucky, Georgia, South Carolina, I am struck by the vivid greenery of which we Californians have been so deprived the past, few years. It is nearly postcard perfect in its cleanliness and park-like beauty through the land of Dixie. No litter or graffiti anywhere in sight. No "Spanish" radio stations. They even have to mow the green grass and abundant vegetation alongside the highways.

I have just finished watching "The Other Israel," a well-researched and very professional documentary of Zionism. I am thoroughly familiar with the content from my own historical and theological studies; there is nothing

•

new in the presentation for me but I am grateful for such a well-reasoned and thoughtful production; I wish every American could see it.

It is helpful, however well studied, to have our memories stirred concerning things that fall into that, increasingly with age, yawning maw of forgetfulness. As with Benjamin Franklin, Winston Churchill warned of Zionism, saying: "Wouldn't it be one of the most malevolent paradoxes of history if both Messiah and the Anti-Christ were to have their human origins in the same people?"

The video was also a good reminder of many things I have written in the past such as the Zionist origins and control of the major media (ABC, NBC, and CBS) using "goi" fronts in their presentation. The Zionist origins of Communism are well known, as are the origins and control of the major moving picture empires (excepting United Artists). The video makes a good point about God's restraining work through history in frustrating Zionism's agenda together with the futility of trying to attack and destroy innocent Jews (non-Zionists) as Hitler and Stalin tried to do.

I have to mention, in passing, the "joke" some "artist" has played on the poor, unsuspecting folks in Atlanta. You can't miss it as you enter the city from the North. It is a huge joke. It rises several stories into the air and can be seen a mile away. It is supposed to represent a ripe peach perched on the tall column. Now this is going to be difficult to explain, let alone believe, without getting too descriptive for younger readers. This immense "peach" stares at you like something you would expect to see in Penthouse or Hustler magazines. Why the people of Atlanta don't rise up in wrath at the city fathers for even hoisting it up for the entire world to see is beyond me. They should certainly be agitating for its removal. Maybe the "artist" was a homosexual. That, at least, would explain the "sculpture" and motive.

Downtown Atlanta is a new city of tall, modern buildings mixed with the old South of gentility and civilized manners. Angilino's though, was housed in an old hotel right next door to the ultra-modern law office building. Using the restroom, I was treated to a ride in an ancient Otis elevator to the second floor where the "facilities" were located. Resplendent (once) of marble-faced decor, the material was cracked and broken pieces had disappeared here and there; but enough remained to remind me of the splendor and nobility the old place once had.

Breakfast is leisurely and delightful. A gentle rain is falling. There is no hint, as yet, of what Hurricane Andrew will do to Florida and Louisiana. My buddy has "sweet tea," the national drink in the South, and I have my usual coffee with breakfast. With our meal finished, we are ready to do some sightseeing. Negro faces predominate everywhere as we stroll about. I wonder aloud to friend, "Whatever is to become of all these people when government largess (our tax dollars) can no longer pay them off or support them?" My friend, I know, has wondered the same thing.

We are on our way to one of the most interesting features of the old city; the Underground, historic site of an old railway; now rows of boutiqueish shops catering to tourists. It is a marvelous display of the old and new Georgia, Calvin Klein and Civil War mementos and curios.

Going into one of the more interesting shops, attracted by the antiquities on display, we have a most interesting conversation with the owner, Grant! What that name meant in Georgia a hundred years ago! Imagine my surprise to learn that Grant was actually from Taft! Incredible; here I am in the very heart of Dixieland and the fellow I am talking to, the owner of the shop, came from my neighboring town back in California! Grant proved to be a really fine and helpful chap. I'm sending him a complimentary copy of Confessions of an Okie Intellectual. I hope he enjoys it.

It is time to leave the Underground for a 2 p.m. appointment with someone my friend has to meet. He has bought a nicely mounted set of minnie balls, those very destructive .50+ caliber bullets from our national tragedy.

After returning to my friend's home I've just taken another, short break from the writing to go sit for a while on the small dock of the lake, more accurately, large pond, near the house. It is nearing suppertime. As I sit, I marvel at the jewel-like perfection of the setting. It is about 78 degrees outside. The humidity is low and a cover of high, thin cirrus permits the sun to dapple the lake with reflected highlights from gentle swells created by the fish rising to take insects. A large dragonfly buzzes near the surface, hunting smaller prey.

Nearby, a beautifully formed Magnolia is budding. There are also grand, red oaks, sycamores, mimosa and the tall, thin, long-needled, white pines. The music of the wind through these reminds me of the same sound my old, digger pines make. Walking paths, soft and plush-carpeted by the pine needles, invite your legs and feet to wander. The bank of the pond is all grass-covered round about. As I sit on the end of the dock, my feet nearly touching the water, the ducks glide up to inspect this "intruder." They expect me to give them some treat and, having nothing with me, I have to disappoint them and promise a rain check. I suppose they believe me since they glide away without a squawk (quack?).

The very large satellite dish nearby reminds me that, notwithstanding the elegiac surroundings, "everything's up to date in Kansas City." Well, back to work.

I have been researching these groups like CIM, The Aryan Nations, etc. for about five years. I am finally getting to the point where I can put a "Human Face" on the groups and their leaders. Our legislators are passing laws with one hand tied behind their backs. They simply don't have the facts and the media is prone to so much distortion that such information from such sources does more harm than good. Can I possibly hope to correct some of these misconceptions? I work in the hope that I can.

After all, I have taught Cultural Anthropology at the college level and am expert in Behaviorism and what we are dealing with, essentially, in regard to the Neo-Nazis, Skinheads, CIM, Aryan Nations, the Klans, is cultures in conflict. Very few in these organizations are truly motivated by racial hatred, particularly those in leadership positions. But there is no denying the fact that as soon as you mention the Ku Klux Klan, the "grandaddy" of all these organizations and movements, you will get a reaction. No one is without an opinion no matter how ignorant or well informed the opinion-giver. You take the "label" and you take all that goes with it.

The next day I'm back on the road again heading for the folks place in Fort Smith. Like Faulkner, I have experienced the "gloom of green." As a true Westerner, too much greenery gets to me and I begin to long for the "Big Emptys" of the West; the mountains and deserts, the huge trees, rugged, granite monoliths and trackless and fenceless wilderness areas. I'm a man who will always want "walkn' 'n' lookin'" room.

Contributing to the dense flora of Arkansas are a great variety of oaks-the Bur, White, Red (Southern, Swamp and Northern), Post, Yellow, Black, Dwarf, Shumard, Water, Blackjack, and Willow. The largest Brown Trout ever caught, a behemoth of 40 lbs., 4 oz., was recently taken by a Mr. Howard Collins in the Little Red River near Heber Springs. A record Blue Catfish of 74 lbs., 13 oz., was caught in Nickajack Reservoir near Chattanooga in neighboring Tennessee. They grow 'em big in the South. All you fellow fishermen eat your hearts out; I am.

About thirty years ago, I had the opportunity to tour all the Western, National parks. It happened that I was asked to be in the wedding of an old college "roomie." I had a '53 Chevy wagon that I had just put a new engine in. It was decided that in return for attending the wedding and bringing the wedding presents back to California, my old buddy would pay for the gas. Good deal. After the wedding (In Minnesota), I pointed the old wagon West and hit every National Park between there and California. You must consider the fact that, lacking the modern Interstate system we have now and the lack of crowds, it would be an entirely different tour than what you would have in the present time. There were no crowds or litter problems. You felt reasonably secure to pull over and park for the night almost anywhere. People were friendly and helpful all along the way and gas was cheap.

In such an enviable environment and time, I toured the Grand Tetons, Bryce, Zion, Mt. Rushmore, Pipestone, Custer, Yellowstone, Wind Cave,

Yosemite and many that escape memory through the passage of time. It was a glorious experience and I have seldom spent my time to greater advantage.

I recalled that marvelous journey as I have crossed the Southern area of the U.S. from West to East and back again. If I still had the old Stinson or Alon, flying would have been far easier but I would have missed a great deal that, even given modern, Interstate travel (much of the time, boring), I was able to stop and enjoy along the way.

I had been "drinking in" the atmosphere of the South while heading toward No. Carolina and pass through Little Rock, Memphis (No, I didn't stop at Graceland. I have the music of Elvis and that is sufficient for me), Nashville (enjoyed the wide selection of music programs on my radio through this neck of the woods), Knoxville, Ashville, Winston-Salem and turn South at Greensboro. My trip to Atlanta goes through Charlotte. The South still lives and so much of my reading of the great, Southern writers comes alive through these historic names of historic cities.

When I return to Fort Smith, the Times-Record is telling of a shoot-out in Idaho involving a CIM-linked man, one Randy Weaver, who has held federal agents at bay for some time. One U.S. Deputy Marshall, William Degan, was killed. The U.S. Marshall's Service has had Weaver's cabin under surveillance off and on for more than a year. Weaver claims the police set him up on a weapons charge. Given my own study of such matters, he may very well be telling the truth. After all, "we" can't let these "uppity white folks" flaunt the "revenoors" and feather merchants from D.C. No tellin' where all that would lead!

Tragically, at last count, Mr. Weaver's wife and 13-year-old son have been shot to death by the "authorities." Someone like so-called "evangelist," Tony Alamo (you remember, the guy I wrote about that seemed to like to watch young girls being paddled in the name of religion to get his kicks?) is back in court trying to get a federal trustee to allow him to resume his "business ventures." And, in Baton Rouge a 20-month-old boy is found dead of thirst in an apartment with his dead mother. The toddler survived, it is estimated, for several days on crackers but couldn't get water. No word, yet, on the cause of death of his mother.

It does make you wonder, doesn't it, about the actual status of the richest and most blessed nation in history? In Lincoln, New Mexico, computer analysis is being used with the one, known, legitimate photograph of William Bonny, aka Billy the Kid, to determine the authenticity of many other pictures and, according to spokesmen for the Lincoln County Heritage Trust Museum, to aid in the same procedures for law enforcement to better identify suspected criminals. Humm, I wonder?

I am very grateful that alcoholism doesn't seem to be in my "gene pool." I can take the stuff or leave it alone; always could. But I always suspected it might, in some manner, be hereditary. Much proof of my suspicion now exists. The Hemingways are prime examples.

The Lord knows I have suffered enough grief that if I had a propensity for alcohol I most surely would have availed myself of such a "liquid solution" long ago. But I can, at least, sympathize with the conditions of some people in a few cases, where the world must, indeed, look better through the bottom of a glass or bottle.

A political cartoon in one Southern paper shows the Clampetts leaving California in their old jalopy with the caption: "I've had it with the crime, gang wars, riots, earthquakes, brush fires, mudslides, high taxes and state budget crises—Step on it Jethro... We're goin' back home!!..." So it was as I discovered crossing the country. A whole lot of people have decided to leave with the Clampetts.

A curious thing- most Southern newscasts and papers pay virtually no heed to the happenings in California. Whether through envy, disdain, or some other attitude, California is ignored by the South. I haven't had anyone spit on my license plate yet (doubtless because they feel sorry for me when they see my vehicle) but the attitude is certainly one of contempt for the "Golden State." I can, naturally, understand the attitude when I think of Willie Brown and our Democratic legislature.

But, my dear, Southern countrymen, you better pay attention; what is happening in California is bound to catch up with y'all as well! It may be California that is saying: "Bar me five" today but hit 'll be y'all t' marrah! After all, Atlanta, like L.A. and so many other major, metropolitan cities, has its own "doorways" of poverty. I've seen them. Metal-cased and sheathed in the old, downtown buildings, the metal rusted and corroded, eaten through by the urine of the indigent, poor and homeless for whom a doorway is "home."

I've also contacted Richard Butler's organization, Christian Identity, in Idaho and, hopefully, he can help "flesh out" some of the popular misconceptions about his organization- especially since the "Feds" are shooting women and 13 year-old boys. In short, I don't trust media to tell the truth about such organizations and want it from the "horse's mouth" whenever possible regardless of the popular (or unpopular) view. Margaret Meade doesn't have the corner on the cultural research market. I would certainly, as one qualified in such research, counter some of her views in any event.

If what I am about may be called a "quest," the term may not be far off the mark. I am searching for Truth, Justice and the American Way. We know we have lost our direction in this nation. Scoundrels and thieves have stolen and sold our birthright for the "pleasures of sin for a season." The Randy Weaver's and others are, primarily, guilty of only trying to do something about it. In the trying, they come up against an evil system of which I have written so much about. It is a system that only those like me understand. Not because of any superiority of individual mind or character, but because of training and experience, particularly in the areas of human behavior, theology and history, not to mention the schools of the ghetto and barrio, and government in general.

It is probably a truism: "Once a teacher, always a teacher." I can't seem to help trying to teach and preach. There is a, largely, it seems, deathless optimism in real teachers. They just don't seem to give up. So, forgive me if I wind up telling you more than you ever wanted to know about some things. I do realize, however, that like family photos, they have little interest to those not "related." But what is happening in our nation requires, for understanding, a great breadth of, often seeming, unrelated facts. It is a given that the great majority of people have little interest in, or knowledge of, Tom Paine, Rousseau, Comte, Voltaire. History is no longer taught in our schools and is virtually irrelevant to this generation.

I think it is a tragedy that Nelson Eddy and Jeanette MacDonald are lost to our posterity. It is a national tragedy that people's lives are so filled with the effluvia, bric-a-brac, things of seeming importance that the things of real value are no longer given credence or a place in our culture.

We've come a long way from the ideals of our Forefathers to the place where our lives do seem to "...consist of the abundance of things which we possess." In spite of Jesus' warning not to lay up "treasure" where moth and rust (and dust) corrupts, the "Lord's people" are intent on letting the detritus of life take the place of the work we are called to.

I enjoy the show, Northern Exposure. I do not enjoy the lack of morality of many of the characters but I do enjoy the setting and the literateness of the scripts together with the fancifulness of some of the players.

Children should be able to enjoy watching and chasing butterflies. Children in Somalia are starving to death. Children in Bosnia are being shelled, bombed and shot. Such children do not chase butterflies. And what are we to say to God of our own nation when a toddler in Baton Rouge is found, with his dead mother, who has died of thirst!

Kierkegaard said we are "not!" but "we are in the process of becoming." Children in most parts of the world are not in the process of "becoming." It takes an enlightened society to allow and encourage children in "becoming." The best civilizations encouraged chasing butterflies.

Comte gave it the name: "Social Science." He and Fourier hoped such "Science" would usher in Utopia. It didn't happen that way. Perhaps they were, like so many others, trying to excuse their own sinful selfishness or, perhaps, they were simply altruistic. I am inclined to the former because of my own, earned, and studied, cynicism concerning human nature.

Just maybe, if Thomas Paine had been a little more inclined to the truth of human nature, he himself might have been more tolerant of the foibles of "priests." As justifiably laudable his self-sacrifices were for the Rights of Man both in America and France, it is one of the misfortunes of history that this great patriot had to face such an ignoble, superstitious lot the churches of his time represented.

It is another tragedy of history that the leadership of the churches of all stripes has never confessed their own sins in this regard. In respect to the blind leading the blind, consider the fact that Paine, Comte, Rousseau, Fourier and so many others never recognized the tremendous debt they owed God and His Word in even being able to formulate the ideals they professed. Had they only recognized the actual Truth of God's Word as opposed to the superstitious, self-serving systems of religion represented as speaking for Him, how different might have been their bitter denouncements of religion and "priestcraft."

As admirable as Paine's work in "pamphleteering" and, even facing death, both here and in England and France, in the cause of liberty, it contrasts sharply with his blind prejudice in regard to God. In few other lives does the truth of Jesus' words that: "No one can come unto me unless the Father draws him" show itself so sharply. That a man so gifted with genius in so many ways could have written so absurdly and childishly when it came to God and the Bible is almost incomprehensible. But, tragically, as with so many other gifted men of genius, such was the case.

Had Paine only resorted to God's Word and let Him speak for Himself rather than taking, as his source, what others were saying, how different it might have been. But he did not. He allowed the "Priests of Baal" to do God's talking for Him and all Paine's "theological" writings show the two-fold impress of his tragic mistake, from his egotistical and juvenile "examples" to his outright, critical errors; even giving credence to the very superstitions, as examples, of the very things he was fighting against. Imagine this great man actually having Eve eating an "apple!" It leaves one wondering if Paine ever resorted to the primary source, the Bible, of his attack or just took "priest's" and "Blackcoat's" word for it! It is always painful to witness a great man making himself look silly. But, alas, such is the case of Thomas Paine. And, sadly, another great man, George Washington, could not countenance such "silliness."

It is almost impossible, in retrospect, to believe Paine could be so blind to the lack of the very things in Scripture, such as myths and fables of the Greeks and Jews, which he used to make his own points! He stands condemned by the very illustrations of which he thought the Bible guilty. It is with a great sadness that I realize how very much he might have gained had he only let God's Word speak for itself to his own need and longing rather than judge it by systems of mere "religion" and false prophets. But how often have we had to witness this very same weakness in men who, by their noble works and deeds, should have known better.

But, as I have written in the past, the very genius of men, no matter the sin and wickedness of the individuals, still gives praise to God and His glory is reflected in the "Thomas Paines" whether the men ever credit God in their lives, words or deeds.

The end result of men like Thomas Paine not recognizing, not being able to distinguish, the sublime Truth and separate it from the false teachers which abounded, was that a system established itself through ignoble thieves and liars which succeeded in simply passing on the torch of corruption from one administration to the next down to the present time. But imagine if you will, these champions of liberty being blind to the very Bible to which they owed all their ideals of liberty, the very Bible which, through men like Luther, Huss, Wycliff, Knox and so many others, they owed the very noble ideals they even had enough knowledge and freedom to express! So, tragically, such champions of liberty as Paine and Rousseau lived, themselves, to see those ideals dashed on the rocks of distortion, unscrupulous men using the human ideals, devoid of the checks and balances of God's Truth, to their own, selfish purposes.

I would like to offer, as an apologetic, the consideration of Washington's later coldness to his old friend the fact that Washington could hardly do other in the face of Paine's attack on the Bible. Even so, I know Washington evidenced enough good sense to heed his old friend's advice as in the following letter from Paine: "When we contemplate the fall of empires, and the extinction of the nations of the ancient world, we see but little more to excite our regret than the moldering ruins of pompous palaces, magnificent monuments, lofty pyramids and walls and towers of the most costly workmanship: but when the empire of America shall fall, the subject for contemplative sorrow will be infinitely greater than the crumbling brass or marble can inspire. It will not then be said, here stood a temple of vast antiquity, here rose a Babel of invisible height, or there a palace of sumptuous extravagance; but here! Ah! painful thought! the noblest work of human wisdom, the greatest scene of human glory, the fair cause of freedom, rose and fell! Read this and ask if I forgot America."

It would have served our leaders well if they had studied such of Paine. Yet, when such words and thoughts no longer inspire, what is to be the course of leadership? The author of The Crisis would be followed by too many noble men for whom "priestcraft" had done incalculable damage, men like Goethe,

Samuel D. G. Heath, Ph. D.

Schiller, Jean Paul, Shelley, Brougham, Byron, Carlyle, Tennyson. If, as one writer said so well: "All that is fresh and lofty and spiritual in the French school of Poetry and Literature is distinctly traceable to Rousseau" then it is easy to understand the feelings of Emerson and Schiller: "...In Rousseau Christians marked their victim - when Rousseau endeavored to make Christians men!"

So it is, in my own writing, when I attempt to make "Christians" men that my own epitaph may well be read in the same words. My efforts at shaming men in places of leadership for allowing women to have the rule over them is based on the fact, that, it matters little whether they profess any kind of religious sentiment, the results are simply more offensive in the case of those that do.

It would also serve his critics well to consider Paine's poem: "The Castle In The Air," To The "Little Corner Of The World," no man who could write such verse as the following could not have had his fair share of the tenderness all great and caring men share:

Delighted to find you in honor and ease
I felt no more sorrow nor pain;
And the wind coming fair, I ascended the breeze, And went back with my
castle again.

If the seeming rebellion of men like Paine and Rousseau could be contemplated in the light of "priestcraft," might even Washington have been able to embrace his old friend? Of a certainty Franklin's advice to Paine to refrain from making his religious views public was given in genuine friendship. But dear Franklin, the pragmatist, was not the man to persuade the fiery Paine whose own prejudices so blinded him.

One only had to consider the case of Lord Nelson and Lady Hamilton to have an appreciation of the struggle of men like Paine and Rousseau. Regardless the scandalous relationships, silly and wicked men and women are quick to forgive the sins of those men of the time who offered deliverance and bury, in shameful humility and ignominy, the women involved.

So it is today that an Anita Hill or Gennifer Flowers must, irrespective of their own designs, give place to the men, the "survivors" of scandal, who promise something to the mob or are the puppets of power. Give David and Solomon their peccadilloes and concubines; let them multiply wives and horses unto themselves as long as I can enjoy my six-pack and TV without undue discomfort.

If the words of Paine and Rousseau no longer inspire, if "The Crisis" is not perceived in moral terms, to be met with moral argument and force of character and righteousness, such a nation of such citizens and leadership will most certainly receive, not only the verdict of history, but the end it most assuredly both deserves and even calls down on its own head!

The greatest and most grievous tragedy to our posterity is the loss the ignorance of such wisdom represents. To many who read this essay, the names Paine and Rousseau are little, if at all, known; let alone the ideas they expressed so very eloquently. Their persons, vile it is true in some respects, still offer the wisdom and genius with which men are distinguished from the beasts of the field. It is Wisdom, justified of her children, to heed the Truth no matter the person of the source. My own vile heart has led me in too many false paths to fail to recognize the need of sound counsel regardless its source.

One of the sagest pieces of advice I have ever encountered is: "A more unreasonable scheme never emanated from Bedlam, than that of plying the masses with reason, on subjects so complicated as are religion and sociology!" This given the understanding the subject of government is a part of that sociology.

If anything of real value is to be derived from the works of men like Paine and Comte, it has to be with the understanding of their having to confront the hypocrisy of the "Blackcoats" who, like the Pharisees of old were devoid of either understanding or compassion; let alone any propensity for the Truth of the Gospel. Men like Paine and Rousseau, like so many others who tried to make "Christians" into real men, as did Sam Clemens, faced an insurmountable task. It is, as I have mentioned, a great tragedy that such great men and thinkers did not give more credit to the very God and His Word whom so many petty tyrants, in both the churches and government, assayed to represent.

For example, though credit was given Luther, it was never Luther's intent to do anything but bring reform to a decadent and self-serving religious system. Luther recognized the great Truths of God's Word and the cause of his "revolution" was to turn the churches back to those Truths. So with Paine and Rousseau, it was not an attempt to destroy but to build up, in liberty and freedom, not iconoclasm, from the darkness of evil hierarchy. It was of the Blackcoats that they said: "They do not wish to let their dupes know that such men as Humboldt and Comte did not believe in the existence of the extra-almighty pedant whom they seat on the throne of the universe."

But such men as Paine did not seek worship; nor would anyone who believes God and His Word be persuaded to give it to any man. Most certainly men such as me find a great deal with which we are in disagreement with men like Paine and Comte. Further, if one understands the circumstances of Paine's plea for the life of the King, it was the politically astute thing to do. Even Robespierre knew that. But, here is Marat who "... once confidently exclaimed, in reference to his known incorruptness: 'A patriot so pure as myself, might communicate with the Devil.'" It was well said: "The appropriateness of his association of personages and attributes, he probably did not suspect!"

So it is that I too grieve over the blindness of those reformers who depend on "principle" and "good intentions" to carry the day. Oh, the tragic history, the inhumanity to man, caused by those whose true vices are the "virtues" they would enslave others to; and, as those Pharisees of old, all in the name of some god. Thusly, the Lord Nelsons get their monuments and the Lady Hamiltons die of starvation in ignominy.

As I said, Luther did not set out to cause factions, to destroy, but to reform, to help, to set free; so with Paine and others of our founding fathers; never with any other intent but liberty. Tragically, even as the Apostle Paul warned, such liberty was never to be an occasion for shameful and wicked license, never to be construed as an excuse for debauchery or to lie, cheat and steal or for sloth or, as is our present case, a system so evil that such things are, in fact, the actual result of "liberty" turned to vice touted in the name of "virtue!"

Alas, for the human condition and nature; it appears axiomatic that selfishness and greed are never to come under the sway of the utopian dreams of social scientists no matter the mountain of data and the persuasiveness of Reason's dictates; "Truth, forever on the scaffold, Wrong, forever on the throne!" So it is that those that will not learn from history are doomed to repeat it! So it is that from time immemorial to the present, the price of liberty is eternal vigilance, a thing of such preciousness that the thieves and robbers are a constant and ever present threat!

But it is not so much ignorance of history that dooms men, it is a lack of the understanding it. History cannot rightly be understood apart from the Bible and Freud (using Freud in the clinically, generic sense). As I mentioned in my last essay, to try to understand why people do the things they do, whether Hitler or your best friend, without knowing the history and psychology of human nature is fruitless. And history, the chronicle of human nature, is religious and sexual.

It was with deep sadness that I returned to California. I miss my mother and stepfather, Ken, immensely. My own father left our mother and Ronnie and me when I was three and my brother, two years of age. We never heard from him again. Ken, on the other hand, has more than filled the role of a father, often going beyond the requirements of one's natural father. He has to be one of the finest men I have ever known and my mother and I are extremely fortunate to have him there for us. Thanks, Ken, for all you have meant to us and for being the kind of man you are.

The folks, and my nephew, David, made things so comfortable and delightful for me that if it had been possible, I would have gladly remained in Fort Smith. But, for the time being, I am a "nomad" and my place of business is California. I don't think of anyplace as home, certainly without a family, and, lonely as it is perhaps that is best under the present circumstances.

It is when I think of my own children, now grown, of Mom and Ken, of my brother John, of David and children throughout our country, of the Randy Weavers, that I know I must follow this work to whatever conclusion is ordained for me. Sensible men must come to power to lead us; not "wet behind the ears" egotists like the "Clintons" or tax-fattened hyenas like the Willie Browns, Cranstons and Rangels.

If fault is to be found with so-called "white supremacists," it would do well to ask, honestly if possible, what our founding fathers, faced with the same circumstances, would have done? Lincoln wanted to found a separate "preserve" for Negroes- a "reservation" if you will. He in no way would have countenanced giving them "equality" with Caucasians. He well understood the utter insanity of such a thing, the destruction of our society that we now live with. The "Great Emancipator" was not an evil man; he was a sincere, caring man who knew the Union could not survive what evil men have done in spite of the pragmatic truth that when cultures come into conflict, just as they did in the inexcusable blood bath of fratricide in our nation, there can only be one "winner." The utter chaos we now live with, the immorality and license to lie, cheat, steal and murder, is all a result of a failed "social experiment" that has run counter to every fact of human nature and history, one the Pilgrims, Founding Fathers and those that delivered us the greatest nation in history would never have imagined nor countenanced. It is not extreme to say that they would all, without exception, have damned and called insane what we live with as "government" today!

As we witness the resurgence of Nazism in Germany, something I said long ago would have to come to pass, it is understandable in the face of human behavior, religion and history. As Serbs "purify" their territory, as Jews and Arabs continue the never-ending internecine hatred, as we attempt to make sense of the nonsensical, as we witness the applause for the likes of a Murphy Brown and decry anyone who stands for morality and the Bible, as both California and our Federal Government face the grim economic realities of the failed "social experiment," as our young people face a future of hopelessness brought on by the utter betrayal of those ideals, rooted in European Christianity, that made us a, once, great nation, what shall history, as Paine pointed out, say of us?

The betrayers of our nation howl "racism, xenophobia, homophobia, sexism, discrimination, pro-choice" and, all the while, each of these "adulterers" and "idol worshipers" is more than willing to sell out our country to satisfy their own selfishness, greed and egos. The shame is that so many are telling the world they stand for God! I will excuse a greedy and egotistical politician far more willingly than the "gospel-peddlers" who shame The Lord every time they take His Name on their vile lips, who quote a verse of Scripture to justify themselves and ignore the real heart of God; as the preacher said to Elmer Gantry: "Mr. Gantry, why don't you believe in God?" And, realistically, what can we expect of anyone who has no real belief in, or genuine fear of God?

Enlightened, far-sighted leadership is the desperate need of our nation. But when we examine the choices we are being offered, there doesn't seem to be much hope of such. In the absence of good men, prisons and welfare will continue to be our "growth industries" and "... evil men and seducers will wax worse and worse.... then, will the end come!"

CHAPTER SIXTEEN

CHRISTIAN PERSPECTIVE

OCTOBER, 1992

Psalm 2

PRESS RELEASE: Randy Weaver from his jail cell today made the following statement: I decided to come down from the mountain for two reasons: First, I didn't want my children exposed to any further danger. These girls were very brave. They stayed by their dead mother all of those days and took care of Kevin Harris and me and the baby. If it weren't for them we might not have made it at all. In the end, they were afraid, as was I, that if we came out we would all be killed.

"I have never believed that I could get a fair trial in a government court. I was assured that Mr. Spence, one of the great lawyers of the country who has spent his life fighting for people and the cause of freedom, would see that I get a fair trial. I believe Mr. Spence will see that my rights are protected. If I did not believe that I would still be up there.

"I have authorized Mr. Spence to undertake my defense understanding that he and I see eye to eye on very few political and religious issues. But one thing he and I agree on- and that is people ought not to be murdered by their own government.

"This case must stand for something. Otherwise my darling Vicki and my dear son Sam have died for nothing. The case must do something for this country that I love. Otherwise mamma's lives and Sam's death were wasted.

"The facts in this case are known to everyone. First they killed our dog, a big, friendly yellow lab. Then they shot Sam, my son. They blew off his arm. Then they shot him in the back. The second day they tried to eliminate all of the witnesses to Sam's murder. They shot me, and then Kevin. Finally they killed my wife as she stood at the doorway of our cabin with our baby daughter in her arms. She fell with her arms still clutching our baby. When I lifted her head, half of her face had been blown away. We did not have enough water to bath her or prepare her body. We kept her with us eight days.

"There is no doubt that she was killed in retaliation for the death of the federal officer. Those officers are all trained and skilled in shooting an identifiable target. They are excellent marksmen. They shot her in the head. I expect the system to do whatever it can to cover this atrocity, but they know, and I know that what I say is true.

"This is my statement: Randy Weaver" (This is Randy's statement in its entirety, unexpurgated, as it was given me by the folks at the Aryan Nations headquarters' compound in Hayden Lake, Idaho.

I'm in Gooding, Idaho with my old school chum, J.L. The years slip away as we talk about the "good" days of long ago in the "old" Kern Valley when the river ran freely, the air was clean, and the total population of Isabella was 36 and 115 in Kernville. The Sequoia National Forest was our playground, there were no locked doors and children lived without fear or drugs. You never even heard the word "homosexual," there were "good" girls and boys and the term was not derisive but honorable.

J.L. is retired from the Air force (as a full "bird" colonel. He could have retired at a higher rank but, like me, he hasn't "changed" enough to give in to an evil system). He has done well, a world-traveler and knowledgeable of so much that my hope is that he will start writing himself. Naturally, since we shared so much of what was a happier and simpler age, an age of innocence and undiluted hope of the future, of the grand vista of life unfolding before us, he should add to the job I have been trying to do in offering these things to our children and grand-children.

But the graver part of his responsibility, one he alone is peculiarly qualified for, is what he has learned of the military and the operation of the "shadow government" that has played such a key role in the betrayal of our nation. As we sit and renew the good times of our childhood, I am more and more impressed with what his experiences have taught him that could help others understand things like the tragedy of Randy Weaver, the tragedy of our children being robbed of hope of a future, the tragedy of a president and congress, unable to do anything of substance to correct the grievous and catastrophic conditions that threaten our very existence as a nation and threaten to make slaves of all of us.

Returning to California I had just finished putting an intercooler in my Maserati. My trip to Idaho had to wait till I met with a fellow who has some interesting contacts in Russia and Germany. As I waited for him to work out the details of a fellow semi-stranded at O'Hare (The fellow had arrived from Russia and didn't have connections to LAX. That took some rapid and expert help from this chap), I wondered about what he might have that would be of mutual benefit that he would be willing to share. The thing that brought about the meeting was my ability in the German language. That and the fact that I am at liberty to travel anywhere and at any time make me a valuable resource person in some schemes. Maybe this will be one of those things; more of that meeting at a later time (A Mercedes "Junk Yard?").

After my meeting it was on to Lake Isabella and quickly throw the stuff into the old Dodge for the trip. I don't trust the Maserati to drive out of state and be stranded by some mechanical problem and no shop nearby to fix the thing. By 2 p.m. I pointed the old wagon out Walker Pass where I picked up highway 395 North. Passing through the beautiful country around Bishop, I kept grinding out the miles and hung a right at Reno on Interstate 80 East. Caught a few winks in the back of the old car outside of Reno and was back in the saddle before sunrise. Talk about desolate country! I keep forgetting just how "empty" most of Nevada is until I travel in it. Some people, understandably, find it forbidding. I find it mind and soul expanding-awesome! And, for me, there are two particularly awesome and inspiring times of day in this great "empty;" sunrise and sunset.

Tahoe was beautiful as always. Since it isn't much out of my way, why not visit Sun Valley? It helped considerably that traffic was almost non-existent (I drove some two-lanes, during my odyssey, for fifty miles without seeing another vehicle). There were a few thunderclouds scattered about, the sun's rays strikingly beautiful as they lanced through the clouds with sheer, near blinding, brilliance. The old Dodge's engine was humming sweetly, the road was smooth and the only noise was that of the tires on the pavement- solitary and serene. But, as the sun rose and the heat began, the utter desolateness of this part of the country across Nevada made me think of the "iron" that had to be in the backbone of those early pioneers who first made the trails that became this interstate highway we now travel in the comfort of air-conditioned luxury. "Where did such men and women come from?" More importantly, where are they to be found now? They must have gone with the passing of our national "soul" and purpose; the end of our "age of innocence."

Now that the words "Patriot" and "Nationalist" have become "politically incorrect," I find my mind wandering to early writers of our nation's history like Thomas Jefferson, Henry Adams and William James. The miles slip away behind me as I muse in the solitary occupation of keeping the old Dodge pointed in the right direction.

The question is still argued in Academia as to Jefferson's hopes for America, mingled with his Virginia prejudices; that science would lead to the "better man." But, with the insight of years and the disappointments of life, with a "That was then, this is now" hindsight, he concluded in 1815: "I fear from the experience of the last twenty-five years that morals do not of necessity advance hand in hand with the sciences."

Henry Adams believed that in the early days of colonization each new settlement "...represented an idea and proclaimed a mission. A great, liberal movement aiming at the spread of English liberty and empire founded Virginia. The Pilgrims of Plymouth, the Puritans of Boston, the Quakers of Pennsylvania, all avowed a moral purpose, and began making institutions that consciously reflected a moral idea. No such character belonged to the colonization of 1800."

But, the disappointment of Adams was, as with Jefferson's that "science" did not, in fact, produce a "better man." He knew the history and the hopes of Francis Bacon, he had studied Karl Marx and his "doctrines of history," he could understand the American physicist, Samuel Langley, waxing lyrical over the Dynamos of the Paris Exposition of 1900 (see Adams' The Dynamo and the Virgin) and understand the "occult" connotation of the Age of the Machine.

Adams had the benefit of being closer to "un-excised" history, of knowing of Talleyrand, Liancourt, Watt, Napoleon, Oersted and Cuvier. His search for the "soul of America" had the advantage of the blooming of Walter Scott, Goethe, Haydn, Kant and Shelley; the works of Descartes and Newton were as much grist for the wheels of his mind as those of Voltaire and Priestly. But, in the end, as with Aquinas, it was all "straw" in the face of the symbiology of the "Virgin." From the Greek genius of Zeno to Montaigne and Pascal, there was no peace or reconciliation to be found for Adams in the merely physical genius of men; let alone an explanation of the, even by then, departed soul of America. Like Jefferson, he could not come to an agreement with that spiritual dimension that drove men like Knox, Huss, Brewster and Bradford. But what a marvelous job he did in laying out, for all to see, the best that both the practical and fine arts of men can do if they have the liberty, of an explanation of the attitude of foreign powers to a nearly mystical America which, to them, appeared a mighty, brawling, undisciplined infant among nations.

Enter William James, the genius of a budding "Behavioral" school of psychology. If, as James maintained, the value of an idea is in its practical consequences to the individual, we have, yet, another great school of thought that could never quite recover the soul of America, could never quite apprehend what "practical consequence" accrued to the Brewster's and Nathan Hale's of that "lost soul" (and, it may turn out, to the Randy Weaver's of today). From the national soul-searching of Jefferson and Adams to the illusory hope of a "mechanistic" model of human behavior of psychology, the animus against any truly spiritual factor as an explanation for our nation's early goodness and greatness has been clearly displayed; but, back to my visit with J. L.

I am more than a little pleased to find Jack London, Robert Service and "Ducks Unlimited" part of J. L.'s. life. The prints on the wall of his home and the shotguns leaning against the wall of the living room tell me he, like myself, still remembers the things that are really important; that and an excellent music station tuned from Twin Falls tell me he hasn't changed in the things that really matter. He seems just a tad creaky in the joints but that is due to "rodeoing" in all probability. Too bad my daughter, Karen, isn't with me. J. L. would have loved talking horses with her. He and I still enjoy shooting but we are taking more and more pleasure in "shooting" the critters and country with camcorders.

We visit the local pub a short walk away (everything in Gooding is a short walk away) where I meet his hunting and fishing buddies; good men all. The easy conversation and camaraderie is a tonic compared to the harshness of the big cities. And, it is marvelous to travel with no signs of litter or graffiti anywhere. People here don't have to lock doors or cars and everyone knows everyone. America.

The next morning, I help J. L. put shocks and a new speedometer cable on his motor home. This will be "home base" for the forthcoming grouse and elk hunting. I wish I could join him but I have much to do and miles to go.

I spend one more night with J. L. and am on my way early the next day. It was a cold night and the morning was especially crisp. Without resetting the choke on the old Dodge, it proved a little resentful but finally calmed down.

I choose the interstate (84) through Boise and hang a right North on two-lane 95. This will take me through Coeur d' Alene to my destination-Hayden Lake.

The farms are the things that strike the eye as you travel this country; they are breath taking! Nowhere have I seen such magnificent, agricultural works of art! They are striking in their size, richness, cleanliness and beauty. And Coeur d' Alene, what a fantastically sparkling gem of a city!

It's a long haul from Gooding to Hayden Lake and I'm pretty well worn by the time I pull in that late afternoon. I have to call to get specific instructions to the headquarters since it is some off the beaten track and you have to know the backwoods to get there. The secretary is most cordial and, since I am known and expected, I don't have any trouble getting the bearings I need.

Seeing the flagpole and emblem of the organization, I know I'm at the right place. The first thing you notice driving in to the compound is the guard shack and motor-driven guard pole for the access road. The sign out front proclaims: Whites Only!

I park the old Dodge and am met by a friendly fellow who determines who I am and what I want. He leads me to the cafeteria where I can get a cup of coffee while he finds Leonard, the fellow I spoke with last and who was to have made arrangements for my visit.

285

Leonard proves an able and affable chap and we strike it off well. One can't help noticing the sidearms many of these men carry. The guards are identified by white-patched caps (and their guns). The camp is run like a military installation, including a tall guard tower that overlooks the compound.

Since it is so late, Leonard gives me a "quick tour." I'm shown the office and church (the repairs from the bombing of the sanctuary some time ago are clearly visible). The entryway to the cafeteria has a bulletin board festooned with newspaper articles about Aryan Nations- none very complimentary. There are a couple of historical articles that include pictures of Hitler and Goering. Inside the combination cafeteria/work-room there are flags depicting the various "Aryan Nations." There are some striking paintings as well but one's attention is immediately drawn to the Nazi flag which is prominently displayed.

I am given dinner; Leonard shows me where I am to bunk for the night and I am left free to wander a bit before turning in. Lights Out is 10 p.m. I am to meet with Mr. Butler the following morning. He is elderly and retires early. He and his wife occupy a building called the "parsonage."

It is about 8 p.m. when Mr. Butler's associate, Mr. Carl Franklin, an intelligent and erudite man, conducts the nightly "Bible Study." I'm bone-tired and can hardly keep my eyes open but listen attentively. Mr. Franklin doesn't have much that I'm not conversant with in his discourse. The question and answer period is interesting but devolves around, mostly, very elementary subjects.

This close to the Canadian Border, it is quite cold that night; I'm glad I was told to bring warm clothing as the work on the bunkhouse is not completed and there is no heat. But, particularly since the loss of my family, I know how to live in rough conditions and between my heavy, winter pajamas, warm socks, stocking cap and sleeping bag I sleep warm enough.

I'm an early riser and beat "reveille." I go to the cafeteria where the coffee is ready and breakfast is being prepared. It's a beautiful, crisp morning and the air is fresh and pine-scented. The compound property is park-like, studded with many magnificent trees.

Smoking is permitted on the grounds but not in any of the buildings. So it is that I enjoy the "fresh outdoors" with my usual coffee and cigarette. Alcohol, drugs and "coarse language" are forbidden at the compound. Guns are permitted if kept locked in your car. Only authorized personnel openly carry guns on the grounds.

Shortly before breakfast is served, Mr. Butler comes in. Everyone stands to attention. The morning prayer is interesting; it is given by Mr. Butler with right arm stretched out in a Roman salute, those in attendance doing likewise.

Breakfast is excellent with some of the best flapjacks I have had in some time. After the meal, Mr. Butler and I are left to ourselves and the conversation enjoined. Among the questions I ask him is what he thinks was Hitler's biggest mistake? He says it was Hitler's alliance with Japan. Historians have long argued the point and I have often considered it myself, but, in retrospect, it would seem that what became the Axis Powers was an "evolutionary expediency."

I understand Mr. Butler's point because of his "theology." Hitler had no business allying himself to an Asian race and was doomed as a consequence because of God's judgment. Of course, when it comes to spiritual/philosophical opinion, the way is open to all sorts of conjecture. Suffice it to say, and I've said plenty about the subject, Hitler made enough mistakes in judgment to presage defeat with or without such an "unholy alliance."

The conversation is genuinely open and interesting. Mr. Butler is exceedingly sharp and intelligent and an excellent speaker; he has no trouble keeping your attention. After about an hour, he has to excuse himself to take care of business and, thanking him for his time and courtesy, I prepare to take my departure.

I was given a packet of "introductory" material when I had arrived but wandered over to the office where I found Mr. Franklin and asked him if he could supply more background information to better prepare me for the writing I intended to do.

He was readily agreeable and gave me what he thought would be helpful and, indeed, it has proved to be so. I am much better informed now about the movement and can share, as I have done with the KKK, some of the "other side of the story."

Please keep in mind the fact that men like Mr. Butler because of their much publicized positions and, especially, in the case of the KKK, cannot approach legislators, not even their own local "representatives." In my own case, I know many influential men who, while sympathetic with some of the points espoused by the KKK and AN's, cannot possibly afford to make their sympathies known. And they know they can trust me not to betray their sentiments by naming them.

There are visits to be made in Washington and Oregon so I hit I-90 to 395. Finishing up business (which I can't discuss) in Washington, I continue into Oregon where I hit a real "duster." The desert side of the state is really dry and the wind does a good job of stirring things up. I come across an old VW with a woman and a couple of kids. She is having real problems in the wind so I tell her to follow me and I keep an eye on her till we get to calmer weather. We Californians aren't the only ones suffering from drought. It is evident throughout the West.

As usual, meeting people at the local businesses, restaurants and rest stops gives me a pretty fair understanding of how Americans are feeling about our nation; and it isn't good! Some of the language you will read in this essay is pretty raw, but it isn't half as raw as what the "common folk" are using against our "leadership."

Somewhere outside Ukiah, I pull into a spot among the trees to get some sleep. It is cold in this high altitude but I have a good "bed" and rest comfortably in "Casa Dodge."

On the road again before sunrise, I make a quick descent out of the tall timber to the valley floor. It is deliciously warm after the cold of the mountains, promising a hot day. I can actually roll the window down and thoroughly enjoy the marvelous, fresh air rushing in. The sky is beginning to lighten, that magic time on the open road in this Big Empty just before sunrise. I nearly run into a small herd (four) of Pronghorns. Fortunately, I have been dodging rabbits and coyotes on this lonesome stretch and I'm on the alert when the Antelope decide to jump out in front of me. I miss them by about fifteen feet. I pass a young, forked horn deer alongside the road that wasn't as fortunate.

I pass through Burns and view the devastation of the recent fire. It left several people homeless and I chat with a lady who is doling out Salvation Army donations. It's a pretty bad scene.

Arriving in the neighborhood of Lakeview, I make my "visit" and continue south into California. I pass through Sacramento and, reaching Stockton, try to call my son Michael but get no answer. Too bad- I would have really liked to have seen him. One of the reasons I am taking old 99 now is to visit him and his sister, Karen, in Merced. Well, maybe she will be at home.

Luck is with me here and she is at home and, since it is late, I spend the night. We have a good visit and, since I still have time, the following day I take her out to visit my old friend, Bill Cox's ranch in Stevinson. Bill is racing in Pomona but Karen gets to "play" with the horses and it is a real treat to see her with them; she has a marvelous gift with animals and it is most evident in watching her with horses, she can really get them to "dance" to her tune.

It is late by the time I get on the road again. I need to stop in Bakersfield before returning to Isabella so I take the Los Banos cutoff to I-5 and spend a comfortable night at the first rest stop. Lots of trucks there and, as usual, I strike up a conversation with some of the drivers and travelers; same story; disgust with government in general and California in particular.

The mood of the nation is not good. Perhaps that is the reason for the proliferation of "conservative" publications like REASON, CHRONICLES, SPECTATOR, CALIFORNIA POLITICAL REVIEW and so many others. As I have noted, publications like National Review and The New American are too tame for today's mood. Not even Rush Limbaugh will (he may not be able to) touch some of the things I am going to bring out. But he, and others that bill themselves as "conservatives," had better take note (not to mention the target of all this anger and frustration, the politicos). There are few like myself that are "Christian" enough to tell the whole story, realizing that there are a few good men in government who need information from primary sources, not what the Zionist-controlled media dishes out.

Having successfully aligned myself with the "lunatic fringe" and disassociated myself from the Jewish Intellectuals that guide (mis-guide) our government and churches; I really throw caution to the winds in the following pages.

¼ INCH-RANDY WEAVER'S STORY: By Louis Beam

In 1985, the FBI approached Randy Weaver, a former Special Forces soldier, and asked him to become an informant for the federal government (The federals have over 12,000 paid informants nationwide, whose job is to spy on the American populace). Weaver refused - then filed an affidavit with his county recorder saying he feared for his life as a result of the refusal.

In August 1992, an eleven-day siege of the Weaver home in North Idaho began. A federal agent charged that Weaver had sold a shotgun with the barrel ¼" too short. Weaver said it was a frame-up for refusing to pimp for the government. Over 500 federal personnel (Marshals, FBI, ATF, U.S. soldiers, some just returning from the killing fields in Iraq) surrounded the Weaver home; and above the ground were crack snipers, trained at the FBI Academy in Quantico, Virginia. Their job was to kill Weaver. Randy had vowed not to surrender to the federals on the phony charges brought on for refusing them.

The siege ended August 31, with the surrender of Weaver, but not before the Red-White-and-Blue-star-spangled-banner-taxpayer-paid snipers had shot Weaver's 14-year-old son Samuel in the back, killing him, and blew Weaver's wife's head apart as she stood at the front door of the cabin, as she was holding their 10-month-old baby in her arms. Your government's sniper bullet shattered Mrs. Weaver's skull (a mother of four) with such force that it exploded, bone fragments penetrated the chest of friend Kevin Harris... causing serious injury and infection to a lung. The baby, covered with the crimson blood of her mother, fell to the floor in screams of un-understanding terror. (Do I say the pledge of allegiance to the flag now, or may I wait till the nausea has passed?) Two other children, 16 and 10-year-old girls, watched in horror as their mother fell dead to the floor, barely escaping injury or death themselves.

The federals have, by these two murders of a child and woman violated the rules of civilized warfare. War is made upon men, not upon women and children. This federal act of barbarity against women and children must be punished in the courts of justice - in the courts of last resort, if not..."

THE MURDERING SWINE! From RESISTANCE, issue #20. Some months ago agents of the Federal Government of the United States decided they would send a few "White Supremacists" from the Aryan Nations to prison on some bogus rap or another. After all, it isn't as if this country has any kind of serious problem with actual crime, is it? Certainly not a serious enough crime problem to justify taking any valuable federal time, funds and manpower away from their vital task of suppressing political dissent and destroying the few remaining tattered shreds of the United States Constitution...Lacking a petty criminal, our Federal hotshots simply create one by framing some poor sucker on a fabricated drug or gun rap...Then the 'droids' in the three-piece suits let the patsy know that his only chance to avoid the great stripy hole is to 'cooperate with law enforcement,' i.e. spy for them... finally get up on a witness stand in a court of law and swear away the lives of innocent people...the garbage in Brooks Brothers threads thought they had found a patsy, a 44-year-old former Green Beret from Naples, Idaho, named Randy Weaver...Who the hell did Randy Weaver think he was, refusing to tell lies on a witness stand when he was ordered to do so, pretending he had rights, acting like he was somebody? Did he not understand that college-educated yuppies who wear three-piece suits and carry little badges and photo IDs from Washington are his superiors? Where the hell did Randy Weaver get off, not doing as he was told by men who draw government salaries five times what Weaver earned through the mere labor of his hands? This uppity racist had to be taught a lesson.

So agents of the United States government taught Randy Weaver a lesson. They shot down 13-year-old Sam Weaver and his mother, Vicki, right before Randy's eyes. Now they are going to bury Randy Weaver alive as a punishment for having defied them, along with a young family friend named Kevin Harris who dared to strike back at the cowardly, blood-drinking Federal jackal who killed the boy. America the Beautiful...."

(If any of you are interested in the entire edition of ARYAN NATIONS, issue #79, from which I have quoted these excerpts, write to: Aryan Nations, P.O. Box 362, Hayden Lake, Idaho 83835)

Hard, harsh language; but can words no matter how hard ever really convey the stunning heinousness of the murders of a woman and child under the cover of my flag, the flag of the United States of America, the flag Randy weaver fought under, the flag the murderers took an oath to preserve and protect?

The people I visited and spoke with at the Aryan Nations compound in Hayden Lake would like, and expect, the murder of Randy's wife and son to be the catalyst of action on the part of patriotic Americans. Is that likely? Not in my opinion. The heinousness of the murders is, undoubtedly, going to be hushed up, as only the federal government knows how to do. After all, the federal government, a self-willed empire, as with education, knows how to "take care of its own;" witness their "handling" of the S&Ls, BCCI, Iran-gate, the banker who, even now, has the White House trembling over the exposure of how it armed Iraq etc. Cover-ups and attempted cover-ups galore; small wonder the government is stymied when so many are so busy covering their backsides they don't have time for the mere problems of unemployment and a bankrupt nation.

Further, the feds may be dumb but they ain't stupid. No one could more gladly pull the switch on the cold-blooded murderers of Vicki and Sam than me. And I emphasize the word GLADLY! The murdering swine have no excuse under heaven for what they did and what they did should raise the bile of everyone with any sense of decency or concern for the rights of others. It was, as stated by those I met, an act that stains, indelibly, the very flag the murderers hid behind and, hypocritically, took an oath to serve and protect. In this instance, the guilt or innocence of Randy Weaver has no bearing. What is a cold-blooded fact is that a mother and her son were callously murdered as an act of "war" against women and children by, what are, obviously, our "keepers." Will they get away with it? I think so. Besides the adroitness of our "slave masters" to get away, literally, with murder, there is the factiousness of the various groups like KKK, Aryan Nations, The Order, etc., that precludes, at present, their ability to act in concert with common goals and objectives. This, more than anything else, is what the government depends on to prevent another Boston Tea-party.

Richard Butler's "sedition" trial was a "mock" trial. The government had no case and, as I said, they ain't stupid; so why the trial of someone who posed no real threat? I'll share a little secret with my readers. They aren't concerned with someone's "funny" religious convictions. They most certainly aren't afraid of some small group whose antics strike the majority of people as strange or, downright weird. You would really have to visit and talk with the leaders of these groups to fully understand the ludicrousness of the government prosecuting and persecuting these people based on any real danger or menace by their minuscule following. Here is what the government, our "keepers," is afraid of: They are afraid of people like me, people who are educated and dedicated to the Truth and know how to write. And, in respect to the Aryan Nations, they write and publish enough to get the fed's attention. It is the power of the pen they are afraid of. And, rightly so!

But, just suppose, as I have often warned, an enlightened and educated leadership should materialize? Then the porkers and jackals in three-piece suits and Washington badges would have just cause to be concerned!

We could reasonably ask why Lyndon LaRouche is being kept in a prison "medical ward." We might ask why Yorie Von Kahl is serving two life terms in federal prison for committing no crime whatever! I, personally, might well ask why the reporters of newspapers I know are literally afraid of printing what I could, personally, tell them of what I know about the "other side of the story." Perhaps, as I have often said, it can only be told by those like me who are both qualified and have nothing to lose.

Once, divine law was a subject in our schools; now it is forbidden and our schools are in shambles. Once, politicians would invoke the name of Jesus Christ; now they don't dare to utter anything in favor of The Bible or Caucasians.

It has become "politically correct" to denigrate Caucasian achievement and bow the knee to multiculturalism- even to the point of vilifying our founding fathers. This makes it possible, of course, for Dan Walters to warn about the hazards of trying to do business with an absolutely corrupt government like Mexico's, of the Mexican driver of the truck that killed seven children to run across the border to safety and nothing can, or will, be done about it. And Mr. Walters can have his say as long as he doesn't mention Jews or show any pride in Caucasian achievement.

If something, as I have often pointed out, is as obvious as the government's desire to keep drugs flowing into our country, there must be a reason. Besides financing our "shadow government," there is the "benefit" of making millions of "spies" through the simple mechanism of making "drug criminals." And, what about the breakdown of morality and law-enforcement across the board which the ridiculous "war against drugs" has accomplished? Can we have any cause to wonder that Berry is back in "business" in D.C.? Can we have any cause to wonder that the husband of Mayor Sandy Freedman of Tampa Florida is in bed with organized crime figures like Santo Trafficante? Not when "the money was just there" and "everybody is doing it!"

"Spanish-speaking people will find it a little easier to file complaints against sheriff's deputies thanks to work of a community advisory group. The Kern County Hispanic Advisory Council to Law Enforcement held a news conference Wednesday to unveil a Spanish-language form used to file complaints of excessive force on the part of deputies...to help the Sheriff's Department."

Insane? I think so. Particularly since the loony gringos can't even get the driver-killer of seven children back from Mexico. Now if he hadn't run away and this form could help him file a lawsuit against deputies trying to arrest him or using "excessive force" in jail...? Hey, MAPA, why don't you inform Fernando Hernandez Flores of his "rights?" Maybe he would come back, give himself up and, with the help of MAPA and this new form, sue Kern County, do a year in jail for killing the seven children and collect a couple of million dollars from the crazy, gringo taxpayers? Come to think of it, he probably wouldn't need MAPA; there are enough greedy gringo lawyers around to do the job. Sure sounds like a plan to me! I'm surprised the Bakersfield Californian hasn't carried this proposition in its editorials. The rag loves its "Hispanic citizens" as its overweening and laughably disproportionate desire to hire and please them testifies. But, by now, I am used to the media's distortionate "pick-and-choose" which is so successful at sucking in the gullible, lazy, ignorant and illiterate and, I might add, doesn't do too badly at gulling those that think themselves educated and "informed" as well.

"The Luechter Report" and "Did Six Million Really Die?" These are not "night-time" or "potty" reading. Nor will they be found on your library shelves or the anteroom of your local legislator. In fact, I don't think anyone in the so-called "public service" sector but David Duke would acknowledge knowing of his or her existence. But they are surely enough to get the feds on your case if you start handing them out, as Richard Butler and Randy Weaver know first-hand.

None of us who are truly literate in history have ever countenanced the story of the "Holocaust" as anything but propaganda, albeit, "necessary propaganda," (we were told) in the light of the historic setting. As with the mythical diary of Ann Frank and the "fixed" photos of death camps, there were enough real atrocities and slave-labor camps to make extraordinary stories believable. What few seem to consider is the fact, that, in order to appease the public need for blood after WWII, the, now well known, kangaroo court of Nuremberg became a vital, propaganda necessity.

Talk about "politically incorrect!" But, for those few willing to consider the facts, devoid of the emotional element surrounding those Apocalyptic years of the war, there has never been any historical evidence that six million Jews died in gas chambers; the demographics and sheer logistics of the whole thing make it an impossibility. Small wonder that the looks of astonishment on the faces of those German leaders at the "trials" were not feigned; they were genuinely dismayed at the charges! One can only wonder what the "architects" of this colossal, evil hoax would have been able to do with the Salem Witch trials!

If the media wished to do so, what do you suppose it could do about the real holocaust of the millions of babies aborted as "contraception" in our nation; again, "pick-and-choose" propaganda.

If you are anywhere near my age, you were well, and, in most cases, understandably, propagandized to hate the "rotten Japs and Knocksies." Our films, comic books, radio programs were used most successfully to instill "patriotic hatred" of the "enemies of Democracy." (Notice they didn't say "enemies of our Republic!").

With the war's end, those hated enemies had to be dealt with in a fashion to satisfy the loss of so many sons and fathers, daughters and mothers. So, it was Nuremberg. Kangaroo Court? Yes; but necessary in the light of political expediency. If we had only had Hitler! But, we didn't.

Nothing in history, not since the mythic of the Trojan Horse itself, has such a hoax like the Holocaust been so successfully perpetrated. And what was, exactly, the need and agenda for such a deception? For the answer to this question and the goals of the traitors who persuaded the goy to haul the horse into our camp, you need a working knowledge of Freemasonry and its Jewish element and leadership. A few of the names connected with the Masonic movement since Jewish leadership (control) emerges as a factor: George Lincoln Rockwell, Ezra Pound, Huey Long, Joe McCarthy, General George S. Patton, Jr., General Douglas MacArthur and Larry McDonald of the John Birch Society (of Korean flight 007, the flight that Richard Nixon was "mysteriously" removed from).

It was no accident that in 1954, the Supreme Court, where eight of the nine justices were Masons, struck a fatal blow to education in the case of Brown v. Board of Education. The, ostensibly, non-Mason was none other than the Jew, Felix Frankfurter, publicly known as the mastermind of the "New Deal" and, according to Theodore Roosevelt, a "Bolshevik!" Of course, we now know T.R. was absolutely correct in his assessment.

I quote prisoner Kahl from his excellently researched article: "Are you aware that the Bank of England is situated in 'The City,' 677 acres in old London. This 'City' also houses the headquarters of numerous other international enterprises, as well as Freemasonry's 'Grand Lodge' - sometimes called the 'Mother Lodge' of England.

By 1721, the Bank of England was rapidly being 'bought out' by numerous Portuguese and Spanish Jews (Benjamin Franklin knew of this. It, along with what he had learned in France, was a primary reason for his trying to exclude Jews, by the Constitution, from entering the United States), and in 1812, the Rothschilds began their great 'buying up' of stock of all franchises being thrown on the market due to the Napoleonic War.

Before the 19th century had passed, France had lost her financial power to the Rothschilds. In fact, in 1876, the desperate French nobility tried in vain to counter the growing threat of a Jewish financial monopoly."

E.C. Knuth published a book entitled The Empire of the City. I quote: "This international financial oligarchy uses the allegoric 'Crown' as its symbol of power and had its headquarters in the ancient city of London, an area of 677 acres, which strangely in all the vast expanse of the 443,445 acres of Metropolitan London alone is not under the jurisdiction of the Metropolitan Police, but has its own private force of about 2,000 men, while its right population is under 9,000...This tiny area of a little over one square mile has in it the giant Bank of England, a privately owned institution; which as is further elaborated hereinafter is not subject to regulation by the British Parliament, and is in effect a sovereign world power. Within the City are located also the Stock Exchange and many institutions of worldwide scope."

For those of you with the genuine interest of separating fact from fiction, try getting any of your Masonic "friends" to get you factual information about the only Masonic Lodge in Israel; I'm sure you will be interested in the reaction. And, while you are at it, take a dollar bill from your pocket and look for the "Star of David" and the Masonic symbols. If I were into "signs and omens," I might try to put the Apocalypse and the thirteen "tribes" and the thirteen colonies into some kind of cabalistic format.

I quote from a speech given in Budapest, Hungary on January 12, 1952, at an Emergency Council of European Rabbis by Rabbi Emanuel Rabinovich: "We will openly reveal our identity with the races of Asia and Africa. I can state with assurance that the last generation of white children is now being born. Our control Commissions will, in the interests of peace and wiping out inter-racial tensions, forbid the whites to mate with whites. The white women must cohabit with members of the dark races, the white men with black women, thus the white race will disappear, for mixing the dark with the white means the end of the white man, and our most dangerous enemy will become only a memory."

Thomas Jefferson said: "Single acts of tyranny may be ascribed to the accidental opinion of the day, but a series of oppressions, begun at a distinguished period, unalterable through every change of ministers, too plainly prove a deliberate, systematical plan of reducing us to slavery."

As Kohl, and myself, have pointed out: in contemporary politics any hint of racism is a "live rail issue," sudden death to anyone maneuvered into contact with it. I would further ask: Why? particularly if no "racist" intent is found other than to acknowledge that Caucasians have rights and our nation and its Constitution are of "Caucasian manufacture and intent for our posterity?"

GERMANY SEIZES WEAPONS: Hamburg, Germany – "Officials confirmed Friday that police raided an apartment belonging to neo-Nazis, uncovering a cache of weapons and a list of names one newspaper called a 'hit list.'

The mass-circulation newspaper Bild reported that the 'hit list' contained the names of about 200 politicians, judges, prosecutors and police officials. Bild said police seized an 'extensive weapons arsenal,' including pistols and rifles and 'containers of poison.' It did not elaborate."

Maybe Bild can't "elaborate" but I can; I have certainly written enough on the subject. Zionism is real. The objectives of a global economy and government under its control are real. What stands in the way? People like Franklin and Jefferson (and, people like little, old me).

It should give pause to wonder to even the most obtuse "liberal" that a piece of real estate about the size of New Jersey, a minuscule number of people of "strange religion," should dominate world history in such a fashion as Israel and the Jews. Those of us who believe in God and know the Bible do not find it strange at all. But pity the poor unbeliever who has to struggle with such a mind-numbing conundrum. It simply does not compute; makes no sense whatsoever. Hitler would have done far better to have believed God's Word rather than his astrologers. But we can only wonder, at present, how Ron and Nancy's "star-gazers" influenced their decisions.

These few paragraphs should, by themselves, silence my enemies as to their attempts to "label by narrow interests." Of a certainty, you won't hear Rush Limbaugh talking about these things. It takes real courage and, I must admit, I'm more than a little surprised at my own in the whole thing! I don't count myself an exceptionally courageous man. It took the event of the murders of Randy Weaver's wife, Vicki, and his son, Sam, to galvanize me to openly saying some of these things that I have known for years! But, maybe, Mr. Bush and Mr. Clinton will be too busy "cooking the books" to notice the ravings of yet another "mad man." Mr. Perot may be another question. And, of course, there is the IRS to consider. The words of a retired, IRS professional who served for 30 years auditing returns: "Hire a professional; don't try to go an audit by yourself!"

Some more "light reading" for those that want to know the real truth should include some of Manfred Roeder's comments on international banking. No, you won't find him in your local library either. But I will provide you one quote from him to pique your interest:

"World economy is nothing but world government. Don't wait for the system to collapse, it never will. The only way to independence is the refusal to make debts and to convince more and more communities to follow the example of Ribeiro." Yves Ribeiro, for those that haven't read what I wrote of him some time ago, is the mayor of a small, Brazilian town who refused to borrow money from the World Bank in spite of the Bank's efforts to coerce him into it. As a result, and free of the restraints of the "money-lenders," and prohibitive, bureaucratic "building codes," the small town prospered by doing for themselves and is one of the few success stories in a failed country.

Certainly I have proved, to my detractors, the truth of the "fool walking where angels fear to tread" by "exhuming" some history that has been "cleansed, sanitized" for "modern consumption." We have, in America, today, a thoroughly brainwashed generation that knows nothing of our early and proud history. We have a generation that would "villainize" Columbus and the early explorers (not to mention the founding fathers) and chooses to ignore the inhumanity and perversion of the so-called "civilizations" they were supposed to have victimized (including that of Aztecs, Mayans, Incas, American Indian) and chooses to, with "smoke and mirrors," make those savage and perverted peoples "noble." But the leaders of such revisionist "histories" know they have little to fear from an illiterate nation. And what can be said for those that will hurl the accusation of "Anti-Semite" against those who hold to the historical evidence that Christianity is not the "Sister Religion of Judaism;" is not a "Judaism for the Gentiles."

The plain and painful truth is that we now live under a De Facto government, not a De Jure one and certainly not the one our founding fathers gave us. But does it take White Supremacists, Neo-Nazis, Ku Klux Klanners, Skin and Onion Heads to rub our noses in this truth? Or is the only alternative more people like Bob Mathews and Gary Yarbrough, the "White Guerrillas?" But I will leave that subject along with The Order and William L. Pierce of The National Alliance for another time.

But keep one thing in mind before you write all this "stuff" off as lunacy; these men know about the results of Potsdam, of Morganthau at the Quebec Conference and Hap Arnold's conversations with George Marshall and Harry Stimson. The fact that most of this was "cleansed" from the history taught in our schools and universities, particularly Morganthau's and Baruch's successful vow of revenge against Germany after the war does not eliminate the truth of it. But, it seems, only the "lunatics" are willing to keep it in print! Knowing what was happening as an orchestrated plot by the Jews against Germany with the collusion of our own government, this great general had to say: "The more I see of people I regret that I survived the war!"

"History records that by 1945 the 'news directors' of the American and British peoples revealed themselves openly as Bernstein, Daniell, Levin and Morgan. Avowed Soviet collaborators such as Harry Dexter White, Henry Morganthau, Herbert Leman, Laughlin Curry, David K. Niles and Alger Hiss carried out the policy of the true president of America's Government, 'Bernard Baruch.'" It certainly isn't pretty but it is certainly true!

In the time of Ezra and Nehemiah, the Israelites (and they weren't all Jews) were commanded to put away "strange wives and children." Failure to do so resulted in excommunication, loss of property and exile. Harsh terms for a harsh time. Yet, miscegenation has proven a "taboo" in most societies. It took an unholy time in our own nation to give approval to this "mongrelization" of our society and culture.

Now, if people like me are going to be considered the "enemy" because we choose to stand up for Caucasians in the face of the multi-cultural claptrap of Hollywood and Zionism, even in the face of "droids" in three-piece suits, so be it. But be warned! I may not be an aficionado of C&W but you ought to be listening to some of the lyrics concerning conditions in this nation. It isn't just truck drivers and waitresses who are madder than hell at the "leadership." There are some "grandmas" carrying guns out there as well!

And, in regard to the so-called *holocaust*, "The Auschwitz Lie," Jahrhundert Betrug and a host of other books are beginning to make a huge dent in the mythological beast and it is, understandably, getting afraid. Remember my warning that no contradiction can last forever; further, you can't shoot and imprison all the Randy Weavers and Manfred Roeders or all their wives and children. Remember one of the famous lines in an old propaganda flick: "There are always survivors!" The present reaction in Germany is due, in large part, to a nation that is beginning to learn the truth of the phony shame that was heaped upon it. Even older Germans who know the truth are getting so fed up that they are beginning to overcome their fear and are speaking out.

When the whole truth comes out, when it is learned what the Bolsheviks and their puppets did to perpetuate the myth, when the truth comes out as to the actual atrocities done in Russia and blamed on the Germans, Zionists would do well to fear since they set the Russian machinery in motion! Don't be surprised when the whole Grundgesetz is opened up for factual inspection, especially if some of the archival evidence from Russia should, now, see the light of day. And if it is, where will you hide and what will your billions of extorted monies be worth? And, once exposed, who, then, will be branded the "traitor?" And the sooner you Christians stop playing stooge for a so-called "holy land" the better. Neither The Lord nor you have any friends there, only "users" who would turn the sword against you quicker than a blink if (when?) conditions allowed!

At this time in history, it seems all the "mad men" are Arabs. And, no, as a Christian I wouldn't trust a Muslim any further than I would a Jew. But, just exactly who is the "enemy?" Isn't he the one who enslaves and makes Americans dance to the tune of oil money and backbreaking debt and taxes? But be warned! I already covered the story of BCCI and who blew the whistle on this attempt to circumvent the Zionist Cartel of the World Bank and won't belabor it further. Suffice it to say, our nation's woes won't go away without turning to the God of our fathers and He is not a Jewish god (or Muslim,

Buddhist, etc.); He is The Father of those children who obey Him no matter what race. Try saying that out loud on a street in Tel Aviv or any place else in Israel or downtown Kuwait. But I'll bet I could do so in downtown Bonn or Berlin!

You know, as much as I chide people like Rush Limbaugh, John McManus and Bill Buckley for being afraid to "tell it like it is," my real anger, much as I love and pray for them, is for people like my old "friend" Gary North. As you may know, Gary touts his own brand of religion but he started something called Institute for Christian Economics some years back. Yet, though he thinks he knows something of economics, he has never addressed the issues I have brought up. Gary even thinks he is somewhat knowledgeable of history. Still, he has yet to speak to the most relevant and important historical issues of the Christian faith, particularly the historic juncture when church leaders began to crawl into bed with the Jews. "Their house left unto them desolate until they say: 'Blessed is he who comes in the name of the Lord?'" Not according to the church's version today!

In fact, it would seem, as I have written for so long, that the majority of Christian scholars of the churches have led us down the garden path for the last two hundred years. And, if this is the extent of people like Gary's knowledge, it is small wonder they are either ignorant and/or afraid.

Now it is freely admitted that my visits with far-right "radicals" leaves some of my few friends shaking their heads over my welfare (and sanity). As long as I am viable enough to recognize this fact, they have nothing to fear. But I do have some degree of fear about the potential for anarchy in this country, and seeking out primary sources rather than secondary is the mark of a scholar.

Too many people are hurting and, as I have often pointed out, there are scapegoats aplenty to go around. One of the things that is real and not melodramatic fiction is something I'm certain the feds are aware of also and that is the fact that desperate times make for some rather strange alliances. One in particular is that of the "mob" and White Supremacists.

Over the past few years that I have undertaken the study of the White Supremacist movements I couldn't fail to pick up the undercurrent of "connections." At first, these were veiled innuendo. Most of it could be easily discounted as phony, macho braggadocio of the kind "Oh yeah, I know this guy and he has contacts. Want someone taken out?"

As not a few can testify, some of these are of the type the feds tried to make of Randy Weaver, people the feds could bribe or coerce into pimping for them; "contract hit men" are just not that easy to come by. This is particularly true of the "mob." As I learned in the gun business, don't trust that smiling face trying to sell you a lower case for your "tamed" M16, it probably belongs to an ATF agent (besides, why buy what any knowledgeable machinist can produce in a simple shop?).

But the connection is a "natural." In a perverted way, it makes sense for those considered extreme radicals to find common cause with the Mafia in some cases. One only has to consider the relationship between Mussolini and Hitler to find its historical basis. It is perfectly common of the fallen nature of men to come to terms with the axiom: "The end justifies the means." Politicians, the FBI, the CIA, and most judges live by this creed; why not the Mafia and the KKK, etc.?

The "Shadow World" is not a nice place. You do, in fact, find psychopaths, people who are more than able to put that pipe bomb in some reporter or judge's car. A few of those on the fed's "payroll" fall into this category. But there are some that are just plain madder than hell at the betrayal of Americans by our government, men and women who, while not psychopaths, are willing to do whatever they believe in for the "cause." One of these men, I'll call him "Joe," is an excellent example. Rambo could well describe his psychological makeup.

Having done a double tour in Viet Nam, he is more than angry at the betrayal of those he fought with and of our nation. Joe is an intelligent and very capable "killer." Skilled in the use of all kinds of small arms and explosives, Joe only needs a "target" he believes the world would be better off without taking up oxygen.

I have met many of the phonies; men who brag about "serving" and never even went overseas. I've met several who have just gotten into the habit of lying, simply to impress the girls, who were never even drafted. Joe is real. It helps, of course, for a person to have my qualifications in psychology to separate the "real" from the "wannabes."

Of the "Joes" I have met, they only need a "leader" who gains their loyalty and trust to become deadly weapons that could turn the entire nation on its ear in anarchy. Yes, as melodramatic as it sounds, there are more than enough "Joes" out there to do that. All they lack, and, are waiting for, is that leader and a target.

Would Joe make common cause with the Mafia? Yes! Particularly since, typically, Joe is not an educated man in the sense of the fine arts and formal, graduate studies but he has learned of the "organization's" abilities in buying politicians and judges, he knows of the network that reaches places where the Aryan Nations, KKK, does not reach. Joe also knows something is dreadfully wrong in our nation, he knows he and those he fought with have been betrayed, he is willing to listen to the most extreme scenarios that will, to him, make sense of a course of action. And Joe is more than willing to shake hands with the Devil and risk his life in such a cause! And Joe is not married; he has no "Vicki or "Sam" to lead into danger! This, of course, helps tremendously in making Joe a very "reliable" and extremely dangerous man!

Granting that Joe doesn't see the "big picture" from the vantage point of the halls of power, he, like all Americans, is reacting to the pain, hurt and anger of the betrayal of America and his flag. And, yes, symbols are important to Joe. Hitler had a firm grasp of the human psyche in this regard. When our Supreme Court decided it was okay to desecrate (yes; that is the right word, I think, in the context of Joe's thinking though not in mine) his flag, the flag he fought for and for which so many "Joes" died, he hated that court and everything that court stood for. It stood, now, for an alien ideology, supported by a De Facto government, which is now an "enemy." The examples could be multiplied, seeming endlessly, of reasons for Joe's anger and hatred.

I have been warning for over twenty years of the dangers of an ultra-conservative backlash to the insane and greedy policies of our government. I am now witnessing the "fruit of prophecy" and most decidedly take no pleasure in seeing it come to pass. Too many innocent, particularly the children, are going to be hurt. It may yet be years away but to those who are "madder than hell and not going to take it any more," the answer is simply: "How can it be any worse than what we have now!" Difficult to refute as we watch our "leaders" in "action" and "duly, constituted authority" murdering innocent women and children and harassing and imprisoning those whose only crimes are "politically incorrect" dissidence!

Well, the old Dodge and I have another 2,800 miles on us and it will take some more essays to tell the "rest of the story."

Protect your Constitutional Right to own and bear arms: Join the NRA Today! Call 1-800-368-5714 NOW! And remember another, precious Right as an American: VOTE!

CHAPTER SEVENTEEN

CHRISTIAN PERSPECTIVE

NOVEMBER, 1992

Jeremiah 8:20

Seems Gore Vidal has hit a new low, just when decent people thought this impossible, with his "Live From Golgotha." It is hardly worth the paper and ink to reply to, let alone quote, some of his outrageous blasphemies. I simply bring the subject up to make a point. America is so far down the path of immorality that it seems "Anything Goes."

An L.A. Superior court ruled, rightly, that illegal aliens must pay full tuition at California State Universities. But university leaders may actually appeal this decision! What, you didn't know California has been subsidizing the education of illegal aliens for years? Shame on you! We give them welfare, medical, food stamps and everything else you could mention, even though poor Whites who are working taxpayers can't even afford a dentist, why shouldn't we pay for their university education as well? "Just another day in the destruction of America." National Review.

It takes the "Gore Vidals" to make for such insanity. One can easily imagine what the reaction of those, to use the "Politically Correct" language of today, Intolerant, Sexist, Racist, White Supremacist, Slave-holding WASPs, otherwise known as our Founding Fathers, would be to such obscenity. But anyone who knows the system of the universities and, in fact, the whole school system in America, is hardly surprised; certainly people like myself who have been through the system and have actually taught in it, who have experienced the worst of such an "education," are not. "Kill any thoughts of America that contribute to, or uphold, the ideals of those Founding Fathers or any pride in Caucasian achievement" has been the focus of the schools for decades.

While my old friend, Gary North, hasn't had my experience in dealing with the system, he is correct in his assessment that secular humanism has "...absolute sovereign (ty) over the granting of terminal degrees: the Ph. D., the M. D., and the J. D." I agree with his point that compulsory funding for education makes a systematic program of comprehensive Christian education impossible. But, if Gary should really agree with Voltaire who "...longed for the

302

day in which the last king would be strangled in the entrails of the last priest" (this in respect to university presidents and the Department of Education) he has come a long way in agreement with some of my own feelings about what needs to be done to have any hope of "Christian Reconstruction." Sadly, while Gary talks a good fight, I don't really believe he has thought the whole thing through.

For example, it reminds me of the Jews whose "heirs" would build monuments to the very prophets their fathers had stoned. It was Jesus' contention that they would (and did, in fact) do worse than their fathers! It has always been the cry of politicians to "hearken" to the voices of the Founding Fathers. But, given the facts about those worthies, just how sincerely are the deeds and beliefs held by them held by those that would like their own names reckoned alongside? I urge you to give me one name of one politician who would, if pressed, say he "belongs in their camp!" It would be political suicide and politicians know it! But it has always made for good July 4th rhetoric.

Consider the facts of the case. The Founding Fathers were just what history says they were. They were White Anglo-Saxon Protestants. Many believed in slavery. They believed only men should have the franchise. They believed, for the most part, that the Bible was divinely inspired. They believed, again, for the most part, in Jesus Christ and the Protestant position of salvation by grace alone apart from any "good works." They believed men (White men) had the responsibility, duty and unalienable right to forge their own, individual, destinies. They were firmly committed to the concept: "That government governs best which governs least."

They were adamantly opposed to any Jewish or Roman Catholic involvement in the government. They were equally opposed to women being given any voice, and most certainly a vote, in government. They were wholly committed to the ethic of "If any not work, neither should he eat!" Government, as set forth by the Founding Fathers, should stay out of the rights of the individual; the individual was to be considered above the government in all cases that did not involve the national interest.

By now you surely realize, particularly my readers of some years that the kind of thoroughgoing, ruthless honesty so desperately needed today is not going to come through the media, particularly not through the likes of Rush Limbaugh. As with so many others of his kind, he talks a good fight but is a sell-out to liberalism ever much as Donohue and King; he is simply more successful at deceiving people into thinking that he is one of the "good guys." But you search in utter vain to find the kinds of things, historical truth, in either his "talk shows" or his vaunted "The Way Things Ought To Be" concerning such things as the Masons, Zionists or the so-called Holocaust. Mr. Limbaugh knows, indeed, which side his bread is buttered on.

I note with wry amusement the articles by magazines that loudly proclaim to speak for "family values" and the "Founding Fathers" but won't touch the subjects of real, historically proven significance. Some even have the temerity to poke fun at the "Brie Eaters" and don't even notice their own affectations of "respectable conservatism." I am particularly disgusted with the so-called "Christian" media, including many periodicals, that think they have "done their part" when they "strongly disagree" with Act Up or Queer Nation or carry sob-pieces about how difficult it is to find "good, Christian entertainment" anymore. These people haven't the foggiest notion of what "Christian" with a capital is really all about and as long as the churches stay in league with Satan (tax-exempt status), doing "business as usual," they will never know!

Time Warner can keep the money rolling in extolling killing cops and bashing Whites but just try to have a radio show extolling any White achievement, calling perversion what it is or actually telling the truth about our own history as a nation! For a real eye-opener, you ought to read about the "trial" of Ernst Zundel of Toronto, Ontario in 1988. A radio station in New Brunswick was fined $25,000 for allowing Aryan Nations Canada leader Terry Long speak on a talk show! But Louis Farrakhan is acceptable.

In Limbaugh's defense, I know he couldn't talk about Eichman's visit to Jerusalem and Golda Meier's (Meyerson) visit to Nazi Germany on behalf of a Jewish State even if he wanted to (but I somehow doubt he would want to). Nor could he ever address the facts of the Zionist cooperation with Nazi Germany to foment conditions that would literally drive Jews from Europe into Palestine even at the cost of the whole of European Jewry!

No, Mr. Limbaugh, your brand of "conservatism," is still a "sell-out" to your puppet masters in the media and I am too thoroughly conversant with where your "panaceas" of tickling conservative ears leads: further down the road to oblivion. The thinking of people like you is always: "As long as we give them the appearance of freedom of speech; that is enough." All your bluster is "wind" when it comes to the issues I am addressing. I'm sure your "masters" find it all, and you, thoroughly amusing; but dangerous to them? That is laughable. I would think such a thing is difficult for an ego like yours, equal to that of Perot's, to live with. Alas, I know: "The money was just there!"

Kudos to Joe Sobran for his excellent piece on Bobby Fischer; I was surprised to find Joe back in the good graces of NR. I thought I might be the only one to find such interest in Bobby's "move" concerning the U.S. Government. Now Mr. Fischer is certainly not high on my list of those I would want as "confidant" but, to quote Joe: "It might avert possible misunderstandings by naive chess players if they (the government) replaced George Washington with the IRS Commissioner on the dollar bill, and excised a few misleading words from the 'Star Spangled Banner.'"

Now I do admire Fischer's handling of the missive from the State Department (he spit on it), but you can, in some respects, treat the government like dirt compared to the IRS, Jews or perverts. Since Fischer hasn't paid taxes since 1976, it will be interesting to see what happens. And thanks, Joe, for your insightful phrase "Darkest California." That was most appropriate.

Notwithstanding Robert Genetski's excellent analysis of the crisis precipitated by the Clean Air Act, Social Security, Medicare and the Tax Reform Act of 1986 (the most grievous blunder by blunderers in Congress), there is still the chicanery of the S&Ls, BCCI, Drugs, uncontrolled borders and illegals, etc. which the criminals are getting away with. In their own way these are as despicable as the criminal and inhumane treatment of the MIA question: Political necessity? Certainly, given the character of the "players!"

Germany and Japan would both like to become permanent members of the U.N. Security Council. Some twenty years ago, I made the point to a group of young people that our society had become so fearful that it would gladly trade liberty for security. This is, in fact, the case.

Not too many people in the U.S. are aware of the tremendously restrictive Canadian laws that Zionists are using to persecute any one they see as a threat to their "World View and New World Order." It is largely because of my taking the trouble to visit the leaders of White Supremacist organizations and get their side of the story that I have become knowledgeable of the facts of the case.

Since I am not in a position to have to worry about what construction others may place on my meetings with such leaders and, since I am not, like Randy Weaver, putting others at risk for my views, I am free to seek out the truth no matter who I have to speak with or where the searching may lead. I am extremely inquisitive by nature. I have always wanted to know what makes things work. I'm the kid who was always taking apart clocks, etc.

The fact that I became professionally well-trained in research has aided tremendously in the present search for the truth in all the "madness" attendant on the inordinate fear so many have of organizations like the KKK and Aryan Nations, fear exemplified by literal "witch hunts" against men like Terry Long, Manfred Roeder, J.W. Farrands and Richard Butler. In regard to Terry Long, the whole weight of Canadian law was brought to bear on one man that seemed to have stirred such passions on the part of the Jewish Establishment that, as with Randy Weaver, it was a "Get him at any cost (to taxpayers)" scene.

Regardless the sentiment toward the seeming outrageousness of the views held by men like Terry Long, it somehow doesn't make sense to treat such people as though they were planting suitcase, thermonuclear bombs at the International Airports or letting out contracts on heads of state! One is left asking, "Just what is it which these Jews and their goy counterparts fear?"

I have come to a few conclusions based on my own research efforts. They are definitely afraid of the truth of the hoax of the Holocaust and the Kangaroo Court at Nuremberg becoming common knowledge. They are afraid of the actual facts of the views of our Founding Fathers becoming common knowledge. They are afraid of the truth being told of the Jewish State of Israel's real attitude and agenda toward all non-Jews. They are afraid of the truth of the real agenda of The New World Order becoming common knowledge and just who is backing it. In sum, they are afraid of the truth from the beginnings of history to the present becoming known! That kind of fear engenders a whole lot of "overkill" in cases such as Richard Butler's "sedition trial," in cases like Terry Long and Randy Weaver's flaunting of the hypocrisy of "free speech" laws. And I repeat my warning concerning Canadian laws: The same thing is in process in this nation! And, like the attempts to take away our Constitutional right to bear arms, the threat is equally real in respect to our freedom of speech. This is already so successful that, as I have mentioned, you cannot take any view of White achievement or pride of White race on the radio, TV or in the print media. The real danger to Bobby Fischer is not his spitting on a piece of paper from the State Department, but his open contempt for Jews and his support of Arabs (his failing to file Income Taxes I attribute to his ignorance alone).

The fact of history is that Jews have always posed a threat to other civilizations for a number of reasons, not the least of which has been their insistence on control of economies and their expertise at using the mechanism of ruinous usury to gain such controls. I found it of extreme interest that in the first presidential debate, none of the three contenders, including Perot, would touch the question dealing with Alan Greenspan and the Federal Reserve! Why should this Jew have these "powerful" men so afraid? If you understood the diabolical system you would understand their fear.

Now the situation as it exists in our nation is one of whether the Founding Fathers "had it in for Jews, Negroes and Roman Catholics?" Since such an obviously extreme view was held by the Founding Fathers concerning all who did not subscribe to WASP membership it may be asked why they believed and acted this way? Only a thoroughgoing ignorance of history would precipitate the question. It is that kind of ignorance, coupled with the agendas of those opposed to the views of the Founding Fathers, which would make similar, contemporary views a threat to our nation!

The average person, I'm certain, knows that the majority of Roman Catholics, Mormons, etc., are "born" to their belief systems; few are, in fact, "converted" to them. As with Jews, Negroes, Mexicans, Arabs, etc., people are born to race, they did not "choose." You cannot change your ethnicity but you most certainly can change a "belief system."

For this reason, there are many who one could describe as not being "good" Catholics, Mormons or Jews. Such people are not firm devotees of the religion; this is particularly true of Jews. I have known too many Jews who would be appalled at being classed with the Zionists. The Zionists, on the other hand, would chop off the heads of such "betrayers."

It is most certainly a fact that the great majority of the membership of any organized religion does not really subscribe to, or is even knowledgeable of, the whole of the belief system to which it belongs. This is equally true of a Baptist, Roman Catholic, Mormon or Jew. In other words, it is the fanatic who poses a "danger," not the "nominal" believer whether Jew or Gentile.

The inability to reconcile the historical truths of the founding of our nation with what has become "politically correct" thinking has its roots in a very common, historical conundrum. If you want to take the position that "people are people" regardless of race or creed, you can only hold such a view when all the "people" are in agreement. Certainly no "fanatics" of an opposing view can be allowed!

Tragically, the view that people are only people doesn't work. The failure of every utopian dreamer and exercise can be laid to the weakness of human nature in our inability to "live and let live." One culture, and only one, will survive in any community, whether the smallest hamlet or the greatest nation. Diversity will be allowed only to a "point" and once that point is transgressed, the transgressor will be punished.

Our Founding Fathers perceived the truth of this historical dictum. Because of their own belief system, opponents and those who were perceived as a threat were excluded in their actions of setting up the Republic. They cannot rightly be faulted for not anticipating the insanity which prevails today of government trying to be all things to all persons. At least the Founding Fathers had sense enough to know this was impossible; so impossible in fact, that it didn't even occur to them to try to circumvent such a thing! In fact, the whole thing regarding "entangling alliances" was utterly anathema to them.

In 1893 Frederick Jackson Turner read his most interesting essay: "The Significance of the Frontier in American History" to the American Historical Association gathered in Chicago to help commemorate the World's Columbian Exposition. If anyone has failed to follow my interest in the history and politics of our early beginnings as a nation, such as the remarks of Jefferson and Henry Adams, my often allusions to men like Emerson and Cooper, I hope the following will enlighten you and prove of value.

The "true grit" of the men and women who first came to these shores never fails to provide inspiration. Whether anyone agrees with the values they held, no one will deny the supreme and sublime character that these early colonists of Plymouth had to have to survive and, more than just survive, begin to carve out a "home in the wilderness." No "revisionist" will ever be able to steal the honor due this unique band of heroes. Nor can one steal what properly belongs in such manner to those "Cavaliers" in the South. As time passed, people of less noble character did begin to arrive. But the situation that existed in 1776 was still such that noble men, for the most part, still held the ascendancy in positions of trust and authority.

The insistent, beckoning of this great nation, falling on the ears of those that considered it a right of free men to explore and, with rugged individualism and determination, carve out their own niche in the daunting wilderness called the hardiest to start moving into the vast areas that presented such a challenge to fulfill their destiny.

I have often used my own "wilderness experience" on the mining claim in the Sequoia National Forest as an example of what I am talking about. To take your gun on your shoulder and intrude yourself into an unexplored unpopulated, wilderness area speaks to a peculiar few, it forms a character unlike that to be found in the cities where the challenges are far different and usually build less desirable traits and values.

For this reason, Dr. Lyman Beecher said, in 1835, that: "It is equally plain that the religious and political destiny of our nation is to be decided in the West." As Turner pointed out, the "battle for the West" shaped our national character in adamant ways. Scoundrels and thieves there were aplenty. But, too, were men of hardy character and virtue in goodly supply.

We thrive on the "shoot-outs" in Westerns where John Wayne and Clint Eastwood are always giving hell to the bad guys. As children of my generation wildly applauded Hopalong Cassidy, Roy Rogers and Gene Autry, so later "Western Heroes" giving it to the bad guys, righting justice and fighting injustice still excited our children.

I pointed out, in a previous essay, the psychological, sexual "high" of war. "Instauration," a publication some may be familiar with, had an article on the "orgy" of war. The point of the writer of the article was perfectly valid; I have made the same point. In war, there is an intensity of life not felt in the ordinary, business as usual, humdrum affairs of day-to-day living. As a valid, psychological principle, it is only when we face death that life itself becomes such a precious thing, that the intensity of living is felt in full force.

The article quoted some Germans who claimed they really lived in those 12 years, 1933-1945, and have not "lived since." Many of our own veterans know exactly what these Germans meant. It is the point of Mr. Turner's essay though he would never have put it in such a way; may, in fact, have been unable to.

The expanding of our frontier to the eventual completion of the Westward movement was, in its own way, our "national orgy." It was not, as with Plymouth Colony, a "moral" thing. It was a seeming vacuum that drew people by the millions for any number of reasons. As other nations perceived us as a "brawling, undisciplined infant" among them, it was true to the extent that we were lacking in the kind of moral discipline that checked many of the abuses of the early colonization of the seventeenth and eighteenth centuries.

We were no longer, in the 1800s, the same nation of our Founding Fathers. Accommodation had already been made to set aside the obvious intentions of those worthies in order to admit the "mixed multitudes." As it was in 1809 with Jacob Henry, so it became with the "settling of the West." While White, Anglo-Saxon Protestantism provided the firm foundation of our Republic; it gave way, here a little, there a little, to a mongrelized perversion of its original intents and purposes.

It takes a lot of history to become "Babylon," were the Founding Fathers right in their exclusivity? Were those that came after, those that began to "accommodate" other "ideas" that subverted the clear intent of the Founding Fathers correct? Realizing that the question may be academic, moot or simply rhetorical by virtue of the seeming impossibility of ever renewing those "ancient landmarks," it does provide a basis of understanding the position of some wanting to "secede" to start their own "colony." The impossibility of such a venture is obvious. As long as the "law of the land" is interpreted so as to try to "be all things to all people" such efforts to divorce from such insanity is doomed. The "inmates of the present asylum" will not allow such to happen.

Turner and so many others engaged in a search for the American Character; but that character had been formed, originally, by Biblical, Protestant, Christianity and a value system that placed responsibility on the individual for his actions and caring for himself and family without government intrusion and welfare hand-outs.

In my travels throughout California, especially, I find the wicked of a wicked system of government "walking on every side" and prospering. The post offices in San Jose, Modesto, Merced and Bakersfield have Spanish interpreters. I wait in long lines of illegals and watch as they buy their money orders to send American dollars to their relatives in Mexico to help more illegals to come and enjoy the largess of the insane gringo system that has cut its own throat economically through such insanity. The welfare offices of California must have interpreters also since the caseloads are heavy with "Spanish surnames." Many of these leeches are so illiterate they can't even read their own language and have to have the interpreter read the forms they are to fill out to bleed honest taxpayers. Thanks to Willie Brown and his ilk.

Short of a national convulsion such as a military coup, there is no way any White group can claim any "land of their own." There are De Facto "nations" within our nation like Watts and East San Jose. But who in their right mind and given any other options would choose to live in such a manner?

God's Word has never failed me in its salutary effect in my life, being the sheet anchor of my soul. It is the final, but not sole arbiter, of the kinship of right thinking. I say "final but not sole" for the reason of close friends who have never failed me. It has been my experience to include, and augment, the wise counsel of God with wise counselors in whom His genius and Spirit are in such evidence. Such friends are Emerson and Thoreau. I have frequently hearkened to them and made the association well known to my readers over the years. They never fail to be timely and their insights in human behavior are a blessing. Their words to the effect that the argument against a standing army should apply to a standing government as well: "Government is at best but an expedient; but most governments are usually, and all governments are sometimes, inexpedient...That government is best which governs not at all!"

Like his inexperience with marriage and children, of which Henry's thorough honesty made no pretense of knowledge, his naiveté concerning the base nature of men led him a false path occasionally. But what is a true friend if he is not a friend "warts and all?" The purity of his gems of truth and faithfulness far outweigh any defects of discernment in regard to the baser nature of men and nations. What a wonderful world where there is no need of standing armies; no need of a government to hold in check the natural depravity and selfishness of the human race! I also, would fain plant ideas rather than beans, corn and cabbages but the one requires the sustenance of the other and cannot exist apart as even Thoreau allowed.

When I'm in Isabella, I write at a desk in the corner of a room framed with windows looking out at the mountains. The lighting is marvelous and I watch the sun come over the hills. The nearly one acre lot has plenty of oak and pine trees, granite boulders that delight my eye. I've done enough work on this old place, Sweat Equity, to feel a part of it. But it has been well worth it. While it is a most humble abode, I know I am "rich" compared to those who suffer under a mortgage they know they will never pay, they are only "renting from the bank," and, consequently, are not only not "laying up for their children, but will lose even the little they have at the least trouble. I am most certainly rich compared to the millions who have no hope of ever owning their own home or the millions who don't even have adequate shelter.

The American Character is still to be found in the Protestant Work Ethic exemplified by Plymouth Colony and the Founding Fathers. When a man can find opportunity, without onerous government intrusion, to provide by his sweat and honest, honorable labor, for himself and his family, which I have written so much about, there you will find the American Character. The loss of Unity of Purpose that so pervades our nation has born bitter fruit in the cruel bondage of slavery to government that has supplanted the honest labor of our hands. We are left vulnerable to a Hitler, a god, who will unite us once more as a nation because, refusing the God of our Fathers, only a Hitler can achieve this!

Utterly lacking in opportunity to do for ourselves because of codes, laws and totally prohibitive, restrictive rules, regulations and concomitant bureaucracies and obscenely, penalizing taxes and endless, ruinous litigations, the only answer is a "god" who will deliver us and unite us, once more, in a goal which will promise "deliverance from bondage" and "purpose in living."

Such a "leader" must surely come for the times cry out for him to make his appearance. We obviously need a "national orgy," a "national blood-letting" which will deliver us from our dreary and pointless lives. Desert Storm was a good start. But the need is for a Desert Storm on a world scale. The fear of hopelessness can only be answered by the kind of thing that led those Germans to say they had "lived for 12 years and hadn't lived since!"

The churches of America, representing only a shameful joke, offer no hope whatsoever. Our bungling and greedy "leadership" offers no hope. The universities, "education" of their kind offers no hope. In fact, they don't even seem to realize the truth, any more than the politicians and churches, that the warfare between Arabs and Jews is something actually desirable to them both; that keeps those people "alive" and gives them unifying purpose! Were it not for their mutual warfare and hatreds, they would be at complete loss and soon find themselves as "lost" hedonistically and materialistically as Americans and Europeans!

It is a fact of human nature to want to live in "delicious danger," a danger that enlivens and quickens the senses. This is one of the reasons for there being no lack of applicants for police jobs or the military. Whether the roller-coaster, advancing on the wilderness with only your gun and your wits, watching the shoot-out at the O.K. Corral and living vicariously through the TV thrillers, a sense of danger puts zest into life.

The impending Apocalypse of Revelation was easy enough for God to predict, given the nature of the Beast. The entire history of mankind is a history of warfare. We have always been preparing for a predestined Armageddon. We must have our Tower of Babel and only by forsaking God, as with those ancient builders, can we hope to have it! And, as I said, our "Nimrod" must soon appear. If honest and God-fearing men could be elected to leadership I would not be so pessimistic but I don't see this happening. If men would heed the sound advice and warnings of Thoreau's Civil Disobedience I would have hope. But they aren't listening. There is an embarrassing abundance of the lessons of history to which men give no heed that could save us and turn us from destruction and hopelessness. So it is that I continue my practice of years of telling young people that there are answers but only for the individual; the mass of humanity has never learned or listened. In spite of the abundance of evidence that work, whether the tilling of the soil or the building with one's hands must have, as its reward, to be both honorable and fulfilling, an end that satisfies our need to provide, by our own efforts, for ourselves and our posterity; not for welfare and church leeches or a leeching government which, in our case in America, has become the new Massa of a nation of slaves.

For a period of time, Turner's essay was construed as engendering Isolationism by glorifying the individual character, as Cooper did, of those Americans who subdued the wilderness and made this a nation from "sea to shining sea." But more recent interpreters of Turner have been more charitable and, correctly, I believe, began to look more at the insights of human nature he provided.

It is grievous to me to know that "gangs" have supplanted "family" in so many cases. I have long recognized, particularly during my tenure in Watts and East San Jose, that gangs were necessary to provide "family" when a family, as such, was non-existent. As one young man told me: "Hey, man, they is my family!" But let's not forget the human need for "danger" as well.

I grieve for the young people of today. Forsaking the ideals and values of the Founding Fathers, the progressively worsening leadership of our nation leaves them as "sheep without a shepherd" and the only "leader" on the horizon seems to be Nimrod. The symptoms of the disease of Godlessness pervade our entire society, a society which has forsaken its moorings in the God of our Fathers, and, as a result, wanders aimlessly without point or purpose. But where are the "prophets" who would call us to national repentance in sackcloth and ashes, the perquisite to reclaiming our heritage? Our own "house" seems to be left to us as desolate as that of the Jews!

Tragically, the only "glory" I see on the horizon is the "glory of evil." No matter the revisionist history of the Third Reich, no one would dispute the fact that Hitler unified the nation in purpose, in a feeling of sacrificial self-worth and gave the people back a dignity that unscrupulous, world leaders had robbed them of. Given the evil agenda and actions of the Zionists and their greedy puppets, the resulting moral and economic disaster cried out for Hitler. Can't you, yourself, hear the same, siren voice today in our own nation? It doesn't take much imagination to see millions, more than willing, "to bow when they hear the music and see the image!"

Jesus made a most telling point when the Jews asked him to tell them by what authority he preached and taught. He told them in turn; that he would answer their question if they would tell him whether they thought the baptism of John was of man or of God? Now understand that John preached repentance and those who came under conviction of their sins flocked to him. We are told that the leaders of the Jews did not do so and so it was that Jesus had made the statement that the "harlots and tax-collectors" had responded to John while the "professional religionists" had not.

These Jews who demanded an answer of Jesus as to his authority reasoned thusly: if they said John was just a man without Divine authority, they were afraid of the people who held John as a true prophet of God; but if they said John and his message was of God, they, in turn, would have to acknowledge Jesus' authority because of the witness and testimony which John had given him as the "Anointed One." Talk about "Catch 22!"

So it was that these Jews tucked their tails between their legs and slunk off proving Jesus' point that sinners who clearly realize the fact of their sinfulness respond to the Gospel, that message bringing both the conviction of sin and the "antidote." But for those, like these Jewish "leaders," the message is repugnant due to their own "righteousness." As Jesus had pointed out, He had come to heal the sick, not those who thought themselves in no need of such "healing" as with the point of the prayers of the Publican and the Pharisee.

Our sorry case today is that there are no leaders in religion or government who have the authority of God to call people to repentance. Whatever the "anointing" to such service is, it most certainly is not upon any that I know of in such positions notwithstanding all the Electronic Caterwauling of the shameless, egotistical charlatans on radio and TV or Snake-oil peddlers like Schuller. Tax-exempt status alone would prevent any who would presume to speak for God from doing so. Caesar will, like Limbaugh, et al., allow the illusion of "freedom of speech" but never the Real Thing!

So it is that our leaders today find themselves on the wrong end of Jesus' confounding of those Jews. They cannot admit to their own unbelief nor can they acknowledge the Truth of God! Rock and Hard Place time! They cannot admit to the truth of the historical facts of our Founding Fathers and those early Pilgrims nor can they, openly, dispute them! To this extent I can almost feel some sympathy for their plight. They are left with nothing to really believe in and, in their own way, are as hopeless as those they rob, cheat and steal from.

I will never forget chatting with a biology professor one time and, as the conversation turned to religion (my fault, of course) he began to share his early, childhood memories of his own church background. There were actually tears forming in his eyes as he said: "How I wish I could believe the things I believed as a child!" I reminded him of the words of Jesus in this respect. I don't know that he found any answer of comfort from what I shared with him but I will always hope so.

The experience of this professor is no different from what many of our national leaders have shared. How many I could name could say the same thing this man did: "If only I could believe the things I believed as a child!" How much simpler life would be if we could hold onto that childhood faith in some of the things we "knew were so" as children.

I've just returned from a visit with a dear friend and lady, Arlene. She and her husband, Frank, have a marvelous place at the foot of a mountain. Arlene and I went to school together in Kernville and Isabella, there was no "Lake" Isabella back then, and we thoroughly enjoy sharing memories of those "good, old days." As we sit and chat in their backyard, a beautiful, gray tree squirrel comes down one of the trees. Arlene hands me some walnuts and, as the squirrel begins to approach, I tap one on the patio bricks and his bright eyes home in on them. I'm thoroughly familiar with squirrel behavior. He quickly scampers over and grabs one, turns away and hurries to his "dinner table" in the tree. In fairly short order, he comes back and we repeat the procedure.

Arlene is sharing her experience with "pet" deer, raccoons and a bobcat. We are agreed that such critters are to be enjoyed outside of cages; like the kit foxes in Stevinson, only when these marvelous animals are in their natural habitat can we really have the benefit of them. It's fun, as Arlene agrees, to "spoil" them a bit, as when the squirrels start climbing on her screens, the uppity little critters demanding nuts, and our throwing grain out for the quail. But the real joy and fun of such critters is being able to watch them in their freedom, just going about their business naturally. Thoreau certainly understood what Arlene and I feel in this regard.

Too many people today are like caged animals. They know their "freedom" is, at best, only an illusion if that. What most don't seem to realize is the need for studied appraisal of their "cages." The first thing an animal does when trapped or in a cage is seek a way out. Now if you provide food and water, comfort, for the animal, many will finally give up and "domesticate," at least as far as their instincts will allow. You will still have to be very cautious with the bobcat or raccoon; even the squirrel will bite.

An armed citizenry still has the ability to "bite" as politicians are fully aware; therefore their concentrated efforts, as with all despots and tyrants, to disarm us. However, once the "teeth and claws" are pulled, any animal, even the lion, becomes only able to roar and, with enough "discipline," even the roar is extinguished.

I just had to "pop" a ground squirrel. These animals, unlike their cousins, the tree squirrels, are totally destructive. They are, in fact, vermin, digging holes that undermine house foundations, killing trees, causing other animals to break legs in their burrows, eating carrion and flea-ridden carriers of plague. There is little good to say about a ground squirrel (I am not referring to those cute little chipmunk-like California Ground Squirrels). You cannot change the behavior of these pests. Their nature is destructive and there is nothing to be done about it.

It seems that in too many cases of education, the churches and government, the system is riddled with "ground squirrels." They have made careers of "burrowing in" and "killing" or "maiming" the innocent. It has, in fact, become so common that, again, as with the ground squirrel, it seems to have become their "nature."

I am not suggesting that a new cadre of Minutemen begin "popping" some of these "vermin" no matter how tempting or how badly, to paraphrase Ma Joad, they might "need killin'!" I am saying that, as per Thoreau, there must be some "friction" applied to the "machinery" that constitutes the energy of the Beast and keeps it grinding away to the destruction of our birthright of freedom and liberty. To this end, I remain the strong advocate of Tom Paine and Thoreau, believing as I do, that the pen will always be mightier than the sword but never forgetting to keep my powder dry in preparation for a "worst case scenario!" I am far from being a "pacifist." For example, I would quickly and without any hesitation "drop the hammer" on any who proved a threat to one of my children! I will willingly forfeit my own life, if required, but don't harm a child within my "range!"

Antoine de Saint-Exupery said: "There are only motive forces, and our task is to set them in motion - then the solutions follow." As with all well reasoned philosophical thought, there is much to ponder concerning this statement and I have often done so. I mentioned my graduate class in Advanced Statistics in a previous essay. I would like to disabuse the casual notion that such studies are comprised of esoterica concerning sterile mathematical concepts and configurations; nothing could be further from the truth. This is the reason the university allowed the substitution of the study for one of its two foreign language requirements.

A group of six university and government physicists have recently started a new company in Santa Fe, New Mexico called "The Prediction Company." That these six men hail from Los Alamos National Laboratory, the University of Illinois at Urbana-Champaign and the University of California at Santa Cruz is not a case of "random selection."

In the early 70s, when I was involved with graduate studies, it occurred to me that there were identifiable patterns in so-called "random" phenomena. Physicists called these things "chaotic" at this time. By the late 70s, physicists began a concentrated study of such complicated behavior. My own particular interest was more concerned with how such theories might apply to seeming random, chaotic conditions of human behavior but I also had an intense interest in the mathematical models as well. I am sure the average person has had thoughts along the same line, though not in the sense of trying to apply the abstractions of mathematical criteria to them. A case in point might be what is popularly called deja vu. There is probably application to much of what is presently construed as ESP or "paranormal" psychology and phenomena.

The purpose of this new company is an attempt to "trend-forecast" (another most interesting field of my graduate work for which advanced statistics is essential) the Stock Market! Ah, ha! That probably got your attention. It certainly got the attention of The World Bank in Washington D.C. and SBC/OC Services, L.P., an options and trading house in Chicago.

Mathematical theorists know the plausibility of such an enterprise succeeding. As with my own, early, interest in the subject, it seemed obvious that if the data base was complete and broad enough, virtually all so-called "chaotic" conditions might reveal mathematically precise patterns underlying them. Astronomers have long believed in such precision rather than the earliest held beliefs of cosmotic chaos. There is, in fact, "order" in the universe, but on such a scale as to thwart the best of computer technology heretofore. But new generations of computer technology are making it possible to at least entertain the notion that such databases might be achievable.

The scale of such enterprises is, in fact, astronomically mind-boggling. Few people are conversant enough in the technology to understand the immensity of the data needed to achieve precise results. That is the challenge facing this new enterprise. As a very simplified example of what I am talking about, suppose you were trying to set up a mathematical probability of the exact time and place of a lightening strike? Given a complete enough database, you could, theoretically, make such a prediction. Given a complete enough database, you could fire a gun into the air and calculate the exact point where the bullet would fall! In other words, prediction of such "chaotic" events is actually possible; but the data base would be of such enormous quantity as to consider virtually everything involved with the event; truly an "astronomical" amount of information. But, in fact, the "randomness" of such events is, theoretically, precisely and mathematically "predictable."

Now, to my point in bringing up such a subtle subject; if I were to assign a "philosophical" name to my own theory it might well be called: "The Great

Number Fear!" In fact, it might well impinge on that old bugaboo of so many religionists, the "Number of the Man of Sin, 666!"

I believe there is a "pattern" to the seeming "randomness" of history and human behavior. I contend that if the "data base" was large enough, you could have predicted the Revolution, Civil War, World Wars I and II, etc. and their outcomes. Therefore, given that database, you could predict horse races, elections and future wars etc. I contend that, given such a database, you could accurately predict human behavior.

Taking the next logical step from such a theory, the theological concepts of "Predestination" and "Prophecy" are easily explainable because the greatest "Mathematician" of all, God, has a sufficient "data base!" But suppose men should, eventually, have the necessary technology to accomplish such "forecasting?" I would assume the only entities which would allow such would make absolutely certain that such a "philosopher's stone" be intensely and jealously guarded for obvious reasons. Can you imagine the success of such an enterprise being able to accurately forecast the Stock Market falling into any but the Zionist's hands? I can't! But I can easily imagine the "Fear" the success of such an enterprise would engender!

The question: Do events control men or do men control events? is a legitimate one. For example, just recently the Supreme Court agreed to resolve a dispute over what has been called "Junk Science." This has evolved from the propensity of lawyers (who else?) to try to win cases on the basis of "expert testimony" by people whose credentials are suspect but try to pass themselves off as knowledgeable simply because they have some letters after their names and a university education. Very good, you say, but! The other side of the coin is the probability, because of the criteria the court will impose, that the decision will disavow any Christian testimony by expert scientists who hold to Special Creation or, for that matter, any issue that would intrude into the area of theistic beliefs. Anyone who tries to present evidence, regardless of his or her scientific expertise, which is founded on belief in the Bible, will be disallowed! The "event" in this case is the ostensible attempt at "fairness." But, this "equity doctrine of fairness" makes good political rhetoric but in trying to be all things to all men, women and children regardless of racial, cultural and religious distinctives is insane in its final throes of destruction and enslavement.

The Great Number Fear will, if mastered, enable "predictability" beyond imagination. Gambling, as such, will no longer be a matter of "chance." Chance will not exist. As it is now, there are those who have mastered the game of Blackjack to such a degree that the known experts in this area are barred from playing. But imagine if you will a mathematical database that removes all "chance" and reliably predicts every throw of the dice, turn of the wheel or card, every pull of the slot machine! These are a few of the more mundane possibilities of the mathematical construct of which I am writing.

Those who "know" it cannot fall into the "wrong" hands must obviously, control such a thing! Most important of all, if any specific person or group should actually control such a methodology, he or they control the world! Not science fiction but grim reality!

In regard to human behavior, if I am theologically correct in my opinion that God Himself had to create a "data base" in order to accurately make His Own predictions concerning history and mankind, the historical account of what happened in creation and the Garden makes imminent sense.

For example, regardless of the simplicity of the problem, a certain amount of raw data must first be evaluated. If you construct a simple plane and roll a marble down its incline, you can determine its terminal velocity with great accuracy. The same thing can be done to measure the velocity of a bullet.

However, certain "variables" come into action during the rolling of the marble and the firing of the bullet which go far beyond such rudimentary elements such as the length and incline of the plane, the weight and configuration of the bullet and amount of powder used in the cartridge, etc. These variables contain influences such as time of day, temperature, earth-gas compositions, altitude, gravity, and, for the utmost reliability precision, even the "weak forces" of planetary configurations, atomic structures, etc. In short, maximum predictability would require a database containing absolutely everything that has a bearing on the outcome! Such an ability to consider all such things in reliably predicting is given to only a few. Savants have a "gift" that is not understood. I am writing about a mathematical "program" that would have the capability of the Savant in every field, not just a narrow aberration!

My study of history, as I have said, has always indicated a "pattern" of behavior. It is almost as though you could have predicted the events as the pattern emerged. You sit watching a horror movie and you find yourself yelling at the person (in your own mind, of course): "Don't open that door!" Why? Simply because you, as a spectator, have information the intended "victim" does not have as to whom or what is behind that door. In the same fashion, if you have the "information," you can "predict" the outcome; you know what is "behind the door."

I can think of nothing that poses as great a danger for humankind as the perfecting of the "predictability" mathematical model these physicists are now working on! It is one of the reasons I have never written my own thoughts about it. You might say it is now too late! I have no doubt that, if they pursue it long enough, they will have what they want in regard to stock predictions. After that! All hell could break loose but for the more hellish fact that it is my contention that the danger is clearly perceived by those "few" in the background and will be held in check by them except for their own, diabolical use. But such a device will give them the power to rule the world!

As I sat outside last night observing the stars, a multitude of thoughts on this theme intruded. There is one variable which I don't believe any mathematical database will be able incorporate successfully; that is the matter of "choice." While "predictors" of even an immense magnitude are achievable, only those that deal with material, insensate phenomena will be reliable. Even choice lends itself to predictability in some cases, for example:

He: "Will you go to bed with me for a million dollars?

She: "All right."

He: "How about five dollars?"

She: "Of course not! What kind of woman do you think I am?"

He: "We've already established that; I'm just trying to negotiate the price!"

One could multiply the examples endlessly as per this old chestnut to make the point. Under certain conditions, even choice is predictable. Another kind of example would include a large enough population as to preclude any but an easily identifiable answer. For example, the vast majority of people will "choose" to be rich rather than poor; will choose to not have to work hard if possible, men would choose a pretty woman and women would choose a wealthy man. It doesn't require much of a "data base" to have reliability when the variables themselves are predictable.

Uncertainty is a problem when the variables are of such magnitude that unknown influences come into play. I have often said that ignorance is a "killer." I can easily build a pattern for a tracer lathe and "predict" that the results will be according to the pattern. The same can be said for an injection mold and over a thousand other like things. I have absolute control because I can expect the material and machinery to conform to the specifications built into them. The only "variables" would be the tolerances that, because of their very nature, would have to be allowed such things according to practical considerations such as cost and application.

Theologically, I have tried to make the point that God, Himself, acquired a "data base" through His various creations including that of man. I believe God, in a sense, was in the process of "learning" through all His efforts and that man was the culmination of His hopes for fulfillment of God's own needs. What sets the religious establishment in howling anathemas against me is the obvious fact that I am saying that God was "ignorant" of certain things until He acquired the necessary database that would provide "predictability." But this is what all experimentation and creativity is directed at. To do and achieve better requires constant work, requires the perfecting of certain skills in order that advancement can be made.

When a certain thing is built for a specific purpose, usually utilitarian in nature, it can be improved as more data is gathered and needs change. Such learning always presumes ignorance. However, since there is no "standard" against which we can specifically measure our knowledge with absolute certainty, except in some specifics as per the application of such knowledge, we lack the necessary criteria against which to measure the degree of our ignorance apart from those same applications.

I have always accepted the dictum that we are all ignorant, just about different things! My battle, particularly as a teacher, is against the kind of hurtful ignorance that is not only ignorant but also prejudicially proud of the fact; like the ignorance that pervades the churches.

I believe God needed the element of choice in His supreme creation, man. By allowing choice, God not only had a creature in His Own image, He accepted the criteria of uncertainty. But it is that matter of choice that makes life what it is, with both its "light" and "dark" sides. That is what love and hate, obedience and disobedience, is all about.

The lack of the variable, choice, makes the mathematical precision of reliability and replication possible with the strictly mechanical model or database. But, under certain conditions, even human choice can be factored in with a certain degree of precision. Slaves, for example, have little choice and, hence, their behavior is fairly predictable. The "society" of a concentration camp or prison is fairly reliable.

On an individual basis, I can predict with fair precision, that if someone attacks someone else, the one attacked will try to protect himself. On a national scale, the only difference would be the factors that would make the threat real enough to arouse an entire populace. A predictable factor for my database would be the psychologically sound principle of the many against the few. If the few can be made a threat to the many, I can easily predict that the majority can be aroused to action against the few.

My part is to pursue my own ideas of making sense of those things in history and human behavior that might provide an "edge" against those who would be our "slave masters." There is a strong, historical case to be made for those that fear the Zionist agenda. There is a strong, historical case to be made for the achievements of White Europeans such as those of Plymouth Colony and the Founding Fathers. What is not nearly so clear, the reason being the purposeful work of the universities, churches, government and media at squelching any discussion of it, is the role of "race" in cultural distinctives and achievement.

Colleges and universities, for example, in their extreme paranoia, academic "bigotry and prejudice," refuse to involve themselves in any kind of "academic freedom" touching on this subject. And for good reason- it is volatile in the extreme! And there are the real enough specters of the extremes of Hitler's Germany in such studies. But, that was no excuse for "throwing out the baby with the bath" in such studies. Refusing to open the subject for honest appraisal and discussion will do nothing but cause a bad situation to become progressively worse. It is almost paradoxical that the greatest institutions of "learning" in our nation are ignorant of some of the very things they pretend an expertise, such as their classes on "cultural anthropology," things which are common knowledge among the supposedly "ignorant!"

It does not take a university education to understand the mechanism of "proving" an assumption by being very "selective" of the "facts and criteria" you use to support your assumption. As with the old bromide: "Figures don't lie but liars figure!"

When cultures come into conflict, as they always must, the only "resolution" is for one culture to achieve dominance. That is an essential factor in any database that attempts to predict human behavior. The dominant culture, may, depending on a number of variables, allow aberrations only to a point where they do not interfere with the flow of the dominant culture. The major problem in societies is the fact that such a "flow" is, invariably throughout history, economic.

I wish everyone would read Thoreau's Civil Disobedience. While we have much more data than he had, his main points are still, as with all Truth, valid enough to be of the greatest importance. For example: "If a plant cannot live according to its nature, it dies; and so a man...I can afford to refuse allegiance to Massachusetts, and her right to my property and life. It costs me less in every sense to incur the penalty of disobedience to the State than it would to obey. I should feel as if I were worth less in that case...Thus the State never intentionally confronts a man's sense, intellectual or moral, but only his body, his senses. It is not armed with superior wit or honesty, but with superior physical strength." In quoting Confucius: "If a State is governed by the principles of reason, poverty and misery are subjects of shame; if a State is not governed by the principles of reason, riches and honors are the subjects of shame."

Jesus, as with Thoreau and me, can make reliable predictions based on the greed and selfishness of men and, especially, those men who have "the rule." The inherent nature of men lends itself to a substantial degree of such predictability. No model of human behavior, to be successful, can exclude this most important factor in its database. Extrapolated to an entire society, the laws and values that govern human behavior must be analyzed thoroughly and factored in as well. Given sufficient, factual data, devoid of political, educational and religious prejudice, a remarkably accurate database would be achievable on both a personal and national level.

Such data, however, would require the most ruthlessly candid appraisal of true facts concerning human behavior- something that, certainly, the universities are unable to deal with. Without the, at least, concept of "the university" in its ideal configuration, with the free exchange of ideas, such a data base is most unlikely to be achieved. As with my contention that an "army" of Christian scholars should undertake the study of a new, systematic theology, an army of scholars coming together for the free exchange of ideas, devoid of hurtful ignorance and prejudices, is badly needed and most unlikely.

On an individual basis, like Thoreau, I will continue to undertake such a study wherever it may lead. Thus far, the search has made many enemies due to ignorance and prejudice. My visits with Klan and Aryan Nations leaders, my ruthless candidness regarding the historical facts of Zionism, Hitler and our Founding Fathers, my religious opinions, are most unpalatable to those whose "comfort" seems to be in coddling their own fears, prejudices and ignorance. But the "works of darkness" always find "light" painful and to be avoided at all costs. No deeply felt hate or prejudice gives way easily to love of the truth.

CHAPTER EIGHTEEN

CHRISTIAN PERSPECTIVE

DECEMBER 1992

Psalm 36:1-4

Merry Christmas; I am planning to run for the State Senate in the 16th district. I am told the filing date will be known sometime the middle of this month.

Many people have encouraged me to run for public office and it seems the time has come to ask them to put their money where their mouth is. If the support is there, I will run. This issue of CP will make my reasons for doing so abundantly clear.

The elections are over and they proved to be an unmitigated disaster to the nation in general and California in particular. They also proved that, far from being a pessimist, I was unusually optimistic in thinking George Bush might actually have a chance. The popular vote was exceptionally close but the Electoral College vote was overwhelming. You will recall that I had counted on people voting more out of fear than anger. The opposite proved to be the case. People are far angrier than even I thought.

We now have an admitted adulterer and draft-dodger as our "Leader." We also have a "First Woman," as she insists on being known, to further the causes of domineering women. California, having achieved the status of a third-rate "Banana Republic," can "boast" two such women as its U. S. Senators. Things do not look good for men, especially not for men like me who still thinks God means what He says. The Church of England has voted to ordain women! It took American churches to open the door to this evil.

Our adulterous, draft-dodging, perversion coddling "President Elect" will probably make good on his promise to force the military to accept perverts into the ranks. He will, undoubtedly, have the help of the courts. I can't think of anything that will have a more demoralizing effect on our military than inviting perversion, under legal sanction, into the ranks.

Another California note: A Sikh who was ticketed for riding his moped without a helmet has asked for exemption from the state's "helmet law" on the basis of his religion. Seems he can't wear the required turban and a helmet both. The judge, M. Lewis, and attorney, understandably, doesn't want to touch this "can of worms" and wanted to dismiss the case, in other words, ignore the law in this case. "NO WAY!" Seems the Sikh, Sadu Singh, wants his day in court. Just another day in the insanity of men's laws carried to their logical extremes. But I ask my readers to go back to earlier essays on this subject.

Things are so bad in California that Barry Keene, the majority leader in the state Senate, has announced his resignation. The reason; he is frustrated by a "Rube Goldberg-like system" that can't pass budget or bills. Quote: "We have a heavy tilt against change at a time when the state is crying out for a coherent vision...The government process as evidenced by the Legislature is in a state of dysfunction and disarray!"

As a matter of fact, while taxpayers are groaning under the load imposed by illegal immigration and welfare abuse, we couldn't even pass a proposition giving the governor authority to address the issues. Why? Because of the David Duke syndrome! No, there weren't any Swastikas or Hoods and Robes involved, at least not directly, but the same thing was at work. Who kept Duke from winning in Louisiana? The Media, Women and Minorities! Who put the Clintons (remember: "Two for the price of one!") into the presidency and "elected" Feinstein and Boxer? The Media, Women and Minorities! Where does that put White, Anglo-Saxon Protestant Males? In the cellar! And where, do you suppose, all of this leads? This is one of the reasons for my contemplating "tossing my hat into the ring."

Another is my great familiarity with the 16th district that covers the areas where I have lived and worked for so many years. The most prominent part of my platform will be the issues of education and the economy. No one can question my qualifications and expertise in the area of education. Neither does any other candidate possess such qualifications.

Having worked in so many California school districts including elementary, secondary and college and having started private schools in retaliation to a failed system of public education, having broad experience in working with minority young people and having a thorough understanding of what needs to be done in this regard, I know I can mount a good campaign on this issue alone.

My further motivation, along with the genuine concern I have always had for young people, is the fact education, more than any other single issue, is the one that needs help from people like me, not the so-called "experts" with worthless "doctorates" in education. I have always said that you cannot expect answers from the same people who created the problem! Most certainly you cannot expect answers from people like state Superintendent Honig!

Few would disagree with the fact that education and the economy are inextricably interwoven. As goes the one, so goes the other. If there is to be any hope for a future for our children, the utter failure of our schools to educate is the single most important factor that must be resolved.

Those that are familiar with my essays on various subjects will be concerned with some of my, considered, "extreme views" on some of these things. I will attempt to alleviate some of your fears in this essay.

Let me begin by saying that most of such views are only considered extreme when taken out of their historical context. Once placed in their proper context, they are not extreme at all. If you will bear with me, I will make this clear.

With the new "leadership" will come passage of federal laws which will give perverts "protected, privileged status" much like Canada's shameful legislation which prohibits even ministers from reading passages of the Bible where God, unmistakably, condemns perversion and calls it an abomination. Adulterers, which God classes along with perverts and murderers, are already free of any cultural restraints, the very concept of adultery being a "joke" in our society. But God still hates divorce and adultery and will not be mocked. What we sow as a nation we will most assuredly reap to our destruction. This, as an example, is not "extreme" in its historical context. Few would argue the historical fact that any nation which treats homosexuality, adultery and divorce lightly or acceptable is on a downhill slide to oblivion.

The New American, Reason and several other conservative periodicals have articles on legislation regarding so-called "Hate Crimes" which is must reading for every Christian and all others who value their personal liberty. You will scarcely be able to believe what Caesar has in store for us in this regard.

There is an old, Latin proverb that states: "He who eats at Caesar's table is Caesar's dog." Americans United is suing a church in New York for Separation of Church and State for the church's accusing Clinton of violating Biblical injunctions against abortion and homosexuality. The complaint, filed with the IRS (read: American Gestapo!) will most assuredly result in the loss of tax-exempt status for the church in question and a hefty fine. To make it even worse, this church even had the gall to ask for "tax exempt" donations to politic against Clinton! As a Christian I am repelled; find utterly repugnant, this leeching hypocrisy by this church.

I have long warned about this very thing. The churches simply cannot "eat at Caesar's table" and declare the whole counsel of God; they are "eunuchs" without any power whatsoever to confront evil, let alone seriously contend against it.

The joke is on those who, like the organization for separation of church and state that brought this suit, think such a thing actually exists! These poor saps think the churches are actually separate! They are not! The churches are a part of the very system this group belongs to. I can hear the howl of "good Baptists" everywhere at that statement. But think it through before you holler too loudly.

When any organization has made the compromises the churches have in order to "enjoy" special privilege and status, such an organization is in the pocket of the more powerful to which such an appeal is made. If the churches insist they should enjoy the privileges of Caesar in order to "do business," they are at the command of Caesar and are allowed to exist at his pleasure.

Robert Schuller and Son will keep smiling and hosting famous personages to give the illusion that the churches are alive and still in the business of promoting the Gospel. They're not. Pat Robertson, like the "old dope peddler," continues to "do well by doing good." While he and his CBN will give some excellent news segments, these will be, invariably, followed by some dewy-eyed "flake" that has just experienced some "miracle" of healing" or a "vision of an angel." Who on earth in their right mind is going to take such nonsense seriously? And who is going to take the flakes that promote such things seriously?

We continue to read numerous articles by well-intentioned individuals in support of the "theory" of our being a "Christian Nation" with concomitant, historically Christian roots. It ain't necessarily so!

Quite some time ago, I raised the question of how a "Christian" nation could have its roots in slavery? I even made the statement that the seeds of our own destruction were sown in not abolishing slavery by our Constitution, something Franklin and Jefferson tried to do without success because of the power of the Southern colonies for the sake of profits. There is also the historical fact that the "colonization" of the Westward Expansion was anything but "Christian;" in most cases, it wasn't even honorable or moral!

Unquestionably the early history of our nation from Plymouth Colony and Jamestown to the Revolution was steeped in Christian theology and traditions. As deserving as the Pilgrims, Puritans and founding fathers are of our highest regard, they are not deserving of "veneration." It is equally unquestionable that their theology was badly flawed in many respects that, ultimately, led to the abuses, even heinous sin, against The Lord and others in his name, slavery and the Salem Witch Trials being infamous cases in point.

The fact is that Christians are so abysmally ignorant of our early history that, as I have often said, many would be thunderstruck at some of the actual events of church history in general and the period of American Colonization in particular. For example, let's look at some of the actual occurrences of

"God's dealing" with those people during the tenure of John Winthrop. I will cite historian Darrel Abel's account:

"If Winthrop's record is a fair sampling of the Lord's dispensations to New England during the first two decades at Massachusetts Bay, He attended much more to punishing the wicked and chastening the faithful than to granting mercy to evildoers and rewarding saints. He dispensed terrible punishments for what seem to 20th century consciences slight offenses. The Lord especially favored drowning as a means of punishing those who, according to Puritan notions, had incurred His wrath. He drowned one child because, his parents having no other sons, they 'had been too indulgent toward him,' and another because his father had worked an hour past sundown on Saturday to finish a pressing task. He drowned a man of Marblehead for 'carrying dung to his ground in a canoe upon the Lord's day,' and a young man for refusing to help his poor father without pay in order that he might work for another man for wages. Others drowned for drinking on the Sabbath and for scoffing at ministers. Lewd sailors were disposed of by having them taken by the Turks and sold into slavery, or by contriving to have them blow up their ships by accidentally setting fire to their gun-powder. The Puritans certainly contributed greatly to the formation of our republic, but nothing in the record supports the ignorant popular notion that they were democratic, or even humanitarian."

It was the Puritan, Calvinistic trait to see a dichotomy in every thing that transpired in their lives. So much so that Cotton Mather, the most prodigious writer of the period could write: "I was once emptying the Cistern of Nature, and making Water at the Wall. At the same time, there came a dog, which did so too, before me. Thought I; 'What mean and vile things are the Children of Men, in this mortal State! How much do our natural Necessities abase us, and place us in some regard, on the same level with the very dogs!'"

Few would argue Mather's "spiritualizing" of our natural, bodily functions but imagine maintaining such a frame of mind at all times! Such constant attention to such a mental state might offer some explanation for Mather's role in the Salem Witchcraft trials that, unlike Samuel Sewall, he never repented of.

It was Mather's constant immersion of mind in such things that has led more than one historian to make the statement: "No doubt he was insane, but if a man's mania is merely a magnification of the chronic insanity of his time it cannot be detected and he will pass with many as a marvelous man." A reading of Mather's Magnalia Christi Americana or The Ecclesiastical History of New England or his Diary would be and eye-opener for any who have the mind-set that our Puritan forebears had their wits, spiritual or physical, about them at all times or should be emulated.

It would be most enlightening for all you "pew-warmers" to examine the "liberty" men like Mather allowed themselves in "translating" Scripture. The Bay Psalm Book, the first book ever printed in America, printed at Jamestown, was revised by Mather to suit his own taste.

On the other hand, we had men like Roger Williams and Samuel Sewall who we would regard as more "enlightened" and humane than the Mather's. Sewall, in fact, put up a "bill for forgiveness" to be read by the minister of the Old South Church while he stood before the congregation for his part in the Salem Witch trials. Even further, Sewall published the first anti-slavery tract in America, "The Selling of Joseph." Curiously, Sewall subsidized much of Cotton Mather's publications and was judged the wealthiest man in Massachusetts. He also published a tract favoring miscegenation. No plaster saint himself, his attention was far more directed at gaining wealth than "good works." Contrasting the two, Mather and Sewall, you begin to get an inkling of the religious confusion that prevailed at the time.

When we leave New England and direct our attention South to Virginia (all the Southern Colonies were spoken of as "Virginia" at this time) we encounter men like Captain John Smith and, later, Robert Beverley. Any study of our history, secular and religious, must take such diversity into account. Only then can any consensus of the truth of our history as a "Christian Nation" be of any trusted use. The Puritan and Southern "Cavalier's" dealing with the Indians is most informative as well.

Beverly's accounts help in understanding why the South was so instrumental in the Revolution. More importantly, such study of the early histories gives insight as to both the economic and spiritual dimensions of the South's rebellion to the Crown.

The single, most obvious problem with which our Puritan forbears had to struggle is still with us today; that is the matter of Law and Grace. The Puritans had separated from the Church of England on the basis that the Reformation was only "half a reformation" as per the state Church. In their attempts to "purify" and reconcile Law and Grace, they, themselves, fell into many a grievous error. The Southern Plantations, continuing to hold to the Mother Church, had no such quandary.

One of the things which was of utmost importance making its contribution to our Civil War was the fact that the Southern Plantations were isolated and, as a result, generated a "class system" with its own rigid codes. Cities were few and far between in the South. New England, on the other hand, had numerous, large cities. The single most important fact of this disparity was in the field of printing.

New England was pouring out huge amounts of printed material indigenous to the Colonies while the South relied on materials from the

Mother Country. In no other case in history has the pen been mightier than the sword and had such far-reaching ramifications than this single factor. This disparity, more than anything else, was to come crashing down on the South in particular and the nation as a whole and result in our national blood-letting beginning April 12, 1861 and from which we never recovered.

If there is to be any understanding of racial or ideological hatred and prejudice, any hope of our children having a future free of these things predominating, it will only come about with men of good will meeting in concert, willing to forego their own preconceptions of "equity of fairness" and deal with truth and facts alone.

Jesus warns against having men's reputations in regard. We are told, explicitly, to look at the works of men in order to determine whether they speak and work for him or against him. But there is a curious thing at work in this respect- especially in regard to our forefathers. But, then again, why should this be any different than the situation Jesus faced when He condemned those Jews who venerated their own "fathers," men who had killed God's prophets? The plain fact of the matter is that few are able to study the history of our nation objectively. As a consequence, many things are believed which are simply not so!

Many years ago I read an article on the Reformation in Collier's Encyclopedia. The article was so definitely biased in favor of Roman Catholicism that I wrote the editors. In their reply I discovered the writer of the article was a Jesuit Priest! Now just how "objective" was the "scholarship" of such a sensitive subject from such a source? So it is that much of our own history can only be rightly interpreted by reading widely and attempting to build a "data base" which would include everything touching on the subject, not just those things which serve to enforce our own biases and prejudices.

A few days ago, I was having dinner with a prominent, Negro Christian publisher and author. When he learned of my research, visits and familiarity with various White Supremacist organizations, he became intensely interested in my views of such. It seems he is contemplating a newspaper directed to the Negro community, which would emphasize Negro achievement, and, it is hoped, Negro esteem. As a Christian, he wants this publication to have a Gospel orientation.

After a lengthy conversation, he asked if I would be willing to contribute some of my own knowledge concerning White Supremacist organizations to the paper. I asked that he read what I have already written, a large task, before we discussed such a thing. A few days later I delivered copies of my books and essays to him and am awaiting his response.

Now several things immediately suggest themselves to my readers of some years. First and foremost is the fact that those that know me well would never accuse me of racial prejudice. Second is the fact that I am equally well known for "saying it like it is." I never engage in flattery to attain position, something that caused me a lot of grief in education, and I will never curry favor for the sake of my own agenda. As a Christian, I am wholly committed to the truth in all matters, even those of race! If I run for the State Senate, I will not equivocate on the views I have already made clear in print.

This Negro publisher faces a hard choice; if he sincerely wants to do something for the cause of the Gospel and to help others, he will only have my assistance as long as I am able to write factually in total disregard of racial considerations. I have explained to him that the only reason I can be privy to the confidences I enjoy with leaders in organizations like the Aryan Nations, the KKK, et al., even some in the "shadow government," is their respect for my being "my own man" and never betraying a confidence.

When he expressed the obvious concern that some of these associations placed me in some danger, I explained that as long as I told the truth and was even-handed in my treatment of all these organizations, I felt I had nothing to fear. But, it hardly needs to be said that an element of danger still exists and only people like me, those with nothing to lose and no family to be concerned with, should undertake such studies and have such associations.

A fact that escapes most people, due largely to media distortion, is one that I have often commented on. The leaders of these various organizations are not "haters." They are, for the most part, people who are intelligent and have a somewhat different perception of the role they have in American culture and society. Extremists? In many cases. I make a distinction between the leaders and the "soldiers" in these organizations. As one leader told me, he could get all the "cannon fodder" he needs to pass out literature and hold rallies but he couldn't get educated people, people he could trust, to join with and support him. Much as police jobs attract people who like to carry a badge and gun and thump heads and education attracts homosexuals because of children, extremist groups attract many, black, brown, yellow, white who have their own peculiar reasons for involvement.

The real danger, as I have often stated, is for some charismatic genius to appear on the scene that would cause all these various factions to coalesce under a common cause. Then the feared race riots nation-wide would be a certainty!

If this publisher wants to do something constructive for people, particularly Negro people, he will deal with the truth, with facts, and not with wishful thinking and the truth, as I told him, is not always some bright, golden shining thing, it is often tawdry, hurtful, grievous, scandalous and shameful. But it is still the only thing which God can bless and which one can place hope to provide remedy for wrong.

In my studies of "Conflict and Resolution," it is a given that the only approach with any degree of hope for success is one that enables those in conflict to be able to engage in honest dialogue and inquiry based on facts alone. The process, to be successful, is based on an ability to set aside preconceptions, biases and prejudices and deal with the truth.

One of these "truths" in regard to race and religion is the fact that only one, dominate culture can survive in a nation. All others will be subservient to that dominant one. We are presently witnessing the killing of Kurds by Kurds, Africans by Africans, Arabs by Arabs, Moslems by Moslems, Whites by Whites (as per Ireland), etc. Our own Civil War claimed over 600,000 lives, brother against brother.

Further, "To Kill a Mockingbird" is a two-edged sword. If the emphasis is placed on ignorance and bigotry, racial prejudice and hatreds, the results are always going to be Burn Baby Burn! with Watts and Harlem always the recipients. If the emphasis is on some altruistic and ethereal concept of "Love Everybody" the results will be the same. Only ruthless and candid facts and truth have a chance of success.

So there is much more than "race" involved with the shedding of blood. The ultimate factor is an ideology, a belief system for which one is obliged to take or give life. Whether "ethnic cleansing" or real or imagined threat to one's life, the lives of loved ones or one's culture, the case must first be made of threat and the "righteousness" of the cause.

The purpose of all propaganda is to muster support for resistance to, and/or, attack against, the perceived threat. There are few contenders for such causes as religion. One may as an individual loot and kill for monetary gain but religion is the *cause celebre* for the coalescing of the "tribe."

Now it doesn't matter whether we call it "religion" or not. As long as the cause has its roots in an ideology, a "brotherhood of believers," it has all the concomitant ingredients of religion. Whether Zionism, Masonism, Mormonism, Muslimism, etc., the ingredients are the same and are able to pit brother against brother. Even the churches had to "take sides" in our own Civil War: so much for the "power" of the churches to be an ameliorating influence. The Roman Catholic Church (and others) was most "circumspect" in dealing with Hitler's Germany. Even now, with Nazism on the ascendancy once more, little is heard of any church "influence" in the process.

Speaking of Germany, it gets ever more interesting. A WWII general, Otto-Ernst Remer, 80, has been sentenced to a year and 10 months for denying the Zionist-media-popularized version of the so-called "Holocaust." While Remer was instrumental in thwarting the 1944 plot to assassinate Hitler, according to W.L. Shirer, and was promoted to major general before the end of the war, he was never prosecuted as a war criminal!

Also, German authorities are investigating the extent of the neo-Werewolf's association with the KKK. But, the problem is that other German "authorities" are involved in the group being investigated! Reminds me of our own CIA/FBI/State Department/Justice/Department gun and finger pointing; my, my, what's to do? When it comes right down to it who is going to have the authority to arrest whom for what?

I am indebted to my old school chum, Gary North, for his letter clarifying his association with David L. Hoggan and, particularly in regard to the contradiction between Hoggan's Ph. D. dissertation for Harvard and his later conclusion of Lord Halifax's supplanting Chamberlain. I do not have the problem Gary has, however, with R.J. Rushdoony's early acceptance of Hoggan. I think this is because I am more familiar with the history of Freemasonry and Zionism than he is.

For those of you who are unfamiliar with Hoggan, I would ask you to try to obtain his "The Enforced War, Myth of the New History" and Rushdoony's "This Independent Republic, Conflict in 1937" and "World History Notes." You might also like to read Olivia Maria O'Grady's "The Beasts of the Apocalypse," though, as Gary rightly points out, this last, as with much of Hoggan's work, is largely un-footnoted.

I also want to thank Gary for clarifying the disposition of the "Center for American Studies, the William Volker Fund" organization and the "Institute for Humane Studies" in Menlo Park where I used to work. I have to wonder at Gary's accusation of Hoggan as an Anglophobe and Germanophile. It has to be to Hoggan's credit that he publicly made his views known at a time when they posed such personal risk and for his serving time in prison rather than fight against Hitler and "for the English." Gary may be right but I rather think Hoggan is to be understood in respect to conscience more than prejudice or politics. This may be the reason for Rushdoony's acceptance of him.

But the kind of "Truth" and "Facts" of which I am speaking demand historical imperatives of truth and facts, even when the facts have to take the "Hoggans" and "Roeders" into consideration. One of these facts is the truth that we no longer have Constitutional De Jure government- only De Facto government. In other words, we have a government based on interpretations of the Constitution that various Supreme Courts have made the law of the land that is diametrically opposed to the intent of the Constitution.

Here are some more "facts." Trachoma is devastating hundreds of thousands of Africans. The simple preventative for this dread disease is to only wash the face at least once a day! Now you might, reasonably, cry: "Good grief, why don't they?"

The point, as I have tried to make clear to multitudes without success is: Cultures In Conflict! An unpalatable fact of our European ancestry is that for centuries such peoples held the belief that bathing was injurious to health! So you never bathed; the invention of perfume and high ceilings in palaces bear mute testimony to this most unsavory fact. Only in relatively recent times have the amenities of washing bodies and teeth, the inventions of undergarments and indoor plumbing brought about near hysteria in hygiene and a multi-billion dollar industry concerned with deodorants and sex appeal.

Another, at first glance, seemingly unrelated fact is that of genetic studies. Only recently have scientists discovered their "facts" based on Mendelvian theory are wrong! Genes do not, always, adhere to this "rule." Some appear the same but will have different characteristics depending on whether they come from the father or the mother! As with recent genome studies in mice, the door stands, not open, but only ajar.

My point is that, while we always pay it lip service, things are not always what they seem; no matter how well intentioned the "believer." I have warned about the charismatic heresy for years. Just recently, a group of "well-intentioned believers" in Korea numbering in the thousands were selling their homes and quitting their jobs because "Jesus is coming!" While most of my religious colleagues were waxing lyrical over the "huge successes" of the "gospel" in Korea, I was warning that this was the result of charlatanism in the guise of real Christianity. My rationale was based on the fact that most of the seeming "work of the lord" was charismatic heresy. The shame attached, and the damage done, to the real work of the Gospel is there for the whole world to see and ridicule as another bunch of loonies gave leave to their senses in exchange for a "religious fix" and "emotional high!"

The field of science has never lacked for "charismatic believers" either. The same egos and "seeking" influences are at work in every endeavor. They are certainly not lacking in the Jim Jones's or their black, brown, yellow or white counterparts.

"Ah!" you say, "He is finally back on the subject." Ah! I say, I never left it! You just fell behind. Now pay attention and keep up. I didn't lose you, you aren't paying attention. You remind me of the fellow who, recently, went outside and found the body of his father on his doorstep covered with a sheet. A local mortuary had picked up the body of the guy's 69-year-old father previously with orders for cremation. Why was the body dumped back on the guy's doorstep? Because he hadn't paid the mortuary! True story. Why do you remind me of this bizarre story? Because you don't think lack of attention to "petty details" will result in the body being dumped back on your doorstep! But it will!

More facts; "petty details." The problems of the Dallas Police, the failure of the anti-pervert initiative in Oregon and the welfare reform initiative in California, the gang violence in the cities, the election of the Clintons,

Feinstein and Boxer, the growing Nazi movement in Germany, GATT and Maastricht, the failure of Canadian "unity" and the burning of Watts are all inter-related. The "data base" grows hugely correspondingly.

As an aside, why did the California proposition for doctor-assisted death fail? Simply because the poor and minorities can vote! Since it doesn't cost them anything for medical care, why should they worry about the catastrophic cost of keeping a "vegetable" alive! The taxpayers can afford it! Richard Lamm's remark that the terminally ill had "A duty to die and get out of the way" only flies with those who have to pay the bills. The dead don't and the welfare living won't.

Would I choose to go on breathing with hoses, tubes and machines at the cost of my children's inheritance? I would not! But if I could steal the money from the taxpayers, ah, that might be a horse of another hue.

Another fact: Mexican illegals murdered four, teen-age girls in a yogurt shop in Austin, Texas. They were tied together and each was shot in the head. The store was then set on fire. Mexican authorities say they have the murderers in custody but will not turn them over. The two Mexican murderers, Porfirio Villa Saavedra and Alberto Cortez, had been sought in Texas for a previous sexual assault and rape. Mexico will not extradite nor does it have a death penalty. If you were one of the parents of one of these poor, murdered girls, how would you now feel about Mexico and Mexicans? Wouldn't you be seeking an organization that promised you justice? I would.

Fact: In his October newsletter, Dr. James Dobson of Focus on the Family made this statement in regard to congressmen ignoring the wishes of the constituency: "Why have so many of our representatives ignored and insulted their constituents in this way? Why would they risk the disapproval of those who sent them to Washington in the first place? The reason is that they are convinced, with some evidence that you and I will not remember on Election Day."

Dear Dr. Dobson: you couldn't be more wrong! The "people" did remember and the Clintons won. You are absorbed in this thing touted as "family values." Fact: "Family Values" as per you and the GOP do not exist in America! "Family Values" as per the Clintons, with divorce, adultery and perversion is now the "norm." The vanishing middle class, women in general and the welfare poor are the norm together with the toadies, like the Clintons and their ilk, who cater to them in order to hold political office!

Those of us who believe The Bible could certainly see, as a result of the Dan Quayle/Murphy Brown debacle that "We the People" really are in contemporary society. When good men cannot lead in their own families, due to punitive legislation and the ease of divorce, when men who believe in God's injunctions concerning the family continue to be bashed, and bashed, and bashed without let, there is no such thing as "family values." When churches ordain women in any capacity, when churches, themselves, contribute so hugely to the "feminist, equality lie" and agenda and continue to eat at Caesar's table, you can no longer have "family" in the context of God's Word. What we have in the churches today are spineless men, weaklings who aide and abet the enemy in placing women in leadership utterly contrary to God's clear injunction against such an abomination.

I'm a musician. Due to that fact, I more often played for dances rather than dancing myself. As a consequence, I was never much of a dancer. But I've watched a lot of dancing and nowhere have I seen such a repertoire of terpsichorean agility (fancy foot-work) as when I've watched and listened to men in the pulpits try to dance around God's clear, unmistakable words such as "Women should keep silent in the churches for it is a shame and disgrace for them to speak, should learn, quietly at home from their husbands, that a woman should never hold a position of authority, or be teachers of men, in the churches."

Further, Dear Dr. Dobson, you too eat at Caesar's table thus making you of very limited effectiveness in dealing with the ugly realities of the very sins you espouse to confront. I don't doubt your good intentions, but you obviously are not willing to let go of this public teat at the cost of your own "empire."

"It's the system!" religious organizations cry. Regardless the cost, as per Thoreau, it would cost far less to be real Men and throw sand into the evil machinery of the system than to succumb to it. Worse, in too many cases, to become such a part of that evil system that the voice of God Himself is silenced!

I repeat, when a nation is morally adrift, even worse, is guilty of repudiating morality; its end is easily prophesied. When adultery, divorce and perversion is legally sanctioned, even approved by so-called churches, when these things are treated as simple "taboos" of an anachronistic past, the constraining influences for good give place to license for every kind of abomination.

When I call for people to get together for dialogue on the basis of the truth and facts alone, setting aside prejudices and biases, I am asking for something of tremendous complexity with monumental amounts of information to digest. The problems and answers are far more, hugely complex than those espoused by the "Little Brown Church in the Vale" or the "One Room Schoolhouse." Such truth and facts must include the Randy Weavers and the Louis Farrakhans.

But if such meetings of men seeking the truth do not come about, violence must increase. Given the present climate of fear, anger and political and religious "leadership," such meetings must be held or things like carjackings and the snipers on Florida highways will become the "norm" along with racial conflict that will escalate to make the Balkans look like a holiday scene.

Bakersfield has been the butt of so many jokes for so long it is difficult for me, a native son, to comprehend the changes that have taken place so quickly. Recently, a business seminar hosted the following at CSUB: Former West German Chancellor Helmut Schmidt, Walter Cronkite, Andy Rooney, Robert McNeil, Jerry Goodman, Rich Little, Cliff Robertson, Zig Zigler, Melissa Manchester and Norman Schwarzkopf. That's a pretty hefty gathering to my mind. How is it that such a range of personages can come together for political purposes but the churches are barren eunuchs by comparison in the spiritual arena? Ignorance, once more, is the "killer!"

Cultural Anthropology is an essential ingredient to understanding. Not of the form so corrupted by the universities and churches, but fact and truth, devoid of prejudice whether of the "liberal" or "conservative" mold. This is one of the reasons I know an entire New Systematic Theology is needed by the churches. Not one which would denigrate or deny the Truth of God's Word, but one which would promote understanding rather than obfuscate or further abet entrenched prejudices and ignorance.

The lessons of history are there for us to profit from, from Aquinas to the Puritans to the present. The blood-letting, confusion and chaos among the churches will only get progressively worse until that "army of scholars" come together, agreeing to set aside their prejudices, and let God speak for Himself as per that first council in Jerusalem without their muddying the water with their "pet doctrines" and "traditions of the fathers" holding sway.

Nathaniel Hawthorne and Melville were closer to the situation of the Puritanical Theocracy of New England than we. Were we not an illiterate society, abysmally ignorant of the facts and literature of our history, there would be more cause for hope. As it is, the Hate Crimes legislation gaining favor will only further alienate and exacerbate an already dangerous situation. Jewish Intellectualism having the ascendancy, gave us such terms as "Homophobic" and organizations with "Diversity Consultants" in order to fan the flames of "Ethnic and Racial Characteristics."

As I have written in the past, oxymora such as "Judeo-Christian" popularized by foolish men like Jerry Falwell and Pat Robertson serve only the agenda of the Zionists and militate against any truthful dealing with facts. When Jewish intellectuals are so successful in capturing, wholesale, the areas of psychology and psychiatry, an entire nation becomes captive to the propagandizing of "Homophobia is a deeply rooted pathology among Christians!" Marxist Theodor Adorno and Daniel Bell.

By "diagnosing" a stand against perversion as a "pathology" to be "treated," Adorno/Bell give legitimacy to an inquisition against any who hold a contrary view, particularly those who believe the Bible. On April 23, 1990, when George Bush signed the Hate Crime Statistics Act, he knowingly played into the hands of the homosexual lobby. In some diabolical way, you might even say he was cooperating with those who would oppose him for a second term as president and, as per the Clintons, carry the evil agenda even further!

As a direct result, following the lead of Canada, the group which now uses phrases such as "Homophobic, Bible-thumping, Hate-mongering Bigots, Mental Dinosaurs, Nazis, etc." are considered "compassionate liberals" while those that quote God are the "Bigoted Racists" which need "professional help!" And, with Caesar's cooperation, such benighted souls will get it through such "treatment" as imprisonment and lobotomies!

Because of the blindness of their own prejudices, anti-Christians such as the Zionists, Malcolm Xs and Farrakhans fail to see how such persecution of Bible believers will come down on the heads of their own followers. In blindly following their own ideological agendas of hatred and persecution, they fan the flames of hatred where scapegoating becomes, as with Hitler's Germany, a necessity of government.

We have treaded a weary and ignorant road to such a debacle of a supposed Republican form of government which flies in the face of every shred of the hopes and aspirations of our forefathers. Far from the dreams of a New Israel of the Colonies, we are a nation divided on just about every front imaginable. Only if enough good men of good will come together with the common cause of absolute truth can we have any hope of anything better for our children. But an objective view of our present circumstances would almost dictate the necessity of a national convulsion of cataclysmic dimensions for the need of such to be perceived as an absolute essential to bring order out of the, presently, prevailing chaos.

The necessary "data base" would have to be exhaustively monumental. A thoroughgoing re-evaluation of theology, history and literature would be a demanding requirement. It's enough to make this Weedpatcher shudder; but if it is not done...?

In one of the more colorful propaganda organs of pseudo-Christianity, Israel My Glory, the ZVI department has the following concerning recent elections in Israel: "One candidate in particular, a rabbi running on the ticket of an ultra-Orthodox religious party, placed an ad in the newspapers stating: 'If you vote for our party, you will earn a place in the Garden of Eden. It will be your passport to paradise...God will judge those who do not give their votes to our political party!'" Not a few of our own politicians, I would guess, wish they had such clout with the "Almighty." Further, it is difficult to fail to see the similarity with such propaganda as that practiced by Arab leaders.

The writer of the article goes on to say that he visited the campaign headquarters of this party and was asked if he knew the Talmud and the 613 Oral Laws. The writer, a professed Christian convert from Judaism, tries to give the impression that he had a "successful witness for Christ" to these Talmudic Jews. I was not impressed.

Not to belabor the point, as I have often pointed out the battle is on ideological grounds, Cultures in Conflict. The basis of every culture is its system of beliefs that dictate its values and "taboos." Even Cotton Mather was some ahead of his more superstitious and ignorant "brethren" in his advocating study and acceptance of things like inoculation for the pox. Such "scientific" inquisitiveness and acceptance didn't, however, keep him from condemning to death those poor souls for witchcraft solely on the words of a few, at least equally superstitious, ignorant and hysterical children.

If Mather were judged "insane" by a more enlightened age and his dementia cloaked by the very culture in which he thrived as a "holy man," it should be patently obvious that those of his contemporaries that would oppose him would, in the context, be judged the insane ones. It is on this basis that I might very well be considered "insane" myself for surely I do oppose most of what tries to pass as "enlightened sociology and theology" in our present times. In its context, I am most certainly an "enemy of the State!" Such "madmen" are not easily suffered by a generation bent on ferreting out the "witchcraft" of reason and a sound mind, particularly when it lies athwart its own agenda: "The truth, it doesn't pay!"

The world has become an ever more dangerous place. Only recently has Russia admitted to the atrocities committed on our MIAs of the Korean War. As I have written in the past, if the Russian archives were fully open, a great deal of the history of the past fifty years would have to be revised, particularly concerning the so-called "holocaust." But, I fear, this subject falls into the category of the purposeful stonewalling going on concerning the Scrolls with the collusion of the Vatican and Jerusalem.

Yet, if honest inquiry concerning such sensitive issues is denied, how can there be any honest history from which to advance in learning? I have made the point in one of my books that there are no "illegitimate" questions of God. I am convinced we "have not because we ask not!" God has said: "... that if any lack wisdom, let him ask and it will be given." If, as God says, "Wisdom is the principle thing...with all your getting, get wisdom," He either made a bad joke or people are asking, as Jesus warned, for the wrong reasons. When it comes to church "leadership," I cannot help but be reminded of the dreadful condemnation of Jesus of those religious leaders of His day:

"Woe to you experts in the law, because you have taken away the key to knowledge. You yourselves have not entered, and you have hindered those who were entering." Things have certainly not improved in the churches of today. They are certainly guilty of taking away the "key to knowledge" and seem to be doing all they can to hinder those who are asking legitimate questions. The Galileo's and Luther's are still "excommunicated" and sycophants continue to hold sway.

In our concourse of trying to make sense of so many diverse questions about so many different things, a certain "stream of consciousness" is necessary. Since I brought it up, I hasten to add that any questions dealing with the subject of animal and human behavior and modification of same requires a thorough grounding in psychological principles together with an understanding of science and history. Even given such a background, intriguing possibilities suggest themselves at every turn and the seeming answers to one question pose even further inquiry.

I will never forget the first time my children, Karrie and Michael, decided to make coffee for their dad. Not knowing how much coffee to put in the filter, they simply filled it up; made sense to them. Now I enjoy strong coffee and this certainly qualified in the extreme. But I drank it and loved them for their thoughtfulness. I did instruct them in the proper proportions just in case they should have any future "attacks" of consideration for me. So it is that in too many cases well intentioned acts don't necessarily bring the desired results. The motive may be pure but the coffee may compare favorably with toxic waste.

Now I refuse to grant any semblance of altruism to the "sociological tinkerers" in government and education. For example, you would have thought it obvious that when education was being gutted of language, math and vocational education in the 60s and the travesty of the so-called "new math" and other equally devastating experiments were being carried out at the cost of children's learning anything of substantive value, people, in general, would have learned better. They haven't.

I've beaten this drum for too many years. My writing on the subject is voluminous from my Ph. D. dissertation on and I won't belabor it at this time. Suffice it to say that the "experts" in local, state and federal positions who were making the decisions to ruin education in this nation didn't listen then and they aren't any more responsive, or knowledgeable, now. Who would have imagined, for example, that the "experts" would have the unmitigated gall to begin touting learning by doing as something "new!" Idiots! And that is the most charitable thing I can call them.

I could wax lyrical, and have, over the most shameless point; the fact that such ivory tower inhabitants haven't the foggiest notion of what "doing" is all about, the so-called "profession" far removed from the real world of labor and earning a living and far too often deserving of the opprobrium: Those that can, do; those that can't (or won't); teach!

The situation isn't any more promising in the churches or academia in general. As I have often said: We couldn't have designed a system for failure any better if we had done so intentionally! Just as there is no "royal" path to knowledge and wisdom, neither is there any such path that will lead to understanding in the issues I have covered in this essay. It will take hard work and sacrifice. Funny how some things simply don't change.

It was a bitter thing for me to watch the exploitation of some young people recently as a TV "special" touted itself as an attempt to get at the problems of gangs. The shameless promoters of this debacle must have thought that just because they had some "real, live gang members" on the "show" they were doing something of value toward "understanding" and was nothing but a mechanism for displaying the utter inanity, futility and hopelessness of a self-serving "orgasm" of idiocy.

The most shameless display of ignorance and selfishness was not from the kids; it was from the "teachers," largely women, one of the most devastating ingredients of the whole problem, who followed the usual party line of mouthing the usual incomprehensible, nonsensical "Educationese" and pseudo-psychological clap-trap (psycho-babble) the schools continue, ignorantly, to shamelessly display as "relevant."

I have often made the point that the schools are paranoid in the extreme because they know they are guilty and they know they are not doing the job they are paid, over-paid, to do. And, as is to be expected, the "bottom line" of these ignorant, self-serving, public leeches, as usual, was to "Give us more money and we'll solve the problem!" I repeat: Use what you are already getting effectively before I ever consider giving you more! And, unlike politicians, including predominantly and equally ignorant school board members, I am well qualified to render that verdict.

What does "Full Gospel" mean to you? It would certainly seem to indicate that anyone who does not "belong" is deficient of the whole truth of God. In other words, if you don't subscribe to the heretical doctrine of the charismatics, you probably aren't even a Christian by their peculiar definition. Such people remind me of the following:

NIGGER

DON'T LET THE SUN SET ON YOU IN LINLOW!

A sign displaying this message was posted at the city limits of this fictional town in Sudie and Simpson, a sensitive examination of racial prejudice and child molestation. But, as with "To Kill a Mockingbird," the sword cuts both ways. In WWII, it was the Dirty Japs and Knocksies! During the Cold War, it was the Dirty Commies. There is always enough racial and ideological hatred around to "do the job" and nowhere does such hatred find such fertile soil as that of the subject of religion. It plays directly into the hands of those that would foment racial strife.

Those "realities" of life that make up so much of our art and literature is ugly in the extreme. No one is more sensitive than me to such themes being treated in depth and sincerity by those who are gifted to do so. This is a needed dimension for any great culture. But the "sword that divides" is forcing children to have to confront adultery, perversion, and violence of every imaginable kind at the time when they should be enjoying just being children. And that is such a tragically short enough time as it is. Why should children have to be exposed at the tenderest of years to the likes of Madonna and MTV? Is it any wonder that we are raising a generation of "devils!" And to attempt to justify this violence and perversion in the hallowed terms of Free Speech, Expression and Art!

There is, at least, one, single element of truth in Hollywood's portrayal of life; that is the actual heart condition, the dark side of men and women devoid of the spiritual conscience that provides the foundation of loving and caring for others and particularly those loving and caring elements essential for "family." Legitimizing this moral vacuum by laws making adultery a joke and divorce as easy to obtain as buying a bottle of shampoo, penalizing men and children in the process, further exacerbates this thoroughly destructive, wicked and hateful process of eliminating "family." And make no mistake; women, by an obscenely disproportionate factor, choose divorce, as they do abortion as contraception, to gain their own selfish ends.

This holiday season, my children and I get to "celebrate" the sixth "anniversary" of their mother's decision to trade us for another man. The grief and destruction this adulterous decision caused the children and I can only be comprehended by those that have experienced it in their own lives; the "joy" of the "holiday season" is nothing but a constant reminder of the "death" of our family just as, every 4th of July, we have to deal with the death of my oldest daughter, Diana. Tragically, this is not "anecdotal;" adultery and divorce are such an insidious and prevailing norm that if a man or woman is dissatisfied with their present mate, they can easily exchange for another without the slightest pang of conscience and with total disregard for "family."

No one wants to touch this problem in all of its ramifications. Such is the inherent selfishness of depravity and perversion. Extrapolated to the ghettos and barrios, welfare laws that actually penalize those that would like to have a family doom women and children to living without a husband and father;

further laws that steal a man's dignity as a man and often prevent even the best intentioned from even trying.

We herald George Whitefield, John Wesley and Jonathan Edwards as "Heroes of the Faith" without ever considering the historical fact that their actions fomented great strife and opened the door wide to every kind of heresy. No, these worthies would have been, and were, appalled at the excesses of emotional hysteria and nonsense that followed their preaching. But, as with Luther and the so-called "Reformation," lacking real discipline, concise doctrine and authority, such excesses are always bound to follow. And the very same principles apply to government and education. When "inner light" becomes the rule for behavior, emotion leads and rational thought becomes subservient thus opening the door for all manner of evil and "visions of angels." Unhappily, emotion is a commonality while critical thinking is not; disciplined, critical thinking is a learned behavior.

The "leadership" across the board has been preaching its doctrines of "Equity Fairness" and "Multiculturalism" (both are emotional, not critical thinking) in the doomed hope that you can legislate morality and fairness. In trying to force a historically doomed "equality" for women and people of foreign cultures, there has been a resulting catastrophe of engendered hatreds. People in the South did not hate Negroes until the punitive laws of the North made them "hateful."

In just such a manner, when the federal government, aided and abetted by foolish "experts" in education, decided that every child would receive an "equal" education, the lowest common denominator became the standard. And until rational, factual differences in culture and ability are once more recognized there can be no hope for any improvement.

No one, by now, would deny the fact that Hollywood, and the media in general, have made the traditional family look like a dinosaur. In fact, if you are not having a dozen, sexual "adventures," you are "missing out." And, of course, the women have to be Venus's and the men, Apollo's. As a classroom teacher of many years, I watched the "sexual revolution" work together with the destruction of learning and authority in the schools to destroy a generation of young people. The Viet Nam War and Nixon's Watergate pounded nails in our national coffin. We are, daily, having our noses rubbed in the fact of national debt that has no hope of being paid, even the inheritance of our grand-children going to the greedy crooks and thieves who profited mightily by selling out our nation and its posterity, casting us, our children and grand-children into slavery.

As with the early failure in our nation to eradicate slavery, the seeds of destruction are, invariably, sown in good intentions by the greed for profits and by ignorance, and ignorance is a killer! But when you have ignorance and its handmaiden's ego and greed working together you have a monstrous alliance of disaster!

Damned as I am by the churches, politicians, minorities and women in general, the Truth remains as fixed as the stars. In all honesty, you have to begin asking why the Truth of these things I write of should stir such anger and hatred? The root of the answer is as ugly as that which caused those early politicians and churchgoers to kill God's prophets, behead John the Baptist and the Apostle Paul and crucify Jesus!

But until the ugly issues of our hastening destruction as a nation are faced and dealt with, factually and truthfully, there can be no hope for our children or our country. In no other instance has the old truth of Honesty is the best policy had such relevance and at no time in our history has such been so badly and critically needed.

We are all in this together. Irrespective of race or creed, "Payday Someday" is here now! Only the most evil and wicked will attempt to thwart attempts at resolutions based on thoroughly ruthless facts and truth! Please keep in mind, at all times, there is no lie so heinous as to be accepted and treated with all "due respectability" by those whose own selfish ends demand it. *Whited Sepulchers* continue to be filled with dead men's bones and every manner of uncleanness regardless their appearance!

CHAPTER NINETEEN

THE OKIE POET

APRIL 1992

First Corinthians 13

Goethe: "Self-respect—the secure feeling that no one, as yet, is suspicious."

There is nothing like a university education to make one continually discontented with the status quo. We are the consummate "Rabble-rousers." Not usually grabbing our musket but stirring people with ideas, a far more dangerous, even deadly, mechanism for change. Philosophers and writers like myself struggle with the "rightness" of our ideas. "A little knowledge is a dangerous thing" and some things are best left alone, never to see the light of day. Unhappily, these "things" brood in the breast of all men.

I was not aware myself of the "Pandora's Box" I was opening in attempting to shed some light on the Civil War. Cause and Effect is a well-known concept. "One thing leads to another" is another way of putting it. So it was that one thing led to another to bring about the Civil War. The problem is its historicity, that is, what "thing?"

The Civil War is America's Iliad, an event of Homeric proportions. Everything is there for a romantic interpretation of our Epic Poem and the list of contributors is exhausting, from Lowell, Bryant, Harris, Cable, Crane, Lindsay, Markham, Sandburg, Benet, Faulkner to "Gone With The Wind." Yet, the definitive explanation eludes the best efforts of genius. "What a great matter a little fire kindleth" may have to, as it usually does, suffice. Yet, even failing to find agreement on ultimate cause, there is always something of value to be recovered from the effect as one sifts through the ashes of our national Conflagration.

The fact remains that the history of man is a history of war. An entire field of psychology exists on the premise that war is not only inescapable, but also even necessary and desirable to human need and advancement. Whether this is true or not, it is a fact that a culture is never able to succeed as a superimposition by force over another. Only one can exist and we call it

344

the "winner." And, I would ask, that you do not make of my own writing, an apologetic for the worship of either Mars or Venus.

One definable element of the war was certainly a difference of the agricultural basis of the economics of the South versus the industrial economics of the North. The two most certainly were in conflict as to their respective cultures and the resulting value systems. "Unsound historical analogies may have present-day effects. The 'explaining' of war is one of the most tricky of subjects." J.G. Randall: "A Blundering Generation."

Hergesheimer called the war the last war fought in the grand manner, the last romantic war that "clad fact in the splendor of battle flags." In his forward to "Dear Blanche" he writes: "Here is a book of swords...of old-fashioned dark roses... [of] the simpler loveliness of the past." His writing, filled with the Gold Spurs of Jeb Stuart and the virtues of a chivalrous South, makes one smell the magnolias and eradicates the misery of death and destruction; "history" the way we would like it.

Many years ago, my old high school chum, Gary North, gave me an excellent volume entitled: "Slavery As A Cause Of The Civil War." I heartily recommend it, like Bowers' "The Tragic Era," to you all. It helps to remember the fact that many politicians of the times, the bravest ones, were making speeches to the accompaniment of the sound of cocking pistols in their audiences. Wonder how Bush, Clinton or Brown would fare in such an environment?

I was talking with one of my young friends the other night. He had recently returned from Washington and the conversation turned to politics as usual. He is a good "churchgoer" and expressed an opinion about "praying for those that have the rule over you" and "those in authority." Further, Christians are told in the Bible to obey their rulers. This presents quite a conundrum to those that take a simplistic and unwarranted "literalistic" view of such Scriptures. It is a very dangerous thing to come to a conclusion on only a portion of God's Word without weighing the whole from cover to cover; something very few are qualified to do.

I pointed out to this young fellow that, if he tried to hold a "doctrine" of non-confrontation to unjust laws and lawmakers based on a simplistic view of such passages he was in a "heap of trouble." By his view, the Colonies would never have confronted King George and the evil system our founding fathers, godly men for the most part, rebelled against and for which many shed their blood and lost all their material possessions in the cause of Justice, Liberty and Freedom.

In that great, vague but intensely interesting, world of "Let's suppose" we could easily make a case for disobedience to God in the founding of the United States of America. Thus, our founding fathers not only rebelled against duly constituted authority but God Himself and our Land of Liberty was, in fact, founded as an evil empire! So it is, once more, that a little knowledge is a dangerous thing. If a person is ignorant of the whole history of the founding of our nation, if he is ignorant of the Spirit, Intent and history of God's Word and has only a smattering of knowledge of the Whole, he is easily led into error. This is the reason God gave, as one of the great gifts to the Church, Teachers and Leaders who proved themselves to be filled with the Spirit, knowledge and wisdom. It is the loss of such leadership that has made the churches such abysmal failures in these "last days" and caused "worshipers" to be deluded in the "comfort and safety of their pews."

A simplistic interpretation of such passages also misses the point that it was their rebellion to "duly constituted authority" that led to the martyrdom of the prophets, the Apostles and the early persecutions of the Church. Why couldn't John the Baptist keep his mouth shut against the sin of Herod? Why did Jesus have to light into the "Leaders of Israel" and Rome's appointees? "Noble lies" and "Fairy-tales" may make men easy in their minds, may help them escape persecution for the truth, but they must, eventually, give an account to God Himself for their failure to confront evil. When "duly constituted authority" commands you to "burn the incense, fall down before the idol" and "carry the Mark of the Beast," where do you suppose most "professing Christians" will find themselves?

I love this young fellow and his family. My heart goes out to him and many like him that are "sheep without a shepherd." Who can they really believe and count on to take a stand against the evil of this generation and lead them in our own required rebellion? They will most certainly not find such leadership in their comfortable, "safe" and "polite" churches. Suppose Canadian law held sway in this country (I'm sure it will eventually) and your preacher would go to prison for simply reading the Scriptures against perversion to his congregation? Ask yourself, honestly, what do you suppose your preacher, priest or rabbi would do? I know what they would do. They would, ever so nicely, tell you to read it for yourself while they got on to more "important" things like the men's and women's "fellowship" groups, "Bible studies" and building church membership and "giving." After all, surely God doesn't want your "leaders" to go to prison for failing to declare the WHOLE counsel of God? Also, we mustn't let folks think we are engaging in "gay-bashing" or "racism." And "Heaven Forbid" that we find ourselves in rebellion to our own "duly constituted authority." There is, obviously, a "need" to interpret God's Word a little differently in respect to these things that doesn't offend anyone or put your preacher at risk! But: Ezekiel 3:16-21 and Hebrews 9:27 among so many others are all still there to confront the false prophet.

In spite of our differences, I still love men like Gary North, my old high school chum. I have among my "souvenirs" a first book of his entitled: The Dominion Covenant. In the front, he inscribed these words: "To Don Heath, without whose intervention, this book would never have been written." Gary has written many books and his organization, I.C.E., provides a worthwhile service to the Christian community. In spite of the fact that my latest writings have been met with his gravest disapproval and dire warnings of hellfire, I love him nonetheless and value his opinions. I read his writings faithfully and, occasionally, share some of his points in my own "epistles."

The Lord needs all the help He can get. He wouldn't have made us and put up with so much from us otherwise. I know He must be lonely at times. I wish people like Gary would be more open and honest in their own contradictory thoughts and admit there is room for more latitude for my own in their views. I wonder if he remembers some of the things we used to be able to share (like my switchblade he borrowed for a part he had in school play) and music, the "parties" in the old SouthBay of our young adulthood? I know he must remember North Redondo Chapel and Lake Hume, the transformation of our own lives as we grew in the knowledge of the Lord together. I do miss your fellowship old comrade. We're both too old to make new "old" friends. But "labeling" our different points of view from "assumed knowledge" will not clarify issues or make a satisfactory substitute for the Truth or our ignorance. It requires the love of the Lord and one another in all humility.

The sun is shining nicely while I write. That helps a lot. I am listening to the velvet voice of Nat King Cole and enjoying the reverie of reminiscences of a kinder, gentler past where all things were possible. Where have love and romance gone? To those of us that lived, as teenagers, the dream of the fifties, the ugliness of the present is a constant reminder of what the real loss has been for our children and grandchildren.

Like many of us, and like young people in general, there was a "first real romance" in my own life, a love that makes all art and poetry real. I would have cheerfully slayed dragons, reached for the moon and stars, lived a life devoted to the happiness of that "One" I cherished who became the definition for my whole life, my reason for being, for existing. I was able, shortly before her death, to share this experience with my daughter Diana. I hope I can do so with Karen also someday. Somehow, in the telling of it, a bond was established that was never before possible. I will never forget her putting her arms around me afterward, kissing me and saying, in a way that made it sacramental, "Dad, I really do love you!" In that moment, as a result of my own, true, "love story," I had managed to communicate that thing that makes life worthwhile to the young and the old have lost, traded for the "cares and concerns" of the "real world."

I am not leaving my sons, Daniel and Michael, out of this in my thinking. Daniel was there at the side of his sister when I told her about this. I know he understood what I was trying to say just as, I'm sure, the other children will also someday. It took many years for me to understand and find the words for it; I don't expect them, or anyone, to come to a full realization of it without paying the price.

Perhaps it was the reality of "first love" that made me a successful teacher of young people. I never "recovered" from the "reality" of that first love and I became understanding of its operation in the lives of my students. But it is the thing that makes me so grieve for the poor exchange our young people have settled for. "How do I love thee, let me count the ways" has been traded for the glorification of evil in the "music" and other things spawned of Satan for this generation. The "needs" are the same but the poor substitutes of real love leave nothing but destruction and hopelessness in their wake.

I do have one important point of understanding in this tragedy. Young people are giving up any hope of love at a younger and younger point in their lives. Divorce, together with pornography, violence, corruption, illiteracy and drugs have taken their toll in the dreams of young people. Chastity is passé and the devil has substituted mere sex in its place. What our young people cannot possibly realize is that knights in shining armor and sleeping beauty are only possible in terms of chastity and morality, in that best part of the child that one loses in betrayal of what really is of value in our lives.

Our present "Civil War" of values rages. Norman Lear and PAW vie with Biblical principles and Kipling's "IF." The lessons of James Dean, Natalie Wood and Sal Mineo in "Rebel Without a Cause" are still to be learned. The "poetry" of the movie lost in the grim "reality" of "it's only a story." I sorrow for the loss of "The sad, silken rustle of each purple curtain while each slowly dying ember wrought its ghost upon the floor," traded for Stephen King, and, Madonna in exchange for the "Lady of the Lake." Who among our young people can now distinguish the "child" in Gatsby and fathom Fitzgerald's own yearning for immortality in the love of that "One?" Who among them knows the dark singleness of the goal, the final bonding in mad purpose, in the hunt for "Ye damn-ed whale?"

The thumping, mindless and sense-destroying, animalistic noise of the "music" my youngest daughter and son listen to is a counterpoint to my choice of "Red Sails in the Sunset." Not because I have not tried to teach them better, but because an entire society is telling them that their poor, deluded and antiquated father just doesn't "understand." They can't possibly know what they are losing in the process; for that, they would have to accept the wisdom and experience of their father and society tells them that I am an anachronism. What chance do such young people have of ever coming to an understanding of real love, of that thing that makes it all worthwhile, when they don't even realize that MTV and the noise they are listening to, the violence they are being taught to "worship" is the antithesis of all that is lovely, is anathema to truth, beauty, hopes and dreams, a mind-destroying, numbing analgesic to living a real life of eternal purpose!

There were several, large old pines on our mining claim. I was able to build a platform in the branches of one of these not far from our cabin. Thither I would resort to do my schoolwork on occasion and, in addition to the usual math and English, I would often take some books for pleasure. Sitting on the planks in the branches of the old tree, I would look out to the dun-colored, sere hills of the east and, moving my eyes north to north-westward, to the majestic, forested and granite grandeur of the mountains, master of all I surveyed from my Aerie. What child could help but imagine all things were possible in such surroundings?

It may well be that the most profound and vital questions of life are the purview of youth. It is in adolescence that all the extremes of life come crashing in on our minds and bodies. It is at this time that we begin to question, for ourselves, what is of real worth and how to begin pursuing our vague goals.

Were "April Love" and "Sixteen Candles" the last vestiges of what our parents had left of the best of their own experiences? When I was forced to leave my playground of the entire Sequoia National Forest for the culture shock of the SouthBay of SoCal, I was seventeen years old. Admittedly, I was ill prepared for the transition. Not that I hadn't lived in metropolitan areas before or was not, to some degree, cosmopolitan in my travel experiences. But the forest and desert, the hunting and fishing had been my choice of lifestyle. The rocks, trees, streams and critters were my soul mates, my community.

To leave my forest fastness and a high school of 72 for the beach cities and a school of 3,000 was a tad difficult. But the "music" went with me. It was the same and American Bandstand and the Top Forty were there to greet me. I played clarinet and saxophone in the band and continued to do so at Mira Costa in Manhattan Beach. I still have my clarinet.

But I was ill equipped to meet the society of my new school. Thanks to my, even then, "antiquated" ideals of romance and chivalry and the morality of my grandparents and James Fenimoore Cooper, I was easy prey to the excitement of my new surroundings. My senior year was attended by events of major proportion; I had full-time employment at Floyd and Gil's Body Shop and got married; pretty "fast" for a kid in his senior year back in 1954. You might say I "acculturated" at an accelerated pace.

Even in those incomparably simpler times, an eighteen-year-old boy and a sixteen-year-old girl still had the deck stacked against them. So it is not surprising that, continuing my "fast pace," I found myself a father of two, divorced and introduced to child-support payments by the time I turned 21.

If there is any doubt that the heart of the romantic still burned brightly, I dispelled it in marrying five more times (twice to the same woman). It is said that a bachelor is a man who has never made the same mistake once. I guess I will never be the stuff of a good bachelor.

Manhattan, Redondo and Hermosa Beaches were my Camelot, a fairy-tale world that only exists in the imagination unless you were fortunate enough to have been young and lived in them in the fifties. The sheer magic of such an environment made anything possible in a slightly different way than the possibilities of my other life in the mountains.

I was young, had a full-time job and a car, a DeSoto convertible. I had my music and my books. The ultimate fulfillment of my contentment and excitement was realized in holding a lovely, soft, warm girl in my arms as we sat in the open convertible watching the waves roll in on an immaculate beach to the music of "Ebb Tide" on the car radio. Gas was twelve cents a gallon, an apartment by the beach was thirty-five dollars a month and you could buy a brand new Chevy convertible for less than eighteen hundred dollars; a house for four thousand at four per cent interest. A dollar or a dollar and twenty-five cent an hour job was sufficient to live a life the rest of the world could only dream or watch movies about.

Far removed from any real want or care, we lived lives of "Lotus Eaters" in an oasis from any turmoil or strife due to drugs or crime. Dean Martin and Jerry Lewis were supplanting Abbot and Costello and TV was an interesting, but not all-pervasive, demanding drain on our time and senses. Andre Kostelanetz, Oscar Levant, Morris Stolof, Jackie Gleason and Frank Chacksfield were not a betrayal of Gershwin, Benny Goodman or Glenn Miller. They were most certainly not "elevator music" to a generation that still retained hope of the future and any heritage of real love and romance in their souls.

What does a man who remembers a first kiss say to a generation that has "done it all" by the time they are fourteen? What does the poet have to offer to young women who are "things" and young men who are emasculated of any manhood? How do you explain the magic of being able to sit for hours, content to simply hold one another while listening to the strains of Billy Butterfield or Mantovani? What tragic, grievous loss!

With that kind of music in the background as I write, I am young once again, I am with that girl and we share the secrets of the universe, the secrets of lovers who blindly trust and have faith that all must be well. We are the true believers in life, a life where you can commit to one another and never for a moment doubt that that trust will ever be betrayed. "Better to have loved and lost than never to have loved at all?" Yes! A thousand times better!

The "girls" have gone but the memories linger on. They, in fact, have never left that better part of the child in me. They are still the innocent and pure, sweet-scented softness of the best part of the man that now lives, no matter how fractured and obscured, in my children. How I wish I could impart to them my store of "precious memories." But how to impart that which is so intensely personal as looking deeply into the eyes of that one you cherish and would cheerfully die for and being able to see into their very heart and soul? And how do you explain the mechanism by which that first love becomes a foul spirit of competition, then combativeness, selfishness, and, in its final death-throes, bitterness and hatred?

A society that makes divorce easy and adultery a "joke" cannot hope for anything better than we now live with. The poet's pen cannot hope to scratch the flint-like, sin-hardened callousness to virtue, the insulated shell that refuses sacrificial love. As an admitted "heretic" I have come to the conclusion that God, Who is Love, had to first learn to love. I admit further that such a conclusion was aided in part from my "...pouring over many a quaint and curious volume of forgotten lore." But the conclusion was far more the result of my acquaintance of God Himself through His Word, His Creation and my giving myself to the loving of others.

If would-be theologians would only be as honest in their own approaches to His mind and nature as some Eastern philosophers, they would admit they have failed, miserably, to convey the love of God to others in any intelligible way. In spite of the equally miserable failure of Eastern philosophies to deal with the subject in all its truth, they, at least, are willing to admit some degree of humanity into it. It is a perversion of God's love to dress it in black, stand it in a pulpit for display and endow it with the hypocritical garb and language of liturgy and religiosity. Such will never entertain the notion, let alone honestly ask: "Lord, is it I?"

Can I hope to understand the wounding of God's own heart unless I have experienced the same thing by looking into that girl's eyes and seeing my own love reflected by hers for me only to have it turned into betrayal? Can the real perversion of what is holy and good by a Judas be reconciled in any other fashion, let alone be made intelligible in any degree? I think not! When, in this temple of clay, we give ourselves to others, there is always the risk that the one loved will turn out to be a betrayer, an impostor. God took that chance and so must we if we are to have any hope of understanding what life is all about. To clothe such a profound truth in religious verbiage is to profane it, to prostitute it to the designs of evil men and women who would put a price on it for which our weak flesh can find the coin without personal sacrifice.

At least I was honest in my forays into irony and sardonic verse and I have found the Lord and the Muses to be far more understanding and forgiving than most of my religious colleagues. It takes much to admit of ignorance, let alone hypocrisy. If that girl and boy could have kept the candle of love lit, what a difference it would have made. But to trade it for the meanness of what this world offers in its place? How very foolish.

The world is a cruel taskmaster. There is no place in it for the idle or foolish dreamers. It rewards industry on the most pragmatic of terms. Even Thoreau had to accept the necessity of making pencils. But, he had the advantage of being able to make it a noble occupation. The secret is being able to do what is required while never losing sight of what is of real value, of keeping the "child" with his magic and dreams alive while earning the man's wage by honest toil.

When I held that girl, I was hers and she was mine; "the two had become one." And so it should have been in that ideal world of true love and romance. But the times were already changing. The truth of the statement "... when lust hath conceived, it bringeth forth sin and sin, when it is finished, bringeth forth death" was lurking in wait for any unwary challenger. When lust is the motive to begin with, how avoid its inevitable result?

What our children have inherited is lust, not love. Glorified by the Silver Screen and TV, by government itself, lust is the operant condition of their lives and they know no other. It may be a most unique legacy to my children that their father knew what it was to love; that he held a girl in his arms without any thought but the exquisite joy of sharing the closeness of one another and that was enough. It took an entire society's cruel devaluation of the fine gold and silver of real love and romance to make the trade for the tawdry brass of sex as the goal rather than the seeking of the other's happiness and a lifetime commitment.

In that definitive treatise on love, the thirteenth chapter of First Corinthians, we are told that love seeks the welfare of the other, not your own. It seems much easier to say what love is not than to explain what it is. But God has defined it for us so perfectly that only those with no interest in what He has to say about it can miss the meaning.

My daughter Karen and I were sharing some thoughts and prayer was mentioned. It has been a curiosity to me that prayer is so natural to people yet little that is intelligible has been written on the subject; if my presumption that few religionists have much real knowledge about the true nature of God that is not surprising. Too often clothed in the language of religion, prayer is made to be a "mystery" and I don't believe God is purposely "hiding" from those that seek Him.

Because of my conversation with Karen, I was reminded of something that came to me many years ago. We like to "teach" our children to say their "Now I lay me's" early on. It is good to kneel with our little ones and come before the Lord in prayer. We hope they will continue, as they grow older. But, a curious thing about prayer became clear as I began to speak with others about the subject; the fact that many of us fall asleep as we lay in our beds talking the day over with the Lord. Most expressed concern about being "rude" to the Lord in doing so.

As I have done with others, I did the other night with Karen; I tried to explain what makes a great deal of sense to me. If God is our Heavenly Father, why should He react any differently than an earthly father who loves his child? I don't think He does. As a well-qualified father, I can think of few things that would give me more pleasure than to have my little one fall asleep in my arms while telling me all about their day's activities, their hopes, dreams and plans. For lo, these many years, I have found it the perfect end of the day to fall asleep talking with the Lord. Many times it has been the only means of finding peace at the end of a dreadful day and the only means of finding badly needed sleep and rest. I'm certain the Lord looks forward to that special time with each of us.

The Psalms are my "prayer book." I have read from them daily for years and go through them about once a month. There is no other book of the Bible that shows the "human" qualities of both God and His people so clearly. The Psalmist found himself, I'm certain, falling asleep in prayer as he communed with the Lord on his bed. What a fine way to find surcease and comfort from the evil of the day!

But the effectiveness of prayer, like any of our dealings with the Lord, depends on sincerity and commitment (faith), not "good intentions." James, in his excellent epistle, spells it out for us in no uncertain terms. All of this leads me to make a point of what has to be one of the things I detest most and, I'm sure, the Lord does also.

There are many ways to prove one's lack of sincerity about the subject. Few people are deluded by the "good intentions" of a shallow character. Unhappily, we all know examples of such people; "those that say and do not." One of the worst offenders of my acquaintance is a young man who used to be one of my high school students. He is now a thirty-six year old "man." I put man in quotes because no one who really knows him would call him much of a man. This phony has never learned what love and commitment is; remaining single and a "momma's boy," he has never had to make any commitment to wife and children, he has missed the best in life by successfully never having to account for his actions or take on any personal responsibility. And when he fails in any endeavor, there is momma to take him in to sponge off her.

He recently said he was coming to visit on a Wednesday. About 10:30 p.m., after I had given up on his arrival and already gone to bed, he called to say he would be up on Friday but wouldn't pull in until about 11:00 p.m. So, we subordinated all our weekend plans to accommodate his visit at that time. We waited up for him, and we waited and waited. Nothing. Not even a phone call. The others finally went to bed but I was worried about him. Something must have happened for surely he wouldn't keep us waiting up for him until the wee hours of the morning without getting in touch? Wrong!

I dozed fitfully until about 4:00 a.m. when I finally conked out but I was awake again two hours later. Groggy and tired with a dull, throbbing headache from lack of sleep, I waited most of the day Saturday for some word. That evening, acting on my experience of years of such incidents with this young fellow, I finally called his mother. He was there. He had changed his mind about coming but it didn't even occur to him to call us and tell us about his change of plans. I let him know in no uncertain terms what I thought of his callous lack of simple courtesy, that you don't treat anyone, let alone those you say you care about or even pretend friendship for, in such a fashion. The most hurtful thing about this young fellow is that he claims to be a follower of Jesus Christ! Yet, in his whole life, he has never exhibited any real, consistent and sacrificial love for anyone but himself. Most hurtful of all is the fact that he never realizes the shame he brings to the Gospel he claims to believe, that the name of Jesus is a profanity on his lips, especially when he is drunk.

Like this young phony, many talk a whole lot about God but know nothing about Him and their lives declare their ignorance to the whole world. They become "living epistles" of their own conceit and selfishness and never come to repentance. The love of God is simply not in them and the lack is plain for all to see except themselves. And, like this young man, they always "intend" to "do better." But very seldom does the transformation take place. Having never truly loved anyone but themselves, their end is one of loneliness and bitterness. I grieve for so many like this young fellow who will never know the joy of real love in their lives. And they will always see the Truth as an attack on them rather than an attempt to bring them to repentance.

Given gifts of intelligence and personality, such people remind me of trying to make silk purses of sow's ears, of treasure thrown in the mud, dogs returning to their own vomit. And, while my words of warning have never resulted in any change in this young man, they may be of benefit to others. I certainly take no pleasure in warning the wicked but it is part of the "prophet's" calling and if I didn't care, I wouldn't bother; far better to come in love rather than wield the rod of correction and instruction. But real love is proven by its willingness to do the hard tasks, not sparing its own heart for their crying. There is so much I long to share with people like this young man, but they are unable to receive it: Time to listen to some Phil Harris to take the bad taste of such a thankless task out of my mouth.

I have a tremendous advantage in having known so many loving people. Beginning with our great-grandmother, our grandparents and our mother, my brother and I grew up in the warm security of people committed to one another. While mom and our grandparents fought like the proverbial cat and dog, Ronnie and I never doubted their love for each other and us. Why? Because, when the "chips were down," they were there for one another and us. Somehow, in spite of the fussing and fighting, the commitment and genuine love came through. These days, the first "disagreement" easily ends in divorce.

I have a great debt of love to these people. I owe mom so much for the music in my life, to my stepdad, Ken, for caring for her and Ronnie, Johnny and me. It has been my great good fortune to know so many loving people throughout my life. In spite of all the grief and tragedy so common to the human condition my memories of those dear ones shines through any gloom and I still hold converse with those gone on before me whose wisdom is, now, so certain.

As I listen to the music of the fifties, I am once more cruising in my beautiful, old '53 Cadillac convertible, top down, sun shining and ocean breeze clean and perfumed with the scent of the sea, through Manhattan, Hermosa and Redondo toward Palos Verdes and Portuguese Bend on Pacific Coast Highway. When I reach the cut toward P.V. I'll take the shore road. I'm now divorced but the world still holds promise of love and beauty. I've left Floyd and Gil's and sanding cars with 320 wetordry by hand until my fingertips bled and am employed at North American Aviation as a machinist; I have the Caddy and a bachelor apartment in Redondo. I'm now meeting other people and, especially, girls.

Ronnie also has his own place but he is going steady with Susan. They will marry, have two children, Jennifer and David, and Susan will divorce him. Danny and Diana are with their mother in Hawaii where, after our divorce, she went to be with her parents. Oh, well. There is still magic and romance in the latter fifties SouthBay; especially if you're young, have a good job, the music and a Caddy convertible.

But Camelot can be a dangerous place for a poet looking for love in all the wrong places. In spite of all the betrayals, no poet worth his salt is going to forego the experience and hurt and chance the loss of the greater goal of an illusive ideal. "Surely," he says, "these things are temporary and will pass; the Truth must lie out there somewhere along with someone with whom to share it?" Don Quixote will find his "windmills." It is the world that is out of step and tune. I know in my bones that "Atlantis's of the Sands" like Ubar are still to be discovered, that there is truth in the mythic of the Arabian Nights and The Talisman and "Good Guys" still win! Purity and Virtue will still triumph over evil!

In defense of our children listening to the noise they call *music* today, I know the music we were listening to in the fifties, much of it from the thirties and forties as well, was based on a culture and society that still lived in hope that things would only get better and better; jobs were plentiful, America was the preeminent world power, we were a nation "on the go" and a phone call or cup of coffee was a nickel.

In contrast to the songs of love, hope and a better future of my time, our children turn to the songs of suicide, violence, sex and drugs as an escape from having to hope in the face of hopelessness. Hard Rock is a mechanism for tuning out the mind and giving in to the animalistic senses that have no responsibility or accountability; an anti-establishment protest against being robbed and cheated of hope. A generation that has lost hope in eternal verities of love and goodness, the triumph of good over evil must opt for the glorification of evil as it gains the ascendance. At least it promises change and excitement and, therefore, must be "better" than the status quo, which dooms them in any event.

A large part of the American Dream still existed in the fifties. I could have gone to Lake Isabella and built my cabin on a few acres without the defeating and strangling codes that now have succeeded in destroying any hope of people being able to do for themselves and provide for their children without becoming slaves to Big Brother and the Bankers. No one to date has ever done the requisite study on this subject which figures so prominently in a nation's fall from its ideals and greatness and virtually enslaves its citizens in perpetual debt through exorbitant property taxes and mortgages which can never be paid off.

It would seem to be obvious that a man must be able to have hope of providing for a wife and children in order for love and romance to survive, to enable that girl to commit herself to a husband and children. The basis of this is a home of their own no matter how humble; remove this hope and you have the generation and the society we presently have; a generation that knows it has been betrayed and is ripe for rebellion and revolution.

You would think that, with all the historical evidence at their disposal, world leaders and geo-politicians would recognize and act on the fact that at the bottom of all revolution is the need for a man to provide for his family, to own his plot of land and with the help of a wife and children, build for a future. Men and women can stand the loss of trying as long as there is hope that they can start again. There is no shame in failing in honest effort but the hope must be there that you can pick up and try again. I recently left off a proposal for property rights with a State Senator of my acquaintance. I await his reply and will share it with you all. He's one of the "good guys" and I know I will get an honest response.

No matter how brightly the sun shines on the grass of a rented house, if a family knows it is only a paycheck away from being on the street they have little incentive in trying; particularly when the fat cats in Congress and the banks are robbing them blind of any hope while stuffing their fat faces and pockets. Such conditions cause intense rage in the breast of the poet.

Ever since F.D.R. threatened to pack the Supreme Court if it did not cave in to his "New Deal" socialism, Big Brother has called the Fifth Amendment with its "taking clause" "arcane". But it is certainly in the interest of the New Reich to remove all property rights and sell our souls to the State. Would F.D.R. and his cohorts have acted any differently if they had known about the man for whom their policies were responsible, who was found living with his small son in an abandoned bus and the boy's legs having to be amputated due to freezing? I doubt it. Being, essentially, an optimist in spite of my knowing the "realities," I still hope men like David Lucas succeed and he gets to build what he wants on his own property. To quote David Kaplan: "In the new order, if you want to love a tree, it would be best to buy one." But, knowing the agenda of men like Kaplan, I know his and my definition of the "New Order" is worlds apart.

Frohnmayer may have been dismissed but we know his "ideals" of art still plague us; perversion sold in the name of "art" cannot elevate a population no matter how evil men try to package it. The average person still sees it for the vile garbage it really is. Tammy Faye gets her divorce from Jimmy (certainly a fore drawn conclusion to the affair), the vandals are getting smart enough to follow upper-middle-class victims to their homes in the suburbs and rob them there instead of preying on the poor of their own ghettos and barrios, congressmen kite bad checks at will without penalty (interest free personal loans), Jurors decide a Swastika placed at the desk of minority fire fighters in San Francisco is not racial harassment, Secretary of State Baker uses obscenity about Israel and American Jews, a Thousand Oaks fifth grader is upbraided by a Jew for wearing a khaki uniform with swastika armband, fake mustache and delivering a speech to her classmates that presented Hitler as being mistreated by Jews (the speech won second place in the oratory contest) and an Indiana man gets stabbed in the chest by a catfish.

Was my brother the victim of a "grammar gene" which precluded his being a writer? Will the CIA open the Kennedy files? Will Darlene Johnson ever get her Norplant now that she has gone back to jail for using drugs? Does the secret agreement our government made with Saudi Arabia in 1948 continue to plague Israel? Has the Secret Service gotten too big for its britches? Will

HBO's success with Real Sex give the Playboy channel any real competition? Will the recent admission of the fact that the whole world is in recession hasten Armageddon? Is there, finally, a proper stage for that "strong man" to take world power in his hands and will the American Jewish Voice, Larry King, have him as a guest? Will we finally get around to castrating child molesters (my sentiment)? Who can deny the logical and winning combination of Jerry Brown and Jesse Jackson? Where is the despicable tyrant, J. Edgar Hoover, when we "need" him? What would he have done about United Way's leaders, like the "old dope peddler, doing well by doing good?"

Chaucer's "The Knight's Tale" is long gone from our curriculum. The "Canterbury Tales" are only, now, a dim reflection in even the eyes of my own generation. But, like the music, they were my companions in my Caddy convertible as we cruised the old SouthBay. The Strand with its grand hotel and the beaches with their sun-tanned "immortals," the pier and the roller coaster at Long Beach, water-skiing out of San Pedro, clipping the wake of the boat and wave tops, out on a thirty-two foot sailor becalmed in the swells and wishing I hadn't eaten that liverwurst sandwich, Big Bear with its magnificent forest, lake and throwing snowballs in the crisp, clean air; all magic.

The Rosenbergs and Tail-gunner Joe were doing their part to change our world but it didn't mean much to someone listening to Noel Coward on their Grundig Majestic and chasing girls "therapy" for a divorce that left me a wreck. The fact that good-intentioned men were trying to make the world safe for Democracy didn't turn on the question of who was going to make Democracy safe for the world; that, too, would come later. The atom was still science fiction in the sense of "War of the Worlds" and "Forbidden Planet."

It's St. Paddy's Day as I write. Everyone is Irish today. It was good to have the Little People honored. It is still good to have Leprechauns, Santa Claus, the Easter Bunny, the Sandman and the Tooth Fairy to rely on. It was good in the fifties to enjoy the exquisite scariness of Dracula, The Mummy, the Wolfman and the Invisible Man even if Abbott and Costello were making fun of them by then.

Vaughn Monroe is singing "Racing With the Moon" and the world is good and full of promise once more. Dancing the Conga and playing Canasta are there somewhere in the recesses of memory. I'm learning new and interesting skills as a machinist and gaining an upper hand in auto mechanics that will be of life-long importance. I have yet to go to college and become a teacher or build my first house but these things will come. I'm young, strong, intelligent, and, the girls say, good-looking. With all that going for me how could I contemplate anything but success and an exciting future?

Ken is working as a machinist and Mom is waitressing at a Chinese restaurant; the kid's mother will do a stint there for a while. Mom was in

Pearl Harbor when it was attacked. She has some marvelous artifacts of the Islands. I am still entranced by the butterfly, abalone and mother-of-pearl artwork, shell necklaces and woodwork boxes; they were always a delight to Ronnie and me. She also has some metal art-works done by Joe Brown, our first step-dad who was a sailor stationed in Pearl. Who was the man that those burned, personal items like the watch belonged to Mom?

There is the marvelous, little restaurant up Trancas Canyon out of Malibu to impress a date or the Albatross with its dining area built out over the surf. Some time later, I will have to stop and cool the brakes of my '57 Continental when traveling the steep canyon road of Trancas. But it presents an opportunity to enjoy the stars, listen to the radio with its great reverb and speaker system and hug the girl.

Hey Pete, do you remember the '64 Chevy Malibu I had with the custom LP player and cruising Hollywood? How about the Kern River and Bull Run Creek where you lost your wallet? I know you will recall one experience we "shared" as my going away present before you went off to the "Nam" and our figuring out the best way for you to smuggle your 9mm Browning over with you. Is your old buddy, Warren, still working on his Hitler book and working for Paramount? Is your virtuoso brother still teaching music at the university? I know you still have a real winner in Joannie. She exhibits such exceptionally rare qualities of discriminating taste and appreciation for the finer things (she married you and thinks I'm a good writer). Congratulations to both of you. I assume you have never told her about some of the Flora and Fauna, especially that "Fauna" John, you and I chanced to come across on our way out of Mojave toward Boron in his Mustang? Don't worry; wild horses couldn't drag it out of me!

Grandad has located in Redondo as well. He has a job at California Handprint. It's good to have him nearby. He has re-married and Dora is a swell lady. Even with the scent of the ocean in the breeze, there is still the smell of the fireplace and the pines of the mountain mining claim in my memory. I still get up to Isabella and out to the desert to shoot and fish. The values of Mayberry and the Waltons are still fresh in my life in spite of the cosmopolitan sophistication of the SouthBay. Huxley's warnings of abstraction and simplification are, at present, lost to me, as is the warning of De Toqueville and so many others. I don't know what a war is yet to rage over the simple verities of decency and justice or the twists and turns of my own life that will draw me into the warfare.

The changes will be the result of those loved ones who taught me from a child to reverence The Lord and His Word. I continue, through the excitement and bright lights of So Cal living, to read the Bible and pray. My life, at this time, bears little outward appearance of Christian living. After my first divorce, I "sow my wild oats" with all the enthusiasm of the most devoted and hedonistic pagan. But it is a sham life because my heart is still directed by values that demand I treat others as I would want to be treated, "honesty is the best policy" and "an honest day's work for an honest day's pay." This is why I cannot take advantage of all the "perks" of a wanton lifestyle.

Mad Dogs and Englishmen Go Out in the Noonday Sun. Since I was working swing shift, I had plenty of time for the noonday sun. It put a small crimp in my nightlife but I was a responsible worker and stuck to it, even taking some classes in Tool and Die making at Santa Monica Tech. But, being young and strong, I didn't need much sleep and managed to burn the candle at both ends.

Years later, I will be subjected to having to sort out the thoughts of some of the professors of one of my alma maters like Ashley Montagu and Victor Frankl. "Man's Most Dangerous Myth: The Fallacy of Race" and the "Existential Vacuum" together with Skinner's "Behavior Modification" are not yet intruding on my mind. Watts hasn't yet burned and I'm not yet teaching at Jordan High. Robert Dahl won't write "After the Revolution?" until 1970. A world and another lifetime away from all this I am simply enjoying the vitality, the youth and beauty of Santa Monica and Malibu. At one time, I have five, lovely, young girls to myself in the Caddy. I have a picture to prove it. A couple of guys in another car pull up and make the statement the situation demands: "Look at that guy; he's got five of them!" Modesty also demands that I point out the fact that I was simply transporting them to a dance, a "mixer," where most of them had dates waiting. But why should I tell those guys?

Time has yet to teach me the truth of the fact that, toward the end of life, you will be able to count your real friends on the fingers of one hand. I haven't yet studied John Stuart Mill's treatise "On Liberty" or figured out that writing and activism, like the Bible and Christians, are both essentials of change (Romans 10:14). Pogo and Walt Kelly are still my political philosophers and critics and Cooper, Edgar Rice Burroughs with Sir Arthur Conan Doyle and so many others offer escape through childhood memory from any tedium of routine. Biola, Cerritos, Cal State Long Beach, Chapman, Cal State Northridge, U.S.I.U. and the love of disciplined learning are yet awaiting my becoming a "professional student."

My eldest son, Daniel, is still living in Torrance and working for Hughes Aircraft. He is keeper of the flame in the SouthBay. He has a really classy '47 Packard and I recently was treated to a drive up to Palos Verdes on my last visit to see him. The territory has changed, very "up-scale," but the view and smell of the ocean are still there to challenge memory. I was, once more, young and in love with, in order, his mother, LaDonna, Julie and the sea. He is old enough to start appreciating the fact that age never dispels that young girl or boy that still lives in the heart of us "oldsters." Put us in the proper environment and youth still springs eternal in our breasts. You will occasionally catch us at it when we get that thousand-yard stare in our eyes and we seem to be reaching for words, haltingly, that are, usually, vain attempts to explain "reasons" for which reason has no words; as the poet says: "The heart has its reasons of which reason knows nothing."

Martin Denny and "Exotica" are stirring memories of Ronnie and I, dressed in three-piece suits, strolling Sunset Boulevard. Some shabbily dressed "radical" character that looks like he ought to be stumping at Pershing Square is passing out some kind of pamphlet. We take a few and start passing them out just for the fun of it; we don't even look to see what it says. It amuses our fancy that such well-dressed and obviously sophisticated young men are advocating the violent overthrow of our government or saving the trees. It causes our dates to wonder what they have gotten themselves into. They settle for our being fun but eccentric.

Some years later, there will be restaurants where Ronnie and Russell will be loath to return because of some "amusing" repartee or riposte of mine. They might have forgotten how to have fun but I never did. But, in my defense, imagine the possibilities in a simple question to a Maitre de or waitress as to how their frog legs are or if the lady would consider dating outside her species? Prince Albert in a can (well, let him out!) and the Burma Shave signs still live in my memory as well. I worry about Gary North and others losing their sense of humor also. Years of working with teenagers have kept my own honed.

I wish more of my friends were writing. I hope there is time to speak of Cabbages and Kings but the adumbration of war drums sound all about us. I need more subscribers like Dorothy who sent in subscriptions for her son and daughter. That dear lady, like Joannie, shows rare perspicacity. Dorothy, you ought to write about your experience of Hitler's Germany and the labor camps of Arvin.

In my reverie, there is a definite need for the old SouthBay of clean air and beaches, no graffiti in sight, of the excitement of being young and the whole world waiting your impress upon it. I need to remember the first issue of "Mad Magazine" appearing and seeing "Shane" in downtown L.A. (Got my first parking ticket then). There was the quaint florist shop at the end of Pier Avenue where I could get orchids and roses for the girls and the marvelous coffee shop next to the beach with its windows giving us a view of the ocean, where we all shared so many profound experiences and the wisdoms of youth.

Such things are more than a catharsis and reaching back to the sanity of simpler times and values. They are some of the best we have to offer our own children in the hope that they will understand the "Way It S'pozed To

Be." Perhaps, in sharing some of these things, some young people may be encouraged to take the reins, get involved and seize opportunities. Not all of it is "gathering rosebuds while ye may." There is work to do. If their own store of "precious memories" is to be of value to their children, they must be given hope that not all is lost to them. It is the poet's task to encourage them and face the evil, even Kings and "those in authority."

Even in Camelot, there are inescapable realities. Dragons need slaying and damsels need rescue. The young knight must know his enemy and keep his sword sharp. A betraying Guinevere or Lancelot should never cause the loss of a crown and the Grail must be sought no matter the cost. Arthur must be true though all others play him false. While it is, as my old friend pointed out, women, who, predominantly and historically get sex and religion all confused, it is still the responsibility of the "Moths" to draw near the Flame and its Keepers, upon whom, Love's Labors are not lost.

What a time it has been! From that small boy's bare feet kicking the gray, summer noon-heatened alkali dust of Weedpatch and Little Oklahoma to cross-country trips by train, bus and auto, grandad and grandma meeting us at the top of the old Grapevine in the '28 Buick, to the mining claim in the forest and, thence, to sun-kissed Lotus Land. Things learned in Cleveland, Las Vegas and Henderson, lakes Mead and Isabella. The times in WWII San Pedro, San Francisco and Oakland, a collage, vignettes here and there, that makes up the tapestry of a life.

Even though Jacob's Staff has been traded for written language, it is still the responsibility of the poet-historian to keep the legends alive and make his marks on "Aaron's Rod." Truth will always sort through the myth and make what is vital real. In the most clouded of memories, sharp spikes of light dart here and there, illuminating what is of real value in the keeping and the sharing with others. We never can guess what is taking root in the minds of our children that will become their own epics.

In the twilight of life, we begin to sort through, even unconsciously, the things that make it all worthwhile; the faces and places that come, often unbidden, to mind. I would make more of fiction were that needed. But reality has been more than enough to pauperize any attempt to clothe it with more than an occasional lapse of memory, which in its kindness, covers many hurts. We are all "builders" and "makers" regardless of the type of "architecture."

I have a love of all kinds of architecture, from the most garish of Gothic and Baroque to the most sterile monuments of glass and steel. Roman or Oriental, it all fascinates me as an expression of cultures. The simplest forms of bare studs and the smell of clean, new lumber always excite something in me. I recently saw a civic center building that had an entryway of a wall of glass brick. How many my age remember when those marvelous blocks of translucent glass adorned so many buildings? When the sun strikes through them, they have the most entrancing array of shades of light. What a glorious touch the veined hues of the different marble and granite used in some of our own creations like Grand Central Station. Such "Cathedrals" invite worship.

Even "tents in the wilderness" had to have their ribbons of color. The nomad needs something to draw his eye and tell him he is a man. Few things attract a man as his honest toil resulting in a structure, no matter how humble, which evidences his ability to do with his mind, back and hands. And, if the effort is directed toward the welfare of his family, what a worker he is! We are inveterate builders but even the cave will show signs of something more than utilitarian shelter. We will hang our pictures and bric-a-brac to declare our "personness." The most humble of abodes will show some indication that "building" is more than providing a roof over our heads. This is the reason for my making so much of removing the onerous bureaucracy that precludes a man doing for himself. You must turn from the seemingly, meaningless disarray of twisted threads and knots of the back of the carpet and look at the grand design of its true face.

In one of my wilderness forays, I came across an old mining shack of rough lumber. The bare, wood walls of the interior were covered over with the comics (funny papers to us oldsters) of a long defunct newspaper. Now any part of the newspapers would have served as well against drafts but the comics?

We are suffering the noisome pangs of politicians, once more, telling us what they are going to do for (more properly "to") us. They will talk of "building" for the future. My grandad built a better privy than what these scoundrels are likely to produce and it smelled better than the odor of these charlatans.

"Pencils" and "Walden" may at times become confusing but the doing for others never does- they should all work together for good. If we are to build with other than wood, hay and stubble, they must. The Ancient Landmarks will stand no matter how evil men and women try to remove them, but the grief and the loss that the attacks on them cause.

Somewhere along the way, we got too busy for the things that really count. The work, books and beauty, the "others," even that "One," are there but they want for attendance. As rich as the endowment may be, it profits nothing to those that will not take heed and invest it properly.

"You have forsaken your first love... I would that you were either hot or cold but because you are lukewarm, I will spew you out of my mouth!" What a word of warning that should be to all! But it falls on deaf ears of those who are more concerned for the cares and "riches" of "reality" than a reality where love conquers all. God's love goes begging as the "professionals" either prostitute it as "religion" or "mysticize" it to some ethereal realm out of existence.

I might have as easily settled for the counterfeit if I hadn't held that girl in my arms, listened to the music and watched the waves roll in. If a true lover's and father's heart hadn't grown out of all these things, I would be no better off than a Jimmy Swaggart or George Bush, unable to distinguish between Heaven and Hell and opting for the glory of evil.

Children should never lose Christmas or Halloween. That young girl and boy must never lose their first love.

But my white pow, nae kindly thowe
Shall melt the snaws of Age
My trunk of eild, but buss or beild,
Sinks in Time's wintry rage.
Oh, Age has weary days,
And nights o' sleepless pain:
Thou golden time, o' Youthfu' prime,
Why comes thou not again!
Robert Burns

But my dear Robert, you surely knew that the youth that learned to love never went away and you proved the truth of it in your own life.

The Way of All Flesh does not have to be the only way. There are precedents aplenty for something better that will carry us through and, in the end, be able to say: "It was worth it!" What will you say?

CHAPTER TWENTY

The Okie Poet

May, 1992

Hebrews 12:1
So kiss me my dear, and don't let us part
And when I grow too old to dream, your love will live in my heart

Come, my dear, grow old with me
The best, by far, is yet to be

The old song like "Silver Threads Among the Gold," like the aged sentiment, is part of a history; a history that was not successfully communicated to the last few generations. It is, tragically, lost to this generation. Part of the reason for this is the fact that while women profess a love of poetry and sensitive prose, few can abide the Poet personally. And, in their defense, it must be pointed out that "fine sentiment" doesn't put a roof over your head or meat on the table. As Melville and I say: "The Truth, it don't pay!" Women, it would seem, are the more "practical" in spite of opinion to the contrary. They would never stand for a "Philosopher King."

It is one of the reasons that Clemens could have been correct in his opposition to women being given the vote. I would certainly not allow welfare recipients the vote. It is only the finer sentiments that lead a nation to greatness. A nation's literature and art guides its values and morals. And it is men, by a vast majority, that are the artists, risk-takers and visionaries. And it is vile and spineless men that have abrogated their responsibility and led our nation to ruin. None can, any more than Adam could, blame women for such failure. But women recognized the need to protect themselves politically from the abuses of law by unscrupulous men; and no better redress could be expected than to have the franchise. I can hardly fault women on this score.

However, it is a commonplace to ascribe the "hand that rocks the cradle" to the making of a nation but that is simply not so in many cases. At the basis of any nation's success or failure is the leadership of men. But it has been to the advantage of unscrupulous and spineless men to pass our failures off on women when the fault is with us men.

In the book of Judges, chapter four, we find an excellent example of God's feelings about the situation. When Barak refused to go to battle without the prophetess Deborah, he was warned that a woman would receive the glory of the victory to the shame of men. Sure enough, a woman, Jael, drove the tent peg through Sisera's head and delivered Israel.

Long ago, Barak, hiding behind women's skirts, began to fill our pulpits and we are living with the results. God never intended it so. Until women are able, once more, to accept their rightful place and men have the backbone to rule their families, there will be no improvement in our society and no hope for a future for our young people.

There is a need for the Nancy Trouts (wife of Focus On The Family co-host Mike Trout) to tell their stories. But men are to lead! If there is a failure of leadership, the fault, ultimately, must be laid at the feet of men, not women. One area of agreement that comes out of the recent riots is that point exactly. The community of Watts and others has evolved into matriarchal, welfare societies that lack male leaders in the home.

As with the McGuffey Readers that shaped the morality and values of that generation, we have departed from the very essence of those things that made commitment and fidelity noble and of great worth. But even McGuffey found himself having to defend his use of Scripture in his lessons. And that, almost a hundred and fifty years ago! So when, exactly, did our nation begin to lose its way toward that star that shone so bright to the generations that sacrificed so much for our liberty and the rights of the individual?

"For the copious extracts made from the Sacred Scriptures, I make no apology. Indeed, upon review of the work, I am not sure but an apology may be due for not having more liberally transferred to the pages the chaste simplicity, the thrilling pathos, the living descriptions, and the overwhelming sublimity of the sacred writings.

"The time has gone by, when any sensible man will be found to object to the Bible as a school book, in a Christian country; unless it be on purely sectarian principles, which should never find a place in systems of general education. Much less then, can any reasonable objection be made to the introduction of such extracts from the Bible as do not involve any of the questions in debate among the various denominations of evangelical Christians.

"The Bible is the only book in the world treating of ethics and religion, which is not sectarian. Every sect claims that book as authority for its peculiar views."

I hope you will all take a few moments to ponder those words of McGuffey before you continue reading his further remarks:

"We often seem to make discoveries; and certainly do make advances in knowledge, by being somewhat importunately interrogated upon topics, with which our previous acquaintance was neither accurate nor extensive. It roused the mind to successful effort, and often strikes out new and brilliant views of a familiar subject. And who, that has made one acquisition of this kind, does not desire frequently to repeat the experiment?"

Ah, my dear McGuffey, who indeed? Would you not look with sorrow upon the cause you championed and for which you gave so much? Would you even recognize the monster it has become? Would you not rather have passed your time in the sighs of the Psalmist and the cloistered, hallowed Halls of Ivy rather than take any credit for the bastardization of your ideal of an education for all children regardless of humble circumstances?

But how could this noble man have guessed that the early detractors of his use of Scripture in his Readers would become such an outcry that the later editions would have to expunge his clear, Gospel message as we rushed, pell-mell to a polyglot, mongrel nation devoid of God, that message which motivated this great educator? Was he simply naive? Or, could it have been, studied as he was in the history of the founding of this nation, never have entertained any notion of its betrayal on such a monumental scale? I suspect that such was the case. Forsake God and the Bible? Unthinkable! At least to McGuffey.

"Let's bring back McGuffey's Readers - it would expose young men and women to good literature, self-discipline, and traditional moral values." Dr. Carl Bode, Professor of English at University of Maryland at College Park. True enough Dr. Bode but it isn't going to happen. Nor, for that matter, should it. We desperately need a "New McGuffey" who will speak to the evil of today to this generation in much more concise and understandable terms. This generation does not have the historical store upon which to base an understanding of McGuffey. That foundation was destroyed and needs to be rebuilt first.

I was a high school teacher for many years. I loved working with adolescents; they hadn't learned what was impossible and could dream. I watched that change to hopelessness in a few, short years. It wasn't long ago that I stood before a group of seniors in Kern Valley High as a substitute for that day and made the following pronouncement:

"Any education you get in high school will be by accident or your own initiative; the schools are not in the business, any longer, to educate or prepare you for the real world!"

There was stunned silence at first. Then, one after another, they began to applaud. Soon the entire class was standing and applauding. Why? As some of them said later, it was the first time in their whole lives that someone of the educational establishment dared tell them what they already knew and no one would listen or cared. I was never invited back by the principal.

It wasn't that the school was any better or worse than many I had taught or subbed for. It was fairly typical and, typically, had long since lost its function of really caring whether young people were being equipped to deal with the real world, had long ago lost the ability to even know how to deal with that real world itself.

I stayed in L.A. and the Antelope Valley U.H.S.D. long enough to be tenured in both districts. I worked temporary contracts in six others as well as starting three private schools. Mixed with this was teaching in the Community College system and a class for graduate students for Chapman College.

It was teaching this graduate class of prospective teachers, fresh B.A.s in hand, that I knew education was doomed. I had read plenty of material about the dismal failure of colleges to educate but here was the proof. These adults, college educated, weren't even capable of writing good undergraduate papers. But their respective colleges had passed them on to be trained as teachers. And Chapman, as per "policy," would have its instructors perpetuate the myth.

I want to thank my old friend, Gary North (who still isn't speaking to me) for his last newsletter. He suggests that the churches pay attention to evangelistic efforts directed toward the aged, particularly those in "homes." But Gary would be surprised at the reasons for my agreement. I know most of those old folks are without hope. How could it be otherwise since that generation "sold us down the river" to the moral holocaust we face today? If any generation needed to repent of its ungodliness it is the one of the elderly! And what were the grandparents, great-grand- parents and great-great-grandparents doing wrong that brought this moral holocaust upon us? They were being led by "Barak."

"Generational Wars?" They are surely coming. "Gray Greed" is the thing that is pauperizing young people; that and the insane greed of politicians who have no other thought than feathering their own nests at the cost of the vanishing middle class. Between the exorbitant costs of government bailouts for the unscrupulous, welfare, medical and social security, we have spent our children and grandchildren's inheritance. And they know it!

Throughout the history of Israel it seems there was a constant failure of the previous generation to pass on to the younger, the claims, commandments and works of God. He had to, repeatedly, send them Judges and Prophets to turn them back to the Truth. Even so, the next generation would not learn the lessons of the past and had to be taught, sometimes ruthlessly, those things they had failed to learn.

Two things were at work here. Teachers failed and those that were to be taught failed. It takes both a good teacher and a good student to effect the desired result. When this nation began to reject the message of the Gospel, began to teach "another way" than the Bible, we began the moral slide we live with today. It was Christianity that made us unique as a nation, not some Jewish, Islamic, Hindu, Confucian, etc. "mush" of deism that did it.

It reminds me of the pompous ass of an English professor that, when one of the students in his class mentioned the Bible, said: "Which bible?" The fact that he was a Jew might have had something to do with his attempt at seeming cosmopolitan, but the fact is when an American in an American school says "Bible," he, even in today's moral vacuum, means the Bible of Christianity and not a collection of Vedic Hymns or the Koran! Dear, dear McGuffey, how could you have thought that our Bible would ever be considered "sectarian" in a "Christian" nation?

My last year at A.V.U.H.S.D., I threw caution to the wind and brought in a quantity of "sectarian" Christian literature. There were New Testaments, Gospel tracts and comic books. The kids loved them. Within a short span of time I witnessed a miracle. The students stopped using profanity, were kinder and more sensitive to each other and gave themselves to their studies in a way they had never done before. I had always kept a Bible on my desk but this was an "experiment" in depth of what God's Word and the Gospel could accomplish. It was what was "normal" in the schools in McGuffey's time.

It wasn't long before I had the Devil's attention in the form of other teachers and the administration. I was told in no uncertain terms that what I was doing was "breaking the law" and to "stop and desist immediately!" Since no one had the guts to confront me directly (a not uncommon situation with the evil one and his system) I still have and prize the letter I was served. I was also in "competition" with a principal who had just been arrested for shoplifting and I knew it was going to be my, as his, last year in the district. The difference was that he would receive a glowing letter of recommendation so the district could get rid of him to some other district. This is the same mechanism by which hospitals get rid of bad doctors: "Recommend them out!" Most school districts get rid of their bad administrators the same way. I did not obey the "law." I continued to make the Gospel clear to my students, even having groups to my home every Friday night; as many as thirty would show up. Thirty teen-agers on a Friday night just to visit with a "Bible-thumping" teacher; who says God isn't in the business of miracles today!

I have discovered that there is an intense desire on the part of young people to try to understand our history and make sense of what went wrong that has robbed them of a future. But they lack credible teachers. By forsaking our historical roots, by forsaking the Gospel, by forsaking the Word of God, we have become a polyglot, mongrel nation of selfish hedonists.

As I trekked the marvelous fastness of my mountain home in the Sequoia National forest so many years ago as a youngster, I would sometimes get off on a "false trail." The sensible and normal procedure was to backtrack and pick up the trail again. It would be imminently sensible for us, as a nation, to do the same thing. But I never had a "guide" in my forest wanderings. Such guides are indispensable for our nation. And the churches must, once more, provide such guides.

Recently, I have visited a couple of small, community churches. They exemplify both the failure and potential I am speaking of. The failure lies in the "hirelings" which fill the pulpits. Ignorant and spineless men who have adopted the "itching ears" format of "preaching," such "men," such "Baraks" can never offer any hope of change for the better. Our only hope is that real men who are willing and able to confront the real evil all around us will begin to fill our pulpits.

My dear old friend, J. Vernon McGee, gave up on the organized churches and started his greatly successful "Through The Bible" radio ministry. He stated that the real work had passed from the churches to radio and home groups. Yet, Jesus founded the Church and the gates of hell cannot prevail against it. But Jesus chose real men to get the organization started, men who would give their lives for the Truth.

Somewhere along the way, we lost our compass heading in this nation. I still see the local churches as the way back; but not without real men who are able and willing to pay the same price as those early leaders. I know from personal experience that any man today, who would choose to declare the "Whole Counsel of God," would soon be looking for another job. For that reason, it will take an "evangelistic" effort of another sort to make it work.

Like Paul, it will require men who can "sew tents" to get the thing started. It will take men who can earn their daily bread and preach and teach without a "church paycheck." But it is that "ministry for a paycheck" that precipitated the crisis and dominates the present, dismal, condition of our churches.

EDUCATION IN AMERICA

The cause of the Gospel and that of good education cannot be divorced. I pray you are bearing with me as I assault the citadels of "holy liars and beggars" and, perhaps, help you evaluate your own concept of "living Christ."

As the Apostle Paul said, the wolves are from within. They are indeed in sheep's clothing and have succeeded to infiltrate to an alarming degree. The warfare has never been so heated as it is today. The famine of The Word is upon us. Not the material lack of it but the starvational lack of knowing it, preaching it in truth, believing of it and the living of it.

In Paul's first letter to Timothy, he catalogs the sins of those who are proud and envious, the perversity of their disputings; their supposing that gain (money, power, and prestige) is godliness. "From such," he says, "withdraw thyself." If we are to be men and women of God, we are instructed to "flee these things;" these things such as envy and riches, "and follow after righteousness, godliness, faith, love, patience, meekness."

"Godliness!" Oh what a mockery we make of it supposing that our lists of conformity to a particular philosophy characterized by the "touch not, handle not" crowd testifies of purity while our own hearts would, if we would but search them, rightly accuse us of the murder of hatred, the lust of the eyes, the envy of positions others hold, the covetousness of what others have, the money spent, not laying up treasure in heaven, but for more, ever more, of what we so often mistake for the necessities of life.

We beggar ourselves amid the riches of God and even blame Him for things not being better or our not having more to satisfy our natural appetites. Of whom was the world not worthy? Of those in caves, wearing the skins of animals, the heroes of faith who counted their lives of no value apart from the truth of God! What of the Godliness of those that are content to pick up and bear the cross daily, of these unsung and unheard heroes of faith who, daily, put their hands to the plow and, not looking back, faithfully day after arduous day, just keep cutting those furrows straight and true?

"You have not because you ask not or you ask to consume upon the gratification of your own flesh!" When did God change His mind to alter the form and content of true Godliness? His law is just and good and perfect. It is His covenanted law, His purity in His law to which His Word testifies. The perfect law of liberty is not an open invitation to change or corrupt God's clear intention that we should follow after righteousness, working out our own salvation with fear and trembling, nothing doubting; certainly not with the thought that we can make a prostitute of God by somehow earning His love or by "buying" it. By His love God has put the seal to any thought of "deserving" His mercy and love. We do not deserve anything and have not earned anything but the wages of sin- death. To think or teach that God's love can be earned by the keeping of any list of "do's and don'ts" is to spit on the free, unmerited gift of God's love. But the fact that God has offered salvation to men will never excuse making a mockery of such love, openly despising such a gift, by living as though God has no claim on our lives.

The wolves may preach a cost-nothing, love everybody, live as you please brand of evangelism, but you better not. "Doers of the Word and not hearers only" is the word of warning. James I:22. To examine ourselves whether we be in the faith is more easily done if we search the Scriptures daily and obey the whole counsel of God, not just those parts that appeal to us.

The writings and nonsensical gibberish and shoutings of a "holiness" meeting may satisfy the needs of the flesh of the charismatic, but true Godliness is not seen in such self-righteous, hysterical nonsense (much of which is, undoubtedly, demon inspired). Neither is true Godliness that flagellation (self-induced) of the flesh that prohibits smoking and drinking but has no love for that same group that the Pharisees derided Jesus for associating with. I would never suggest that our Jesus engaged in any sinful act or thought but he certainly enjoyed the company of a group of people that could never be accepted by the fundamentalist brethren.

I see little difference between the self-righteousness of a door to door Mormon or Jehovah's Witness that cheers himself for doing "God's work" and the good Baptist or Presbyterian who is too "good" to associate with "sinners." There is a world of difference, my believing brother or sister, between knowing we are sinners and truly recognizing the other sinners for whom Jesus died.

The average person in our society sees religion as a denomination represented by the churches on the various corners; Baptist, Church of Christ, Presbyterian, Lutheran, Pentecostal Holiness, Assembly of God, Nazarene, Episcopal and a host of others. No wonder he is confused. How do you try to make sense of God's simple plan of salvation to someone when that simplicity of God's love is so distorted by laying such a weight of "doctrine" on it as to totally obscure it?

The average person, unsaved and hell-bound, is not a pupil to be instructed in the niceties of the liturgy or communion service, the "proper" phraseology of prayer or eschatological differences between lapsarianism and supralapsarianism, or soteriology, hermeneutics, homiletics, demonology, angelology or any other "ology." He needs to be told with all the authority of God's plain Word, There are literally millions of people who are without the knowledge of salvation because professional religionists have beat the drum of their peculiar "label" to the virtual extinction of the Gospel message. There are legitimate questions and answers that the children of God are responsible for. But the first question of import that we should never fail to answer is that of the Phillipian jailer: "What must I do to be saved?" To fail by answering with denominational claptrap is to fail in the greatest work God has entrusted to us, that of being ambassadors for Christ, speaking The Word of God Himself by His authority entrusted to us II Corinthians 5:17-21.

To obscure the simple plan of salvation by indulging in erudite (or, most often, not so erudite) discussion displaying your vaunted knowledge of "spiritual" things is to be guilty of shutting the door to heaven against those seeking to enter Ezekiel 3:18-21.

Adults have been taught that there is no such thing as a "free lunch," that no one does something for nothing. It is for that very reason that Jesus said,

"Except ye become as a little child, ye cannot enter the Kingdom of Heaven." Mark 10:15.

A child, a little child, understands and accepts selfless love. The small child does not prostitute the parent's love by asking, "What do I have to do for it?" No! Such a question is asked by those who have forgotten or never known what selfless love is.

The failure of so many not having an absolute and clear understanding of the Gospel leads to a failure in living for God and instructing children. Part of the wholesale failure of the church leadership may even be attributed to such lack of understanding or the obscuring of the message by layer upon layer of "instruction" or the "prophecy bandwagon" or the continued attempts to feed meat to those who have never had the milk of the Word clearly taught to them.

My experience as a pastor and with Christian schools has led to some very difficult conclusions. The parents of many children in Christian schools have not instructed their children in God's Word; now either they can and wont, or, they cannot.

I know that many of them are guilty of thinking that just because the school is "Christian" that they may be complacent about Bible instruction in the home. The hectic pace of our modern lives easily leads to thinking you are doing your best for your children by sacrificing to send them to a Christian school. All the while you may be ignorant of what is actually being done in the school and failing to provide at home.

Nothing can truly take the place of a Father and Mother's instruction of their young. God has so constituted us and ordained it to be so. While it is true that the Godly family needs all the help and support it can get from school and church, there is no way of circumventing familial responsibility.

The Church and Its leadership are needed to shepherd the flock. But if the leadership of the home is abdicated, the best that others may do may not be enough. Even secular schoolteachers are right in criticizing parents who do not involve themselves in their children's instruction (it must be pointed our, however, that teachers do not usually welcome such involvement).

If an ungodly institution like the state school can understand such a lack and necessity on the part of parents, how much more are Christians expected to do so! As we observe the destructive influence of Satan's work in daily life, in government, industry, education, how can we not cry out to God to bring us to our knees in true repentance for our cold and uncaring indifference.

Isn't it a shame that so many without children seem to think they have no responsibility for the young? This is another aspect of the problem I will not pursue at this time. I raise it later.

I grieve to see the failure of the great, Christian publishing houses that have given themselves to the emotional "trash" and claptrap of the "experience" crowd; that, not godly scholarship is what sells today. I grieve to see organizations like Youth For Christ, Inter-Varsity Fellowship, The Salvation Army, the Y.M.C.A. and Y.W.C.A. join the crowds of infidelity, thinking they can trade on a religious heritage and fool God.

Small wonder that ungodly organizations like The World Council of Churches and National Council of Churches can do as they do with impunity. Where are the Elijah's of God! Small wonder that the qualifications for a deacon or elder in the churches, if strictly adhered to would eliminate all women from such offices and leave only a hand-full of men at best.

Is it any wonder that God will not bless the pitiful attempts of religiosity that most are deluded are acceptable as a substitute for true holiness? Gone are the mourner's benches and true altars of God as an unrepentant generation seeks in vain to please God by frenzied extravaganzas of the flesh. In their place we find Hollywood productions, dead formalism, the electric church, the "emotion and money" crowd (God made a beggar) yelling for you to send so-called "love gifts" and "offerings" for their dubious ministries.

As God is robbed of the true gifts, tithes and offerings of broken and contrite hearts, can He bless our feeble prayers of "gimme, gimme, gimme?" The time would fail me to tell all I know of the thieves in the temple.

As a parent fills out a check for Christian school tuition, does he think he has fulfilled his duty to his children? As he pays off like a slot machine to the various so-called ministries is he really and truly Biblically aware of what that ministry is really doing for the building of the Kingdom of God?

Worst of all, does "J. Normal Christian" really believe that God will accept anything of lesser value than a heart that is true to Him? Will men rob God? of course! They do it all the time. We are hearing from some evangelical brethren that God is calling our nation to repentance. This is usually accompanied by a litany of woes and transgressions. This is not in and of itself wrong, but where is the real knowledge of God manifested? We can whip people up to the frenzy necessary to delude themselves that something of great, spiritual import is transpiring, but, as with the typical charismatic who is always running hot or cold, such things lack the ability to instill real repentance followed by consistent, Christian living.

No small part of that consistency is to see that children are not only educated, but that they learn relevant skills with both their hands and minds. I have been heavily involved with vocational education at the high school level. Unhappily, it costs a small fortune to adequately equip schools with such facilities.

Virtually no Christian school is able to offer such training to teens. If I were speaking here of "missions" I would have much to say about our failure to properly prepare young people for the "world of work." Few of even the Lord's people have an adequate appreciation of what is involved here.

Christians, especially, should be responsible for recognizing the emphasis God places on providing, by honest labor, things honest in the sight of men and God. Yet there is the delusion that God will wave His "magic wand" and our children will acquire the needed expertise to build, repair, invent, in spite of apathetic effort on the part of adults. In fact, we will let ungodly institutions do the work for us and make us ever more reliant on them for goods and services. This is as good a place to digress and provide a little autobiographical information. It is followed by an extract of a sermon I preached some time ago:

When I was born, circumstances were such that I was to be, for the most part, raised by my maternal grandparents and a great-grandmother. Born in 1935 on a cotton farm in a tiny "dust bowl" crossroads south of Bakersfield called, appropriately, Weedpatch, the world I came into was laughably simplistic by today's "sophisticated" standards.

Coal oil lamps and outdoor toilets were still relatively commonplace at that time. I was old enough, by the time of the start of World War II, to be caught up in, and enchanted by, the patriotic fervor of our nation at war. The rationing, the war stamp and bond drives, watching planes practice mock combat in the skies over Bakersfield. I was old enough to see and understand the meaning of the small pieces of fabric that hung in the windows of homes, some displaying one or more blue stars, some gold. To you younger people, the blue stars were proudly proclaiming a member of the family was in the armed forces; the gold proclaimed the "ultimate" sacrifice.

We were all proud to be a part of the greatest nation in the world, defending the rights of other nations against the aggressor. Many years later I would study and understand the evil machinations that were at work during the war years.

But my society during that period believed in America. Sons were sent willingly to give their lives so the world would have peace and freedom. That is the point; the little people sacrificed and believed while evil men grew rich and powerful. The seeds of destruction were planted long before this.

When I was a boy, people still respected preachers and teachers. Government was not yet truly synonymous with corruption. Even the films, radio shows and magazines were ludicrously naive by today's so-called production values. Pornography was not a part of our life or vocabulary. The majority of children did not know the meaning of the word *homosexual* if, in fact, they ever heard it. People believed the Bible was the Word of God and there weren't comparisons between the relative merits of Buddhism vs. Christianity or Confucius and Jesus. But we were a simple people. It was enough to simply believe God's Word and trust Him. There were heroes in those days. Men who gave their word and a handshake was a contract; just a bunch of dumb "Okies" who believed in God and Country.

It has been no accident that recent events have brought our nation to choices of evils rather than between good and evil. God declared plainly that He will not be mocked. What a man or nation sows it will assuredly reap. Time after time He has given us space to repent but we have continually chosen to follow and obey men rather than God. The power has gone from the nation's pulpits; The Glory has departed. There may no longer be time because the "great falling away" is taking place. Mockers on every hand "heaping to themselves teachers, having itching ears," hearts grown too cold by unbelief to be touched by the Gospel.

God may be giving America over to judgment (AID's, terrorism, the economy, etc.?). This is not the ranting, pulpit-thumping, radical cry of an extremist, doomsday prophet. I only voice the fears of all the "experts" as they speak themselves. It is the verbalization of years of considered, thoughtful observation, study and experience.

The unbelieving world is, in large part, already in agreement with this pronouncement even though they certainly are not saying it in this way, not understanding, of course, that this is God's judgment. Many, in fact, believe we are simply only going to have to tighten our belts and conserve. How deluded such thinking is. Modern America knows very little of the severity of God's wrath in judgment. God ordained that I be born at a time and such circumstances that I can understand what has and is happening; after all, what claim do we have, as a nation, on God's continued protection and blessing above other nations?

When I was a child, a praying mother was not exceptional. A drunkard was just that- a drunkard. Sin was still understood by young and old as transgression against God. There was a thing called virtue that was not sneered at. "Good girls didn't" and a "good boy didn't try." Boys could be "chums" and men could kiss and embrace in true, manly love for each other without evil connotation. Women were on their rightful pedestal as the strength of purity in the home. Dad could be depended on for guiding the family, providing for it and being the spiritual leader. A happy compatibility existed.

Oh; but now I hear the sarcastic and cynical voices raised against my overly simplistic generalization of the time. But; I do know about the brutality of men against women, even then, using their strength and vaunted positions in the world to humble, abase and abuse their wives and children. Yes, the double standard was at work then and prejudice was ugly and overt. But have you truly considered what I am saying? I have not said these things did not exist in that simpler world. I have said we were a Godlier nation and the home was still the exalted institution God ordained it to be.

But, as this nation turned from God and Godliness, wicked men became exalted. We began to lose interest in the things of God. The churches began peddling a pseudo-gospel of the better society and self-actualization. Mother's hair used to stand on end if her boy's room yielded a novel with the word's damn or hell in it. Now mother's hair does not respond to pornography, drugs or prophylactics. In fact, it might be, as easily, daughter's room. The enemies today are indeed, often, those of one's own household; mother against daughter, father against son, brother against brother.

Not only do the courts not dispense justice, they cannot! When men are no longer under conscience, enlightened by God's law and grace, the law cannot be just to all. What men will not do for the fear of God, they have license to do without God.

Our society is in an absolute shambles; the wicked walk on every side. The vilest men are exalted, distress of nations and men's hearts failing them for fear. At no time has God's Word seen such fulfillment, yet, at no time has it gone so unknown, unheeded or been so misunderstood and misrepresented.

Jesus said: "When ye see these things come to pass look up for you know that your redemption draweth nigh." There is a moment yet to work before "the night cometh when no man can work." Will you be found doing His work when He comes? As Christians, we watch in sorrow as this age rushes headlong toward destruction. Men are more and more willing to accept Antichrist if he only promises world order, peace and prosperity.

Even as Christian parents try to raise their children in the knowledge of God, they see their authority virtually eroded on every side. Satan now offers so many attractions to demand our time and allow our families to disintegrate. The pervading atmosphere of lust, materialism and a nearly absolute vacuum of moral standards hasten the process.

I have wondered where the Billy Sunday's, D. L. Moody's, Spurgeon's, and Luther's are today. I think I know and I share my answer with you with great sorrow. This age has a form of Godliness while denying the power thereof. God is not going to cast His pearls before swine. His Spirit, He warned, will not always strive with that of man's. I believe the time of striving is drawing rapidly to a close.

An evil and adulterous generation is now fully committed to seeking a sign (charismatics especially) But God is sending "a strong delusion that they will believe a lie." Satan's ministers, even now, enjoy the prestige of "angels of light." In the world's desperate search for an answer apart from God, it is ripe for destruction- swift and sudden as death itself. I wonder and pray even now, "Lord, who am I speaking to?" The need for laborers in the harvest field is on every hand.

Consider carefully what I am now going to say about persecution. In times past, Christians died at the stake, went to the lions and were hacked to pieces for the sake of the Gospel. In more recent times, the greatest cost to Christians has seldom been anything more than to suffer a little inconvenience by attending church or being branded a fanatic for taking The Lord seriously.

Of course, persecution unto death has always, and even now, gone on in some places in the world. There are still places, particularly in Communist and Muslim countries, where the preaching of the Gospel leads to imprisonment, torture and even death.

When America and England did the work of preaching, teaching and sending out missionaries, God opened the windows of heaven in the richest blessings known in history to any nations. But, as God's Word began to be impugned, ignored and treated lightly, we notice the power and influence of these two great nations begin to decline.

Satan's work was insidious. Being a creature, and neither omnipotent nor omniscient, he has learned by past mistakes. By allying the organized churches to himself through false doctrine and other means, he has had far greater success than he ever enjoyed through persecution tactics.

The slow but sure cancer of worldliness and pride in human achievement in science has so eroded the professing church that the power and influence of the churches for the true Gospel has nearly evaporated. They sit now as the harlot of Revelation saying they have need of nothing and do not know that they are naked, poor and powerless.

We have not yet resisted unto blood as Paul put it. What a joke! Unto blood? Why we haven't even resisted unto perspiration let alone blood. Will not the righteous Judge of the universe not keep His Word and judge every act of men? He has said He will. He will judge our failure to warn the wicked of his way and our failure to rebuke the righteous when in error (Ezekiel 3). We delude ourselves if we think for a moment that we can hold anything more dearly in this world, whether it be loved one, friend, lands, home or riches than our Father in Heaven.

What is it that holds you, dear brother or sister, from following God's clear and unmistakable will for your life as we find it in Romans 12:1,2? Does a mere job or mortgage suffice for an excuse in eternity? I know of Christians who wouldn't do God's will if it cost them a "$50 a month cut in wages. Are you so far in debt to the world that you can't lay up treasure in heaven? Is your heart so hardened by easy living and false prosperity that you do not even mumble a prayer at mealtime? God help you!

Did the Lord make a bad joke when He asked us to pray for laborers and that they would be few? Do you know why there are few? Because YOU won't work! How do many Christians in this country allocate their time; four hours of TV and four minutes for bible reading (if at all)? Do you have a family Bible study and pray as a family? Or, do you, as so many, simply do your "duty" of going to church and think that is enough?

We read these words in the epistle of Jude: "Go to now and weep and howl for your misery that is to come upon you." Can we imagine any Christians weeping and howling if they lose their jobs and possessions? If God in righteous judgment allows them to suffer in any way after the manner of their brethren in foreign lands; what if we have no gasoline or heat for our houses? What if our money turns worthless overnight? It can happen you know. Even now we know the world has so drastically altered that our children can never hope to have anything like the so-called American Dream of home, security or liberty as my generation enjoyed and so dishonored.

Over-population, the rape of natural resources resulting in pollution world-wide, the poisoning of our land, waters and air, the potential for nuclear terrorism and catastrophe, abortion on demand, perversion being legitimized, illiteracy and a thoroughly, morally bankrupt and corrupt government; this is our legacy to our children. And, you say, "God does not see and will not require it at our hand." God have mercy on you!

The sheer hypocrisy that this nation now represents to the other nations of the world is a shame to the Gospel and a stench in the nostrils of God Almighty! While some are telling us that God will forgive and bless if our country repents and turns from its wickedness, I am convinced it is too late. That does not mean I am going to stop preaching repentance for without repentance there is no forgiveness and no hope. We must continue to encourage others to repent of their wickedness. But as a nation, we may well have run our course and God will not be mocked. He must judge America if only as a witness to the world of His righteousness. The only question is where will you stand during this time and on that day?

God in His great love and compassion has promised to restore the years that the locusts have eaten. The question is not what shipwreck have you made of your life up to now but what will you do with the rest of it? Will you, can you, continue on as you have, deceiving and being deceived that somehow you will not have to give account? God help you!

The first business of Christians is to obey God, the second is to obey God and the third is to obey God. Now this one wants to obey but he must first take care of something else. This other one wants to obey but he also has to take care of other matters...and so it goes.

379

What are you putting before obedience to God's clearly revealed Word? Do you really believe in your heart of hearts that our heavenly Father is trying to cheat you? Or, are you only living like it? What does the world see when it looks at you as a representative of God? The world loves its own; have you come to terms of peaceful co-existence with the enemy not knowing that the friendship of the world is enmity against God?

When one is in love, the heart, mind and soul are united in proving that love. But as love grows cold and less ardent, the object of that love feels it. Was there a time in your life when there was sheer joy in God's Word, in prayer and witnessing? And now?

Oh, the coldness of heart that pervades our whole society concerning the things of the Lord! Yet, if we tune in on radio or TV any Sunday, what a broad spectrum of religious programming meets us. If we were to gauge the Gospel by this we would have to say, "Surely The Word is going out."

Yes, great is the company publishing The Word but in Isaiah we read, "Go and tell this people, Hear ye indeed, but understand not; and see ye indeed, but perceive not. Make the heart of this people fat and make their ears heavy, and shut their eyes; lest they see with their eyes and hear with their ears, and understand with their heart, and convert and be healed."

Jesus put it this way: "For this peoples heart is waxed gross and their ears are dull of hearing and their eyes they have closed; lest at any time they should see with their eyes and hear with their ears and should understand with their heart, and should be converted and I should heal them."

It will do no good to preach to such a people. They will not hear nor understand. God has said: "Go to ye despisers and wonder and perish. Behold, I work a work in your days that though a man declare it unto you ye will not believe."

I love my country and I sorrow for its uncleanness and unbelief. But, I can no longer wave my flag with a true heart. We have sunk so far in the pit of depravity that perversion is the acceptable rule, no longer the exception. The wicked grow bolder day by day saying, "Who will hear or see or judge?"

The vilest deeds are glorified in our literature and on magazine racks and in movie houses. Little children have a vocabulary of profanity that adults would have been ashamed of in years past. Junior high school pupils carry guns and knives to school and are addicted to alcohol and drugs.

Untold millions of dollars are being expended on hopeless rehabilitation programs. Millions more are spent to imprison criminals who increase in number daily. Sex perversion and venereal disease are rampant. People are afraid to walk their neighborhood streets day or night.

Millions and millions of dollars go to provide subsistence to the poor who cannot or will not work. An entire welfare society is now in its third generation with no end or solution in sight. Our history has been one of righteousness but that degenerated to only a form. We have attempted to replace true Godliness with legalism and have been trapped even as ancient Israel was. In committing ourselves to humanism and emotionalism as a religion, we lack the moral fiber and genuine integrity to face our enemies with Godly strength, courage and conviction.

God will not fight for a nation that has backslidden as far as ours. He has told us that He uses the nations as His rod of iron to correct and chastise. If ever a nation deserved His chastening it is the United States of America. How else will His people turn from their wicked ways and repent of their evil and lack of holiness?

In any event, where is our first allegiance to be placed, in God or our country? Yes, we must pray for our nation and its leadership, but above all else it is required of the steward of the Lord to be faithful to Him. Such faithfulness requires us to put our hand to the plow, not looking back; to pray without ceasing; to study to show ourselves approved unto God.

My dearest brothers and sisters, how many of you need to start from the very beginning and learn once again what be the first principles of the oracles of God; can there be, in fact, any hope for a nation where believers themselves squander their wealth on things that have value only to the flesh? Am I indeed now considered beside myself, even your enemy, because I tell you the truth? Am I to be cut off from the assembly of the saints because, like the prophet of old, I cannot tell you things "pleasant to the ear?"

The Lord knows His own. I know that some of you will be pricked in your hearts; that the Holy Spirit will convict of sin and righteousness and judgment to come. To such, who repent and turn to God, He promises His help in meeting the days ahead.

God wants you and will use you. Get down on your knees and pray for Him to move your hard heart. He, who cannot lie, says, "My grace is sufficient for you. My strength is made perfect in your weakness." Freely admit, with me, that we desperately need His strength, courage and wisdom which He says He will freely give us if only we will empty ourselves of self.

Do we continue to grumble and complain when we see the wicked seemingly grow more prosperous and influential than we? Can't we believe God has put their feet in slippery places and has promised us, not only life everlasting but will make us "rulers of kingdoms and judges of angels?"

Knowing what we do, God says, "What manner of persons ought we to be?" He says: "Make no provision for the flesh, to fulfill the lusts thereof." Oh foolish people! Oh foolish, foolish generation!

So many have deluded themselves that the churches are strong because of their many "ministries" and social involvement; but revival, which is so desperately needed, tarries because so many simply do what is right in their own eyes; so many are saying, "I am of Apollos" and others "I am of Paul." Such division and fragmentation of God's people! Small wonder the world looks in vain for a common standard among the saints!

Is it not strange that the single criteria Jesus gave of discipleship, that should witness of the Truth to the world, would be our love, one to another? Can we accuse him of making such a standard impossible of attainment while the fault lies in us?

Are we not told that if one of the family of God sins against us and repents, even "seventy times seven" in a day, we are to forgive? Only the love shed abroad in our hearts by the Holy Spirit can be so forgiving. On the other hand, do you nourish bitterness because of such wrongs and refuse to forgive even as you have been forgiven? Will He not require it of you in that day when every thought, word and deed will come to light?

In the midnight of your soul, when the heavens seem as brass and your prayers go no higher than the ceiling; do you truly search your heart for some unconfessed sin? David put it very plainly: "If I regard (cherish) iniquity in my heart, the Lord will NOT hear me." Plain speech; make the crooked straight and enjoy the fruit of your salvation.

I will never forget my brother telling me one day, "You know, stealing is wrong!" You may smile but this was a revelation to one who, like the majority of people, had rationalized theft on the basis that there were degrees of stealing so that some theft was okay and others not.

Stealing is wrong and so are lying, cheating, revenge and impenitence. Nothing can improve on Bob Jones Sr.'s succinct motto: "Do right." When you do right, all the consequences are in God's hands. Yes, be defrauded by a brother and forgive; the consequences are in God's hands; He will judge righteous judgment.

It is always hazardous to venture using oneself and one's own experiences as examples. Knowing this, I want, nevertheless, to share something with you.

When I turned to God it seemed the most natural thing for me to immediately begin studying God's Word and try to witness to others. While I met many failures I began to realize that I was growing in the Lord and He was using me. I made a lot of mistakes. All babies have their falls as they learn to walk. But as long as I kept a singleness of purpose, to know God's Word and make it known to others, God blessed me with the closeness of His presence.

I suffered real shipwreck on several occasions because of the betrayal of loved ones, not realizing, as with Joseph of old, that while they meant it for my harm, God intended it for my good. He was allowing me to go through the fiery furnace in order to prepare me for the real testing to come. And now, after several fiery furnace trials, I know that He is always at my side and will never leave or forsake me.

God's Word becomes increasingly real to those who believe it. He deals with us as a heavenly Father who does indeed know, absolutely, what is best for us. He does not give more than we can bear, either in tribulation or riches. As His children we are only asked to trust and obey. What delight there is in such children! Are they not worthy of the boasting of the proud parent? Even as God said to Satan of Job, "Is there such a one on earth such as he?" And how Satan hated that old patriarch! How his slings and arrows tormented this poor man. Yet, as God allowed such testing, Job says in triumph: "Though he slay me yet will I trust him!" What heights of glory are found in that statement of absolute trust and obedience!

As we read the litany of those faithful heroes of faith in the Eleventh chapter of Hebrews, and as we study the history of each, can our hearts fail to burn within us as we realize that they, like us, were subject to failure and weakness and yet they share, with us, like precious faith? They triumphed and the world was not worthy of them. Yes, America, once a nation dedicated to proclaiming the Gospel may have run its course. There remains a fearful looking for of judgment. We who still believe God is ordering events must work while it is still day. The night fast approaches when no man can work. Will you decide right now to commit yourself to the Lord, to hold nothing back and give yourself as a living epistle, known and read of all men? Will you give yourself as a living sacrifice that is your reasonable service?

Make God the very focus of your life and you will not only lay up treasure in heaven, you will find the joy of your salvation and peace unto your soul. As this world system hastens to destruction, you can stand sure and steadfast with our Heavenly Father as the anchor of your soul. Then the light will be ever dawning and the Day Star arise in your heart. He is faithful Who has promised it and He will keep you against that day. "Happy is that servant, who, when his Lord returns, is found doing what his master has asked."

I have had to say much about the Gospel and the problems we face as Christians in dealing with the confusion of religion all about us but it has been necessary to "clear the air" in order to begin attacking the troubles in education. I thank you for bearing with me and hope some of you find my words profitable in understanding as I address the hard issues we face if there is to be any hope for a future for our children.

CHAPTER TWENTY-ONE

THE WEEDPATCHER

MARCH 1992

Galatians 6:7

If you would not be forgotten
As soon as you are dead and rotten,
Either write things worth reading
Or do things worth the writing. B. Franklin

One of my little known and most unique talents is my ability to understand and translate the languages of certain reptiles and amphibians. The other day I chanced to hear a quip among a group of local frogs that deserves my passing on: "Time's sure fun when you're having flies." A real chirker, that. Most people don't even know frogs have a sense of humor. Seriously, folks, it is this unusual talent of mine that enables me to understand the language of most reptilian and amphibian dialects (like those of politicians) and pass on to you the real meaning of the president's recent State of the Union address, Clinton's disclaimers of adultery and other such slippery non-speak.

For instance, well after a year of this on-going recession, the President suddenly realized it was happening (Sununu just couldn't bring himself to tell him). Talk about quick-witted. No Johnny-come-lately he. Boy, when he found out about it, he came straight out (as straight as any reptile can come) and really lit into the Congress. But I was left with the curious impression that, due to the lengthy and enthusiastic applause of the, in Peter Grace's words, "Bunch of Clowns," that they really believed the president was one of their own. Now, I know this had to be a misperception on my part because our own senator Cranston had just called them all crooks.

"Cheer up, things could always get worse!" My reply: "You bet, and Congress, the Supreme Court, the President, together with a host of lesser 'evils' are working on it!" For those that feel I'm a tad hard on the snakes, I follow the dictum of "Scratch where it itches, not where it looks the best." Granted, my "scratching" is a bit raw and, as a result, does not appear, or is likely to, in Reader's Digest, The New American or Ladies Home Journal and other such "polite" forums.

You can't imagine how I felt to be told "We the People" had "won" the cold war. I simply glowed with pride that we had overcome the "evil empire" and without getting nuked in the process. One thing troubles me though; does this mean that, as with Japan following WWII, we are now responsible for rebuilding the Kremlin? Does Russia now qualify for more modern factories than ours or will we do the smart thing and send them our "experts" in education and welfare programs? If the latter, we could, at least, insure the empire never again being a threat. Probably wouldn't hurt to send them a couple of our "Televangelists" just as additional insurance.

In spite of our huge "success" can we easily dismiss the threat of, in the inimitable and immortal words of Tom Lehr's: "Who's Next?" Nuclear proliferation; it sure looks like Iran and Iraq are really "askin' for it!" Or is it just remotely possible that these poor A-rabs are just pawns in a larger "game?" Watch for more "outrages" such as the menacing and strong-armed tactics against UN inspectors in Iraq and Iran's building a bomb; "Lusitania's" all over, inviting "Just" wars!"

Some of you will, undoubtedly, recognize my "sour grapes" for what it is; I enjoy a good, rousing hand of genteel poker with friendly gentlemen, a good cigar but I wish Uncle Sugar and his co-conspirators would give me a teensy look at the cards. They could at least play with an honest deck and give me some idea of what the hand they dealt me is worth and what the stakes are. Further, the only ante I see in the pot is taxpayer money.

Some things stick in people's minds (or craws, depending); like "sayings" for example. A couple that I remember for their "oddity" are: "I don't trust anyone who doesn't smoke" and "I never trust a man who can't be bought." The first one is just plain peculiar but the second, Ah! That one at least makes a kind of perverse sense; admitting that an honest man is as scarce as hair on a frog makes sense of the statement. It is this "principle" upon which the world, including Congress, I may say, especially Congress, operates.

Reminds me of the time Grandad and I decided to make a killin' on rabbit hides. My grandparents had the largest rabbitry in Kern County during WWII; 600 breeding does. I remember it well because it was my job to keep the critters watered and fed. Some of the hutches were three tiers high. During the Bakersfield summers, I had to keep the burlap on the hutches wet to cool the bunnies.

Well, we had moved to the mining claim in old Kernville and some of the livestock went with us, including a selection of rabbits. I had come of age to be totally responsible for the firewood and the breeding and care of the furry creatures. Being an avid woodsman, reading Field and Stream and

Outdoorsman, the National Rifleman, etc., I asked my grandad one day "Why don't we send some of the rabbit hides to one of these places that advertise in the magazines for pelts?" Grandad agreed it sounded like a plan.

It never occurred to me to ask what Grandad did with all the pelts he accumulated in Bakersfield; one of the mysteries of life. But, after butchering a rabbit, I would always, dutifully, stretch the hide over a wire frame for drying. I had read articles on curing pelts and had followed the instructions well as I could. At the time of this experiment in fur entrepreneurial activity, about sixty pounds of pelts sat at the ready.

Selecting one of the advertisers at random, we boxed and shipped off the hides. The cost of shipping came to $1.64. This was a long time ago. Anticipating sudden riches, I waited impatiently for the check to come in the mail. In about six weeks it did; in the amount of 68 cents. We had lost 96 cents on the deal, not to mention all the time and trouble of skinning, stretching, curing, boxing and shipping. It was at this point that a good, vocational counselor should have recognized my genius and groomed me for work in the Pentagon or Congress. Another of life's opportunities missed because of the failure of the schools to help the "best and the brightest."

It was about this same time that I was learning taxidermy by correspondence school (another sure-fire scheme gleaned from one of the outdoor magazines). I managed a trout and a squirrel, Frankenstein couldn't have done better, and then tried a dove. The grandparents raised pigeons and doves and, as children, one of our favorite treats was fried pigeon or dove eggs sunny side up. Such cookery required a delicate touch. The squab was good also.

I had read that birds like doves had to be soaked in kerosene before peeling the critters. Obtaining one deceased dove, I obediently followed the procedure for soaking the hapless bird. In about five hours, following the directions, I removed it from the bucket of kerosene and set it out to dry and went squirrel hunting.

Occasionally, grandma had a hankering for roasted dove. I returned from the hunt to discover my dove plucked and my grandma complaining of a strong odor of kerosene on the bird. Her first thought was of grandad who had doused the rabbits one night by mistaking a gallon jug of kerosene on the top of a hutch for a bobcat. The .410 had done a satisfactory job of "killing" the jug and drenching the inhabitants. For whatever reason, I never did get around to stuffing birds.

I mentioned Melville's remarks about the "Truth" in last month's newsletter. Some people expressed curiosity about his exact meaning such as "Tell the Truth and go to the Soup Societies" so I will amplify. Lying comes natural to us all from childhood. The strongest language in Scripture from the mouth of Jesus was directed at the religious leaders of His time: "Generation of Vipers, Lying

Hypocrites, Children of the Devil!" Now a "Lie" such as that which God says He hates is an untruth which is told to both deceive and either do harm to another or get an advantage for selfish reasons. God is not talking about the imaginative inventions of childhood or the "Whoppers" of fishermen.

A child, caught in a lie will do one of two things; he will react in anger and further denial of the facts or he will be ashamed, confess and repent. This pattern does not change with adulthood. It is a commonplace for people, caught in a lie, to even attack those that have confronted them with the truth even as those religious leaders attacked the Jesus and Stephen, the Church's first martyr.

The heartbreak of a parent who has a child that continues to react in anger when caught in a lie cannot be described. The parents of such children realize that they are raising a little "devil" who will suffer and cause the parents much suffering. The time would fail me to cite the examples I know personally. It's a litany of woe.

Lyndon LaRouche may well be the "political prisoner" he claims to be. Since Reagan and Bush are proven liars, since We the People know our "leadership" is capable of the most heinous acts, it is easy enough to believe that people like LaRouche who challenge the status quo can be "put away;" virtually any citizen can be "dealt with" who is seen as a threat, who confronts the evil system with the truth.

Regardless of one's opinion of LaRouche, he makes a great deal of sense and made some uncanny predictions about this nation's trials. I think he is accurate in describing the present recession as an "Economic Mudslide" rather than the "Crash" most economists equate with a failed economy. One fact alone, that the government is playing with fiat money, money that has no real value, should make the point. The United States is on its way to becoming an "economic leper." Whether the European Community calls it an "ecu" or not, it will have a real, value foundation and could bury us in the years to come. This has not escaped, I'm quite certain, the attention of the "leadership." The fact that all we can presently offer Russia is an economic "band aid" should speak for itself; small wonder that the United Nations now poses such a threat to U.S. dominance. Bush is now the "Master" of the "Ship of State" but the name of the "Ship," if you look closely, seems to be the "Titanic."

THE WEEDPATCHER

APRIL 1992

II Peter 3:8,9

Life has taught me many useful lessons. It's hazardous to stick a knife in the toaster to loosen a recalcitrant piece of toast and you don't try to put Coca Cola in a thermos. "A little wine for your stomach's sake and your often infirmities" is good but getting falling down drunk is in very poor taste. Don't try to impress people, especially the ladies, if you smell of terminal B.O. and always wear a clean pair of shorts and socks. I'm glad I have made a habit of the latter because I did have an accident once that required emergency treatment. A broken leg, arm, ribs and sundry other injuries did somewhat lessen my concern about clean shorts but you can imagine my relief, coming out of the anesthesia, that I had not "offended" the doctors and nurses by a lack of personal hygiene.

It is not good, either, to live with a limited suspicion of oneself. A veritable garden of delights await those that are willing to take the plunge and give in to their proclivity for anything from bashing "Moonies" to O-D'ing on Twinkies. Rush Limbaugh recently made the point that we ought to be soaking the poor instead of the rich in order to balance the budget. Makes sense to me. You sure can't make the rich pay so go after the poor. He does have a legitimate point however. The poor, mostly black and brown, many illegal, take and take but put nothing in the pot. "Hitlerian Solutions" are well on the way to becoming the only "choices" and I have to thank Mr. Limbaugh for expressing to millions of listeners the "dark thoughts" that only men like me have raised: "Kill the poor!" Of course, the "leadership," with the help of people like Spike Lee, will have them killing each other; so much tidier that way.

Spike Lee, the latest "expert" on Apartheid and Black affairs made an interesting comment to students at the University of Michigan recently in regard to his film, "Do the Right Thing;" quote: "Many whites stayed home to watch it in the comfort and safety of their living rooms, rather than be confronted with an angry, black, raging mob." Now I don't know about you but it seems to me that avoiding an "angry, black, raging mob" is an imminently sensible thing to do on the part of us white folks. If Mr. Lee thinks we ought to "pay dues" to his "genius" by getting shot or cut in order to enhance his revenues at the box office or take a chance on such by playing a vicarious part in the "Negro Experience," I think he remains unclear on the concept of a White America.

On the other hand, illiterate America showed its face at another University recently, West Virginia U. It seems the Russian Nobel Poet, Joseph Brodsky, appeared and none of the "students" showed up to hear him! That's right, this 1987, Nobel Prizewinner stood at the podium facing an empty auditorium! If I were the leader of this school, I would hide in shame and terminal mortification at such an outrage. Now if Spike Lee had shown up instead...?

I just took a drive up the canyon to my mountain retreat. I pulled off to enjoy the Kern River and the new grass and wildflowers. The day was sunny and mild; the scent of the river and all the new vegetation in bloom together with the clear water moving in its course around the granite boulders was a tonic for my jaded nerves. There was a huge, old Cottonwood with which I have been acquainted for over forty years right on the riverbank. I strolled over to renew our acquaintance and pulled up short; one of the large limbs of the tree, about ten inches in diameter and stretching itself out about twelve feet from the trunk had been defaced by Mexican barbarians with a can of black spray paint. The graffiti was that of a Mexican gang, spelled out in large characters and preceded by a four letter word for fornicate. Is the Kern River now to be claimed by the "animals" that have no regard whatsoever for even the simplest morality? I am angered at such animalistic behavior exhibited in the cities. But now do we have to begin to accept its intrusion into the only sane places left to us, the "great" outdoors? I miss Arthur Godfrey and the simplicity of his Lipton Tea show.

Is the Knesset a puppet of the Vatican? The Israeli Antiquities Authority has cooperated with the Pontifical Biblical Institute to keep the Scrolls from being published. I warned of this in previous letters. But I warn you once more, as information about the Scrolls becomes public knowledge, the results could be devastating to the "professing churches" and Jews are going to have to "overhaul" their own theology. The Moslems and other religions together with "modernists" are going to have a field day. Look for Robert Eisenman's book, "Deception," to be compared with Rushdie and his Satanic Verses.

With so much going on that portends gloom and despair, I have to on occasion give vent to my sense of humor if only to prove to myself that I haven't yet lost it. For that reason, I engage in some whimsy in this letter. While having its source in much that is true, the names and places are changed to protect, not the innocent, but those that perceive themselves to be so, for we are all guilty of, at least, Spike Jones' "Shades of Night Falling."

So, by way of endless introductions, I'm going to double check to see if that's a fly or cigarette ash in my coffee cup and continue in a lighter vein. Just a couple more "quickies" before I begin the "Culpepper Chronicles." I quote David Gates' comment about Apartheid, American Style. "Andrew Hacker is a political scientist known for doing with statistics what Fred Astaire did with hats, canes and chairs." Gunnar Myrdal had come to the conclusion (as Tocqueville and others before him) in 1944 that blacks could not escape the caste condition into which they were born in this country. Hacker's dry statistics prove the point, devoid of the usual political rhetoric and emotionalism that I have made in my own analysis of the situation: Negroes and other minorities have no chance against America's "caste system;" one form of slavery was simply exchanged for another much crueler.

Hacker proves statistically the case against any hope of "multiculturalism." His book, "Two Nations," "A book that charts the great, racial divide," is

$24.95. You got the same information in a much more readable format from me for a great deal less. But, unlike Hacker, when asked how he would go about "fixing things," said: "I wouldn't know where to begin!" I, at least, stick my head in the noose by telling it like it really is and my books are cheaper. Hacker knows, as a great but scared scholar, that my conclusion is the only one likely; that minorities will wind up getting poorer and poorer, killing one another faster and faster until the situation demands the "fixes" I have pointed out. And that "situation" will be crises-laden, self-fulfilling "prophecy."

Olivet College in Lansing Michigan has its woes at trying to keep the fiasco of "integration" alive. Caucasian and Negro students are at each other's throats, each group accusing the other of racism; and this on a private "Liberal Arts" campus? I read with sadness the remark of one Negro student to white students: "Our need for an education will supersede your want!" All I can say is: "Lots 'a luck."

Funny, isn't it, that the International Monetary Fund has now been linked with BCCI? Imagine my surprise? That, along with Adolf Hitler making a comeback together with a Roman leader and a Chinese Emperor in commercials for a fast food outlet that the Taiwanese really go for, gives one pause.

We have all heard about "Uncle Ed" by now. This 50-year-old pervert, a Mr. Ed Savitz has AIDS and has molested an unknown number of young boys. He was arrested on charges of involuntary deviate sexual intercourse, sexual abuse of children, indecent assault and corrupting the morals of minors. Bail was set at three million dollars but this pervert is rich. He just might make bail! There are probably a few congressmen wiping their brows at the news.

Show and Tell has a new meaning at Casa Loma Elementary School. A third grader brought in a .22 handgun to entertain her classmates. The principal, one Evelyn Chatman, no slouch she, promptly sent the youngster home. Boy, talk about strict discipline! However, she "forgot" to notify anyone, teachers, police, or parents, of the incident and was "unavailable" for comment after first flatly denying the incident to a reporter. Reminds me of all the schools where I have taught; "Don't Make Waves!" This is the first commandment of administrators to teachers. They learn this in one of the more valuable "*practicum's*" for their administrative credentials at the universities. I would at least like to know if the little girl had a quality Colt or Smith or if her parents are riff raff who make her do with a cheap Saturday Night Special. I have met parents who treated their children in such a shabby manner. Maybe the child was hoping to shame her parents into buying her an Uzi like the other kids have? Alas, as long as this "principle" is in hiding, we may never find out.

At least one out of five children in this country (the vast majority, black and brown) is living in virtual poverty and we can't even hope for any improvement. It will only get worse.

"So, then, to every man his chance - to every man, regardless of his birth, his shining, golden opportunity - to every man the right to live, to work, to be himself, and to become whatever thing his manhood and his vision can combine to make him - this, seeker, is the promise of America." Thomas Wolfe.

We have a debt to Wolfe and others for carrying on the hope of such things. We have a "debt" to those that have betrayed and stolen that hope. It may have been his Southern background that made Wolfe write as he did. But the "promise" he speaks of is only possible where men are free to choose and build, to dream and hope. In his discourse on the use of language in the "Truth of Intercourse," Robert Louis Stevenson writes: "That the one can open himself more clearly to his friends, and can enjoy more of what makes life truly valuable - intimacy with those he loves."

My own writing is an attempt to share, first and foremost, with those I love, those that "...make life truly valuable." It is for that reason that I will begin the Culpepper Chronicles with this edition of the Weedpatcher. But I warn you; only subscribers will get the whole story. If you want the whole thing, get your subscriptions in.

I know in my bones that George Will wishes he had never written that dreadful parody on "pushin', eighteen-wheelers." Here is a "fish out of water." He made himself look foolish in this instance.

A couple of senators have called me recently. They are scared. They, as I have written before, cannot share their fears in speeches or print. And if I were not an honorable man, they wouldn't feel free to share their concerns with me. When I asked one of these men what he thought I could do to help he said: "Just keep doing what you have been doing." Folks what I have been doing is trying to warn of what is coming in this nation so those of you that can do so will be prepared for the "holocaust" in the streets and cities.

I will never cite men by name who trust me to keep a confidence. Further, there is always the risk that the brush used against me may tar these good men. But I put it to you that if men in the "seats of authority" feel frightened and helpless, we should be doing our utmost to be prepared for what is surely coming. But rather than take up more space on this theme, just review my previous books and essays. It's all happening. Just one example of many; euthanasia:

Katie Lyle, in Newsweek: "Why can't we treat fellow humans as humanely as we treat our pets...is a gentle death for a human being always the worst answer?" Lyle is actively involved as a volunteer on three boards advocating "on behalf" of the handicapped. Not to worry Katie, the New Reich will "solve" the dilemma.

Jonathan Pollard is found guilty of espionage. He sold our secrets to Israel and they, in turn are selling to the Chinese.

"Lawmakers" simply look at who is voting how on what bills and vote according to how it will affect their political future, not at the bills themselves. Special Interest groups still determine the final outcome. Will Jerry and Jesse make a difference? NO! How about H.R. Perot? NO! LaRouche? Possibly, but the country probably wouldn't survive the drastic surgery needed. Buchanan? Not a chance. As good a conservative as he is, the Pope still dictates his morality.

Prayer wastes away in the heat of circumstances and Gary takes after Nobel Prize winner, R.H. Coase for his "misbegotten conclusions" in economics and takes Franky Shaeffer Jr. to task for "whining" about the lack of morality in this country while making violent, teen sex films and joining the Greek Orthodox Church.

THE WEEDPATCHER

MAY, 1992

Acts 4:12

It's beginning to feel like summer here in my hometown, Bakersfield. I don't like being removed, even temporarily, from the trees, rocks and critters, but for the time being I am in town and doing my best to keep my spirits up in the heart of the Asphalt Jungle.

There are a lot worse places to be. We read of them and watch what's happening in our country and around the world and have to admit: "Yes indeed, there are worse places to be than Bakersfield; even in summer."

At least the mountains are nearby and I can look east and remember the old days when, as a child, I would look at the purple hills through the haze and imagine marvelous things and adventures while listening to "Jack Armstrong, The All-American Boy" on the radio. A little later in the evening, Grandad would put "Dusty Skies" on the wind-up Victrola and I would, unconsciously, memorize the lyrics to this old tune.

Weedpatch and Little Oklahoma are not the same places of my childhood. Gone are most of the empty fields where you could catch luckless lizards. I still like the little fellows but a surprising thing has happened over the years; they run faster than they used to! I know this is true because I can't catch them as well as I could when I was a kid; probably something to do with the hole in the ozone layer or air pollution. Maybe the dinosaurs will make a comeback when we foolish humans get through fouling our own nest and killin' each other off.

But it was magic, drinking a bottle of strawberry Nehi, and, kicking back in the shade of Faith Grocery's porch at Cottonwood and Padre, watching the sun shine through the glass tank of the Mohawk gas pump in front of the store. The war in Europe and Asia was still going strong and our comic book collections were filled with Superman, Captain Marvel and other heroes fighting the Japs and Knocksies.

Dee Dee and I had our picture taken sitting in the new Jeep that the kids at Mt. Vernon Elementary had bought with their war stamps. That made us "big shots" since the picture appeared in the Bakersfield Californian. "Purple mountain's majesty" and "Amber waves of grain" were, like, Columbia, the gem of the ocean, still popular tunes and without a hint of hypocrisy attached; simple times and precious memories.

There are few Heart's Companions in my life like Thoreau. Like he, I would fain have planted "... sincerity, truth, simplicity, faith, innocence, and the like" rather than "beans." There is time for "beans and pencils" and they should not be in competition with those heart's longings for that which encourages the spirit and gives hope of better than meeting only physical needs or gaining the wealth of this world.

Like Thoreau, I sow in hope. While many have called much of what I write "inflammatory", I do not promote anarchy but love and understanding. I am not an "incendiary" but do hope to "ignite" hearts to a better calling than the evil system that does promote lawlessness and greed; and if, as was the case of my soul brother, I provide some of the "friction" to an evil machine, so much the better. In some cases, the system is of such a complexity that the simplest solution may well be to take an ax to such a Gordian Knot. Unhappily, the "Knot" has its guardians who, unless they be subdued first, will inveigh, with all their might, against all who oppose them. It will take a good many "ax-men" to win such a battle.

The Christian is called to Civil Disobedience against unjust laws. He had rather obey God than men when the choice is presented. For that reason, he must cry out against injustice and fight for an end to those laws that would murder the innocent whether by the mechanism of "legal" abortion as contraception or adultery and divorce by whim. He is called to confront evil men from the pulpit and the pew, from within the home and at his work place. His very life must testify of the Godly "steel" in his backbone that will not tolerate injustice and murder or blind obedience to the State that requires the sacrifice of his children to slavery.

The very complexity of the evil system of government leads directly to the attempt at "simple solutions" such as the "ax." This is an historical imperative and most often leads to slavery or revolution. It is an historical imperative for the very reason that men's hearts are evil and seldom do they seek the welfare of others but are motivated by the desire to live without honest toil, by the desire to steal, lie, cheat and engage in every form of immorality freely and without restraint.

So it was early recognized that Law was an absolute necessity to restrain evil and punish the evildoer. Though this would seem to be self-evident, it is still required for each generation to teach the next. As I said in a previous essay, our failure to educate our young people to the facts of our national history and the great men and women who sacrificed so much to give us the greatest and freest nation the world has ever seen has led to a generation that neither knows "Joseph" nor the "God of Joseph."

It took "hirelings" in the pulpits of America to bring us to this sorry pass. When America's pulpits were good, America was good. When the pulpits began to be filled with spineless, evil men, America began the slide to the holocaust of immorality we now live with. My own knowledge and experience, my earnest studies of the subject over the past thirty years allows of no other conclusion.

We rightly decry the abysmal condition of our institutions of society, government, education, the homes, the churches. But I do not overemphasize the role of the religious "leaders" in causing the demise of our nation. It is from the pulpit that this nation was set on a course of righteousness and liberty and it was from those pulpits that our slide to perdition began and is now hastened.

The personal responsibility and value of each individual is a hallmark of the Gospel. It was the profound belief in Jesus and God's Word that motivated those early heroes, whether "churched" or "unchurched," that led to our founding as a nation. Even the "Ben Franklin's" bowed to that motive and exclaimed it being the only sensible course for men who would be free and exercise such freedom responsibly with due consideration to the general welfare and posterity, proving that one can recognize the Truth yet, like the Rich Young Ruler, make baser choices.

To leave that "plain trail" and go off on evil tangents required the teaching of a "pseudo-gospel" that led to our present, polyglot, mongrel status with no king over us but greed and selfishness, each one doing what is right in his own eyes. The failure can be seen historically, reaching back over two hundred years. I have said the seed of our destruction was sown in allowing slavery to remain an institution by the framers of our Constitution. Not heeding Franklin's advice to abolish slavery, it led to our bloody Civil War and the hatred, prejudice and bigotry, the cruel hoax and slavery of a welfare state that followed. It might well be pointed out, and I have done so in other writings, that one cannot rightly accuse the churches of the time of our founding fathers for not being able to stand against the history of slavery as an accepted institution of all nations throughout recorded time.

But in spite of its historical imprimatur, one cannot help but wonder, with all the wisdom our founders showed in so many other areas, why they could not have dealt with this evil at the time? And, once perceived as an evil that would divide this nation, why could not the pulpits of America gather in agreement as to the course of action that was so obviously required to stem the evil? The profit motive of both slavery and our "War for Independence" cannot be discounted in coming to any conclusions.

It seems little known, and certainly present textbooks do not treat of it, either Christian or secular, that the "worm" was alive and well even during the time of the Revolution. It is no accident that men like Edwards and Whitefield were "sent packing" and, as Franklin so well pointed out, that the churches were, even then, more given to making "good Presbyterians" than good citizens.

I have to conclude, given the history of the case, that Franklin put his finger, neatly, on the very problem that led to our national demise and the failure of the churches. Incredible as it seems to our modern senses, the very liberty of conscience and ability to worship freely as we choose led to the paralysis of the churches in the face of ever increasing evil. We might have escaped the yoke of a King but the yoke of divisiveness among believers was firmly fit. It was this very divisiveness with its ancient history of rebellion against God that hampered our forefathers in their efforts to clearly perceive the future evil their omission would precipitate.

It has always seemed a quirk of the time that Franklin and not a man of the cloth, called upon the Convention to pray for God's leading and help. It might well be asked, where were the church leaders at this time? Of course! They were busy making "Good Presbyterians!"

Are today's churches any different? YES! They are WORSE! Far from confronting the Beast, they are busy with a multitude of things of "great, eternal magnitude" like paying for the preacher or priest and paying off the mortgage of their comfortable and impressive mausoleums, of denouncing the dread sins of smoking and drinking, of the problems all those "righteous" folk have in living in such a sinful world that, for some reason they cannot quite apprehend, doesn't take them seriously as "Soldiers of the Cross" in the comfort and safety of their pews and pulpits.

The hope of America is still to be found only in the Church. I encourage everyone to belong to a church, to fellowship with those like-minded. I only hope I can change a few minds so that the sinful and obfuscating "business as usual" mentality can be disturbed enough to fire a million false prophets and get some men with backbone in their place; men who will not play to the "itching ears crowd!"

So it was that, lacking the consensual agreement and encouragement of the organized churches, the framers of the Constitution were left, largely, without such wise counsel and did the best they could as honest and reasonable men. And, considering the magnitude of their success, who can find fault? The amazing thing is that they did as well as they did. Tragically, it wasn't good enough and slavery remained to bring a nation to its knees with the system of evil we live with today. Only knowledge of history can excuse these good men for such a grievous error. The churches can solicit no such absolution. They should have known better.

If some of you wonder at my call for a New Systematic Theology, there is no better example of its need than the study of what went wrong at our Constitutional Convention. I am proud of these men who gave us the greatest nation in the history of the world. I am not deluded that I would have acted any differently than they. I, too, might have ignored Franklin's advice to abolish slavery by the Constitution. Historical hindsight has only one, real value: Understanding and acting on that understanding. With that view backward, I can go even further to Luther and the Reformation. I can study the earliest writings of the church fathers and the early councils and creeds and gain even more insight as to what went wrong: "Professing themselves to be wise, they became fools." Romans 1:22

With the first three chapters of Romans, we have the basis of understanding our own condition in this nation. With a complete reading of the Bible and the ways in which God has dealt with men and nations, we should be able to reach a consensus of what to do about it. But the historical record is not encouraging.

Wisdom is justified of her children but men have a poor track record of responding to wisdom. Religious people reject much of the wisdom that reacts to people and events pragmatically. Men like Franklin, Emerson and Thoreau, Cooper, Clemens and Melville go wanting while the churches continue to honor the Schuller's who safely engage in pious rhetoric thus avoiding the most difficult questions of real, eternal significance.

Even when pious people have read their Bibles from cover to cover, if they have not read the secular histories and literature, they are unlikely to become the "realists" that are necessary to confront evil in a pragmatic and empirical way. Today with religious confusion rampant, with the pulpits filled with hirelings and false shepherds, where to be found the voices in the wilderness crying out: "Make a straight way for the Lord!"

I have spent my years with hammer and saw, mic, lathe and torque wrench, getting grease under my fingernails. I have confronted the fact that while the world rewards its own, there is not much room, any longer, for the Poet, Statesman, Philosopher or Artist. Certainly I have discovered that women, especially, are most uncomfortable with "impractical" men who lack their definition of "common sense." Nor can I particularly blame them for my own lack of not being more concerned for a paycheck than a society that will love children and value chastity and ideals.

My "heretical" status is well established and I make no apology or attempt to recant to curry favor with even those I love. The devil leers and the door is ajar and he certainly knows how to hurt us. But, to quote Melville: "To write other, I cannot altogether do!" Even though it leads to grubbing in the custom house and the loneliness of the "impractical," living without benefit of putting my arms around a "Heart's Companion," it seems my lot to confront the Beast and follow the dread course of poets and prophets: "The Truth; it don't pay!"

To those that accuse me of making too much of the importance of religion, as they see it, I accuse them of hurtful ignorance. Such people are a product of twentieth-century, revisionist history that has, for the most part, ignored the single most important issue of our nation's history; its Christian, religious history. It is from this that all the issues that now confront us have sprung. Therefore, ignorance of this most important part is to be ignorant, even stymied, of any sensible solutions or understanding of the problems; such people face a dead end at every trail they pursue.

I have said that each generation is responsible for passing on the torch of knowledge to the next. When such knowledge is corrupted and twisted, the results are corrupted and twisted young. It is easy to mark much of this in the attempts of vile and corrupt leaders and teachers to destroy the ancient landmarks, the attempts to smear our noble leaders and statesmen of time past; all, of course, in the interest of "de-mythologizing" and "truth." But the universities traded a noble heritage for what we live with today. Oddly, those that should have known what was happening joined hands with those that were set on destroying our nation. I will explain.

Over the years, I have confronted the kind of hurtful ignorance among the "saints" that knows nothing of the early history of the church. I have advised many to get a good history and read for themselves what was happening in those first centuries. Few, regrettably, as with my injunction that they read the Bible for themselves before taking other's word for what it says, have done so. As a result of such intellectual laziness, most "church-goers" are woefully ignorant of how their peculiar form of "worship" came into being. Not a few, I am certain, would throw up their hands and cry: "How in the world did we ever come to this?" Lacking historical knowledge due to the failure of early generations to pass on such knowledge, we are left to our own devices to seek answers. They most assuredly are not going to come from pulpits today!

A generation is always coming that does not know the Lord and must be taught by the previous generation. The failure of the preceding generation is compounded by the ignorance of the next and so on. In retracing our historical steps, it is easy to discover why we are in such a case today that the name of Jesus and the Bible is vilified or made a joke by an ignorant and unbelieving generation. An understanding of this is easily gained by watching and listening to what tries to pass itself off as "worship" by the electronic "churches" and "ministries." They are a confused, ridiculous, shameful caricature of religious entertainment trying to pass itself off as legitimate teaching and worship; the local pulpits of lesser "lights" that haven't made it to the "big-time" are no better.

We lost, many centuries ago, the Council in Jerusalem, where the issues of the Church were settled. Since history is really, since A.D., a history of the Church, it is only sensible to study it to arrive at understanding. To understand my focus on the root causes of the evil today, it is necessary to explain some of my "heresy."

I have taken the position from history and God's Word, His natural creation and Man, made in His image, that God is not perfect by our dictionary definition. In fact, if we were to ask anyone their definition of "generic perfection," the answers would be as varied as the number of people asked.

My accusation of intellectual laziness applies, primarily, to those that pretend understanding of God and His Word and Works. These are the people that assume the role of the arbiters of truth and morality in our society; the "pulpiteers." These are those that pretend a knowledge that is only belief and not a very well studied belief at that.

Mine is not the heretical pedigree of a Harold Bloom of Yale and his seeking a Gnostic behind every bush. I credit Joseph Smith with, not the "originality" of Mr. Bloom's applause, but with being, like Mary Baker Eddy and Amy "Simple," finding a "gimmick" that could deceive those wishing to be deceived. But Mr. Bloom is correct in one instance, religion that is exclusively "American," like the moderate Baptist, is woefully ignorant and prejudiced.

My own heretical mode is more of the contemporary one of a Cormac McCarthy who deals with the evil of ignorance on a personal basis and invites the attack of those that have thoroughly confounded their "belief system" with what they think they know and teach the resulting pap and porridge as fact. Like McCarthy, I find myself in a kind of limbo between accepted "orthodoxy," whatever that is, and the truth of an evil system that is bent on aiding and abetting the Enemy, the Beast, by its tortured, twisted and obscure attempts at religious respectability all the while making the ridiculous claim of "Historical Christianity!"

Mostly concerned with their own egos and a paycheck, the earliest precedents of such men and the major problem that has dogged the Church since its founding can be found in the nature of man and the earliest problem confronting the Church in its inception: Preaching for a paycheck and the applause of men! I have met more than my share of those that like to be called "Rabbi," those that "make long their robes" and show favor to those that can help them on the "career ladder." It took the medium of TV to expose, to a worldview, the greed and insanity of "Religion in America." But its roots are still back there in the beginning, where Paul wept with those early believers knowing that the wolves were waiting in the wings to ravage the flock, those wolves that would come from the flock and not outside agitators.

The enemy without is easily recognizable. He wears the enemy's uniform and answers to a different general and bugle call. The enemy within is a betrayer, a Quisling, working himself into the confidence and trust of those he seeks to destroy. I may face an honorable antagonist sword-to-sword but the traitor? He is much the most dangerous and despicable of all whether as close as my own home or my most trusted comrade in arms! He is the Absalom, my heart's desire, who has lifted his heel against me!

In the schools and in the churches I have witnessed the demise of our nation. The leadership in the schools and churches has no concept of reality; both are led of "hirelings" and false shepherds. As ICHABOD began to be written over the doors of the churches, the schools, more and more began to have to assume the role the churches once filled. As government began to address itself to "social programs," the churches fell away from providing for the poor, the widows and orphans. The STATE now reigns supreme; Caesar now does the job the churches and parents were to have done. But the backstabbing, "play-to-the-crowd," self-aggrandizing, social-gospel bunch of hirelings and false teachers sold our birthright for a mess of potage.

As went the churches, so went the schools. Now we live with what ancient Israel went through time after time. Having forsaken the Lord, He has to try to get our attention. He has always done this by using men and nations as His "Rod of Iron."

If I had the time and means to do so, I would willingly devote myself to writing a history of what went wrong from the time of the first century to the present day. But I don't. All I can hope for is to provide the roughest "map" and hope some will be able to follow. It will take an army of godly scholars to do the job that needs to be done. It is all there in the histories of both religious and secular writers for anybody to read. Through all this time, God had that faithful Remnant that held to the Truth and their work is easily discerned from that of the false prophets. Such men and women, like John Bunyan, Knox and Huss were not "for sale!"

Departing from the way of the Lord, so long ago, we live with division and chaos. The "Hitlerian solutions" I have warned about are all that seem to be left to us; it is the Historical Imperative of all ungodly nations and men.

We are now hard up against the racism I have written so much about. A "Black Korean" is quoted in Newsweek as saying the history of racism in this country goes back 500 years. How naive. Why should racism in this country be unique to the whole history of mankind? Does some poor, mistreated Korean have a claim to discrimination that her "noble" country missed? I hardly think so. Just where do such people come from, outer space? Her remarkably ignorant and prejudicial statements about the "American Dream" being a promise of "equality for all regardless of color" is to overcome, somehow, by the use of mirrors, magic wand or chicken entrails, and succeed in denying human nature? It flies in the face of hard, cruel reality throughout the world and its history.

As I have said many times, the miracle is that so many colored are able to make any advances at all. Nowhere else in the world do minorities enjoy so many privileges at the cost of the majority population. And, quite frankly, those of us that are Caucasian are getting more than a little sick of the whole racist thing, of being called guilty for the "crime" of being white, with European ideals and culture and, at the same time, being forced to pay the bills for those that are accusing and using us! It simply won't wash!

Not many years ago, I sat in state senator Ed Davis' office in Sacramento trying to convey some sense of what desperately needed to be done in education. I had started corresponding with him while I was a teacher in Lancaster in the Antelope Valley U.H.S.D. He was then Chief of Police in L.A. I saw him then as a concerned man who had the backbone to confront the hard issues. He had been encouraging in his correspondence to me and, when elected to the legislature, granted me an appointment to speak with him.

My dissertation on "Accountability in Educations" had been suppressed. The schools were, even then, so paranoid because of the abysmal failure and incompetence rife throughout, that no one would approach a factual assessment of the problem. Then State Superintendent Riles would have nothing to do with my study. I know better than even suggest it to Mr. Honig.

Well, Ed was cordial but it was soon evident that he was more interested in his image as a "statesman" than anything a lowly Ph. D. who was only concerned for the welfare of children and the status of education had to offer. The "interview" was a dismal failure and I was "kicked upstairs" to Gary Hart who was head of "education matters." The best I could do with him was to leave some of my material with a secretary. I never heard from Mr. Hart.

Failure of leadership? I have encountered it everywhere in the churches, schools and government. Presently, I am privileged to know a few, good men in government but I am still looking for some in the churches and schools. They seem conspicuous by their absence.

So I will continue to "beat the drum" and hope to get their attention. I know, as Elijah, that God has good men out there somewhere. But we better get our act together and start doing the job in concert. I realize the incompetents and those that are greedy and ignorant in the churches, schools and government have rightly perceived me as a "dangerous" man, by those that are trying to protect the "status quo." As a friend and school psychologist once told me, "Don, if you would only keep your mouth shut, you could write your own ticket anywhere!" He was right of course. As a qualified "loudmouth" in the pulpit or the schools, I have an enviable track record of being *persona non-gratis* in both institutions. I am gratified at attaining the same status among most politicians as well. I am an enemy of the Scoundrels and Carpetbaggers, the time-servers and greedy thieves that are robbing our children and grandchildren of a future.

In respect to the churches, since I am writing CHRISTIAN PERSPECTIVE for them once more, I am reminded of a conversation I just had with a good man who has experienced, first hand, the hard things I put in my other publications which are not for "church consumption." He complimented the work of C.P. and I am sure a lot of other church people agree with him. But while C.P. is needed, along with the testimonies of those that want others to know about the Lord's work in their lives, the real issues, the Beast, the Evil, is where the battle is. I do not receive compliments from "good, church people" for this work.

My heart goes out to this good brother because he was sharing with me the results of what he considers "bigotry and prejudice" in a nearby community called Oildale. Now I know Oildale very well. I am not surprised that the residents don't want a group of Mexicans gaining a foothold in their community regardless of the worthy cause they purport to represent.

What this poor brother had to face was the reality of what confronts all of us and is leading to those "Final Solutions," the "dirty work," that I am called of God to rub "good" people's faces in. The insanity of the whole thing is that, what this good brother and those Assembly of God Mexicans are trying to force Oildale to do is let them settle where they are not wanted. This may become a "legal" issue but the real war is whether an American can ever choose to live among his own kind in his own country without the courts forcing him to live with an alien, even criminal, one. Once more, a community that wants to maintain its own culture may be forced by the courts to open its doors to an alien culture by force of law.

Does it occur to anyone that if I wanted a Caucasian enterprise, church or "rehab" center in Watts, Harlem, East San Jose, I wouldn't last one night? Since when does it become White Racism because the Oildale folks don't want the problems of Watts in their own community? Just who and what kind of people is trying to make Oildale swallow this anyhow? What color is their skin? What is their "politics?" What "vested interests" are usually involved in this kind of thing? I have seen it countless times. Look under the rocks and you will find, beyond the fine rhetoric of "Equality, fairness, multi-cultural clap-trap," the Beast trying to pass himself off as an Angel of Light.

I know Oildale. I know its relative freedom from the kind of crime and violence, predominantly Negro and Mexican that plagues places like L.A. Do I blame those folks for not wanting to risk importing such things to their community? I do not. Do I wish everyone could act with true Christian charity toward others regardless of skin color or culture? I do! Will people act in such a way? No! Are they afraid? You bet! Are they right to be afraid? Absolutely! No matter how "Christian" this group of Mexicans is, they have relatives who are not of their noble character. Experience has shown that once any group of these people gain a foothold the others are bound to follow along with the attendant crime and violence. The wonder of it is that so many "good" church people have no idea of what the real warfare is all about and are surprised when people react in just the way God says men are at heart. Those hearts do not change with the titles of Senator, Governor, President, Head of the Chamber of Commerce, etc.

Now if Oildale is forced to sell property to this group and forced to allow them to operate a church, drug rehab facility, etc. in their community; which will cater to a foreign, barbarian and criminal, culture, we can reasonably expect the residents to react in a strong manner. These Oildale folks are not bad people. They still believe that America is supposed to be for Americans, not Asians, Africans or Mexicans. They don't, any more than I do, believe in "hyphenated Americans."

Are we then forced to look at race as the battleground? Yes. At least as long as men's hearts are what God says they are, desperately wicked and perverse and God is the only cure for such hearts. The historical imperative is, as I keep saying, a fact that no nation can be divided along racial and cultural lines and survive as a nation. One will reign no matter what the cost. Only one can possibly be the "winner." In our case, the power and authority is Caucasian and that, regardless of the cost in lives or manner of living conditions, will win.

All attempts at legislative coercion have, and will, serve to only reinforce the resistance to such forced "equality." The battle will rage hotter and hotter until the circumstances prevail demanding "strong medicine" in the form of police and dictatorial power that will make us a nation of slaves to the State. If it were a matter of choice, it might be different. But we no longer have any good choices- only bad and worse. Christians better get their heads on straight to the fact that God expects us to take a stand against the evil all about us and call on Him to lead hearts to repentance. He has not called us to promote "multiculturalism," social programs at the expense of others or forced equality with foreign cultures that are alien, even opposed to, and antagonistic to God and God's Word! And if the same denomination that gave us Jimmy Swaggart, Mr. Gorman and their ilk is behind it, I would look askance at the Oildale "proposition" in any event! Leave it to the charismatic hand-wavers and gibberish spouters to lead the way into every kind of error and heresy; all in the name of the Lord of course.

One cannot overlook the "profit" motive in doing "good." Politicians and Realtors make a cozy duo in such schemes. By presenting a "righteous face" with cries of "discrimination" and "racism" it isn't unlikely that when the rocks are turned over, you will find evidence of this kind of thing crawling around underneath.

But such a call to national repentance is not about to be heard from the churches and their "hirelings." Such a call requires the power and authority of God to be effectual and the churches no longer have such power and authority. Also, such a call will bring the wrath of an ungodly leadership down on our heads. The "leadership" knows it is dealing with a bunch of hypocrites like themselves and fear nothing from the churches.

Can't you just hear the "call" from the local pulpits: "Oh, brothers and sisters, we live in such an evil society, sin all around, ungodly people, pornography, and wickedness everywhere; what are we to do? We must pray for our leaders and those in authority! We must pray for God to keep us from the evil and the evil hour! Watch that we don't fall into their evil ways! Have nothing to do with the works of darkness! Let's just keep faithful, keep trusting the Lord and keep coming to church and keep those donations coming in and we will have done our part! Be faithful in Sunday school and evening service and surely God will keep us from the hour of His wrath! Please rise and turn to hymn number..." No wonder Sam used the phrase: "He was as happy as if church had just let out!"

About the Author

Samuel D. G. Heath, Ph. D.
Other books in print by the author:
BIRDS WITH BROKEN WINGS
DONNIE AND JEAN, an angel's story
TO KILL A MOCKINGBIRD, a critique on behalf of children
HEY, GOD! What went wrong and when are You going to fix it?
THE AMERICAN POET WEEDPATCH GAZETTE for 2008
THE AMERICAN POET WEEDPATCH GAZETTE for 2007
THE AMERICAN POET WEEDPATCH GAZETTE for 2006
THE AMERICAN POET WEEDPATCH GAZETTE for 2005
THE AMERICAN POET WEEDPATCH GAZETTE for 2004
THE AMERICAN POET WEEDPATCH GAZETTE for 2003
THE AMERICAN POET WEEDPATCH GAZETTE for 2002
THE AMERICAN POET WEEDPATCH GAZETTE for 2001
THE AMERICAN POET WEEDPATCH GAZETTE for 2000
THE AMERICAN POET WEEDPATCH GAZETTE for 1999
THE AMERICAN POET WEEDPATCH GAZETTE for 1998
THE AMERICAN POET WEEDPATCH GAZETTE for 1997
THE AMERICAN POET WEEDPATCH GAZETTE for 1995-1996
THE AMERICAN POET WEEDPATCH GAZETTE for 1993-1994

Presently out of print:
IT SHOULDN'T HURT TO BE A CHILD!
WOMEN, BACHELORS, IGUANA RANCHING, AND RELIGION
THE MISSING HALF OF HUMANKIND: WOMEN!
THE MISSING HALF OF PHILOSOPHY: WOMEN!
THE LORD AND THE WEEDPATCHER
CONFESSIONS AND REFLECTIONS OF AN OKIE INTELLECTUAL
or Where the heck is Weedpatch?
MORE CONFESSIONS AND REFLECTIONS OF AN OKIE
INTELLECTUAL

Dr. Heath was born in Weedpatch, California. He has worked as a manual
laborer, mechanic, machinist, peace officer, engineer, pastor, builder and

developer, educator, social services practitioner (CPS), professional musician and singer. He is also a private pilot and a columnist.

Awarded American Legion Scholarship and is an award winning author.

He has two surviving children: Daniel and Michael. His daughters Diana and Karen have passed away.

Academic Degrees:

Ph. D. – U.S.I.U., San Diego, CA.

M. A. – Chapman University, Orange, CA.

M. S. (Eqv.) — U.C. Extension at UCLA. Los Angeles, CA.

B. V. E. – C.S. University. Long Beach, CA.

A. A. – Cerritos College. Cerritos, CA.

Other Colleges and Universities attended:

Santa Monica Technical College, Biola University, and C.S. University, Northridge.

Dr. Heath holds life credentials in the following areas:

Psychology, Professional Education, Library Science, English, German, History, Administration (K-12), Administration and Supervision of Vocational Education and Vocational Education-Trade and Industry.

In addition to his work in public education, Dr. Heath started three private schools, K-12, two in California and one in Colorado. His teaching and administrative experience covers every grade level and graduate school.

Your writing is very important. You are having an impact on lives! Never lose your precious gift of humor. V. T.

You raise a number of issues in your material ... The Church has languished at times under leaders whose theology was more historically systematic than Biblical ... (But) The questions you raise serve as very dangerous doctrines. John MacArthur, a contemporary of the author at Biola/Talbot and pastor of Grace Community Church in Sun Valley.

You have my eternal gratitude for relieving me from the tyranny of religion. D. R.

Before reading your wonderful writings, I had given up hope. Now I believe and anticipate that just maybe things can change for the better. J. D.

I started reading your book, The Lord and the Weedpatcher, and found I couldn't put it down. Uproariously funny, I laughed the whole way through. Thank you so much for lighting up my life! M.G.

Doctor Heath, every man with daughters owes you a debt of gratitude! I have had all three of my girls read your Birds With Broken Wings book. D. W.

I am truly moved by your art! While reading your writing I found a true treasure: Clarity! I felt as if I was truly on fire with the inspiration you invoked! L. B.

You really love women! Thank you for the most precious gift of all, the gift of love. Keep on being you! D. B.

Your writing complements coffee-cup-and-music. I've gotten a sense of your values, as well as a provocativeness that suggests a man both distinguished and truly sensual. Do keep up such vibrant work! E. R.

Some men are merely handsome. You are a beautiful man! One of these days some wise, discerning, smart woman is going to snag you. Make sure she is truly worthy of you. Desirable men like you (very rare indeed) who write so sensitively, compellingly and beautifully are sitting ducks for every designing woman! M. G.

Now, poet, musician, teacher, philosopher, friend, counselor and whatever else you have done in your life, I am finally realizing all the things you say people don't understand about a poet. They see, feel, write and talk differently than the rest of the world. Their glasses seem to be rose colored at times and other times they are blue. There seems to be no black or white in the things they see only soft pastel hues. Others see things as darker colors, but these are not the romantic poets you speak of. C. M.

You are the only man I have ever met who truly understands women! B. J.

Dr. Heath;
• You are one of the best writers I've had the privilege to run across. You have been specially gifted for putting your thoughts, ideas, and inspirations to paper (or keyboard), no matter the topic.
Even when in dire straits, your words are strong and true. I look forward to reading many more of your unique writings. T. S.